D0742979

Christian Theology

EMERY H. BANCROFT

Christian Theology

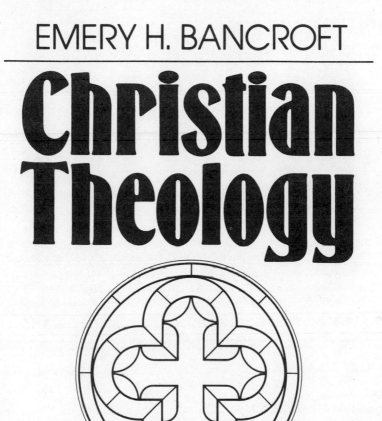

SYSTEMATIC AND BIBLICAL
Second Revised Edition
Ronald B. Mayors, Editor

 ZONDERVAN
PUBLISHING HOUSE
OF THE ZONDERVAN CORPORATION
GRAND RAPIDS, MICHIGAN 49506

CHRISTIAN THEOLOGY
Second Revised Edition
Copyright © 1976 by Baptist Bible College

Copyright 1925 by Practical Bible Training School. Copyright 1929 by E. H. Bancroft.
Copyright 1930 by Echoes Publishing Company. Copyright 1946 by Johnson City Publishing
Co. Copyright transferred 1949 to J. F. May Press, 733 A Street, Hayward, California.

Published by Zondervan Publishing House
Grand Rapids, Michigan

First Zondervan printing 1955
Revised edition 1961
Twentieth printing 1982
ISBN 0-310-20440-2

Contents

Preface to the Second Revision

It has been a joyous, if time-consuming, task to revise Emery Bancroft's *Christian Theology* since this was the text that first introduced me to systematic theology at Baptist Seminary, the same school at which Dr. Bancroft used his compilation as a classroom textbook.

This revision has concentrated in attempting to make the book more generally useful and readable by incorporating the numerous notes into the text itself and by noting various sources and citations by the usual method of footnoting. Various mechanical facets, such as the manner in which Scripture passages are referenced, have been standardized, while the new index should make this book a finer reference tool. While some comments have been updated and others deleted, the doctrinal tenor of this book is still as Dr. Bancroft originally intended. May it yet be used by another generation of students at Baptist Bible College and School of Theology, now of Clarks Summit, Pennsylvania (formerly Baptist Bible Seminary), and other Bible colleges and seminaries to the praise and glory of "our great God and Savior Jesus Christ."

RONALD B. MAYERS, TH.M., PH.D.
Grand Rapids, Michigan

Preface to the First Revision

This volume of theology was designed by Dr. Bancroft to be a compilation of the best writings on the whole area of theology. In the original preface originality was claimed only for compilation and arrangement rather than for contents. The resultant treatise was used by the original author with demonstrated success during many fruitful years of teaching until his death in 1944. Since that time the book has continued to be a valuable collateral textbook in Systematic Theology in the school of which he was the dean as well as in many other Christian schools in America and across the seas.

The present work of revision has been undertaken, not with the idea of any major change of the original edition, but with the desire to eliminate many mechanical errors which have crept into the book. The greatest number of changes in the book will be of this minor nature, and will, thereby, assist the student in making the best possible use of the book. In several places new material has been inserted to replace notes which have become outdated through the passage of time. Some clarification of wording and phrasing has been made in those places where ambiguity seemed to be present. The chapter on Bibliography has been removed from its position in the sequence of systematized theological thought. New information has been inserted in some areas to clarify more fully doctrinal positions, and to make the theological discussion more relevant to contemporary trends.

The value of this volume will be increased through this revision, and will, therefore, accomplish more fully its original purpose of providing for those called into the service of God a better understanding of the great truths of the scriptures.

WILLIAM R. FOSTER, TH.D.

Introduction to the First Revision

A one-volume "Christian Theology" usually leaves much to be desired. In the case of Dr. Emery H. Bancroft's systematic and biblical *Christian Theology*, however, we find a book which has fulfilled the author's objective, namely: an original compilation and arrangement of the best that could be found in a variety of sources. The resultant work is interesting reading of a mass of material in all areas of theology.

The book is sound in its doctrine, scholarly in its approach, and apologetical in its defense. The student who has mastered this volume knows why he believes what he believes.

The need for revision was evident, primarily because of a number of mechanical errors, and Dr. William R. Foster has done a commendable work in its accomplishment. The present edition should be of maximum service to the students at Baptist Bible Seminary, where Dr. Bancroft was the first dean, and to readers in America and abroad who recognize Bancroft's Theology as a standard textbook of the biblical dispensational and premillennial position.

FRANK L. WASSER, TH.D.

Christian Theology

CHAPTER ONE

INTRODUCTION:
THE MEANING AND PURPOSE
OF THEOLOGY

THE DEFINITION OF THEOLOGY

Theology is the science of God and of the relations between God and the universe. Though the word "theology" is sometimes employed in dogmatic writings to designate that single department of the science which treats of the divine nature and attributes, prevailing usage has included under that term the whole range of Christian doctrine.

THE AIM OF THEOLOGY

Its aim is the ascertainment of the facts concerning God and the relations between God and the universe, and the exhibition of these facts in their rational unity, as connected parts of a formulated and organic system of truth.

1. It is the work of theology as a science, not to create, but to discover facts. Schiller, referring to the ardor of Columbus's faith, says that if the great discoverer had not found a continent he would have created one. But faith is not creative. Had Columbus not found the land — had there been no real object answering to his belief — his faith would have been a mere fancy. Because theology deals with objective facts, we refuse to define it as "the science of religion." Both the facts and relations with which theology has to deal have an existence independent of the subjective mental processes of the theologian.

13

2. The work of theology as a science also includes the recognition and manifestation of the relations between these facts, and the synthesis of both the facts and the principles which unite them in the comprehensive, rightly proportioned, and organic system. Science is facts plus relations.[1]

3. As theology deals with objective facts and their relations, so its arrangement of these facts is not optional, but is determined by the nature of the material with which it deals. A true theology thinks over again God's thoughts and brings them into God's order, as the builders of Solomon's temple took the stones already hewn and put them into the places for which the architect had designed them.

> No hammer fell, no ponderous axes rung;
> Like some tall palm, the mystic fabric sprung.

THE NECESSITY OF THEOLOGY

1. Theology is necessary as a means of expressing the meaning of Christianity because man is reasonable as well as emotional.

2. It is necessary in order to define Christianity. The definitions may not be exhaustive, for the objects and experiences involved are beyond our capacity for knowing, in some of their aspects. But we may apprehend what we can not comprehend. We may know in part if not in full. We may know truly if not exhaustively.

3. It is necessary in order to defend Christianity against attack.

4. It is necessary in order to propagate it. Christianity is a missionary religion; it is aggressive and diffusive in motive and aim. But no possible success can attend the propagation of Christianity without doctrine. The truth is employed to produce experience, then experience gives a new appreciation of truth.

THE POSSIBILITY OF THEOLOGY

The possibility of theology has a threefold basis.

1. It is grounded in the existence of God who has relations with the universe. It has been objected, however, that since God and these relations are objects apprehended only by faith, they are not proper objects of knowledge or subjects of science. We reply:

    a. Faith is knowledge, and a higher sort of knowledge than that obtained by mere sense preception.

b. Faith is knowledge conditioned by holy affection (Gal. 5:6).
c. Faith, therefore, can furnish, and only faith can furnish, fit and sufficient material for scientific theology. As an operation of man's higher rational nature, though distinct from occular vision or from reasoning, faith is not only a kind but the highest kind of knowing. It gives us an understanding of realities which to sense alone are inaccessible, namely God's existence, and some at least of the relations between God and His creation.

2. It is grounded in the capacity of the human mind for knowing God and certain of these relations. But it has been urged that such knowledge is impossible for the following reasons:

a. Because we can know only phenomena. We reply —

(1) We know mental as well as physical phenomena.
(2) In knowing phenomena, whether mental or physical, we know substance underlying the phenomena, as manifested through them and constituting their ground of unity.
(3) Our minds bring to the observation of phenomena not only this knowledge of substance, but also knowledge of time and space, of cause and right, realities which are in no sense phenomenal. Since these objects of knowledge are not phenomenal, the fact that God is not phenomenal cannot prevent us from knowing Him.

b. Because we can know only that which bears analogy to our own nature or experience. We reply —

(1) It is not essential to knowledge that there be similarity between the knower and the known. We know by difference as well as by likeness, by contrast as well as by comparison.
(2) Our past experience, though greatly facilitating new acquisitions, is not the measure of our possible knowledge.
(3) Even if knowledge depended upon similarity of nature and experience, we might still know God, since we are made in God's image and there are important analogies between the divine nature and our own.

c. Because we can know only that which we can perceive in the sense of forming an adequate mental picture or image. We reply —

(1) It is true that we know only that which we can perceive if by

the term *perceive* we mean our distinguishing in thought the object known from all other objects.

(2) But the objection confounds conception with perception which is only the frequent accompaniment and help, namely, the picturing of the object by the imagination.

(3) That the formation of a mental image is not essential to conception or knowledge is plain when we remember that, as a matter of fact, we both conceive and know many things of which we cannot form a mental image of any sort that in the least corresponds to the reality — for example, force, law, space, or our own minds. So we may know God, though we cannot form an adequate mental image of Him.

d. Because we can know truly only that which we know in whole and not in part. We reply —

(1) The objection confounds partial knowledge with the knowledge of a part. We know the mind in part, but we do not know a part of the mind.

(2) If the objection were valid, no real knowledge of anything would be possible, since we know no single thing in all its relations. We conclude that although God is a being not composed of parts we may yet have a partial knowledge of Him, and this knowledge though not exhaustive may yet be real and adequate to the purposes of science.

3. It is grounded in the provision of means by which God is brought into actual contact with the mind, or in other words, in the provision of a revelation of God Himself and certain of these relations. As we do not in this place attempt a positive proof of God's existence or of man's capacity for the knowledge of God, so we do not now attempt to prove that God has brought Himself into contact with man's mind by revelation. Our aim at present is simply to show that, granting the fact of revelation, a scientific theory is possible. This has been denied upon the following ground: that revelation as a making known is necessarily internal and subjective — either a mode of intelligence, or a quickening of a man's cognitive powers — and hence can furnish no objective facts such as constitute the proper material for a science. To this objection, urged mainly by idealists in philosophy, we reply:

a. We grant that revelation, to be effective, must be the means of including a new mode of intelligence or, in other words, must be understood. We grant that this understanding of divine

Gen. Rev. thru:History, Conscience, + nature
Ps. 19:1-4   Rom 1:19-20   Acts 14:15-17
Job 12:7-9   Isa. 40:12-14

things is impossible without a quickening of man's cognitive powers (1 Cor. 2:14). We grant, moreover, that revelation, when originally imparted, was often internal and subjective.[2]

b. But we deny that revelation is therefore useless or impossible. Even if religious ideas sprang wholly from within, an external revelation might stir up the dormant powers of the mind. Religious ideas, however, do not spring wholly from within. External revelation does impart them. Man can reveal himself to man by external communication, and if God has equal power with man, God can reveal Himself to man in like manner. If idealists can teach by books, can God not do the same?

c. Hence God's revelation may be, and is in great part, an external revelation in works and words. The universe is a revelation of God. We claim, moreover, that in many cases where truth was originally communicated internally, the same Spirit who communicated it has brought about an external record of it so that the internal revelation might be handed down to others besides those who first received it.

d. The external record is given under proper conditions a special influence of God's Spirit that so quickens our cognitive powers that the external record reproduces in our minds the ideas with which the minds of the writers were at first divinely filled.[3]

e. Internal revelation, thus recorded, and external revelation, thus interpreted, both furnish objective facts which may serve as proper material for science. Although revelation in its widest sense may include, and as constituting the ground of the possibility of theology does include, both insight and illumination, it may also be used to denote simply a provision of the external means of knowledge, and theology has to do with inward revelations only as they are expressed in, or as they agree with, this objective standard.

We have suggested the vast scope and yet the insuperable limitations of theology. So far as God is revealed, whether in nature, history, conscience, or Scripture, theology may find material for its structure. Since Christ is not simply the incarnate Son of God but also the eternal Word, the only Revealer of God, there is no theology apart from Christ, and all theology is Christian theology. Nature and history are but the dimmer and more general disclosures of the

Special Revelation   II Pet. 1:21   II Tim 3:16-17

Miracles, prophecy, person + work of Christ, scriptures

Divine Being, of which the Cross is the culmination and the key.

THE SOURCES OF THEOLOGY

God Himself, in the last analysis, must be the only source of knowledge with regard to His own being and relations.[4] Theology therefore is a summary and explanation of the content of God's self-revelations. These are, first, the revelation of God in nature; secondly and supremely, the revelation of God in the Scriptures.[5]

The Theology of Nature

By nature we here mean not only the physical facts, or facts in regard to the substances, properties, laws and forces of the material world, but also spiritual facts or facts with regard to the intellectual and moral constitution of man and the orderly arrangement of human society and history. The universe is a source of theology. The Scriptures assert that God has revealed Himself in nature.

1. The outward witness to His existence and character is in the constitution and government of the universe (Ps. 19:1-6; Acts 14:17; Rom. 1:20).

2. The inward witness to His existence and character is in the heart of every man (Rom. 1:18-20; 2:15).

There are two books: nature and Scripture — one written, the other unwritten; and there is need of studying both. The systematic presentation of these facts, whether derived from observation, history, or science, constitutes natural theology, or the theology of nature.[6]

The Theology of the Scriptures

The Christian revelation is the chief source of theology. The Scriptures plainly declare that the revelation of God in nature does not supply all the knowledge which a sinner needs (Acts 17:23; Eph. 3:9). True science and the Scriptures throw light upon each other. The same divine Spirit who gave both revelations is still present, enabling the believer to interpret the one by the other and thus, progressively, to come to the knowledge of the truth.

Because of our finiteness and sin, the total record in Scripture of God's past communications is a more trustworthy source of theology than our conclusions from nature or our own private impressions of the teachings of the Spirit. Theology therefore looks to Scripture itself as its chief source of material and its final standard of appeal.

Study Questions on Theology

1. Define theology.
2. What is the aim of theology?
3. Give four reasons for the necessity of theology.
4. What is the threefold ground of the possibility of theology?
5. Discuss the various objections to this threefold ground for the possibility of theology and the replies to each.
6. What, in the last analysis, is the only source of theology?
7. Of what is theology a summary and an explanation?
8. What is meant by *nature* in terms of theology?
9. In what twofold way does the Scripture assert that God has revealed Himself? Quote one passage with each.
10. What is the chief source of theology?
11. What do the Scriptures plainly declare concerning the revelation of God in nature? Quote one passage.
12. What is the relation of true science to Scripture?
13. Why is the record in the Scriptures of God's past communications the most trustworthy source of theology?

Notes

[1]Scattered bricks and timbers are not a home; severed arms, legs, heads and trunks from a dissecting room are not living men; and facts alone do not constitute science.

[2]The revelation on the way to Damascus would not have enlightened Paul had it been merely a vision to his eye. Nothing can be revealed in us. The eye does not see the beauty of the landscape nor the ears hear the beauty of the music. So flesh and blood did not reveal Christ to us. Without the teaching of the Spirit, the external facts will be only like the letters of a book to a child who cannot read (Gal. 1:16).

[3]We may illustrate the need of internal revelations from Egyptology, which is impossible so long as the external revelation in the hieroglyphics is uninterpreted; from the ticking of a clock in a dark room, where only the lit candle enables us to tell the time; from the landscape spread out around the Rigi in jswitzerland, invisible until the first rays of the sun touch the snowy mountain peaks. External revelation (Rom. 1:19, 20) must be supplemented by internal revelation (1 Cor. 2:10, 12). Christ is the organ of external, the Holy Spirit the organ of internal, revelation (2 Cor. 1:20; Eph. 1:17). In Christ, "the yea" and "the Amen" — the objective certainty and the subjective certitude, the reality and the realization. Objective certainty must become subjective certitude in order to be a scientific theology. Before conversion we have the first, the external truth of Christ; only at conversion and after do we have the second, "Christ formed in us" (Gal. 4:19). We have objective revelations at Sinai (Exod. 20:22); subjective revelation in Elisha's knowledge of Gehazi (2 Kings 5:26).

[4]Ambrose wrote: "To whom shall I give greater credit concerning God than to God Himself?"

[5]Von Baader said: "To know God without God is impossible; there is no knowledge without Him who is the prime source of knowledge."

[6]God is present in nature and is still speaking thru it. Someone once said that Spurgeon told of a godly person who, when sailing down the Rhine, closed his eyes lest the beauty of the scene divert his mind from spiritual things. The Puritan turned away from the moss-rose saying that he would count nothing on earth lovely. But this is to despise God's works. "The Himalayas are the raised letters upon which we blind children put our fingers to spell out the name of God."

CHAPTER TWO

BIBLIOLOGY: THE DOCTRINE
OF THE SCRIPTURES

Support, like a bedpost

The Bible, the inspired Word of God, is the fulcrum of the Christian faith. It is the medium of God's addressing man and the means of man's knowing of the incarnation, crucifixion, and resurrection of Jesus Christ. Since all intelligent faith in the supernatural rests ultimately upon the divine origin, plenary inspiration, and infallible authority of the Bible as the Book of God, it is only natural that this book becomes the very center of both the attack and the defense of the whole system of Christianity.

In light of this, as well as the twentieth-century crisis as to the possibility of knowledge and thus truth, the believer is challenged to examine anew the question and evidence of the superhuman authorship and divine authority of the Bible. It is not too much to say that while the Bible holds its place firmly in the minds and hearts of men as the Word of God, as God's own Book, as inbreathed of the Holy Spirit, and to be believed and trusted in every part as a divine guide to doctrine and duty, all that is most precious in our Christian faith and life holds its place in our convictions and confidence; but if the Bible loses or loosens its hold upon us as an infallible standard of truth and action, everything else, as we are beginning to realize, goes down with it into the same abyss of doubt.

For these reasons, among others, it is first of all needful for all believers to have an intelligent, rational, unshakable confidence in God's Word as divine in origin, inspired of the Holy Spirit, a safe

21

guide in belief, and a sure pattern for practice. We say an intelligent and reasonable faith. The "collier's faith" has long been ridiculed as a specimen of blind credulity. "What do you believe?" asked Whitefield of a Roman Catholic worker in the coal pits of Cornwall. "What the Church believes," was the answer. "And what does the Church believe?" "What I believe." "And what do you both believe?" "The same thing." To believe only what, and only because, others believe may be perpetuating false teaching, helping on what Cyprian called "the old age of error." The Spirit of God enjoins disciples to "be ready always to give an answer to every one that asketh a reason for the hope" that is within them (1 Pet. 3:15). The more intelligent and reasonable faith is, therefore, the more pleasing and honoring to God, the more helpful to men, and the more restful and forceful to oneself.

THE BIBLE AS A BOOK

The Designations of the Book

The Bible. Our English word *Bible* comes from the Greek words *biblos* (Matt. 1:1, "The book [*biblos*] of the generation of Jesus Christ") and *biblion* (diminutive form; Luke 4:17, "And there was delivered unto Him the book [*biblion*] . . . and when He had opened the book" [*biblion*]) which mean book![1] Ancient books were written on the *biblus* or papyrus reed, and from this custom came the word *biblos*, which finally came to be applied to the sacred books (see Mark 12:26; Luke 3:4; Acts 1:20; 7:42). The Bible is not merely a book, however. It is the Book — the Book that from the importance of its subjects, the wideness of its range, and the majesty of its Author stands high above all other books as the heaven is high above the earth.

This term *Bible* is one that affirms two things — unity and preeminence. The appropriateness of such a title can hardly be questioned: this conception of oneness through all its parts, of unity and diversity, has been endorsed by the Christian consciousness and has had far reaching influence.

The Old and New Testaments. The application of the term *testament* carries us beyond the simple fact of books or writings to some indication of their main theme. Woven into the very texture of the Old Testament is the idea of a covenant between God and man, first made with Adam, then with Noah, also with Abraham, with the nation of Israel, and with David. Reference to it occurs again and again throughout history, psalm, and prophecy, as the relation into which God entered with His chosen people. In Jeremiah, prophecy reaches its heights in the sublime prediction of the New Covenant, a prediction declared by the writer of the Epistle to the Hebrews to be fulfilled in Jesus Christ.

The phrase *New Covenant* was appropriated by Christ at the Last Supper and is claimed by Paul as the substance of the ministry to which he was called (see Luke 22:20; 1 Cor. 11:25; 2 Cor. 3:6). The word *testament* means *covenant* and is the term used to designate the relation that existed between God and His people. The term *covenant* was first of all applied to the relation itself and afterward to the books which contained the record of that relation (2 Cor. 3:6, 14; Heb. 9:15; 12:24).

By the end of the second century we find the "Old Covenant" and the "New Covenant" as the established names of the Jewish and Christian Scriptures; and Origen, in the beginning of the third century, mentioned "the divine Scriptures, the so-called Old and New Covenants." The Old Testament deals with the record of the calling and history of the Jewish nation, and as such it is the Old Covenant. The New Testament deals with the history and application of the redemption wrought by the Lord Jesus Christ, and as such it is the New Covenant.

The Law and the Prophets. The books of the Old Testament fall into several divisions, the grouping of the English version differing from that of the original. The Hebrew Scriptures are divided into the Law, the Prophets, and the Writings. Probably the three divisions mark three stages in the process of collecting the sacred writing — in other words, in the history of the canon. The earliest Jewish Bible was the Law, the five books of Moses or Pentateuch. Later on, this expanded into the Law, and the Prophets. Later still, a final group was recognized as of divine authority, its general title suggesting the miscellaneous character of its contents; and the canon was complete — Law, Prophets, and Writings.

The New Testament references to this ancient grouping of the Jewish Scriptures are interesting. The first division is referred to as "the Law" in many places where there is clearly an allusion to or a quotation from the Pentateuch (Matt. 12:5; 22:36; 23:35; Luke 10:26). But in accordance with the peculiar reverence attached by the Jews to this portion of the sacred writings, the term *Law* becomes a designation of Old Testament Scripture generally and is so used in reference to citations from the Psalms (John 10:34; 12:34; 15:25) and from Isaiah (1 Cor. 14:21).

A fuller title for the Old Testament combines the first two of its three divisions, "The Law and the Prophets" (Matt. 5:17; 7:12; 22:40; Luke 16:29; 24:27; Rom. 3:21). Only once is there a distinct reference to the threefold grouping: "That all things must needs be fulfilled which are written in the Law of Moses and the Prophets and the Psalms concerning me" (Luke 24:44, ASV). Here either the "Psalms," as the first book of the Hagiographa, stands for the whole of the third division, or our Lord adds to the Law and the Prophets the one other Old Testament book which is most familiar and precious, as well as clearest in its messianic prediction.

The Scripture and the Scriptures. The Bible is called "the Scripture" (Mark 12:10; 15:28; Luke 4:21; John 2:22; 7:38; 10:35; Rom. 4:3; Gal. 4:30; 2 Peter 1:20). It is called "the Scriptures" (Matt. 22:29; Mark 12:24; Luke 24:27; John 5:39; Acts 17:11; Rom. 1:2; 2 Tim. 3:15; 2 Peter 3:16).

The name applied in the New Testament to the books of the Old Testament collectively is "the Writings," or in Latin, "the Scriptures." Once we find the phrase "Holy Scriptures," and once with a different form of the Greek word "Sacred Writings." When the singular occurs, it is with reference not to the whole but to some particular passage, e.g., "Today is this Scripture fulfilled in your ears" (Luke 4:21), following a quotation from Isaiah 61. The collective use of "Scripture," familiar to us and embodying the sense of oneness already referred to, was still in the making. The earlier usage is "Writings, books"; the later, though not the less true, is Scripture. These terms mean that the Scriptures are Holy Writings. By the early Christians the most common designation for the whole Bible was "the Scriptures."

The Word of God. Of all the names given to the Bible, "The Word of God" is doubtless the most significant, impressive, and complete (see Mark 7:12, 13; Rom. 10:17; Heb. 4:12; 1 Thess. 2:13). The Bible as the Word of God is sufficient to justify the faith of the weakest Christian. It gathers up all that the most earnest search can unfold. It teaches us to regard the Bible as the utterance of divine wisdom and love — as God speaking to man.

The Symbols of the Book

Symbols are used within Scripture to illustrate the power and value of the Word of God. These may be classified under seven divisions.

1. The revealing power of the Word is illustrated by the symbol of

the mirror (James 1:23-25).

2. The generative power of the Word is illustrated by the symbol of the seed (James 1:18; 1 Peter 1:23; see also Matt. 13).

3. The cleansing, purifying power of the Word is illustrated by the symbol of the laver and water (Eph. 5:25-27; John 15:3; Ps. 119:5, 11; John 17:17).

4. The illuminating, guiding power of the Word is illustrated by the symbol of the lamp and the light (Ps. 119:105).

5. The power of the Word to equip for the work and warfare of life is illustrated by the symbols of weapons and implements — sword and hammer (Heb. 4:12; Jer. 23:29).

6. The enriching and adorning power of the Word is illustrated by the symbols of gold and fine apparel (Ps. 19:10; 1 Peter 3:3-5).

7. The nourishing, sustaining, and satisfying power of the Word is illustrated by the symbols of milk, meat, bread, and honey (1 Peter 2:2; 1 Cor. 3:1, 2; Matt. 4:4; Job 23:12; John 6:35, 51; Heb. 5:12-14; Ps. 19:10).

THE BIBLE AS A DIVINE REVELATION

The Definition of a Divine Revelation

Revelation may be defined as a supernatural communication from God to man, either oral or written. The term is usually understood of a written communication. Horne says revelation is "a discovery afforded by God to man of Himself, or of His will, over and above what He has made known by the light of nature, or reason."[2]

The Reasonableness of a Divine Revelation

A divine revelation is possible. Granted the existence of a personal God, omniscient and omnipotent, there can be no insurmountable difficulty to belief in such a revelation as that claimed for the Scriptures.

A divine revelation is probable. Granted the sovereign grace and wisdom of God, it is logical to expect that these would prompt Him as man's creator and ruler to communicate with man. Philosophers of all ages have thought a divine revelation probable and have expected it.

A divine revelation is credible. Granted that a special divine revelation is both possible and probable, it is natural and easy to believe that one has been given. Human nature is more credulous than incredulous. Thus, in all ages, mankind has been prone to believe in alleged supernatural revelations. Witness the wide acceptance of such so-called sacred books as the Koran, the Book of Mormon, Zend-Avesta of the Parsees, records of Spiritism, Mrs. Eddy's *Science and Health with Key to the Scriptures.*

A divine revelation is necessary. The imperfect light of nature calls for the perfect light of revelation. Nature throws no light on the trinity, the atonement, pardon, method of worship, personal existence after death, etc. Even the truth to which we arrive by our natural powers needs divine confirmation and authority when it addresses minds and wills perverted by sin. To break this power of sin and to furnish encouragement to moral effort, we need a special divine revelation of the merciful and helpful aspect of the divine nature. While conscience gives proof that God is a God of holiness, we have not, from the light of nature, equal evidence that God is a God of love.

Reason teaches man that, as a sinner, he merits condemnation; but he cannot from reason alone know that God will have mercy upon him and provide salvation. His doubts can be removed only by God's own voice assuring him of redemption in Christ's blood — the forgiveness of sins according to the riches of His grace, and revealing to him the way in which that forgiveness has been rendered possible.

The dense ignorance, low morality, and abject helplessness of man in his natural state demands the illumination, righteousness, and power which the Scriptures reveal and provide. The Babylonians worshiped nature; the Egyptians, animals; the Greeks and Romans deified passion and powers of men.

Man's spiritual longings require the satisfaction which revelation alone can fulfill (Job 31:35).

Man needs a final authority for creed and conduct, for faith and practice, which can be had only in an authoritative revelation from God.

The Certainty of a Divine Revelation

The above grounds afford strong presumption for the reasonableness of believing in a revelation from God; that is, the Holy Scriptures. But we are not left without absolute certainty that the Bible is such a revelation. By the twofold proof of attested miracle and fulfilled prophecy God has certified His Book.

The Attestation of Miracles:

1. First definition: A miracle is an event obvious to the senses, produced for a holy purpose by the immediate agency of God; an

event, therefore, which (though not necessarily conflicting with any law of nature) the laws of nature, if fully known, would not, without this immediate agency of God, be competent to explain. This definition corrects several erroneous conceptions of a miracle.

a. A miracle is not a suspension or violation of natural law, since natural law is in operation at the time of the miracle just as much as before.

b. A miracle is not a sudden product of natural agencies — a product merely foreseen by him who appears to work it; it is the effect of a will outside nature.

c. A miracle is not an event without a cause, since it has for its cause a direct volition of God.

d. A miracle is not an irrational or capricious act of God, but an act of wisdom, performed in accordance with the immutable laws of His being, so that in the same circumstances the same course would be again pursued.

e. A miracle is not contrary to experience, since it is not contrary to experience for a new cause to be followed by a new effect.

f. A miracle is not a matter of internal experience, like regeneration or illumination, but is an event obvious to the senses, which may serve as an objective proof to all that the worker of it is divinely commissioned as a teacher of revealed truth.[3]

2. Alternative definition: A miracle is an event in nature, so extraordinary in itself and so coinciding with the prophecy or command of the divinely commissioned teacher or leader, as fully to warrant the conviction, on the part of those who witness it, that God has wrought it with the design of certifying that this teacher or leader has been commissioned by Him. This definition involves the following conclusions:

a. It recognizes the immanence of God and His immediate agency in nature, instead of assuming an antithesis between the laws of nature and the will of God.

b. It regards miracle as simply an extraordinary act of the same God who is already present in all natural operations, and Who through them is revealing His general plan.

c. It holds that natural law as the method of God's regular activity in no way precludes unique exertions of His power when these will best secure His purpose in creation.

d. It leaves it possible that all miracles may have their natural explanations and may hereafter be traced to natural causes, while both miracles and their natural causes may be only names for the one and self-same will of God.

e. It reconciles the claims of both science and religion — of science, by permitting any possible or probable physical antecedents of the miracle; of religion, by maintaining that these very antecedents together with the miracle itself are to be interpreted as signs of God's special commission to him under whose teaching or leadership the miracle is wrought.

3. The possibility of miracles. An event in nature may be caused by an agent in nature yet above nature. This is evident from the following considerations:

a. Lower forces and laws in nature are frequently counteracted and transcended by the higher. For example, mechanical forces and laws are counteracted and transcended by chemical forces and laws, and these in turn by the vital or living, and yet these lower forces and laws are not suspended or annihilated by the higher.

b. The human will acts upon its physical organism, and so upon nature, and produces results which nature left to herself never could have accomplished, while yet no law of nature is suspended or violated. Gravitation still acts upon the axe, even while man holds it at the surface of the water — for the axe still has weight (cf. 2 Kings 6:5-7).

c. In all free causation, there is an acting without means. Man acts upon external nature through his physical organism, but in moving his physical organism he acts directly upon matter. In other words, the human will can use means, only because it has the power of acting initially without means.

d. What the human will, considered as a supernatural force, and what the chemical and vital forces of nature itself are demonstrably able to accomplish cannot be regarded as beyond the power of God, as long as God dwells in and controls the universe. If man's will can act directly upon matter in his own physical organism, God's will can work immediately upon the system which He has created and which He sustains. In other words, if there be a God, and if He be a personal being, miracles are possible. The impossibility of miracles can be maintained only upon principles of atheism or pantheism.

e. This possibility of miracles becomes doubly sure to those who see in Christ none other than the immanent God manifested to creatures. The Logos, or divine Reason, who is the principle of all growth and development can make God known only by means of successive new impartations of His energy. Since all progress implies addition or increase, and since Christ is the only source of life, the whole history of creation is a witness to the possibility of miracles.

4. The probability of miracles:

   a. We acknowledge that, so long as we confine our attention to nature, there is a presumption against miracles. Experience testifies to the uniformity of natural law. A general uniformity is needful, in order to make possible a rational calculation of the future and a proper ordering of life. Miracle, however, likewise presupposes the uniformity of law. Where there is no law, no settled order, there can be no miracle. Miracle presupposes law. The uniqueness attributed to miracle is in light of the recognition of law.

   b. We deny, however, that this uniformity of nature is absolute and universal.

      (1) It is not a truth of reason that can have no exceptions, like the axiom that a whole is greater than its parts.

      (2) Experience could not warrant a belief in absolute and universal uniformity, unless experience were identical with absolute and universal knowledge.

      (3) We know, on the contrary, from the record in Genesis, that there have been changes in this uniformity, such as the introduction of vegetable, animal, and human life, which cannot be accounted for except by the manifestation of supernatural power.

   c. Since the inworking of the moral law into the constitution and course of nature shows that nature exists, not for itself, but for the contemplation and use of moral beings, it is probable that the God of nature will produce effects aside from those of natural law, whenever there are sufficiently important moral ends to be served thereby.

   d. The existence of moral disorder consequent upon the free acts of man's will, therefore, changes the presumption against miracles into a presumption in their favor. The nonappearance of miracles, in this case, would be the greatest of wonders.

e. As belief in the possibility of miracles rests upon our belief in the existence of a personal God, so belief in the probability of miracles rests upon our belief that God is a moral and benevolent being. He who has no God but a god of physical order will regard miracles as an impertinent intrusion upon that order. But he who yields to the testimony of conscience and regards God as a God of holiness will see that man's unholiness renders God's miraculous interposition most necessary to man and most becoming to God. Our view of miracles will therefore be determined by our belief in a moral, or an amoral, God.

f. Since God is not merely the intellectual but the moral reason of the world, the disturbances of the world order which are due to sin are the matters which most deeply affect Him. Christ, the Life of the whole system and of humanity as well, must suffer; and, since we have evidence that He is merciful as well as just, it is probable that He will rectify the evil by extraordinary means when merely ordinary means do not avail.

5. The plausibility of miracles. The amount of testimony necessary to prove a miracle is no greater than that which is requisite to prove the occurrence of any other unusual but confessedly possible event.

Hume, indeed, argued that a miracle is so contradictory of all human experience that it is more reasonable to believe any amount of testimony false than to believe a miracle to be true. The argument maintains for substance that things are impossible because improbable. It ridicules the credulity of those who "thrust their fists against the post, and still insist they see the ghosts," and holds with the German philosopher who declared that he would not believe a miracle even if he saw one with his own eyes.

a. This argument is based upon a false premise of making our own personal experience the measure of all human experience. The same principle would make a proof of any absolutely new fact impossible. Even though God should work a miracle He could never prove it.

b. It involves a self-contradiction since it seeks to overthrow our faith in human testimony by adducing to the contrary the general experience of men, of which we know only from testimony. This general experience, moreover, is merely negative, and cannot neutralize that which is positive, except upon principles that would invalidate all testimony whatever.

c. It requires belief in a greater wonder than those which it would escape. That multitudes of intelligent and honest men should, against all their interests, unite in deliberate and persistent falsehood, under the circumstances narrated in the New Testament record, involves a change in the sequences of nature far more incredible than the miracles of Christ and His apostles.

6. The evidential value of miracles:

a. Miracles are the natural accompaniments and attestations of new communications from God. The great epochs of miracles — represented by Moses, the prophets, and the first and second comings of Christ — are coincident with the great epochs of revelation. Miracles serve to draw attention to new truth, and they cease when this truth has gained currency and foothold.

b. Miracles generally certify to the truth of doctrine, not directly but indirectly; otherwise a new miracle must needs accompany each new doctrine taught. Miracles primarily and directly certify to the divine commission and authority of the teacher or messenger, and therefore warrant acceptance of his doctrines and obedience to his commands as the doctrines and commands of God, whether these be communicated at intervals or all together, orally or in written documents.

c. Miracles, therefore, do not stand alone as evidences. Power alone cannot prove a divine commission. Purity of life and doctrine must go with the miracles to assure us that a teacher is come from God. The miracles and the doctrine in this manner mutually support each other and form parts of one whole. The internal evidence for the Christian system may have greater power over certain minds and over certain ages than the external evidence.

d. The Christian miracles do not lose their value as evidence in the process of ages. The loftier the structure of Christian life and doctrine, the greater the need that its foundation be secure. The authority of Christ as a teacher of supernatural truth rests upon His miracles, and especially upon the miracle of His resurrection. That one miracle to which the church looks back as the source of her life carries with it irresistibly all the other miracles of Scripture record; upon it alone we may safely rest the proof that the Scriptures are an authoritative revelation from God.

e. The resurrection of our Lord Jesus Christ — by which we mean His coming forth from the sepulcher in body as well as in spirit — is demonstrated by evidence as varied and conclusive as that which proves to us any single fact of ancient history. Without it Christianity itself is inexplicable, as is shown by the failure of all modern rationalistic theories to account for its rise and progress.

f. Christ's evaluation of miracles is seen in Christ's declaring that the eternal fate of Chorazin and Bethsaida resulted from their disregard of His miracles (Matt. 11:21, 22). John the Baptist was to be confirmed in his faith in Him as the Messiah by the record of His miracles (Luke 7:22). Jesus declares explicitly that the work which He did, and which the Father had given Him to finish, bore witness of Him that the Father had sent Him (John 5:36). If men would not believe Him they were asked to believe His works (John 10:25, 26, 37, 38). Jesus emphasized the fact that it was sin on the part of His countrymen not to believe in His miracles (John 15:24).

The Attestation of Fulfilled Prophecy. Prophecy is here considered in its limited meaning as referring to prediction. Prophecy thus is the foretelling of future events by virtue of direct communication from God — a foretelling therefore which, though not contravening any laws of the human mind, those laws, if fully known, would not, without this agency of God, be sufficient to explain. Or, prophecy is the communication by God to man of a knowledge of events still future, which otherwise he could not have discovered.[4]

1. Requirements for prophecy to be an evidence of revelation. There are certain criteria by which prophecy must be judged and on which its evidential value must depend. Here one is justified in saying that Bible prophecy amply fulfills these criteria.

a. It must concern events which no human sagacity could discover. Philosophical historians or statesmen may forecast national convulsion or social revolutions by studying the annals of the past and watching the development of current events, but the predictions of the whole Bible are almost wholly outside the range of probability or precedent.

b. It must be known before the event takes place, and its utterance must be distant from the event. Moses' prediction of Israel's history in Deuteronomy 28 covers this and the preceding point. Clearly predicted long before their actual occurrence, how improbable were the Babylonian captivity, the Roman seige, the present scattered, persecuted, and yet expectant condition of the Jewish people. Take again the prophecies of Isaiah, Jeremiah, or Ezekiel concerning the downfall of the great capitals of Nineveh and Babylon, the desolation of Tyre, and the debasement of mighty Egypt, to say nothing of their predictions and those of others concerning the personal history of the Messiah.

c. It must be sufficiently clear in statement, and yet sufficiently minute in detail, to identify its fulfillment beyond the possibility of dispute. Biblical prophecy enters astonishingly into details. An examination of the subject has shown that in each of the more prominent subjects of prophecy, there are from twenty to forty particulars, while in those concerning the Messiah there are no less than three hundred minutiae, making the chances of accidental coincidence less than one in ten thousands of millions.

d. It would add to the evidential value of prophecy did it contain an element of obscurity or mystery which only the fulfillment could explain. The elements of mysteriousness and obscurity are not lacking from many of the Bible predictions.[5] The paradoxes which they contain add greatly to their supernatural character. For example, any one can see that many of the events and circumstances foretold of Israel are as far as possible from being such as would in the day of their utterance have naturally occurred to the mind of the patriotic Israelite endeavoring to forecast the future of his nation and his country. Indeed, they were offensive to his pride and contradictory to the fixed religious beliefs of his nation, in evidence of which we have the fact that they were almost unanimously disbelieved by the great majority of the people to whom they were addressed. The prophets were severely persecuted and sometimes put to death for giving utterance to such things (see Jer. 7:4; Ezek. 11:2, 3; Mic. 3:11).

e. There must be no collusion or fraudulent intention of fulfillment on the part of the human agents concerned. Bible prophecy fulfills this qualification because of its distant re-

moval in time from its fulfillment and also because often those
who uttered it were not aware of that which was involved in its
fulfillment.
    f. It should be worthy of God in its character and design. Bible
        prophecy is noticeably characterized by the absence of the
        sordid and trivial and by the presence of that which gives it a
        high moral value.[6]
2. Evidential value of fulfilled prophecy. Prophecy, like miracles,
does not stand alone as evidence of the divine commission of the
Scripture writers and teachers. It is simply a corroborative attestation which unites with miracles to prove that a teacher of truth
has come from God and speaks with divine authority. We cannot,
however, dispense with this portion of the evidences — for unless
the death and resurrection of Christ are events foreknown and
foretold by Himself, as well as by the ancient prophets, we lose
one main proof of His authority as a Teacher sent from God.
    In Isaiah 41:21-23 we have what is probably the most remarka-
ble challenge to be found in the Bible. "Produce your cause, saith
the Lord; bring forth your strong reasons, saith the King of Jacob.
Let them bring forth, and show us what shall happen; let them
show the former things, what they be, that we may consider
them, and know the latter end of them; or declare us things for to
come. Show the things that are to come hereafter, that we may
know that ye are gods."
    This Scripture has both a negatve and a positive value. Nega-
tively, it suggests an infallible criterion by which we may test the
claims of religious impostors; positively, it calls attention to an
unanswerable argument for the truthfulness of God's Word.
Jehovah bids the prophets of false faiths to predict successfully
events lying in the far distant future, and their success or failure
will show whether or not they are gods or merely pretenders and
deceivers. On the other hand, the demonstrated fact that God
alone grasps the ages, and in His Word declares the end from the
beginning, shows that He is God and that the Scriptures are His
revelation to mankind.
    Again and again men have attempted to predict future events,
but always with the most disastrous failure; the anticipations of
the most far-seeing and the precautions of the wisest are mocked
repeatedly by the bitter irony of events. Man stands before an
impenetrable wall of darkness; he is unable to foresee the events
of even the next hour. None knows what a day may bring forth. To

the finite mind the future is filled with unknown possibilities. How then can we explain the hundreds of detailed prophecies in the Scriptures which have been literally fulfilled to the very letter hundreds of years after they were uttered? How can we account for the fact that the Bible successfully foretold hundreds, and in some instances thousands of years beforehand, the history of the Jews, the course of the Gentiles, and the experiences of the church?

The most conservative of critics and the most daring assailants of God's Word are compelled to acknowledge that all the books of the Old Testament were written hundreds of years before the incarnation of our Lord; hence, the actual and accurate fulfillment of these prophecies can only be explained on the hypothesis that "Prophecy came not in any time by the will of men: but holy men of God spake, moved by the Holy Ghost."

The Method of Divine Revelation

The method by which divine truth is communicated to man is threefold: revelation, illumination, and inspiration.

Revelation. Revelation, as distinguished from either illumination or inspiration, may be defined as that act of God by which He communicates to the mind of man truth not known before and incapable of being discovered by the mind of man unaided. Thus used it is also to be distinguished from the term *revelation* as descriptive of the truth thus communicated. This mode of the divine action in communicating new truth operated variously: by mental suggestion, by external vision, and by oral statement.

Illumination. Illumination is the divine quickening of the human mind in virtue of which it is enabled to understand truth already revealed. By "truth already revealed" is meant the truth of the Holy Scriptures. "What light is to the eyes, illumination is to the mind." (Luke 24:32, 45; Matt. 16:17; 1 Cor. 2:12, 14.)

Inspiration. Inspiration means that operation of the divine Spirit which renders a speaker or writer infallible in the communication of truth, whether or not that truth is previously known.

Or, to give an alternate definition: By the inspiration of the Scriptures we mean that special divine influence upon the minds of the Scripture writers in virtue of which their productions, apart from errors of transcription and when rightly interpreted, together constitute an infallible rule of faith and practice.[7]

Let us consider further the meaning of inspiration. *Inspiration*, as a general term, may be used to include all those kinds and degrees of the Holy Spirit's influence which were brought to bear upon the minds of the Scripture writers in order to secure the putting into written and permanent form the truth which God has communicated to man.

Inspiration may often include revelation, or the direct communication from God, of truth to which man could not attain by his unaided powers. It may include illumination, or the quickening of man's cognitive powers to understand truth already revealed. Inspiration, however, does not necessarily and always include either revelation or illumination. It is simply the divine influence which secures a transmission of needed truth to the future, and according to the nature of the truth to be transmitted, it may be only an inspiration of superintendence, or it may be also and at the same time an inspiration of illumination or revelation.

It is not denied, but affirmed, that inspiration may qualify for oral utterance of truth, or for any other service to which one may be called of God. For illustration of this, see Exod. 31:1-11; 35:30-35. It is not, however, in the general sense that we use it with reference to the Bible; but in the particular sense, i.e., that God guided, directed, and controlled the human writers and His will to man. This revelation of God and His will is found in the Scriptures and can be found nowhere else.

Theoretical Views of Inspiration

The Intuition Theory, or Natural Inspiration. This holds that inspiration is but a higher development of that natural insight into truth which all men possess to some degree; a mode of intelligence in matters of morals and religion which gives rise to sacred books, as a corresponding mode of intelligence in matters of secular truth gives rise to great works of philosophy and art. This mode of intelligence is regarded as the product of man's own powers, either without special divine influence or with only the inworking of an impersonal God. It denies that there is anything supernatural, mysterious, or peculiar in the mode of the Spirit's operation in and upon the Scripture writers. It claims that they were no more inspired than were Milton, Shakespeare, Muhammad, or Confucius. With regard to this theory we remark —

1. Man has, indeed, a certain natural insight into truth and we grant that inspiration uses this, as far as it will go, and makes it an instrument in discovering and recording facts of nature or history.

2. In all matters of morals and religion, however, man's insight into truth is vitiated by wrong affections, and unless a supernatural wisdom can guide him, he is certain to err himself and to lead others into error (see 1 Cor. 2:10, 11; Num. 12:6-8).

3. The theory in question, holding as it does that natural insight is the only source of religious truth, involves a self-contradiction: if the theory be true, then one man is inspired to utter what a second is inspired to pronounce false. The Vedas, the Koran, and the Bible cannot be inspired to contradict each other. The Vedas permit thieving, and the Koran teaches salvation by works; these cannot be inspired and the Bible also.

4. It makes moral and religious truth to be a purely subjective thing — a matter of private opinion — having no objective reality independent of men's opinions regarding it.

5. It logically involves the denial of a personal God who is truth and reveals truth, and so makes man to be the highest intelligence in the universe. This is to explain inspiration by denying its existence; since, if there be no personal God, inspiration is but a figure of speech for a purely natural fact.

The Illumination Theory, or Universal Christian Inspiration. This regards inspiration as merely an intensifying and elevating of the religious perceptions of the Christians, the same in kind, though greater in degree, with the illumination of every believer by the Holy Spirit. It holds, not that the Bible is, but that it contains the Word of God, and not the writings, but only the writers were inspired. The illumination given by the Holy Spirit, however, puts the inspired writer only in full possession of his normal powers, but does not communicate objective truth beyond his ability to discover or understand.

With regard to this theory we remark —

1. There is unquestionably an illumination of the mind of every believer by the Holy Spirit, and we grant that there may have been instances in which the influence of the Spirit, in inspiration, amounted only to illumination. For illustrations see applications and interpretations of Old Testament Scripture (John 1:29; Acts 2:27).

2. We deny, however, that this was the constant method of inspiration, or that such an influence can account for the revelation of new truth to the apostles and prophets. The illumination of the

Holy Spirit gives no new truth, but only a vivid apprehension of the truth already revealed. Any original communication of truth must have required a work of the Spirit different not only in degree but in kind.

3. Mere illumination could not secure the Scripture writers from frequent and grievous error. The spiritual perception of the Christian is always rendered to some extent imperfect and deceptive by remaining depravity. The subjective element so predominates in this theory that no certainty remains even with regard to the truthworthiness of the Scriptures as a whole.

4. The theory is logically indefensible, as intimating that illumination with regard to truth can be imparted without imparting truth itself, whereas God must first furnish objective truth to be perceived before He can illuminate the mind to perceive the meaning of that truth.

The Dictation Theory, or Mechanical Inspiration. This theory holds that the inspiration consisted in such a possession of the minds and bodies of the Scripture writers by the Holy Spirit that they became passive instruments, or amanuenses' pens, not penman of God.

1. We grant that there are instances when God's communications were uttered in an audible voice and took a definite form of words, and that this was sometimes accompanied with the command to commit the words to writing (see Exod. 3:4; Dan. 4:31; Acts 9:5; Rev. 19:9; 21:5).

2. The theory in question, however, rests upon a partial induction of Scripture facts — unwarrantably assuming that such occasional instances of direct dictation reveal the invariable method of God's communications of truth to the writers of the Bible.

3. It cannot account for the manifestly human element in the Scriptures. There are peculiarities of style which distinguish the productions of each writer from those of every other.

The Verbal Plenary Theory, or Full Inspiration. By verbal inspiration we mean that the very words of Scripture were given by the Holy Spirit, that the writers were not left absolutely to themselves in the choice of which words they should use, but were divinely directed in their selection. This understanding opposes the concept or thought theory, which claims that only the concepts or thoughts of men were given by inspiration.

By plenary inspiration we mean that the Scriptures are fully and equally inspired in all their parts. This opposes the teaching of partial inspiration expressed in the statement "The Bible contains the Word of God."

Those who hold this view claim it not for any version or translation, but for the Scriptures as they first appeared, i.e., the original manuscripts. But someone may say, "Is not this question after all only academic? What is the use of contending for an inspired original when we do not possess it? No one claims the original autographs to be now existent; we have only translations at the best. Why then insist upon an inerrant source?"

The answer is, in the first place, that consistency demands it. The Scriptures themselves claim such an inerrant source. In the second place, God's honor is at stake. To quote an apt though homely remark of another, "A man who wears a pair of patched trousers may have little interest in knowing that they were whole when they came from the tailor's hands, but not so in the case of the tailor. His reputation demands that they shall have been perfect when they were delivered." We have no right to say that God may have given a revelation of Himself and His will to man which contains a single error, any more than we have a right to say that He created a world in which sin existed. In the third place, there is a scientific reason for this claim. What is the use or value of textual criticism if there be no perfect source of Holy Writ?

Why do Bible scholars make so much of words and phrases and shades of meanings, comparisons and manuscripts and versions, if at the basis of it all there is no ground of certainty? If men drive pilings into the earth, it is because they expect to find bottom somewhere, and if men dig into the original roots of the Scriptures, it is because they expect to find, and feel the necessity of finding, a solid footing at the end. And, as a matter of fact, they have found this footing. This is not to say that in the present translations of either the Old or New Testaments we have in every instance the word of the original, but this is so nearly so as to make it practically true.

As far as the Old Testament is concerned, scholars can point out the variant readings and the places that are in doubt here and there, which is the same as to say that the remainder is not in doubt; and the remainder is so nearly the whole that if all the doubtful readings were omitted altogether, they would not affect one essential historical fact or doctrinal teaching. As to the New Testament, in nine hundred and ninety-nine cases out of every thousand, we have the very word of the original.

The Scriptural View of Inspiration

The verbal, plenary theory, or full inspiration, accords with the general teaching of the Scriptures. Inspiration is as much a matter of divine revelation as is justification by faith or any other Bible doctrine. It stands upon the authority of the Scriptures themselves, which must be the final court of appeal on this subject, as on every question of revealed truth. What the Bible teaches about its own inspiration is a matter purely of divine testimony, and our business is simply to receive the testimony as such.

Not only does the Bible claim to be a divine revelation, but it also asserts that its original manuscripts were written "not in words which man's wisdom teacheth, but which the Holy Spirit teacheth"(1 Cor. 2:13). The Bible nowhere claims to have been written by inspired men; as a matter of fact some of them were very defective characters — David, for example — but it insists that the words they uttered and recorded were God's words. When we speak of the inspiration of the original Scriptures, we are speaking of the record only; that is, of the writings and not necessarily of the human writers themselves or any of the human speakers who are referred to or quoted from. This is a distinction necessary to be kept in mind in order to avoid confusion of thought and apparently contradictory statements. For example, the human writers were themselves more or less mistaken and at times unholy in their thought (see Exod. 32:32; Num. 20:10-12; 1 Sam. 20:6; Acts 23:5; Gal. 2:14).

But while the writers may have been mistaken in their thought, the only consistent theory of inspiration is that they were never so as to their words written in the Holy Scripture. The writings were always inspired, though the writers were not always inspired men. The teaching of the Bible concerning the inspiration of the Scriptures is clear and simple and uniform throughout. Its writers were conscious that their utterances were a message from God in the highest meaning of the word. This accords with the statement of 2 Tim. 3:16 that all Scripture is *theopneustic*, that is to say, all is given by the Spirit or by the breath of God. It admits of no exception; it is the whole Scripture, all that is written, that is, the thoughts that have already put on the clothing of language. It admits of no restriction; all Scripture is so far a work of God that it is represented to us as given by the breath of God, in the same manner as the word of a man is given by the breath of his mouth.[8]

The teachings of the Scriptures concerning their own inspiration may be exemplified by the following:

1. The nature of the inspiration of the Scriptures as attested by Christ. Jesus Christ knew whether the Scriptures were true, inspired, and authoritative. He knew the writers. Whatever He said about the Scriptures is therefore true and final to every believer.

   a. His testimony concerning the Old Testament Scriptures. Christ endorsed the Mosaic authorship and inspiration of the Pentateuch (Matt. 22:23-32; Mark 7:8-13; 12:26; Luke 16:29-31; 24:25-27, 44, 45; John 5:46; 17:17). He endorsed the miraculous narratives of the Old Testament as true (Creation — Matt. 19:4; the Flood — Luke 17:27; the destruction of Sodom — Luke 17:29; Lot's wife — Luke 17:32; Jonah — Matt. 12:40; Naaman — Luke 4:27). He endorsed the Psalms and prophetical books as inspired (Matt. 24:15; Mark 12:36; Luke 4:17-21).

   b. His testimony concerning the New Testament Scriptures. Not one word of the New Testament had been written when Christ departed from the earth; but we have His express authority for receiving it as the inspired Word of God. He said plainly that He would leave the revelation of truth unfinished and that it should be completed after His departure (John 16:12, 13). He chose certain persons to receive such additional revelations and to be His witnesses, preachers, and teachers after His departure (Matt. 28:19, 20; John 16:13; 15:27; Acts 1:8; 9:15-17). Knowing beforehand what they would write, He gave their words precisely the same authority as His own (Matt. 10:14, 15; Luke 10:16; John 13:20;17:20).

2. The extent of the inspiration of the Scriptures as indicated —

   a. By the testimony of Christ (John 6:63; 8:47; 12:48; 14:10; 17:8; Matt. 5:18).

   b. By the testimony of the writers (Moses — Exod. 4:10-12; 34:27; Balaam — Num. 22:38; 23:12-16; David — 2 Sam. 23:2; Solomon — Prov. 30:6; Isaiah — Isa. 6:5-8; Jeremiah — Jer. 1:7, 9; 36:1, 2; Zechariah — Zech. 7:7; Paul — 1 Cor. 2:13; Jude — Jude 3, 17).

We conclude, therefore, upon the testimony of Christ and the writers themselves, that the Scriptures are verbally inspired — that the Holy Spirit gave the words. The notion that the inspiration is in the concept and not in the words is contrary to the express declaration of the witnesses who knew.

Proofs of the Inspiration of the Bible
  External proofs:

1. The Bible's place in literature. In nature there are conspicuous phenomena which demand explanation. The boulder is such a phenomenon. Whether or not man's science can satisfactorily account for it, the boulder is an indisputable fact and as such must be dealt with. The science would be blind and the philosophy folly that would deny or dispute its existence.

In the world of letters there are also phenomena which call for investigation and explanation, and foremost among them all is the Bible. Hitherto human science and philosophy have failed to account for it on any purely natural basis. Nevertheless, the Bible is a fact, no less to be denied than the boulder. Within its pages may be found its own explanation. It claims to be a supernatural revelation. If this perspective be accepted, it adequately accounts for the Book.

This Book occupies the peerless place in the literature of all ages. Hence its name "the Bible," attributed to "John of the golden mouth" (Chrysostom). At a time when all literature was but in its beginning, there appeared a Book that rather befits the ending. When the foundation for the pyramid of letters was being laid, there was brought forth one stone of matchless symmetry, itself a little pyramid, the only fit apex to complete and crown the whole structure, a capstone whose lines and angles might well determine the dimensions and proportions, lines, and angles of the pyramid. Whence came this capstone, while as yet the cornerstone of literature was scarce laid? In what quarry was it found and by what hand was it hewn? It is, moreover, of no common material, but a precious stone, a colossal gem, the like of which is found in none of the richest quarries or mines of the earth.

Thus to describe the Bible is not merely to indulge in the poetry of rhetoric, but to state the most prosaic fact. This is the one book which neither belongs to nor befits the infancy of the race, and yet it was found among men in the early days of the world's history; and with all the boasted learning and wisdom of the twentieth century, it still defies all competition. The philosopher and sage cannot equal it, neither shall it be exchanged for all the jewels and fine gold of the noblest poetry and richest products of the imagination. Human hands had indeed to do with it; scores of different writers contributed to its pages. But this, instead of accounting for it, rather deepens our perplexity as to its origin, unless there was manifestly behind and above these human composers and compilers some one true author who at least superintended and controlled the whole.

2. Historical testimony. The general acceptance of the Scriptures, of both the Old and New Testaments — according to the historical records — constitutes a strong presumption in favor of their claims to inspiration. In this connection the following testimonies are worth recording: Clement of Rome, who lived about A.D. 90, said, "The Scriptures are the true words of the Holy Ghost."

Augustine contended for the infallible accuracy of every word of Scripture.

The dean of Westminster, in an address delivered in Westminster Abbey on 3 December 1904, said, "If the Bible was inspired by a Divine Spirit, how could it record what did not actually take place? If an element of human misconception and mistake was to be recognized in the Bible, how could we regard it any longer as an inspired Book, or use it as an infallible guide of life?" And then, after speaking of some of the Bible difficulties, he said, "Behind and beneath the Bible, above and beyond the Bible, was the God of the Bible." Herein lies the true and only explanation of the mystery of inspiration.

Even the Roman Catholic Church — in spite of its inconsistent attitude toward the Bible — declared at the Vatican Council of 1870 that the Scriptures "contain a revelation without error. Having been written by the inspiration of the Holy Ghost, they have God for their Author." Similar language was also used at the Council of Trent, and later at Vatican II where it was said that "since everything asserted by the inspired Authors of sacred writers must be held to be asserted by the Holy Spirit, it follows that the books of Scripture must be acknowledged as teaching firmly, faithfully, and without error that truth which God wanted put into the sacred writings for the sake of our salvation."[9]

3. Its preservation. The survival of the Bible through the ages is difficult to explain if it is not in truth the Word of God. Books are like men — dying creatures. A very small percentage of books survives more than twenty years, a yet smaller percentage lasts a hundred years, and only a very insignificant fraction represents those which have lived a thousand years. Amid the wreck and

ruin of ancient literature the Holy Scriptures stand out like the last survivor of an otherwise extinct race, and the very fact of the Bible's continued existence is an indication that like its Author it is indestructible.

When we bear in mind the fact that the Bible has been the special object of never-ending persecution, the wonder of the Bible's survival is changed into a miracle. Not only has the Bible been the most intensely loved Book in all the world, but it also has been the most bitterly hated. Not only has the Bible received more veneration and adoration than any other book, but it has also been the object of more persecution and opposition. For two thousand years man's hatred of the Bible has been persistent, determined, relentless, and murderous. Every possible effort has been made to undermine faith in the inspiration and authority of the Bible, and innumerable enterprises have been undertaken with the determination to consign it to oblivion. Imperial edicts have been issued to the effect that every known copy of the Bible should be destroyed, and when this measure failed to exterminate and annihilate God's Word, then commands were given that every person found with a copy of the Scriptures in his possession should be put to death. The very fact that the Bible has been singled out for such relentless persecution causes us to wonder at such a unique phenomenon.

4. Argument from the nature of the case. The proposition may be stated thus: The Bible is the history of redemption of the race, or from the side of the individual, a supernatural revelation of the will of God to men for their salvation. But it was given to certain men of one age to be conveyed in writing to other men in different ages. Now all men experience difficulty in giving faithful reflections of their thoughts to others because of sin, ignorance, defective memory, and the inaccuracy always incident to the use of language. Therefore it may be easily deduced that if the revelation is to be communicated precisely as originally received, the same supernatural power is required in the one case as in the other.

5. Testimony from archaeology. Archaeological research in Bible lands during the last half of the nineteenth century has enabled us to bring forth much testimony for the credibility and authority of the Old Testament. These archaeological discoveries, the fruit of the pickax and the spade, include such things as inscriptions on rocks or temple walls, statues, obelisks, pavement slabs, clay

tablets, papyrus rolls, coins, seals, pottery, and other objects, dug up from the old buried cities of the past and now preserved in the great museums of London, Paris, Istanbul, Berlin, New York, and other cities of the world. All the discoveries in Egypt and other Bible lands which have any relation to Scripture speak with one united voice, testifying to the accuracy of the statements of the Bible.

6. Its adaptability. While the Bible has its beginning in the infancy of the human race and the latest contribution to it was made at least eighteen centuries ago, its message is as vital and applicable to human life and experience of the present as at any time in the past. It is the Book for young and old, rich and poor, lofty and lowly, wise and unwise — for all who need the Savior and look for the life beyond, for all who need comfort and consolation, counsel and guidance along the way. There is no point in human experience at which this Book does not touch us. Though oriental in its origin, it fits the need of those of every nation and kindred and people and tongue. Surely a book of such marvelous adaptability is beyond the possibility of mere human production and demands divine authorship to account for it.

7. Its transforming power. The greatest sign of the quality of any book is the residue it leaves behind as it flows through the mind. As in streams where sulfur abounds, the green deposit is on the stones; and where iron abounds, the red hue is in the bed; and where gold is found, its luster is on the very sand — so when a book flows through the mind, the supreme testimony to its quality is what it leaves behind. Is it vice or virtue; is it magnanimity or pusillanimity; is it carnality or spirituality? The greatest proof, perhaps, that the Bible is the Book of God is that it leaves as residuum the gold of heaven wherever it flows.

The contents of the Scriptures have supplied themes for the greatest artists, musicians, and poets the world has yet produced, and they have been the mightiest factor of all in shaping the moral progress of the race. Take down from the walls of our best art galleries those pictures which portray scenes and incidents in the history of Israel and the life of our Lord, and you have removed the richest gems from the crown of human genius. Take away such sublime oratorios as *Elijah* and the *Messiah*, and you have taken out of the realm of music something which can never be duplicated; destroy the countless hymns which have drawn their inspiration from the Scriptures, and you have left us little else worth singing. Eliminate from the compositions of Tennyson, Wordsworth, and Carlyle every reference to the moral and spiritual truths taught in God's Word, and you have stripped them of their beauty and robbed them of their fragrance. Remove from our statute-books every law founded upon the ethical conceptions of the Bible, and you have annihilated the greatest factor in modern civilization. Rob our libraries of every book devoted to the work of elaborating and disseminating the precepts and concepts of Holy Writ, and you have taken from us that which cannot be valued in dollars and cents.

The Bible has done more for the emancipation and civilization of the heathen than all the forces which the human arm can wield put together. It is like the banyan tree: its very branches bend down and take root. It spreads over whole continents, and could not be eradicated without tearing up the very soil of society. Someone has said, "Draw a line around the nations which have the Bible and you will then have divided between barbarism and civilization, between thrift and poverty, between selfishness and charity, between oppression and freedom, between life and the shadow of death." Even Darwin had to concede the miraculous element in the triumphs of the missionaries of the Cross.

Internal proofs:

1. Biblical claims of inspiration. The strongest witness to the inspiration of the Bible is the claim of the Bible itself. Nor can it be said that this is reasoning in a circle. If one thinks that to accept the claims of the Bible to its inspiration is like taking a man's own word that he speaks the truth, the reply is that we are not now referring to the truth of the Bible at all, but only to its inspiration. The truth or credibility of the Bible is assumed, being established by well-grounded proofs. If the Bible then is proven to be true, if its statements of facts are credible, we are certainly justified in opening its pages to see what it says about itself.

The Bible plainly teaches that its words are inspired and that it is the Word of God. This teaching may be considered under three kinds of evidence.

   a. Direct testimony. In the five books of Moses, in the books called historical, and books included under the general title of poetry, such expressions as the following occur hundreds of times: "Thus saith the Lord"; "The Lord said"; "The Lord spake"; "The Lord hath spoken"; "The saying of the Lord";

and "The Word of the Lord." There is no other thought expressed concerning inspiration than that the writers spoke and wrote the very words that God gave them (see Exod. 4:10-12; 34:27; Num. 12:6-8; 22:38; 23:26; Deut. 4:2; 18:20; 2 Sam. 23:2; Jer. 1:6-9).

Turning to the books called the prophetical, we find Isaiah saying, "Hear the word of the Lord"; and no fewer than twenty times does he explicitly say that his writings are the "words of the Lord." Almost one hundred times Jeremiah says, "The word of the Lord came unto me," or declares he was uttering the "words of the Lord" and the "word of the living God." Ezekiel says his writings are the "words of God" nearly sixty times (see as examples Ezek. 3:10, 11; Dan. 10:9; Hos. 1:1; Joel 1:1; Amos 3:1; Obad. 1:1; Jonah 1:1; Mic. 1:1; Nah. 1:12; Hab. 2:2; Zeph. 1:1; Hag. 1:1; Zech. 1:1; Mal. 1:1).

For the testimony of the New Testament Scriptures see the following: Mark 12:36; 13:11; John 5:19; 12:49, 50; 17:8; Acts 2:1-4; 2:7, 11; 1 Cor. 2:13; 1 Thess. 2:13.

The Bible thus uniformly teaches the doctrine of verbal inspiration. *It is the Word of God.* This is the invariable testimony of the Book itself. It never, in a single instance, says the thoughts of the writers were inspired, or that these writers had a concept. The Scriptures are called "the Oracles of God" (Rom. 3:2); "the Word of God" (Luke 8:11); "the Word of the Lord" (Acts 13:48); "the Word of Life" (Phil. 2:16); "the Word of Christ (Col. 3:16); "the Word of Truth" (Eph. 1:13); and "the Word of Faith" (Rom. 10:8). By these and similar statements do they declare, more than two thousand times, that the Bible is the Word of God — that the words are God-breathed or inspired.

b. Inferential testimony. By inferential testimony is meant that which is assumed by the Bible and the natural implication belonging to many of its statements. The Bible assumes to be from God in that it meets man face to face with drawn sword and says, "Thou shalt!" and "Thou shalt not!" and demands immediate, unconditional, and irreversible surrender to the authority of heaven and submission to all the laws and will of God, as made known in its pages. This of itself would not signify a great deal, though unique, were it not for the striking and significant results of such submission; but the natural inference of such assumption is that the words of demand and command are from God.

c. Resultant testimony. There are certain results which follow believing the Word and submission to its requirements which cannot be accounted for on any other basis than that it is inspired of God.

First, it will impart spiritual life and save the soul (John 6:63; 2 Cor. 5:17; James 1:21; 1 Peter 1:23; 2 Peter 1:4). The power and life of the Almighty lie hidden in the words of the sacred record; they are God-breathed; and that power and life will be manifested in the case of everyone who receives them and submits to their requirements. None of the books which men have written can do this. Second, it has cleansing power. "Wherewithal shall a young man cleanse his way? By taking heed thereto according to thy Word" (Ps. 119:9; see also John 15:3; Eph. 5:26). Finally, it is by the Word that we are kept from evil and the power of the evil one (Pss. 17:4; 119:11; John 17:14, 17).

2. Argument from unity. The Bible is assumed to be a phenomenon, wholly unrivaled in the world of letters, even by its judgmental enemies. One of its most important features is its unity, which is as marvelous as it is conspicuous. Every circumstance connected with its preparation and production was calculated to prevent and prohibit such unity. Here are sixty-six different books, written by some forty different authors in three different languages, and the periods of authorship cover approximately sixteen centuries. These human writers were brought up in different countries and were so remote from each other in time and space that they could have had no mutual acquaintance and could neither have conspired for an evil end nor combined for the best purpose. The subjects on which they wrote are very diverse, some historical, some prophetical, some devotional, some ethical. The form of their writings is in some cases prose and in others poetry, and yet, notwithstanding all these divergent elements, they have produced essentially one book. Not only is the Bible as a whole an unrivaled phenomenon, but its features are all phenomenal, and none more so than this convergence of contents like rays toward one common focal point.

a. The unity is structural. The Bible is built up on a definite plan. In the New Testament the four Gospel narratives are not mere repetitions, but designed to present many aspects of the life and career of the Lord Jesus Christ; then the Book of Acts immediately follows, showing what He continued to do and teach by the Holy Spirit in the Church, and how the Pentecostal baptism prepared the church for her witnessing ministry in Judea, Samaria, and then among Romans and Greeks. There are five epistle writers: Paul, especially the Apostle of Faith; Peter, of Hope; John, of Love; James, of Good Works; and Jude, of Warning Against Apostasy. Thus, without human design or intentional cooperation, all the necessary ground is covered without overlapping. fitted to teach or instructive

b. The unity is didactic and ethical. There is no inconsistency in the moral teaching from beginning to end; or, if at first any is apparent, a further and more careful examination reveals harmony. The whole Bible consistently teaches, on the basis of natural religion, with creation as its cornerstone, an original and universal fatherhood of God and brotherhood of man. However, only on the basis of spiritual redemption, with the new creation as its cornerstone, is found again the true fatherhood or brotherhood which sin lost or forfeited. Around these dual conceptions of man's natural and spiritual relations to God and his fellowman all ethical teaching of the Bible moves.

c. The unity is historic. The Bible, however, is not a history of the race, but rather of the kingdom of God. It centers about a chosen family, the family of Abraham, and so a chosen nation — Israel.

d. The unity is prophetic. Here again Israel and the kingdom of God form the central idea. Adam, the original creation-king, lost his scepter in the Fall and Satan obtained it by right of conquest. The second man, espousing Adam's cause, overcame his victor and so regained the lost scepter; and in Him — the Last Adam — the restored kingdom will stand forever and the gates of hell will not prevail against it. All prophecy ultimately relates to this new King, the divine head of the Adamic race, and to His kingdom; to His first coming and its militant period, to His second coming and its triumphant period.

e. The unity is organic. It is the unity of a living organism in which there is a pervasive, vitalizing spirit, making all parts living members and organs, all necessary to the whole body and to each other.

3. Argument from the credibility, integrity, and trustworthiness of

the Scriptures. These belong to the province of Christian Evidences and will not be dealt with here, but nevertheless, as established by sufficient proof, they constitute strong presumption in favor of inspiration.

4. The completeness of the Bible. The completeness of the Bible demonstrates its divine perfection. The antiquity of the Scriptures argues this, for the compilation of the Bible was completed more than eighteen centuries ago while the greater part of the world was yet uncivilized. And since John added the capstone to the Temple of God's Truth there have been many wonderful discoveries and inventions, yet there have been no additions whatever to the moral and spiritual truths contained in it. Today we know no more about the origin of life, the nature of the soul, the problem of suffering, or the future destiny of man than did those who had the Bible eighteen hundred years ago. Through the centuries of the Christian Era, man has succeeded in learning many of the secrets of nature and has harnessed her forces to his service, but in the actual revelation of supernatural truth nothing new has been discovered. Human writers cannot supplement the divine records, for they are complete, entire, "wanting nothing."

5. The character of its teaching. The teaching of the Scriptures is infinitely superior to all the moral or ethical systems of men. God declares that "My thoughts are not your thoughts" — that is, God's conceptions of things are not man's conceptions. The method God uses to express this is to remind us how high the heavens are above the earth — thus high are His ways and thoughts above those of men.

The first impressive feature of the teaching of the Scriptures is the importance which is everywhere attached to holiness. Judging from what we know of systems of human origin, a religion from man would either have spent its force on ritual observance, or have allowed active service on its behalf to make amends for the neglect of other duties. Islam gives the highest place to those who fight and fall in conflict. Hinduism rewards most the observance of ritual worship. Jewish tradition teaches that all Jews are certainly saved. The Scriptures, on the contrary, bring all men into the presence of a Being of infinite holiness, before whom the most exalted human characters fall condemned; and they declare plainly that nothing we can say or do in the cause of Christ can make up for the want of practical virtue. Those who have preached in the name of Christ are to be disowned if they be workers of iniquity, and the reception of the true faith makes Christian holiness only the more incumbent because it is only thus possible. Add to this the fact that Scripture seeks to regulate the thoughts and motives of men and is content with nothing less than a state of heart which refers all our actions to God's will; and it must be felt that the morality of the gospel is not of man. Bad men could not have taught such truths, and good men would not have deceived the people.

But there is another peculiarity in the morality of Scripture, equally true in itself and striking. Sin is everywhere spoken of as an evil against God, and everywhere it is not the instrument or human agent who is exalted but God alone. The first notion is inconsistent with all heathen philosophy, and the second with the natural tendency to the human heart. In Scripture, on the contrary, sin is represented as an evil and bitter thing, because it is dishonoring to God. This distinctly appears in the Old Testament and indeed forms one of its most marked peculiarities (see Exod. 17:16, asv; Num. 20:12; 1 Sam. 2:29, 30; 2 Sam. 12:9; 2 Kings 19:22-37; Ps. 51:4; Dan. 5:23; Rom. 1:21, 28; Heb. 3:19).

The candor and sincerity of the inspired writers are not less remarkable than their moral precepts, and they are quite incompatible with either fanaticism or imposture. They denounce the sins of the people (Deut. 9:24; Judg. 2:19; 1 Sam. 12:12). The inspired historian records with all fullness the sins of the patriarchs (Gen. 12:11-13; 49:5-7; Exod. 32; Lev. 10; Num. 20:12; 27:12-14; Deut. 32:51). In the same spirit the Evangelists notice their own faults and the faults of the apostles (Matt. 8:10, 26; 15:16; 16:7-11; 18:3; 26:31-56; John 10:6; 16:32). With equal truthfulness the Scriptures record the humiliation of our Lord, His sufferings and dejection (Matt. 27:46; Heb. 5:7). The apostle Paul records unreservedly the disorders of the churches which he himself had planted and even adds that his own apostolic authority had been questioned among them (1 Cor. 1:11; 5:1; 2 Cor. 2:4; 11:5-23; 12:20).

6. The scientific accuracy of the Scriptures. The God of all truth cannot, in any of His utterances, contradict Himself. His kingdom cannot stand and be divided against itself. Manifestly His works and His words must, in all essentials, agree. Hence the question as to the attitude of the Bible toward sciences cannot be avoided. There is a scientific element in the Word of God, though it is not in any proper sense a scientific treatise, and for obvious

reasons should not be, since there is no need of any supernatural revelation of scientific facts which may be ascertained in natural ways.

On the other hand, while this may be conceded, the God of the Bible being also the God of nature, it is equally plain that on whatever theme the omniscient One — who is the only infallible Scientist — speaks, incidentally and casually, He must show Himself to be thoroughly familiar with his subject and consistent with His own moral character. The all-knowing God cannot be supposed to betray ignorance on any subject, nor the God of all truth to lend Himself to falsehood. The Bible claims divine authorship. Infinite veracity cannot lend sanction to what is essentially erroneous, nor can omniscience conceal itself behind the veil of popular illusion and delusion, prevailing superstition, or careless inaccuracy.

We adduce the following statements in support of the above position:

— Without anticipating scientific discovery directly, biblical language properly interpreted does not contradict established facts.

— A poetic phraseology is often used, which by the flexibility of figurative or imaginative terms allows room for expansion and accommodation to facts when known. Hence the Bible is a scientific marvel. It belongs to the oldest class of literature, yet it is the youngest and newest in adaptation to scientific discovery and perpetually keeps abreast of human progress.

— Tested by cosmogony, astronomy, geology, zoology, physiology, and comparative anatomy, natural philosophy, sanitary science, etc., this Book evinces superhuman knowledge and wisdom.

a. As to cosmogony — the mother of all sciences — which is the science of creation, the Bible says this: "In the beginning God created the heavens and the earth." Herbert Spencer devotes a chapter to the consideration of what he calls the most general forms into which the manifestation of the unknown are redivisible, and these forms he finds to be these five: space, time, matter, motion, force. Now, if the starting point of religion is really scientific and these conclusions are correct, it must follow that these five forms, which are the factors of all phenomena, ought to make their appearance at an early age in her scheme. We shall not, of course, expect to find them expressed in the terminology of science, but shall look for their theological equivalents. In the first two verses of Genesis we find these five forms suggested: "In the beginning" — time; "God created the heavens" — space; "And the earth" — matter; "And the Spirit of Elohim" — force; "Moved" — motion.

b. Geology — the science of the earth's structure and constitution, treating of the operation of its physical forces and the past history of its developments — is one of the youngest of the sciences. A department of knowledge thus first really explored in the eighteenth century would, therefore, be most unlikely to prove in accord with the opening chapter of the earliest book of the Bible, if it were a merely human production. The correspondence, however, is remarkable. Geology, so far as it may claim to have settled anything, outlines the story of Creation somewhat thus: chaos, chemical light, expanse of atmosphere, appearance of land, vegetation in three forms, animal life from the protozoan to the higher vertebra, and finally man — exactly Moses' order in the first chapter of Genesis! First chaos; then God says "Let light be" and light was; then an expanse of atmosphere, called in the English Bible "the firmament," but in the Hebrew, *Raqia* — an expanse — a marvelously accurate word; then the continent, the dry land; vegetation in three forms; and then life — "the waters brought forth life"; then, bye and bye, higher animals; and at the end of *Mammalia*, man himself.

c. Comparative anatomy shows an order in the animal creation — from the lowest forms to the highest, rather than the reverse — the question of rank among vertebrate animals being determined by the proportion of brain to the spinal column. In fish it is 2 to 1; in reptiles 2½ to 1; in birds 3 to 1; in mammals 4 to 1; then in man it takes a leap, and the proportion of brain to the spinal column is 33 to 1, which raises man far above any other animal. Common sense and observation might have shown Moses that man is far above mammals as a class, and the mammals higher than most fishes and birds; but no common sense or ordinary observation would have shown that the fish belongs below the reptile, or the reptile below the bird. Yet thousands of years before comparative anatomy took rank among the sciences, Moses followed the correct order of classification in this story of Creation. A candid and rational scientist, looking at that first chapter of Genesis, must ask how any unaided human mind could have guided the hand that wrote these words.

d. Anthropology is the science of man's constitution. Was there any science in the days of Moses to teach him how man was constituted? Doubtless not; yet in Genesis 2, with the boldness of certainty, he writes, "God formed man out of the dust of the ground and breathed into his nostrils the breath of life" (Hebrew — "the breath of lives") as though this phrase included both the animal life man has in common with the animal creation, and the spiritual life he received in common with God.

According to the Word of God, man is a combination of spirit, soul, and body; as taught in Ecclesiastes 12, when "the dust returns to the earth as it was," "the spirit returns unto God who gave it" — death being the dissolution and separation of that which God brought into original unity. This is a plain reference to the original record in the second chapter of Genesis. The human body suggests little if any similarity in composition to the earth. Moses had no knowledge, as a human writer, that his body was one with the ground, but modern chemical analysis detects at least fourteen elements in the human body identical with the "dust" — such as oxygen, hydrogen, nitrogen, silicon, magnesium, sodium, phosphorus, carbon. Yet nothing could be more unlike matter in its highly organized form in the human body than the "dust" of the ground from which that human body is divinely declared to have been formed. It was reserved for modern analytical chemistry to demonstrate that what Moses wrote is exactly true.[10]

7. Attested miracles.[11]

8. Fulfilled prophecy.

Study Questions on Bibliology

1. Give a brief summary of the need and importance of examining the credentials of the Bible.
2. Discuss the designations of the Book.
3. Give the sevenfold symbolism of the Book and cite one passage with each.
4. Give definition of divine revelation as it refers to the Bible.
5. Discuss the fourfold manner in which the reasonableness of a divine revelation is shown.
6. What is the twofold proof by which God has certified the Bible as a divine revelation to man?
7. Give the preliminary definition of a miracle, and discuss the several erroneous conceptions of a miracle which this definition corrects.
8. Give the alternate definition of a miracle.
9. What conclusions are involved in the alternate definition of a miracle?
10. Discuss the five considerations which reveal the possibility of miracles.
11. Discuss the six considerations which deal with the probability of miracles.
12. Discuss the plausibility of miracles with the threefold refutation of the theory that miracles are impossible — because improbable according to human experience.
13. Give the evidential value of miracles.
14. Define prophecy in its limited meaning as referring to prediction.
15. Give the distinction between the attestation of prophecy and of miracles to divine revelation, and show the advantages which the former has over the latter.
16. Give the requirements for prophecy to be an evidence of divine revelation.
17. Show how the feature of mysteriousness and obscurity is especially conspicuous in the prophecies concerning the Messiah.
18. Discuss the law of double reference as applied to the fulfillment of prophecy.
19. Discuss the evidential value of fulfilled prophecy.
20. Quote Isaiah 41:21-23, and discuss negatively and positively the divine challenge contained therein.
21. Give the threefold method by which divine truth is communicated to man, and define each.

22. Show the distinction between revelation, illumination, and inspiration; and give Scriptural illustrations where these have ᕀ acted cooperatively and separately.
23. Give further considerations of the meaning of inspiration.
24. Discuss the Intuition Theory of Inspiration and the objections raised against it.
25. Discuss the Illumination Theory of Inspiration and the replies to it.
26. Discuss the Dictation Theory of Inspiration and the remarks made concerning it.
27. What is meant by Verbal, Plenary Inspiration?
28. Show the reasonableness of contending for the claim of inspiration for the original manuscripts only and not for any translation or version.
29. Discuss the scriptural view of inspiration.
30. Discuss the teachings of the Scriptures concerning the nature and extent of their own inspiration.
31. Discuss the external proofs of the inspiration of the Scriptures.
32. Discuss the internal proofs of the inspiration of the Scriptures.

Notes

¹It is curious that this title should have been due in part to a mistake. *Bible* is the English form of the name given to the Latin Scriptures, *Biblia*. This also is a singular, but in turn it is the Latin form of the Greek word *biblia* which is not singular, but the plural of *biblion* (book), a diminutive of *biblos*, a name given to the outer coat of the papyrus reed. This was stripped off and glued together to form writing material; thus by transference from material to the use made of it, *biblos* came to mean book and *biblion* a little book. In the New Testament the term *biblos* and *biblion* are applied to a single book of the Old Testament or to such a group as the Pentateuch. In the Old Testament we find the plural used of the prophets (Dan. 9:2). It was this plural use that passed over into the Christian church: from the middle of the second century the Scriptures are spoken of as "the books," the "holy," "divine," or "canonical books." The same notion of plurality rather than unity is seen in another term applied to the Scriptures by certain of the Latin fathers and later writers, *Bibliotheca*, "Library," or the "Divine Library." But when once the Greek plural noun *Biblia* was adopted in Latin, its original force was forgotten. *Biblia* in grammatical form may be either a neuter plural or a feminine singular; and so, by error, out of *biblia* (books) came *biblia* (book), i.e., Bible. In our study of the Bible we may need to return to the primitive and proper significance of the term, considering first the parts rather than the whole. But we may also thankfully retain the changed significance as one that has wonderfully helped to give sharpness and fixity to the conception of one Word of God, constant and uniform amid all the separateness and diversity of His words to men. The Bible is at once a Library and a Book.

²Thomas Hartwell Horne, *An Introduction to the Critical Study and Knowledge of the Holy Scriptures* (New York: Robert Carter and Brothers, 1860), I, 15.

³The definition given above is intended merely as a definition of the miracles of the Bible, or, in other words, of the events which profess to attest a divine revelation in the Scriptures. The New Testament designates these events in a twofold way, viewing them either subjectively, as producing effects upon men, or objectively, as revealing the power and wisdom of God. In the former aspect they are called "wonders" *(terata)* and "signs" *(semeia)*: Acts 2:22; John 4:48. In the later aspect they are called "powers" *(dunameis)* and "works" *(erga)*: Matt. 7:22; John 14:11.

⁴Miracles are attestations of revelation proceeding from divine power; prophecy is an attestation proceeding from divine knowledge. Only God can know the contingencies of the future. The possibility and probability of prophecy may be argued upon the same ground upon which we argue the possibility and probability of miracles. As an evidence of divine revelation, however, prophecy possesses two advantages over miracles, namely: (a) the proof, in the case of prophecy, is not derived from ancient testimony but is under our eyes; (b) the evidence of miracles cannot become stronger, whereas every new fulfillment adds to the argument from prophecy.

⁵This feature of mysteriousness and obscurity is especially conspicuous in the prophecies concerning the Messiah. For example, He was to be a "root out of dry ground," and yet a "fruitful branch"; a sufferer unto death, and yet not holden of death; without offspring, yet possessing numerous seed; condemned as a malefactor, yet justifying transgressors. These contradictions, it has been well said, present a problem no human wisdom was able to solve. To Jewish rabbis they seemed altogether irreconcilable and suggested the idea of two Messiahs united in the one great work.

⁶Certain prophecies apparently contain a fullness of meaning which is not exhausted by the event to which they most obviously and literally refer. A prophecy which had a partial fulfillment at a time not remote from its utterance may find its chief fulfillment in an event far distant. Since the principles of God's administration find recurring and ever enlarging illustration in history, prophecies which have already had a partial fulfillment may have their complete fulfillment yet before them. This is called the law of double reference.

⁷Revelation concerns the discovery of truth; illumination, the understanding of truth; inspiration, the communication of truth. These may act cooperatively or separately. Instances of this are as follows:

1. Inspiration without revelation (Luke 1:1-3; see also Acts).
2. Inspiration including revelation (Rev. 1:1, 11).
3. Inspiration without illumination, as in the prophets (1 Peter 1:11).
4. Inspiration including illumination, as in the case of Paul (1 Cor. 2:12).
5. Revelation without inspiration, as in God's words from Sinai (Exod. 20:1, 22).
6. Illumination without inspiration, as in modern preachers (1 John 2:27).

[8]The verbal, plenary theory of inspiration is largely based on the teaching of 2 Tim. 3:16. The American Standard Version has an erroneous and misleading translation at this place: "Every scripture inspired of God is also profitable." The reader might infer from it that there is some Scripture that is not inspired. If Paul had said, "All Scripture that is divinely inspired is also profitable," he would virtually have said, "There is some Scripture, some part of the Bible, that is not profitable," and therefore not inspired.

This is what the spirit of rationalism wants, namely, to make human reason the test and judge and measure of what is inspired and what is not. One man says such-and-such a verse is not profitable to him, and a third may select another verse entirely as not being profitable to him, and the result is that no Bible is left. Is it possible that any need be told the flat and sapless tautology that all divinely inspired Scripture is also profitable? Paul dealt in no such meaningless phrases. The word *kai* translated "also" does not mean "also" here — it means "and." Its position in the sentence shows this.

[9]"Dogmatic Constitution on Divine Revelation," *The Documents of Vatican II*, ed. Walter M. Abbott (New York: Guild Press, 1966), p. 119.

[10]These are illustrations of the scientific accuracy of the Scriptures to which others could be added.

[11]Attested miracles and fulfilled prophecy have been dealt with under the heading, "The Certainty of a Divine Revelation" (pp. 26ff.).

CHAPTER THREE

THEOLOGY PROPER:
THE DOCTRINE OF GOD

THE EXISTENCE OF GOD

False and True Systems of Theology and Theories of God

Deism. This view represents the universe as a self-sustained mechanism from which God withdrew as soon as He created it, leaving it to a process of self-development. Deism acknowledges God's relation to the universe as Creator, but denies that He sustains to it any providential relation. Deism says in effect, "God is the maker, not the keeper of the watch"; "An absentee God, sitting idle ever since the first Sabbath at the outside of the universe, and seeing it go." It regards the universe as perpetual motion.

Modern views of the dissipation of energy have served to discredit this theory. "Will" is the only explanation of the forces in nature, but according to deism, God builds a house, shuts Himself out, locks the door, and ties His own hands in order to make sure of never using the key.

Atheism. This view denies God's existence.

Skepticism and infidelity. These two terms mean a doubt or disbelief in the existence of God, especially the God of revelation.

Agnosticism. This is a denial that God can be known. Etymologically, *agnostic* and *ignoramus* mean the same thing. The former is from the Greek, the latter from the Latin.

Pantheism. This view maintains that the universe in its ever-changing conditions is but the manifestation of the one ever-changing universal substance which is God; thus everything is God, and God is everything. God is therefore a necessary but unconscious force working in the world.

Polytheism. This is the doctrine of many gods.

Theism. This is belief in the existence of a personal God — Creator, Preserver, and Ruler of all things.

Monotheism. This view teaches that there is but one God. Christianity, Judiasm, and Islam are monotheistic religions.

Definitions of God

Scriptural designations: "God is Spirit" (John 4:24); "God is light" (1 John 1:5); "God is love" (1 John 4:16); "God is a consuming fire" (Heb. 12:29).[1]

Theological definitions:

1. "By God we understand the one absolutely and infinitely perfect Spirit who is the Creator of all" (Catholic dictionary).

2. "The eternal source of all that is temporal" (Ebrard).

3. "The Infinite Spirit" (Kahnis).

4. "An eternal, uncaused, independent, necessary Being, that hath power, life, wisdom, goodness and whatsoever other supposable excellency, in the highest perfection, in and of itself" (John Howe).

5. "A Spirit, eternal, unchangeable, in his Being, wisdom, power, holiness, justice, goodness and truth" (Westminster Catechism).

6. "The first cause and the last end of all things" (Andrew Fuller).

7. "God is the infinite and perfect Spirit, in whom all things have their source, support and end" (Augustus Strong).

The Origin of the Idea of God   *Rom 1:18-23; 32; 2:12-16*

The idea of God is an intuition of the moral reason, i.e., it is innate in the human race. The knowledge of God's existence is a rational intuition; logically, it precedes and conditions all observation and reasoning; chronologically, only reflection upon the phenomena of nature and of mind occasions its rise in consciousness. Intuition simply means direct knowledge; it is to be distinguished from observation and reasoning, which give knowledge by indirect means. Belief in a personal God is a *primary* or *first truth.*

The nature of first truths in general:

1. Negatively, a first truth is not a truth written prior to consciousness upon the substance of the soul — for such passive knowledge

implies a materialistic view of the soul.

It is not actual knowledge of which the soul finds itself in possession at birth — for it cannot be proved that the soul has such knowledge.

It is not an idea undeveloped at birth but which has the power of self-development apart from observation and experience — for this is contrary to all we know of the laws of mental growth.

2. Positively, a first truth is a knowledge which, though developed upon occasion of observation and reflection, is not derived from observation and reflection — a knowledge on the contrary which has such logical priority that it must be assumed or supposed in order to make any observation or reflection possible. Such truths are not, therefore, recognized first in order of time; some of them are assented to somewhat late in the mind's growth. By the great majority of men they are never formulated at all, yet they constitute the necessary assumption upon which all other knowledge rests; and not only has the mind the inborn capacity to evolve them as soon as the proper occasions are presented, but the recognition of them is inevitable as soon as the mind begins to give account to itself of its own knowledge.

The criteria of first truths. The criteria by which first truths are to be tested are three and may be applied to the existence of God as a first truth.

1. Their universality. By this we mean not that all men assent to them or understand them, when propounded in scientific form, but that all men manifest a practical belief in them by their language, actions, and expectations. Belief in God as a first truth meets this test: No race or tribe has ever been found without at least a rudimentary conception of the existence of a Supreme Being.[2]

2. Their necessity. By necessity is meant, not that it is impossible to deny these truths, but that the mind is compelled by its very constitution to recognize them upon the occurrence of the proper conditions, and to employ them in its arguments to prove their nonexistence. Belief in God as a first truth meets this test: Infinity is the inevitable correlative of finiteness; the race has an innate capacity for religion; the denial of God's existence involves the logical processes, the validity of which rests upon the assumption of His existence.

3. Their logical independence and priority. By this is meant that these truths can be resolved into no others and proved by no

others; that they are presupposed in the acquistion of all other knowledge and can therefore be derived from no source other than an original cognitive power of the mind. Belief in God meets this test also. The intuition of an absolute reason is —

a. The necessary presupposition of all other knowledge, so that we cannot know anything else to exist except by assuming first of all that God exists;

b. The necessary basis of all logical thought, so that we cannot put confidence in any of our reasoning processes except by taking for granted that a thinking deity has constructed our minds with reference to the universe and to truth;

c. The necessary implication of our primitive belief in design, so that we can assume that all things exist for a purpose only by making a prior assumption that a purposing God exist;

d. The necessary foundation of our conviction of moral obligation, so that we can believe in the universal authority of right only by assuming that there is a God of righteousness, who reveals His will both in the conscience and in the moral universe at large.

Belief in God as a first truth. We cannot prove that God is, but we can show that in order for the existence of any knowledge, thought, reason, or conscience in man, *man must assume that God is.*

— As Reason, in which man's mental processes are grounded;
— As Power, awakening a sense of dependence;
— As Perfection, imposing law upon the moral nature;
— As Personality, recognized in forms of worship and prayer.

False suppositions concerning the sources of the idea of God's existence:

1. External revelation, whether communicated through the Scriptures or through tradition — for unless man had from another source a previous knowledge of the existence of God from whom such a revelation would come, the revelation itself could have no authority from Him. A revelation takes for granted that he to whom it is made has some knowledge of God, though it may enlarge and purify that knowledge.

   We cannot prove God from the authority of the Scriptures, then also prove the Scriptures from the authority of God. The very idea of Scripture as a revelation presupposes belief in a God who can make it. We cannot derive from a sundial our knowledge of the existence of a sun. The sundial presupposes the sun and cannot be understood without previous knowledge of the sun.

2. Experience, which comes individually from sense perception, followed by reflection. But God is supersensible and hence does not come within the range of experience. If by experience is meant the accumulated results of the sensations and associations of past generations of the race, it may be asked, "How did the original generation or first man at the head of the series acquire the belief in God to transmit, except as a rational intuition?"

3. Reason, which often brings into consciousness the belief in God, but cannot cause it. The actual rise of this knowledge in the majority of minds is not the result of any conscious process of reasoning. The strength of men's faith in God is not proportionate to the strength of the reasoning faculties; on the contrary, men of great logical powers are often inveterate skeptics, while men of unwavering faith are found among those who cannot even understand the arguments for God's existence.

Corroborative Evidences of God's Existence

The Scriptures do not attempt to prove God's existence. It did not seem to occur to the writers of either the Old or New Testaments to produce arguments for it; everywhere and at all times it is a fact taken for granted, assumed and affirmed. The sublime opening of the Scriptures announces the fact of God and His existence, and they further declare that the knowledge of God is universal (Romans 1:19-21, 28, 32; 2:15). Nowhere in them is the rise or dawn of the idea of God in the mind of man depicted. God has inlaid the evidence of this fundamental truth in the very nature of man, so that nowhere is He without witness.

The existence of God apart from revelation is incapable of direct proof. There is, however, a fivefold line of indirect proof which corroborates our rational intuition. By indirect proof is meant evidence which points to God's existence as the necessary ground and condition of the existence of anything else. The five arguments for the divine existence are as follows: the cosmological, the teleological, the anthropological, the Christological, and the argument from congruity. These arguments may not prove conclusively that God is, but they do show that for the existence of any knowledge, thought, reason, or conscience in man, we must assume that God is. As it is said of the beautiful, "It may be shown but not proven," so we say of the existence of God.

These arguments are probable, not demonstrative. For this reason they supplement each other and constitute a series of evidences which is cumulative in its nature. If taken separately, none of them can be considered absolutely decisive; but in total they furnish a corroboration of our primitive conviction of God's existence which is of great practical valué and is in itself sufficient to bind the moral action of men. *Heb 3:4   Rom 1:20*

The cosmological argument, or argument from change in nature. *Cosmological* comes from the Greek word *kosmos* — world or orderly arrangement. Every phenomenon or substance owes its existence to some producing cause. The universe, at least as far as its present form is concerned, is a thing begun and owes its existence to a cause which is equal to its production. This cause must be indefinitely great, a sufficient cause for that beginning. That the world could not come into being or into its present state of being of itself seems obvious: no more than nails, bricks, mortar, wood, and paint can form into a house or building of themselves.

While the cosmological argument proves that the cause of the universe must be indefinitely great, it cannot prove —

— Whether this cause is a cause of substance or of phenomena only;
— Whether it is a cause apart from the universe or one with it;
— Whether it is a caused or an uncaused cause;
— Whether it is finite of infinite;
— Whether it is intelligent or unintelligent;
— Whether it is one cause or many causes.

Ps. 8:3
Ps. 19:1
Ps. 94:9
The teleological argument, or argument from order or useful arrangement in nature. *Teleological* comes from the Greek word *telos* — end or design. Order and arrangement pervading a system respectively imply intelligence and purpose as the cause of that order and arrangement. Since order and arrangement pervade the universe, there must exist an intelligence adequate to direct this arrangement to useful ends.

The major premise of this argument expresses a primitive conviction which is not invalidated by the objection that order and useful arrangement may exist without being purposed, since we are compelled to deny this in all cases where the order and arrangement pervades the system. Neither is it invalidated by the objection that order and useful arrangement may result from the mere operation of physical laws and forces, because these very laws and forces imply an originating and superintending intelligence and will.

The minor premise of this argument expresses a working principle of all science, namely, that all things have their uses, that order pervades the universe, and that the methods of nature are rational methods. This premise is not invalidated by the objection that we frequently misunderstand the end actually subserved by the natural events and objects — for the principle is not that we necessarily know the actual end, but that we necessarily believe that there is some end in every case of systematic order and arrangement. It is also not invalidated by the objection that the order of the universe is manifestly imperfect, since this does not preclude contrivance or purpose, but indicates some special reason for imperfection, which reason we believe to be the sin of man.

While the teleological argument proves that there exists an intelligence and will adequate to the contrivance of the universe in its present form, it cannot prove —

— Whether this intelligence and will is personal or impersonal;
— Whether Creator or only Fashioner;
— Whether one or many;
— Whether finite or infinite.

The anthropological argument, or argument from man's mental and moral nature. Anthropological comes from the Greek word *anthropos* — man. This is an argument from the mental and moral condition of man to the existence of the Author, Lawgiver, and End. It is sometimes called "the moral argument." This argument may be divided into three parts.

Ps. 32:3
Ps. 38:1-4

1. Man's intellectual and moral nature requires for its author an intellectual and moral Being. Mind cannot evolve from matter, nor spirit from flesh, consequently a Being having both mind and spirit must have created man.

2. Man's moral nature proves the existence of a holy Lawgiver and Judge, otherwise conscience cannot be satisfactorily explained.

3. Man's emotional and volitional nature requires for its author a Being who can furnish in Himself a satisfying object of human affection and an end which will call forth man's highest activities and ensure his highest progress. Only a Being of power, wisdom, holiness, and goodness — and all these in indefinitely greater measure than can be found on earth — can meet the demand of the soul of man. Such a Being must exist. We must believe that He does, or else believe that the very root of our nature is a lie.

While this argument assures us of the existence of a personal Being who rules us in righteousness, and who is the proper object of supreme affection and service, it cannot of itself prove —
- — Whether this Being is the original Creator of all things or merely the Author of our own existence;
- — Whether He is infinite or finite;
- — Whether He is a Being of simple righteousness or also of mercy;

The Christological argument. Christological comes from the Greek word *Christos* – the Anointed, i.e., the Messiah. This argument rests on the following premises: the Bible must be accounted for; the fulfillment of prophecy must be accounted for; miracles must be accounted for; the supernatural character and the divine mission of Christ must be accounted for; the influence of Christianity in the world must be accounted for; the fact of conversion — the moral and spiritual change in men — must be accounted for; these things cannot be accounted for severally or together apart from the existence of God.

The argument from congruity. Congruity refers to a state of logical or practical agreement or harmonious relationship; the state of being harmoniously related or united; adaptation.

If we have a key which fits all the wards of the lock, we know it is the right key. If we have a theory which fits all the facts in the case, we know we have the correct theory. Belief in a self-existent, personal God is in harmony with all the facts of our mental and moral nature, as well as with all the phenomena of the natural world. If God exists, a universal belief in His existence is natural enough; the irresistible impulse to seek a first cause is accounted for; our religious nature has an object; the uniformity of natural law finds an adequate explanation; and human history is vindicated from being a vast imposture. Atheism leaves all these matters without an explanation and makes, not history alone, but our moral and intellectual nature itself an imposture and a lie.

While not one of the foregoing arguments taken by itself may be considered an absolute proof of God's existence, yet taken together they constitute a series of evidences which is both cumulative and conclusive.

THE ATTRIBUTES OF GOD

In contemplating the word and acts of God, as in contemplating the words and acts of individual men, we are compelled to assign uniform and permanent effects to uniform and permanent causes. Holy acts and words, we argue, must have their source in a principle of holiness; truthful acts and words, in a settled proclivity to truth; benevolent acts and words, in a benevolent disposition. Moreover, these permanent and uniform sources of expression and action — to which we have applied the terms *principle, proclivity*, and *disposition* — since they exist in the same person, must themselves inhere and find their unity in an underlying spiritual substance or reality, of which they are the inseparable characteristics and partial manifestations. Thus we are led naturally from the work to the attributes, and from the attributes to the essence of God.

The attributes of God are those distinguishable characteristics of the divine nature which are inseparable from the idea of God and which constitute the basis and ground for His various manifestations to His creatures. We call them attributes because we are compelled to attribute them to God as fundamental qualities or powers of His being, in order to give account of certain constant facts in God's self-revelation.

[margin annotation: Attribute Defined]

The Relation of the Divine Attributes to the Divine Essence

The attributes have an objective existence. They are not mere names for human conceptions of God, conceptions which have their only ground in the imperfection of the finite mind. They are qualities objectively distinguishable from the divine essence and from one another.

The attributes inhere in the divine essence. They are not separate existences; they are attributes of God.

The attributes belong to the divine essence as such. They are to be distinguished from those other powers or relations which do not appertain to the divine essence universally.

The personal distinctions in the nature of the one God are not to be denominated attributes; for each of these personal distinctions belongs not to the divine essence as such and universally, but only to the particular person of the Trinity who bears its name, while contrariwise all of the attributes belong to each of the persons.

The relations which God sustains to the world, moreover, such as creation, preservation, and government, are not to be denominated attributes; for these are accidental, not necessary or inseparable from the idea of God. God would be God even if He had never created.

The attributes manifest the divine essence. The essence is revealed only through the attributes; apart from its attributes it is unknown and unknowable. But though we can know God only as He reveals to us His attributes, nevertheless we do, in knowing these attributes, know the Being to whom these attributes belong. That this knowledge is partial does not prevent its corresponding, as far as it goes, to objective reality in the nature of God.

All God's revelations are, therefore, revelations of Himself in and through His attributes. Our aim must be to determine from God's words and works what qualities, dispositions, determinations, and powers of His otherwise unseen and unsearchable essence He has actually made known to us; or in other words, what are the revealed attributes of God. Scriptural illustrations are found in the following passages: Matthew 5:8; 11:27; John 1:18; 1 Timothy 6:16.

Methods of Determining the Divine Attributes

We have seen that the existence of God is a first truth: It is presupposed in all human thinking and is more or less consciously recognized by all men. This intuitive knowledge of God we have seen to be corroborative and manifested by arguments drawn from nature and from mind. Reason leads us to a causative and personal Intelligence upon whom we depend. This Being of indefinite greatness we clothe, by necessity of our thinking, with all the attributes of perfection.

The two great methods of determining these attributes are the Rational and the Biblical.

The rational method. This is threefold.

1. The way of negation, which consists in denying to God all imperfections observed in created beings

2. The way of climax, which consists in attributing to God in infinite degree all the perfections found in creatures

3. The way of causality, which consists in predicating to God those attributes which are required in Him to explain the world of nature and of mind

Though this method is valuable, it has insuperable limitations, and its place is a subordinate one. While we use it continually to confirm and supplement results otherwise obtained, all chief means of determining the divine attributes must be from the Scriptures. Spurgeon says, "The old saying is, 'Go from Nature up to Nature's God!' But it is hard work going uphill. The best thing is to go from Nature's God down to Nature; and if you once get to Nature's God and believe Him and love Him, it is surprising how easy it is to hear music in the waves, and songs in the wild whisperings of the winds, and to see God everywhere."

The biblical method. This is simply the inductive method applied to the facts with regard to God that are revealed in the Scriptures. Those who accept the Scriptures to be a revelation from God, inspired in every part, may properly look to them as the decisive authority with regard to God's attributes.

Classification of the Attributes

The attributes may be divided into great classes: Absolute or Immanent, and Relative or Transitive.

By Absolute or Immanent Attributes we mean attributes which respect the inner being of God, which are involved in God's relations in Himself, and which belong to His nature independently of His connection with the universe.

By Relative or Transitive Attributes we mean attribures which respect the outward relations of God's being, which are involved in God's relations to the creation, and which are exercised in consequence of the existence of the universe and its dependence upon Him.

Under the heading of Absolute or Immanent Attributes, we make a threefold division into Spirituality, with the attributes therein involved, namely, Life and Personality; Infinity, with the attributes therein involved, namely, Self-Existence, Immutabulity, and Unity; and Perfection, with the attributes therein involved, namely, Truth, Love, and Holiness.

Under the heading of Relative or Transitive Attributes, we make a threefold division, according to the order of their revelation, into attributes having relation to Time and Space, as Eternity and Immensity; attributes having relation to Creation, as Omnipresence, Omniscience, and Omnipotence; and attributes having relation to Moral Beings, as Veracity and Faithfulness, or Transitive Truth; Mercy and Goodness, or Transitive Love; and Justice and Righteousness, or Transitive Holiness.

Schedule of Attributes[3]

1. Absolute or Immanent Attributes

   a. Spirituality, involving
   - (1) Life
   - (2) Personality

   b. Infinity, involving
   - (1) Self-existence
   - (2) Immutability
   - (3) Unity

   c. Perfection, involving
   - (1) Truth
   - (2) Love
   - (3) Holiness

2. Relative or Transitive Attributes

   a. Related to Time and Space
   - (1) Eternity
   - (2) Immensity

   b. Related to Creation
   - (1) Omnipresence
   - (2) Omniscience
   - (3) Omnipotence

   c. Related to Moral Beings
   - (1) Veracity and Faithfulness, or Transitive Truth
   - (2) Mercy and Goodness, or Transitive Love
   - (3) Justice and Righteousness, or Transitive Holiness

Spirit, Infinite and Perfect,

GOD IS the Source, Support and End of all things.

Absolute or immanent attributes:

1. Spirituality. In calling spirituality an attribute of God we mean, not that we are justified in applying to the divine nature the adjective *spiritual,* but that the substantive *Spirit* describes that nature (John 4:24; Rom. 1:20; 1 Timothy 1:17; Colossians 1:15). These passages imply, negatively, that God is not matter: Spirit is not a refined form of matter, but an immaterial substance, invisible, uncompounded, indestructible. They also imply that God is not dependent upon matter. It cannot be shown that the human mind, in any state other than the present, is dependent for its consciousness upon its connection with a physical organism; much less is it true that God is dependent upon the universe as His sensorium (nervous system) — the material medium through which His spirit-being functions. God is not only Spirit, but He is pure Spirit. He is not only not matter, but He has no necessary connection with matter.

La Place, the astronomer, swept the heavens with his telescope, but could not find anywhere a God. "He might just as well," says President Sawyer, "have swept his kitchen with a broom." Since God is not a material being, He cannot be apprehended by any physical means.

Those passages of Scripture which seem to ascribe to God the possession of bodily parts and organs, as eyes and hands, are to be regarded as anthropomorphic and symbolic. When God is spoken of as appearing unto the patriarchs and walking with them, the passages are to be explained as referring to God's temporary manifestations of Himself in human form — manifestations which prefigure the final tabernacling of the Son of God in human flesh. Side by side with these anthropomorphic expressions and manifestations are specific declarations which repress any materializing conceptions of God — as, for example, that Heaven is His throne and the earth His footstool (Isa. 66:1), and that the heaven of heavens can not contain Him (1 Kings 8:27).

We come now to consider the positive meaning of the term *Spirit.* The Spirituality of God involves the two attributes of Life and Personality.

a. Life. The Scriptures represent God as the living God (Jer. 10:10; John 5:26; 14:6; 1 Thess. 1:9; Heb. 7:16; Rev. 11:11). Life is a simple idea and is incapable of real definition. We know it, however, in ourselves, and we can perceive the insufficiency or inconsistency of certain current definitions of

Josh 3:10
I Sam 17:26
Ps. 84:2
Mt. 16:16
I Tim 3:15
Rev. 7:2

it. We cannot regard life in God as —

— Mere process, without a subject; for we cannot conceive of a divine life without a God to live it.

— Mere correspondence with outward condition and environment; for this would render impossible a life of God before the existence of the universe.[4]

Life is rather mental energy, or energy of intellect, affection, and will. God is the living God as having in His own being a source of being and activity, both for Himself and others.

b. Personality. Scripture represents God as a personal being. By *personality* we mean the power of self-consciousness and self-determination. By way of further explanation we remark —

(1) Self-consciousness is more than consciousness. This last the brute may be supposed to possess, since the brute is not an automaton. Man is distinguished from the brute by his power to objectify self. Not only is man conscious of his own acts and states, but by abstraction and reflection he recognizes the self which is the subject of these acts and states.

Exo. 3:14
Isa. 45:5
I Cor. 2:10

(2) Self-determination is more than determination. The brute shows determination, but his determination is the result of influences from without. There is no inner spontaneity. Man, by virtue of his free will, determines his actions from within. He determines self in view of motives, but his determination is not caused by motives. He himself is the cause.

Job 23:13
Rom. 9:11
Eph. 1:9-11
Heb. 6:17

Intellect
Gen 18:19
Exo 3:7
Acts 15:18
sensibility
Gen 6:6
Ps.103:8-14
John 3:16
Volition
Gen 3:15
Ps.115:3
Jn. 6:38

God, as personal, is in the highest degree self-conscious and self-determining. The rise in our own minds of the idea of God as personal depends largely upon our recognition of personality in ourselves. Those who deny spirit in man place a bar in the way of the recognition of this attribute of God. The declaration in Scripture concerning God and His relations to the universe and men clearly reveals personality in God: personal presence (Exod. 3:14); personal characteristics (Gen. 6:6; Ps. 139:1-4; Prov. 6:16; 1 Cor. 2:11; Eph. 1:9, 11); personal relationship (Gen. 1:1; Ps. 75:6, 7; 104:27-30; Rom. 8:28; Heb. 1:3). God is not the everlasting "It is" or "I was," but the everlasting "I am."

2. Infinity. By *infinity* we mean, not that the divine nature has no

known limits or bounds, but that it has no limits or bounds. That which has simply no known limit is the indefinite. The infinity of God implies that He is in no way limited by the universe or confined to the universe; He is transcendent as well as immanent. Transcendence, however, must not be conceived of merely as freedom from spatial restrictions, but rather as unlimited resource, of which God's glory is the expression. Scriptural examples (1 Kings 8:27; Job 11:7-9; Ps. 145:3; Isa. 66:1; Rom. 11:33).

In explanation of the term *infinity* we may notice —

— That infinity can belong to but one Being and therefore cannot be shared with the universe. Infinity is not a negative but a positive idea. It does not take its rise from the impotence of thought, but is an intuitive conviction which constitutes the basis of all other knowledge.

— That the infinity of God does not involve His identity with "the all," or the sum of existence, nor prevent the coexistence of derived and finite beings to which he bears relation. Infinity implies simply that God exists in no necessary relation to finite things or beings, and that whatever limitation of the divine nature results from their existence is, on the part of God, a self-limitation: for example, see Psalm 113:5, 6: ". . .that humbleth himself to behold the things that are in heaven and in the earth" (cf. Ps. 78:41).

— That the infinity of God is to be conceived of as intensive, rather than extensive. We do not attribute to God infinite extension, but rather infinite energy of spiritual life. That which acts up to the measure of its power is simply natural and physical force. Man rises above nature by virtue of his reserves of power; but in God the reserve is infinite. There is a transcendent element in Him, which no self-revelation exhausts, whether creation or redemption, whether law or promise.[5]

Of the attributes involved in infinity, we mention —

a. Self-existence. By *self-existence* we mean that God has the ground of His existence in Himself. Every being must have the ground of its existence either in or outside of itself. We have the ground of our existence outside ourselves. God is not thus dependent. God's self-existence is implied in the divine name in Exodus 3:14; 6:3.

But lest this should be misconstrued, we add that God exists by the necessity of His own being. It is His nature to be. Hence the existence of God is not contingent, but a necessary existence. It is grounded, not in His volitions, but in His nature.[6]

b. Immutability. By this we mean that the nature, attributes, and will of God are exempt from all change. Reason teaches us that no change is possible in God, whether of increase or decrease, progress or deterioration, contraction or development. All change must be to better or to worse. But God is absolute perfection, and no change to better is possible. Change to worse would be equally inconsistent with perfection. No cause for such change exists, either outside of God or in God Himself (Ps. 102:27; Mal. 3:6; Jas. 1:17). Heb. 1:12

The passages of Scripture which seem at first sight to ascribe change to God are to be explained in one of three ways.

(1) As illustrations of the varied methods in which God manifests His immutable truth and wisdom in creation. Mathematical principles receive new application with each successive stage of creation. The law of cohesion gives place to chemical law, and chemistry yields to vital forces, but through all these changes there is a divine truth and wisdom which is unchanging and which reduces all to rational order. Immutability is not stereotyped sameness, but impossibility of deviation by one hair's-breadth from the course which is best.

(2) As anthropomorphic representations of the revelation of God's unchanging attributes in the changing circumstances and varying moral conditions of creatures. Genesis 6:6 — "It repented Jehovah that He made man" — is to be interpreted in the light of Numbers 23:19 — "God is not a man, that He should lie: neither the Son of Man, that He should repent" (cf. 1 Sam. 15:11 with 15:29). God's unchanging holiness requires Him to treat the wicked differently from the righteous. When the righteous become wicked, His treatment of them must change. The sun is not fickle or partial because it melts the wax and hardens the clay — the change is not in the sun but in the objects it shines upon. When a man bicycling against the wind turns about and goes with the wind instead of going against it, the wind seems to change, though it is blowing just as it was before.

(3) As describing executions, in time, of purposes eternally

existing in the mind of God. Immutability must not be confounded with immobility. This would deny all those imperative volitions of God by which He enters into history. The Scriptures assure us that creation, miracles, incarnation, and regeneration are immediate acts of God. Immutability is consistent with constant activity and perfect freedom. The abolition of the Mosaic dispensation, for instance, indicates no change in God's plan; it is rather the execution of His plan. Christ's coming and work were no sudden make-shift to remedy unforeseen defects in the Old Testament scheme: Christ came rather in "the fullness of the time" (Gal. 4:4) to fulfill the "counsel" of God (Acts 2:23).

c. Unity. By this we mean that the divine nature is undivided and indivisible, and that there is but one infinite and perfect Spirit (Deut. 6:4; Isa. 44:6; Mark 12:29; John 17:3; 1 Cor. 8:4; 1 Tim. 1:17; 6:15; Eph. 4:4, 6).

Against polytheism, tritheism, or dualism, we may urge that the notion of two or more gods is self-contradictory, since each would limit the other and thus destroy his godhead. In the nature of things, infinity and absolute perfection are possible only to one. It is unphilosophical, moreover, to assume the existence of two or more gods when one will explain all the facts. The unity of God is, however, in no way inconsistent with the doctrine of the Trinity; for, while this doctrine holds to the existence of hypostatical, or personal, distinctions in the divine nature, it also holds that this divine nature is numerically and eternally one.

3. Perfection. By *perfection* we mean not mere quantitative completeness, but qualitative excellence. The attributes involved in perfection are moral attributes. Right action among men presupposes a perfect moral organization, a normal state of intellect, affection, and will. So God's activity presupposes a principle of intelligence, affection, and volition in His inmost being, and the existence of a worthy object for each of these powers of His nature. But in eternity past nothing existed outside or apart from God. He must find, and He does find, the sufficient object of intellect, affection, and will in Himself. There is a self-knowing, a self-loving, a self-willing which constitute His absolute perfection. The consideration of the immanent attributes is, therefore, properly concluded with an account of that truth, love, and

holiness which render God entirely sufficient to Himself (Deut. 32:4; Ps. 18:30; 19:7; Matt. 5:48; Rom. 12:2).

a. Truth. By *truth* we mean that attribute of the divine nature in virtue of which God's being and God's knowledge eternally conform to each other. In further explanation we remark —

(1) Negatively, the immanent truth of God is not to be confounded with that veracity and faithfulness which partially manifest it to creatures. These are transitive truths and they presuppose the absolute and immanent attribute (Deut. 32:4; John 17:3; 1 John 5:20).

Truth in God is not a merely active attribute of the divine nature. God is truth, not only in the sense that He is the being that truly knows, but also in the sense that He is the truth that is known. The passive precedes the active; truth of being precedes truth of knowing. He is not simply the medium, but also the object of all knowledge. Christ as the revealer of God is the truth (John 14:6; Eph. 4:21).

(2) Positively, all truth among men — whether mathematical, logical, moral, or religious — is to be regarded as having its foundation in this immanent truth of the divine nature and as disclosing facts in the being of God.

This attribute, therefore, constitutes the principle and guarantee of all revelation, while it shows the possibility of an eternal, divine self-contemplation apart from and before all creation. It is to be understood only in the light of the doctrine of the Trinity.

b. Love. By *love* we mean that attribute of the divine nature in virtue of which God is eternally moved to self-communication (John 17:24; Romans 15:30; 1 John 3:16; 4:8). In further explanation we remark —

(1) Negatively, the immanent love of God is not to be confounded with mercy and goodness toward creatures. These are its manifestations and are to be denominated transitive love.

Love is not the all-inclusive ethical attribute of God. It does not include truth, nor does it include holiness. Nor is God's love mere regard for being in general, irrespective of its moral quality. God's love is not a merely emotional affection, proceeding from sense or impulse, nor is it prompted by utilitarian considerations.[7]

(2) Positively, the immanent love of God is a rational and voluntary affection grounded in perfect reason and deliberate choice. Since God's love is rational, it involves a subordination of the emotional element to a higher law than itself, namely, that of truth and holiness.

The immanent love of God, therefore, requires and finds a perfect standard in His own holiness and a personal object in the image of His own infinite perfections. It is to be understood only in the light of the doctrine of the Trinity.

The immanent love of God constitutes the ground of the divine blessedness.[8] Since there is an infinite and perfect object of love as well as of knowledge and will in God's own nature, the existence of the universe is not necessary to His serenity and joy.

The love of God involves also the possibility of divine suffering; the suffering on account of sin, which holiness necessitates on the part of God, is itself the atonement (John 10:17).

c. Holiness. *Holiness* is self-affirming purity. In virtue of this attribute of His nature, God eternally wills and maintains His own moral excellence. In this definition are contained three elements: first, purity; second, purity willing; thirdly, purity willing itself (Exod. 15:11; 19:10-16; Isa. 6:3; Heb. 12:10, 14; 1 Peter 1:15; Rev. 4:8). These passages show that holiness is the opposite to impurity, that it is itself purity. In further explanation we remark —   I Jn. 1:5   Jn.17:11   Isa. 59:1

(1) Negatively, holiness is not —   Luke 5:8

(a) Justice, or purity demanding purity from creatures. Justice, the relative or transitive attribute, is indeed the manifestation and expression of the immanent attribute of holiness, but it is not to be confounded with it.

(b) A complex term designating the aggregate of the divine perfections. On the other hand, the notion of holiness is both in Scripture and in Christian experience, perfectly simple and perfectly distinct from that of other attributes.

(c) God's self-love, in the sense of supreme regard for His own interest and happiness. There is no utilitarian element in holiness.

(d) Identical with, or a manifestation of, love. Since self-maintenance must precede self-impartation — and since benevolence has its object, motive, standard, and limit in righteousness — holiness the self-affirming attribute can in no way be resolved into love, the self-communicating.

(2) Positively, holiness is —

(a) Purity of substance. In God's nature, as necessarily acting, there are indeed the two elements of willing and being. But the passive logically precedes the active; being comes before willing; God is pure before He wills purity. Since purity, however, in ordinary usage is a negative term and means only freedom from stain or wrong, we must include in it also the positive idea of moral rightness. God is holy in that He is the source and standard of the right.

(b) Energy of will. This purity is not simply a passive and dead quality; it is the attribute of a personal being; it is penetrated and pervaded by will. Holiness is the free moral movement of the Godhead.

(c) Self-affirmation. Holiness is God's self-willing. His own purity is the supreme object of His regard and maintenance. God is holy in that His infinite moral excellence affirms and asserts itself as the highest possible motive and end. Like truth and love, this attribute can be understood only in the light of the doctrine of the Trinity.

Relative or transitive attributes: Non- Moral

1. Attributes having relation to time and space.

   a. Eternity. By this we mean that God's nature is without beginning or end, is free from all succession of time, and contains in itself the cause of time (Gen. 21:33; Deut. 32:40; Ps. 90:2; 102:27; Rom. 1:20; 1 Tim. 1:17).

   Eternity is infinity in its relation to time. It implies that God's nature is not subject to the laws of time. God is not in time. It is more correct to say that time is in God. Although there is logical succession in God's thoughts, there is no chronological succession; yet we are far from saying that time, now that it exists, has no objective reality to God. To Him, past, present, and future are "one eternal now," not in the sense that there is no distinction between them, but only in the sense that He sees past and future as vividly as He sees the present. With Creation time began, and since the succession of history is veritable successions, He who sees according to truth must recognize them.

b. Immensity. By this we mean that God's nature is without extension, is subject to no limitations of space, and contains in itself the cause of space. Immensity is infinity in its relation to space. God's nature is not subject to the laws of space. It is more correct to say that space is within God; yet space has an objective reality to God. With Creation space began to be, and since God sees according to truth, He recognizes relations of space in His creation.

2. Attributes having relation to Creation.

a. Omnipresence. By this we mean that God, in the totality of His essence, without diffusion or expansion, multiplication or division, penetrates and fills the universe in all its parts (Ps. 139:7-10; Jer. 23:23, 24; Acts 17:27, 28). In explanation of this attribute we may say — Ps. 145:18   Mt. 28:20

(1) God's omnipresence is not potential, but essential. We reject the Socinian representation that God's essence is in heaven, only His power on earth. When God is said to "dwell in the heavens" we are to understand the language either as a symbolic expression of exaltation above earthly things, or as a declaration that His most special and glorious self-manifestations are in heaven (Pss. 113:5; 123:1; Isa. 57:15).

(2) God's omnipresence is not the presence of a part, but of the whole of God in every place. This follows from the conception of God as incorporeal. We reject the materialistic representation that God is composed of material elements which can be divided or sundered. There is no multiplication or diffusion of His substance to correspond with the parts of His dominion. The one essence of God is present at the same moment in all. While in mathematics the whole is equal to the sum of its parts, we know that with the Holy Spirit every part is equal to the whole. Every church, every true body of Jesus Christ, has just as much of Christ as every other, and each has the whole Christ (1 Kings 8:27; Isa. 57:15; Matt. 18:20). [9]

(3) God's omnipresence is not necessary, but free. We reject the pantheistic notion that God is bound to the universe as the universe is bound to God. God is immanent in the universe, not by compulsion, but by the free act of His own will, and this immanence is qualified by His transcendence.

God might, at will, cease to be omnipresent, for He could destroy the universe; but while the universe exists, He is and must be in all its parts. God is the life and law of the universe (this is the truth in pantheism), but He is also personal and free (this pantheism denies). Christianity holds to a free as well as essential omnipresence, qualified and supplemented, however, by God's transcendence. The boasted truth in pantheism is an elementary principle of Christianity and is only the stepping stone for a nobler truth — God's personal presence with His church. God's omnipresence assures us that He is present with us to hear — and present in every heart and in the ends of the earth to answer — prayer.

> The parish priest of austerity
> Climbed up in a high church steeple,
> To be nearer God so that he might
> Hand His Word down to the people.
> And in sermon script he daily wrote
> What He thought was sent from heaven
> And he dropt it down on the people's heads
> Two times one day in seven.
> In his age God said, "Come down and die,"
> And he cried out from the steeple,
> "Where art Thou, Lord?"
> And the Lord replied,
> "Down here among My people."
>
> — Selected

(b) Omniscience. By this we mean God's perfect and eternal knowledge of all things which are objects of man's knowledge, whether they be actual or possible, present or future.[10]

(1) The omniscience of God may be argued from His omnipresence, as well as from His truth or self-knowledge in which the plan of redemption has its eternal ground, and from prophecy which expresses God's omniscience.[11]

(2) Since it is free from all imperfection, God's knowledge is

Exo. 3:7   Matt 6:8,32   Ps. 147:4   Mt. 20:29

immediate, as distinguished from the knowledge that comes through sense or imagination; simultaneous, as not required by successive observations or built up by processes of reasoning; distinct, as free from all vagueness or confusion; true, as perfection corresponding to the reality of things; eternal, as comprehended in one timeless act of the divine mind.

An infinite mind must always act, and must always act in an absolutely perfect manner. There is in God no sense, symbol, memory, growth, reflection, or reasoning — His knowledge is all direct and without intermediaries. God was properly represented by the ancient Egyptians, not as having eyes, but as being Eye. His thoughts toward us are "more than can be numbered" (Ps. 4:5), not because there is succession in them, now a remembering and now a forgetting, but because there is never a moment of our existence in which we are out of His mind; He is always thinking of us (Gen. 16:13).

(3) Since God knows things as they are, He knows the necessary sequences of His creation as necessary, the free acts of His creatures as free, the ideally possible as ideally possible. God knows what would have taken place under circumstances not now present; knows what the universe would have been, had He chosen a different plan of creation; knows what our lives would have been, had we made different decisions in the past (Isa. 48:18).

(4) The fact that there is nothing in the present condition of things from which the future actions of free creatures necessarily follow by natural law does not prevent God from foreseeing such actions, since His knowledge is not mediate, but immediate. He not only foreknows the motives which will occasion men's acts, but He directly foreknows the acts themselves. The possibility of such direct knowledge without assignable grounds of ascertainment is apparent if we admit that time is a form of finite thought to which the divine is not subject.

(5) Prescience is not itself causative. It is not to be confounded with the predetermining will of God. Free actions do not take place because they are foreseen, but they are foreseen because they are to take place.[12]

(6) Omniscience embraces the actual and the possible, but it

does not embrace the self-contradictory and the impossible, because these are not objects of knowledge.

(7) Omniscience, as qualified by holy will, is in Scripture denominated *wisdom*. In virtue of His wisdom, God chooses the highest ends and uses the fittest means to accomplish them.[13]

c. Omnipotence. By this we mean the power of God to do all things which are objects of power, whether with or without the use of means (Gen. 17:1).[14]

(1) Omnipotence does not imply power to do that which is not an object of power. For example, self-contradictory things are not included in the exercise of God's omnipotence — such as the making of a past event to have not occurred (hence the uselessness of praying: "May it be that much good was done"); drawing a shorter than a straight line between two given points; putting two separate mountains together without a valley between them. Things contradictory to the nature of God are not overruled by His own omnipotence: for example, for God to lie, to sin, to die. To do such things would not imply power, but impotence. God has all the power that is consistent with infinite perfection — all power to do what is worthy of Himself.

(2) Omnipotence does not imply the exercise of all His power on the part of God. He has power over His power; in other words, His power is under the control of wise and holy will. God can do all He will, but He will not do all He can. Else His power is mere force acting necessarily, and God is the slave of His own omnipotence.

(3) Omnipotence in God does not exclude, but implies, the power of self-limitation. Since all such limitation is free, proceeding from neither external nor internal compulsion, it is the act and manifestation of God's power. Human freedom is not rendered impossible by the divine omnipotence, but exists by virtue of it. It is an act of omnipotence when God humbles Himself to the taking of human flesh in the person of Jesus Christ.

3. Attributes having relation to moral beings.

a. Veracity and Faithfulness, or Transitive Truth. By *veracity* and *faithfulness* we mean the transitive truth of God in its twofold relation to His creatures in general and to His redeemed people in particular (Num. 23:19; Ps. 138:2: John 3:33; Rom. 3:4; 2 Cor. 1:20; Titus 1:2; Heb. 6:18; 1 Peter 4:19).

(1) In virtue of His veracity, all His revelations to creatures consist with His essential being and with each other. In God's veracity we have the guarantee that our faculties in their normal exercise do not deceive us; that the laws of thought are also laws of things; that the external world, and second causes in it, have objective existence, that the same causes will always produce the same effects; that the threats of the moral nature will be executed upon the unrepentant transgressor; that man's moral nature is made in the image of God's; and that we may draw just conclusions from what conscience is in us to what holiness is in Him. We may, therefore, expect that all past revelations, whether in nature or in His Word, will not only not be contradicted by our future knowledge, but will rather prove to have in them more of truth than we ever dreamed. Man's word may pass away, but God's word abides forever (Isa. 40:8; Matt. 5:18).

(2) In virtue of His faithfulness, God fulfills all His promises to His people, whether expressed in words or implied in the constitution He has given them. In God's faithfulness we have the sure ground of confidence that He will perform what His love had led Him to promise to those who obey the gospel. Since His promises are based, not upon what we are or have done, but upon what Christ is and has done, our defects and errors do not invalidate them as long as we are truly penitent and believing.

First John 1:9: "Faithful and righteous to forgive us our sins" — faithful to His promise and righteous to Christ. God's faithfulness also insures a supply for all the real wants of our beings, both here and hereafter, since these wants are implicit promises of Him who made us (Pss. 84:11; 91:4; Matt. 6:33; 1 Cor. 2:9).

b. Mercy and Goodness, or Transitive Love. By *mercy* and *goodness* we mean the intransitive love of God in its twofold relation to the disobedient and to the obedient portions of His creatures (Matt. 6:44, 45; John 3:16; Rom. 2:4; 8:32; Titus 3:4; 2 Peter 1:3; 1 John 4:10).

(1) Mercy is that eternal principle of God's nature which leads Him to seek the temporal good and eternal salvation of

those who have opposed themselves to His will, even at the cost of infinite self-sacrifice.

(2) Goodness is the eternal principle of God's nature which leads Him to communicate of His own life and blessedness to those who are like Him in moral character. Goodness, therefore, is nearly identical with the love of benevolence.

c. Justice and Righteousness, or Transitive Holiness. By *justice* and *righteousness* we mean the transitive holiness of God in virtue of which His treatment of His creatures conforms to the purity of His nature — righteousness demanding from all moral beings conformity to the moral perfection of God, and justice visiting nonconformity to that perfection with penal loss or suffering (Gen. 18:25; Deut. 32:4; Pss. 5:5; 7:9-12; 18:24-26; Matt. 5:48; Rom. 2:6; 1 Peter 1:16).

These passages show that God loves the same persons whom He hates. It is not true that "He hates sin, but loves the sinner"; He both hates and loves the sinner himself — hates him as he is a living and willful antagonist of truth and holiness, loves him as he is a creature capable of good and ruined by his transgression. There is no abstract sin that can be hated apart from the persons in whom that sin is represented and embodied. Thomas Fuller found it difficult to starve the profaneness but to feed the person of the impudent beggar who applied to him for food. Mr. Finney declared that he would kill the slave-catcher, but would love him with all his heart. In our civil war, Dr. Kirk said, "God knows that we love the rebels, but God also knows that we will kill them if they do not lay down their arms."

The complex nature of God not only permits but necessitates this same double treatment of the sinner, and the earthly father experiences the same conflict of emotions when his heart yearns over the corrupt son whom he is compelled to banish from the household. Remember it is always the sinner who is punished, not the sin.

(1) Because justice and righteousness are simply transitive holiness — righteousness designating this holiness chiefly in its mandatory facet, justice chiefly in its punitive aspect — they are not mere manifestations of benevolence, or of God's disposition to secure the highest happiness of His creatures, nor are they grounded in the nature of things as something apart from the above God.

(2) Transitive holiness, as righteousness, imposes law as conscience and Scripture and may be called "legislative" holiness. As justice, it executes the penalties of the law and may be called "distributive" or "judicial" holiness. In righteousness, God reveals chiefly His love of holiness; in justice, chiefly His hatred of sin.

(3) Neither justice nor righteousness, therefore, is a matter of arbitrary will. They are revelations of the inmost nature of God, the one in the form of moral requirement, the other in the form of judicial sanction. As God cannot but demand of His creatures that they be like Him in moral character, so He cannot but enforce the law which He imposes upon them. Justice just as much binds God to punish as it binds the sinner to be punished.

(4) Neither justice nor righteousness bestows rewards. This follows from the fact that obedience is due to God instead of being optional or a gratuity. No creature can claim anything for his obedience. If God rewards, He rewards in virtue of His goodness and faithfulness, not in virtue of His justice or righteousness. What the creature cannot claim, however, Christ can claim, and the rewards which are goodness to the creature are righteousness to Christ. God rewards Christ's work in us and for us (Matt. 25:31, 46; Luke 17:7-10; Rom. 6:23).

(5) Justice in God, as the revelation of His holiness, is devoid of all passion or caprice. There is in God no selfish anger. The penalties He inflicts upon transgression are not vindictive but vindicative. They express the revulsion of God's nature from moral evil, the judicial indignation of purity against impurity, the self-assertion of infinite holiness against its antagonist and would-be destroyer. But because its decisions are calm, they are irreversible.[15]

THE TRINITY OF GOD

The Trinity of God is His tri-personal existence as Father, Son, and Holy Spirit. In the nature of the one God, there are three eternal distinctions which are revealed to us as three equal persons. The tri-personality of the Godhead is exclusively a truth of revelation. It is clearly, though not formally, made known in the New Testament, and intimations of it may be found in the Old Testament (Isa. 48:16; 61:6; 63:9, 10).

Scriptural Foundation of the Doctrine

In Scripture there are three persons recognized as God: the Father (John 6:27; 1 Peter 1:2); Jesus Christ the Son (John 1:1, 18; Titus 2:13); the Holy Spirit (Acts 5:3, 4). These three are so described in Scripture that we are compelled to conceive of them as distinct persons.

1. The Father and the Son are persons distinct from each other.

    a. Christ distinguishes the Father from Himself as "another" (John 5:32, 37).

    b. The Father and the Son are distinguished as the sender and the sent (John 10:36; Gal. 4:4).

    c. The Father and the Son are distinguished as the begetter and the begotten (Ps. 2:7; John 1:14; 3:16).

2. The Father and the Son are persons distinct from the Holy Spirit.

    a. Jesus distinguished the Spirit from Himself and from the Father (John 14:16, 17).

    b. The Spirit proceeds from the Father (John 15:26).

    c. The Spirit is sent by the Father and by the Son (John 14:26; 15:26; Gal. 4:6).

Refutation of Heretical Misunderstandings

1. The tri-personality of the divine nature is not merely economic or modal in manifestation, or temporal, but immanent and eternal. There are scriptural proofs of this.

    a. There are passages of Scripture which speak of the existence of the Word from eternity with the Father (John 1:1, 2; Phil. 2:6).

    b. There are passages that assert and imply Christ's preexistence (John 1:18, ASV; 8:58; Col. 1:15-17).

    c. There are passages implying intercourse between the Father and the Son before the foundation of the world (John 17:5, 24).

    d. There are passages which assert that the world was created by Christ (John 1:3; 1 Cor. 8:6; Col. 1:16; Heb. 1:2, 10).

    e. There are passages which assert and imply the eternity of the Holy Spirit (Gen. 1:2; Ps. 33:6; Heb. 9:14).

2. This tri-personality is not tritheism, for though there are three persons, there is but one essence.

    a. The term *person* only approximately represents the truth. Although this word more clearly than any other single word expresses the conception which the Scriptures give us of the relation between the Father, the Son, and the Holy Spirit, it is not itself used in this connection in Scripture, and we employ it in a qualified sense, not in the ordinary sense in which we apply the word *person* to Peter, Paul, and John.

b. The necessary qualification is that though three persons among men have only a specific unity of nature or essence (that is, have the same species of nature or essence), the persons of the Godhead have a numerical unity of nature or essence (that is, have the same nature or essence). The undivided essence of the Godhead belongs equally to each of the persons — Father, Son and Holy Spirit; each possesses all the substance and all the attributes of deity. The plurality of the Godhead is, therefore, not a plurality of essence, but a plurality of hypostatical, or personal, distinctions. God is not three and one, but three in one. The one indivisible essence has three modes of subsistence.[16]

c. This oneness of essence explains the fact that while Father, Son, and Holy Spirit, as respects their personalities, are distinct subsistences, there is an intercommunion of persons and an immanence of one divine person in another which permits the peculiar work of one to be ascribed, with a single limitation, to either of the others, and the manifestation of one to be recognized in the manifestation of another. The limitation is simply this, that although the Son was sent by the Father, and the Spirit by the Father and the Son, it cannot be said, vice versa, that the Father is sent, either by the Son or by the Spirit. The Scripture representations of this intercommunion prevent us from conceiving of the distinctions called Father, Son, and Holy Spirit, as involving separation between them.

The Three Persons Are Equal

1. These titles belong to each of the three persons.

a. The Father is not God as such; for God is not only Father, but also Son and Holy Spirit. The term *Father* designates that personal distinction in the divine nature in virtue of which God is related to the Son and, through the Son and the Spirit, to the church.

b. The Son is not God as such; for God is not only Son, but also Father and Holy Spirit. The Son designates that distinction in virtue of which God is related to the Father, and is sent by the

Father to redeem the world, and with the Father sends the Holy Spirit.

c. The Holy Spirit is not God as such; for God is not only Holy Spirit, but also Father and Son. The Holy Spirit designates that distinction in virtue of which God is related to the Father and the Son, and is sent by them to accomplish the work of renewing the ungodly and sanctifying the church.

2. These titles are qualified in their use.

Like the word *person*, the names *Father*, *Son*, and *Holy Spirit* are not to be confined within the precise limitations of meaning which would be required if they were applied to men.

The Trinity Is Inscrutable Yet Not Self-Contradictory

1. The mode of this triune existence is inscrutable. It is inscrutable because there are no analogies to it in our finite experience. For this reason, all attempts to represent it adequately are vain.

   a. From inanimate things — as the fountain, the stream, and the rivulet, trickling from it; the cloud, the rain, and the rising mist; color, shape, and size; the actinic, luminiferous, and calorific principles in a ray of the sun.

   b. From the constitution or processes of our minds — as the psychological unity of intellect, affection, and will; the logical unity of thesis, antithesis, and synthesis; the metaphysical unity of subject, object, and subject-object.

   c. No one of these furnishes any proper analogue of the Trinity, since in no one of them is found the essential element of tri-personality. Such illustrations may some time be used to disarm objection, but they furnish no positive explanation of the mystery of the Trinity and unless carefully guarded may lead to grievous error.

2. The doctrine of the Trinity is not self-contradictory. This it would be only if it declared God to be Three in the same numerical sense in which He is said to be One. This we do not assert. We assert simply that the same God who is one with respect to His essence is three with respect to the internal distinctions of that essence, or with respect to the modes of His being. The possibility of this cannot be denied, except by assuming that the human mind is in all respects the measure of the divine. The fact that the ascending scale of life is marked by increasing differentiation of faculty and

function would rather lead us to expect, in the highest of all beings, a nature more complex than our own.

Study Questions on Theology Proper

1. Name and define six false views of God.
2. Define *Theism* and *Monotheism*.
3. Give four designations of God, with references.
4. What is the origin of the idea of God?
5. What is a rational intuition viewed both logically and chronologically?
6. What is the simple meaning of *intuition* and from what it is to be distinguished?
7. Give three negative definitions of a first truth and the reasons against them.
8. Give a positive definition of a first truth.
9. What does the logical priority of a first truth provide?
10. How many and what are the criteria by which first truths are tested?
11. What is meant by *universality, necessity,* and *logical independence and priority* as criteria of first truths, and how does belief in God meet these tests?
12. What is the fourfold content of belief in God's existence as a first truth or rational intuition?
13. Give three supposed sources of the origin of the idea of God and show how these are impossible as such.
14. What is the attitude of the Scriptures and the writers of the Scriptures toward the existence of God?
15. What do the Scriptures announce and declare concerning God?
16. What fivefold line of corroborative truth may be given of the existence of God?
17. What may be said concerning the value of these arguments, and why?
18. Give the meaning, value, and defects of the cosmological, teleological, and anthropological arguments.
19. Give the content and value of the Christological argument.
20. Define *congruity* and explain the argument therefrom.
21. What are we compelled to do through the contemplation of the

words and acts of God and those of man?

22. Define the term *attributes of God*.
23. Why do we call them attributes?
24. What kind of an existence do the attributes of God have, and from what are they distinguishable?
25. From what personal distinctions and personal relations are the divine attributes to be distinguished?
26. Of what are the attributes of God the manifestation and the medium?
27. Name and define the two methods of determining the divine attributes.
28. What are the two great classes into which the divine attributes may be divided? Give definition of each.
29. What is the threefold division of the "absolute" or "immanent" attributes and what are the subdivisions of these.
30. Give the divisions and subdivisions of the "relative" or "transitive" attributes.
31. What is meant by *spirituality* when applied to God?
32. What is taught in the passages of Scripture cited concerning God's nature with reference to matter and in relation to the material?
33. How are the passages to be regarded which ascribe bodily parts and organs to God?
34. How are the appearances which God made to the patriarchs to be explained?
35. What two attributes does the spirituality of God involve?
36. Quote one passage of Scripture which represents God as the living God.
37. Give the two negative and one positive definitions of *life*.
38. What is meant by *personality?*
39. What are self-consciousness and self-determination to be distinguished from, and why?
40. Give three declarations made in Scripture which express personality, and quote one passage with each.
41. What is meant by *infinity?*
42. Where does the idea of infinity take its rise?
43. What does the infinity of God not involve nor prevent?
44. What does infinity in God imply with reference to relations and limitations?
45. In what sense are we to conceive of the infinity of God, extensively or intensively?

46. What do we mean by *self-existence?*
47. What kind of an existence does God have — necessary or contingent — and in what is it grounded?
48. What is meant by *immutability?*
49. What does reason teach us concerning change in God, and why?
50. In what three ways may the passages be explained which seem to ascribe change to God?
51. What is meant by the *unity* of God?
52. Quote one passage proving the unity of God.
53. Why is the notion of two or more Gods self-contradictory?
54. What do we mean by the *perfection* of God?
55. What does right action among men and the activity of God presuppose?
56. What did God's previous solitary existence necessitate concerning Himself?
57. What threefold capacity must have been possessed by God from all eternity?
58. What do we mean by *truth* as applied to God?
59. With what is the immanent truth of God not to be confounded, and why?
60. Why is truth in God not merely an active attribute?
61. How is all truth among men to be regarded?
62. Of what is the attribute of truth the principle and guarantee?
63. What do we mean by *love* in God? Quote one passage illustrating it.
64. Define the immanent love of God.
65. Define *holiness* as applied to God and quote one passage of Scripture proving that God is holy.
66. Negatively and positively discuss God's holiness.
67. Define the *eternity* of God and quote one passage proving it.
68. What does *eternity*, as infinity in relation to time, imply?
69. In what sense are past, present, and future "an eternal Now" with God?
70. What is meant by *immensity* as applied to God?
71. Define *omnipresence* and quote Psalm 139:7-10 proving it.
72. Give three negative statements concerning God's omnipresence.
73. Define *omniscience* and quote one passage proving it.
74. From what three facts may God's omniscience be argued?
75. Give some of the objects of knowledge which are included in

God's omniscience.

76. Is prescience causative? Relate prescience to God's predetermining will.
77. What does God's omniscience embrace and not embrace?
78. Discuss omniscience as qualified by holy will.
79. Define *omnipotence* and quote one passage proving it.
80. What two things does omnipotence not imply, and what one thing does it not exclude?
81. What is meant by *veracity* and *faithfulness* as applied to God?
82. In virtue of His veracity, what is true of God? Of His faithfulness?
83. Define *mercy* and *goodness* in general and particular.
84. Define *righteousness* and *justice* in general and in particular.
85. What are the two aspects of transitive holiness represented respectively by righteousness and justice? What else may they be called?
86. Why can neither righteousness nor justice bestow rewards upon creatures?
87. Of what is justice in God devoid, and of what nature are the penalties which He inflicts upon transgression?
88. Define *the Trinity*.
89. In what threefold sense is God recognized in Scripture?
90. What does the scriptural description of the members of the Trinity compel?
91. Give the threefold way in which the Father and the Son are shown to be distinct from each other, with references.
92. Give the threefold way in which the Father and the Son are shown to be distinct from the Holy Spirit, with references.
93. Give the fivefold proof that the tri-personality of the divine nature is not merely economical and temporal, but immanent and eternal. Quote one passage with each.
94. From what is *tri-personality* to be distinguished, and why?
95. What qualification is necessary to show the distinctions between the unity of nature among men and that of the persons of the Godhead?
96. To whom do the titles of the Trinity belong and why?
97. In what sense are the titles of the members of the Trinity to be used?
98. Why is the doctrine of the Trinity inscrutable?
99. When would the doctrine of the Trinity be self-contradictory, and why does not the present interpretation make it so?

Notes

[1]Technically speaking, these are not definitions, but descriptions of God's nature and character.

[2]Moffatt, who reported that certain African tribes were destitute of religion, was corrected by the testimony of his son-in-law, Livingstone: "The existence of God and of a future life is everywhere recognized in Africa."

[3]This schedule, like much of this theological synopsis, is attributed to Augustus Hopkins Strong, *Systematic Theology* (1907). It will be observed, upon examination of the schedule, that our classification presents God first as Spirit, then as the Infinite Spirit, and finally as the Perfect Spirit. This accords with the definition of the term *God* as previously given. It also corresponds with the order in which the attributes commonly present themselves to the human mind. Our first thought of God is that of mere Spirit, mysterious and undefined, over against our own spirits. Our next thought is that of God's greatness; the quantitative element suggests itself; His natural attributes rise before us; we recognize Him as the Infinite One. Finally comes the qualitative element; our moral natures recognize a moral God; over against our errors, selfishness and impurity, we perceive His absolute perfection. It should also be observed that this moral perfection, as it is an immanent attribute, involves relation of God to Himself. Truth, Love, and Holiness, as they respectively imply an exercise in God of intellect, affection and will, may be conceived of as God's self-knowing, God's self-loving, and God's self-willing.

[4]We have here, at best, only a definition of physical and finite life; and even this is insufficient, because the definition recognizes no original source of activity within, but only a power of reaction in response to stimulus from without. We might as well say that the boiling teakettle is alive.

[5]Transcendence is not mere outsideness; it is rather boundless supply within. God is not infinite by virtue of His filling a space outside of space — rather He is infinite by being the pure and perfect Mind that passes beyond all phenomena and constitutes the ground of them. The former conception of infinity is simply supra-cosmic; the latter alone is properly transcendent. God is the living God and has not yet spoken His last word on any subject. God's life operates unspent; there is ever more to follow. The legend stamped with the Pillars of Hercules upon the old coins of Spain was *Ne Plus Ultra* ("nothing beyond")—but when Columbus discovered America, the legend was fitly changed to *Plus Ultra* ("more beyond"); so must it ever be with God. See Pss. 71:15; 78:41; 89:2; 113:4-6; Isa. 52:10; John 1:16, 50; 2 Cor. 4:17.

[6]God's essence is not His act, not only because this would imply that He could destroy Himself, but also because before willing there must be being. Those who hold God's essence to be simple activity are impelled to this view by the fear of postulating some dead thing in God which precedes all exercise of faculty.

[7]Of the two words for *love* in the New Testament, one designates an emotional affection, which is not and cannot be commanded (John 11:36), while the other expresses a rational and benevolent affection which springs from deliberate choice (Matt. 5:44; 19:19).

[8]Blessedness is not itself a divine attribute; it is rather a result of the exercise of the divine attributes. It is a subjective result of this exercise, as glory is an objective result. Perfect faculties, with perfect objects for their exercise, ensure God's blessedness. But love is especially its source (John 17:24). Happiness is grounded in circumstances, blessedness in character.

[9]"Though God extends beyond Creation's rim, each smallest atom holds the whole of Him." From this it follows that the whole Logos, or preexistent Christ, can be united to and be present in the man Christ Jesus, while at the same time He fills and governs the whole universe; and so the whole Christ can be united to, and can be present in, the single believer as fully as if that believer were the only one to receive of His fullness.

[10]God knows His inanimate creation (Ps. 147:4). He has a knowledge of brute creatures (Matt. 10:29); of men and their works (Ps. 33:13-15); of the hearts of men and their thoughts (Ps. 139:2; Acts 15:8); of our wants (Matt. 6:8); of the least things (Matt. 10:30); of the past (Mal. 3:16); of the future (Isa. 46:9, 10); of men's future free acts (Isa. 44:28); of men's future evil acts

(Acts 2:23); of the ideally possible (1 Sam. 23:12; Matt. 11:23); from eternity (Acts 15:18). His knowledge is incomprehensible to men (Ps. 139:6; Rom. 11:33); related to wisdom (Ps. 104:24; Eph. 3:10).

[11]It is to be remembered that omniscience, as the designation of a relative and transitive attribute, does not include God's self-knowledge. The term is used in the technical sense of God's knowledge of all things that pertain to the universe of His creation. As the flash of the cannon is "heard" before the sound of its discharge, so God flashes the light of prediction in His Word before the arrival of the event itself.

[12]Seeing a thing in the future does not cause it to be, any more than seeing a thing in the past causes it to be. Foreknowledge perceives future events, it does not construct them.

[13]Wisdom is not simply estimating all things at their proper value; it has in it also the element of counsel and purpose. It has been defined as "the talent of using one's talents."

[14]He performs natural wonders (Gen. 1:1-3; Isa. 44:24; Heb. 1:3); spiritual wonders (2 Cor. 4:6; Eph. 1:19; 3:20); He has power to create new things (Matt. 3:9; Rom. 4:17), after His own pleasure (Ps. 115:3; Eph. 1:11). There is nothing impossible to Him (Gen. 18:14; Matt. 19:26).

[15]Anger, within certain limits, is a duty of man (Ps. 97:20; Eph. 4:26). The calm indignation of the judge who pronounces sentences with tears is the true image of the holy anger of God against sin. Gaston de Foix, the chronicler, admirably wrote: "He loved what ought to be loved, and hated what ought to be hated, and never had a miscreant with Him" (see also 1 Kings 11:9 and Ps. 101:5, 6). Even Horace Bushnell spoke of the "wrath-principle" in God. Jesus' anger was no less notable than His love. The love of the right involved hatred of the wrong. Those may hate who hate evil for its hatefulness and for the sake of God. Hate sin in yourself first, and then you will hate it in itself and in the world. Be angry only in Christ and with the wrath of God.

[16]Judaism finds in the tri-personality an irreconcilable element because of its strong insistence upon the unity of God, and therefore the Christian doctrine appears to be a clear case of tritheism. Judaism overlooks the fact that the unity which it asserts upon the basis of Deut. 6:4 may involve *a distinction* in that unity (Gen. 2:24; 6:3; Ps. 2:7). The Jehovah's Witnesses accuse the orthodox churches of being tritheistic, but misunderstand the doctrine of the Trinity. The New Testament applies to Jesus Christ passages which the Old Testament applies to Jehovah (Phil. 2:10 — Isa. 45:23; Rev. 1:17 — Isa. 44:6).

CHAPTER FOUR

CHRISTOLOGY: THE DOCTRINE OF JESUS CHRIST

THE PERSON OF JESUS CHRIST

Historical Preparation for His Coming

Since God had from eternity determined to redeem mankind, the history of the race from the time of the fall to the coming of Christ was providentially arranged to prepare the way for this redemption. The preparation was twofold.

Negative preparation — in the history of the heathen world. This showed the true nature of sin, the depth of spiritual ignorance, and the depth of moral depravity to which the race, left to itself must fall.

It also showed the powerlessness of human nature to preserve or regain an adequate knowledge of God, or to deliver itself from sin by philosophy or art.

Positive preparation — in the history of Israel. A single people was separated from all others, from the time of Abraham, and was educated in three great truths: the majesty of God in His unity, omnipotence, and holiness; the sinfulness of man and his hopelessness; and the certainty of coming salvation.

This education from the time of Moses was conducted by the use of three principle agencies.

1. The law — Mosaic legislation: by its theophanies and miracles, cultivated faith in a personal and almighty God and Judge; by its commands and threatenings, awakened the sense of sin; by its priestly and sacrificial system, inspired hope of some way of

pardon and access to God.

2. Prophecy — two kinds.

a. Verbal — beginning with the protoevangelium in the garden and extending within four hundred years of the coming of Christ.

b. Typical — in persons such as Adam, Melchizedek, Joseph, Moses, Joshua, David, Solomon, Jonah; and in acts, such as Isaac's sacrifice and Moses' lifting up the serpent in the wilderness.

3. Judgment — repeated divine chastisements for idolatry culminated in the overthrow of the kingdom and the captivity of the Jews. The exile had two principal effects.

a. Religious — in giving monotheism firm root in the hearts of the people, and in leading to the establishment of the synagogue system, by which thereafter monotheism was preserved and propagated.

b. Civil — in converting the Jews from an agricultural to a trading people, scattering them among all nations, and finally imbuing them with the spirit of Roman law and organization. Thus a people was made ready to receive the gospel and to propagate it throughout the world at the very time when the world had become conscious of its needs and through its greatest philosophers and poets was expressing its longings for deliverance.

Historical Survey of Views of the Person of Christ

Ebionism (c. A.D. 100). Ebionism was the denial of the divine nature of Christ. It held our Lord to be merely man, whether naturally or supernaturally conceived. As a man, however, it was believed that he held a peculiar relation to God in that, from the time of His baptism, an unmeasured fullness of the divine Spirit rested upon Him. Ebionism was simply Judaism within the pale of the Christian church, and its denial of Christ's Godhead was occasioned by an apparent incompatibility of this doctrine with monotheism.

Cerinthianism (c. A.D. 100). This heresy originated with Cerinthus, a heretic who lived in the days of the apostle John. It was an offshoot of Ebionism, holding that there was no real and essential union of the two natures of Christ prior to His baptism. This error founded the deity of Christ, not on the supernatural birth, but on

His baptism and endowment by the Spirit.

Docetism. The term comes from a Greek word signifying "to seem or appear." This error flourished from the last part of the first to the latter part of the second century. It denied the humanity of Christ and was attacked by the apostle John in his first epistle (4:1-3). In denying the reality of Christ's body, Docetism showed its connection with Gnosticism and Manichaeism. This view was the logical consequence of the assumption that matter is inherently evil. If matter is evil and Christ is pure, then Christ's human body must have been merely phantasmal. Docetism was simply pagan philosophy introduced into the church.

Arianism. Arius, a presbyter of the church of Alexandria in Egypt in the fourth century, denied the deity of Christ and also His eternal generation from the Father. This heresy was condemned at the Council of Nicea, A.D. 325. Arius regarded the Logos, who united himself to humanity in Jesus Christ, not as possessed of absolute Godhead, but as the first and highest of created beings. This view originated in misinterpretation of the scriptural accounts of Christ's state of humiliation, and in mistaking temporary subordination for original and permanent inequality.

Apollinarianism. Apollinarius, bishop of the church of Laodicea in the fourth century, denied the completeness of our Lord's human nature. Accepting the threefold division of man's nature as body, soul, and spirit, Apollinarius denied to Christ a human soul, replacing it with the divine Logos. In this way he made Jesus only two parts human. He regarded the human soul as the seat of sin; Christ was sinless, therefore Christ could not have possessed a human soul. This heresy was condemned at the Council of Constantinople, A.D. 381.

Nestorianism. Nestorius, bishop of the church at Constantinople in the fourth century, denied the unique personality of Christ by separating and erecting the two natures into distinct persons. Thus he made our Lord two persons instead of one.

Eutychianism. Eutychus, an abbot of Constantinople in the fifth century, denied the integrity of our Lord's two natures and held a mingling of both into one which constituted a tertium quid, or third nature. Since in this case the divine must overpower the human, it follows that the human was absorbed into or transmuted into the divine, though the divine was not in all respects the same after the union as it was before. Hence the Eutychians were often called "Monophysites" because they virtually reduced the two natures to one.

The orthodox interpretation. Promulgated at the Council of Chalcedon, A.D. 451, this holds that in the one person, Jesus Christ, there are two natures, a human and a divine, each with completeness and integrity. These two natures are organically and indissolubly united, yet so that no third nature is formed thereby. In brief, the orthodox doctrine forbids us either to divide the person or to confound the natures.

The Preexistence of Christ

The Scriptures clearly and distinctly teach that, as the second person of the Trinity, Jesus Christ existed before His incarnation (John 1:1-5; 8:58; 17:5, 24; Col. 1:13-17; Heb. 1:2; 2:10).

The nature of this preexistence was twofold, that is, as to God and as to Creation. As to God, Jesus Christ was "the only begotten of the Father," being begotten not in time, but in eternity. Theologically this truth is called "the eternal generation of the Son." In the historical development of the doctrine of the Trinity in the Scriptures, not the Father (the First Person), but Christ (the Second Person) is first revealed. His sonship was the infinite and positional relation which He sustained to the other members of the Trinity from all eternity (see with the above passages 2 Sam. 7:12-17; Pss. 2:7-9; 89:24-29).

As to Creation, Jesus Christ is "the first-born" (Rom. 8:29; Col. 1:15, 18). In Colossians 1:15 Jesus is declared to be "the first-born of every creature" ("of all creation," ASV); and in verse 18 He is declared to be "the first-born from the dead." These then are the two relations in which He is first-born — creation and resurrection. As applied to Christ, believers cannot share the title "only begotten," but by spiritual sonship and resurrection we share with Him his title of "first-born" (Gal. 4:6; Heb. 12:23). In the latter passage the Greek word "first-born" is in the plural (see Rev. 3:14).

The character of the preexistence of Christ cannot be better expressed than that of primeval glory (John 17:5; Phil. 2:6, 7; Col. 1:15; Heb. 1:3). Just what this principal glory was we do not know. Jesus is spoken of as being in the bosom of the Father (John 1:18) and of being loved by the Father "before the foundation of the world" (John 17:24). These and other phrases express ineffable relationships within the Godhead which we cannot comprehend.

Old Testament appearings. From Genesis to Malachi there are frequent instances of Christophanies, or appearings of Christ to His ancient people. These were two kinds, namely, material symbols and manifestations in human form. The latter were theophanies, or Christophanies proper. (*Theophany* means an appearance of God; *Christophany*, an appearance of Christ.)

1. Material symbols. From the days of the Garden of Eden till the time of the destruction of Solomon's temple, there was a sensible representation of God upon the earth. Our first parents were permitted to come into close contact with Jehovah Himself (Gen. 3:8). In this verse the word *presence* is literally *face*; here there was a divine manifestation to both the eye and the ear. After the Fall God placed at the entrance to Eden cherubim and a flaming sword, visible manifestations of His presence. It was before this presence of God, doubtless, that Cain and Abel brought their offerings, and from it that Cain fled (Gen. 4:4, 5, 16).

   To the patriarchs the Lord both appeared and spoke in a manner sensible to the eye and ear (Gen. 17:1; 18:1; Acts 7:2). Again, to Moses at the burning bush, Jehovah appeared and spoke (Exod. 3:1-6). Finally, in a pillar of cloud and fire and in the Shekinah glory in tabernacle and temple, Jehovah repeatedly appeared and spoke to His servants Moses and Joshua and made known His will to Israel (Exod. 13:21; 14:20; 19:24; 20:1-26; 40:34-38; 1 Kings 8:10, 11; 2 Chron. 5:13, 14). There was no visible manifestation of the presence of Jehovah in the temple of Zerubbabel or in the temple of Herod.

2. Manifestation in human form. In the Old Testament, mention is made of an august, celestial Personage "who acts in the name of Jehovah," whose name is used interchangeably with that of Jehovah, and who received divine honor and reverence. The more prominent names give to this heavenly being are "the Angel," "the Angel of Jehovah," "the Angel of the Presence (or Face)," and "the Angel (or Messenger) of the Covenant." He can be none other than the Jehovah of the Old Testament or the Christ of the New Testament — He who became the incarnate Word or Logos (Gen. 16:10-13; 22:11, 15; Exod. 23:20-25; 32:34; 33:21-23; Josh. 5:13-15; Judges 13:3-20; Isa. 63:9; Zech. 1:11, 12; Mal. 3:1).

3. Identity of material symbols and personal manifestations. The identity of the material symbols of the preexistent Christ with His manifestations is clear from such passages as Exod. 3:2 and 14:19. Nor is there any doubt that these symbols and theophanies were manifestations and appearances of the preexistent Christ. "The

glory of the Lord" and the "Word of the Lord" are frequent Old Testament names for the sensible representations of God — the former describing them as they appealed to the eye, and the latter as they appealed to the ear. In the first chapter of John these same descriptive expressions are applied to Christ (1:14). Modern Bible students feel the necessity of proving the deity of Christ. This was not true of John; his contention was that He whom we now know as the second person of the Trinity, the angel of Old Testament revelation, became incarnate in Jesus of Nazareth.

Prophetic pictures. There are three pictures of the preexistent Christ, so striking and beautiful as to deserve special attention and emphasis.

1. The Slain Lamb. This is a picture of the Passover Lamb (Exod. 12). John the Baptist identified Christ as the sacrificial Lamb (John 1:29; 1 Cor. 5:7). John the seer on Patmos had a vision of our Lord as the bleeding Lamb (Rev. 12:11) slain from the foundation of the world (Rev. 13:8).

2. The Obedient Servant. This is the picture of Christ portrayed in Psalm 40:6-8 (see Heb. 10:5-10). Undoubtedly the primary reference of these passages is to Exodus 21:2-6, where we read of the Hebrew bondslave who, unwilling to claim rightful liberty because of his love for his master, wife, and children, submitted to having his ear bored with an awl as the seal of voluntary and perpetual service. In Psalm 40:6, the word *opened* means "digged" or "bored" — a reference to Exodus 21:6. This picture of our Lord is fulfilled in the Gospel of Mark, which represents Him as the Servant of Jehovah.

3. The Beloved Son. This is the picture presented in 2 Samuel 7:14-16; Psalms 2:7; 89:26-29. At the baptism of Jesus, the Father identifies Him as the well-beloved Son (Matt. 3:17; Mark 1:11; Luke 3:22). This was repeated at the Transfiguration (Matt. 17:5; Mark 9:7; Luke 9:35; see also Isa. 42:1; Eph. 2:18).

THE INCARNATION OF CHRIST

The word *incarnation* is derived from the Latin word meaning, literally, "enfleshment," i.e., the assumption of humanity. Scripture teaches, by both prophetic utterance and historical statement, that the Son of the Old Testament became incarnate in Jesus, who was the Christ, the Messiah of God (Gen. 3:15; Ps. 2:7, 12; Isa. 9:6; Matt. 1:18-25; Luke 1:26-35; John 1:14; Acts 10:38; Rom. 8:3, 4; 1 Tim. 3:16; Heb. 2:14). It also teaches that the purpose of the Incarnation was redemption (Gen. 3:15; Isa. 53:4; Matt. 1:21; 20:28; Luke 1:68-75; John 3:16, 17; Gal. 4:4, 5; 1 Tim. 1:15; 1 John 3:8; 4:10).[1]

The Two Natures of Jesus Christ

  The humanity of Christ:

1. Its reality as demonstrated in that —

    a. He expressly called Himself and was called "man" (John 8:20; Acts 2:22; Rom. 5:15; 1 Cor. 15:21; 1 Tim. 2:5);

    b. He possessed the essential elements of human nature — body, soul, and spirit (Matt. 10:12, 28; 26:38; Luke 23:46);

    c. He was moved by the instinctive principles and exercised the active powers which belong to a normal and developed humanity — hunger, weariness, sleep, love, compassion, anger, fear, groaning, weeping, and prayer (Matt. 4:2; 8:24; 9:36; 14:23; Mark 3:5; 10:21; John 4:6; 11:33, 35; 12:27; 19:28; Heb. 5:7);

    d. He was subject to the ordinary laws of human development both in body and in soul (grew and "waxed strong in spirit"): asked questions; grew in wisdom and stature; learned obedience; suffered, being tempted; was made perfect through sufferings (Luke 2:40, 46-49, 52; Heb. 2:10, 18; 5:8);

    e. He suffered and died (bloody sweat; gave up His spirit; was pierced in the side, and "straightway there came out blood and water"): Luke 22:44; John 19:30-34.

2. Its integrity as both complete and perfect in that —

    a. It was of miraculous conception. We must not lose sight of the fact that there was essentially something supernatural surrounding the birth of Christ (Matt. 1:18; Luke 1:35). "On this wise" indicates that this birth was different from those recorded before it. Luke 1:35 is explicit about this matter. To assail the virgin birth is to assail the virgin's life. He was of "the seed of the woman," not of the man. (See Luke 1:34 — "How shall this be, seeing I know not a man?") No laws of heredity are sufficient to account for His generation. By creative act, God broke through the chain of human generation and brought into the world a supernatural being.

    The narrative of the virgin birth need not stagger us. The abundance of historical evidence in its favor should lead to its acceptance. All the manuscripts in all the ancient versions contain the record of it. All the traditions of the early church recognized it. Mention of it is made in the earliest of all the creeds — the Apostles' Creed. If the doctrine of the virgin birth is rejected, it must be on purely subjective grounds. If one denies the possibility of the supernatural in the experience of human life, it is, of course, easy for him to deny this doctrine. To one who believes that Jesus was human only, it would seem comparatively easy to deny the supernatural birth on a purely theoretical basis. The preconceptions of thinkers, to a great degree, determine their views. It would seem that such a wonderful life as that lived by Christ, having as it did such a wonderful finish in the Resurrection and Ascension, might — indeed, should — have a wonderful and extraordinary entrance into the world. The fact that the Virgin Birth is attested by the Scriptures, by tradition, and by creeds and is in perfect harmony with all the other facts of that wonderful life should be sufficient attestation of the truth.

It has been thought strange — if, as it is claimed, the Virgin Birth is so essential to the right understanding of the Christian religion — that Mark, John, and Paul should say nothing about it. But does such silence really exist? John says, "The Word became flesh"; Paul speaks of "God manifest in the flesh." This argument from silence is sufficiently met by the consideration that Mark passes over thirty years of our Lord's life in silence; John presupposes the narratives of Matthew and Luke; and Paul does not deal with the story of Jesus' life.

b. It was free from both hereditary depravity and actual sin. This is shown by His never offering sacrifice, never praying for forgiveness, teaching that all but He needed the new birth, challenging all to convict Him of a single sin.[2]

c. It was ideal human nature. It furnished the moral pattern which man is progressively to realize, though with limitations of knowledge and activity required by His vocation as the world's Redeemer (Ps. 8:4-8; 1 Cor. 15:45; 2 Cor. 3:18; Phil. 3:21; Col. 1:18; Heb. 2:6-10; 1 John 3:2).

d. It was a human nature that found its personality only in union with the divine nature. In other words, it was a human nature impersonal in the sense that it had no personality separate from the divine nature and prior to its union therewith.[3]

e. It was a human nature germinal and capable of self-communication. Thus it constituted Him the spiritual head and beginning of a new race, the Second Adam, from whom fallen man individually and collectively derives new and holy life (Isa. 53:10, 11; John 5:21; 15:1; 17:2; 1 Cor. 15:45; Eph. 5:23, 30; Rev. 22:16).[4]

The deity of Christ:

1. He is expressly called God. In John 1:1 the predicate precedes the verb by way of emphasis, to indicate progress in thought — the Logos was not only with God, but was God. The Word was distinguishable from God, yet the Word was God, of divine nature; not "a God," which to a Jewish ear would have been abominable, nor yet identical with all that can be called God, for then the definite article would have been inserted.

   In John 1:18, "the only begotten God" must be regarded as the correct reading and as a plain ascription of absolute deity to Christ. He is not simply the only revealer of God, but He is Himself God revealed. In John 20:28, the address of Thomas — "my Lord and my God" — since it was unrebuked by Christ, is equivalent to an assertion on His own part of His claim to deity.

   Titus 2:13 is to be regarded as a direct, definite, and even studied declaration of Christ's deity — "the appearing of the glory of our great God and Savior, Jesus Christ." In Hebrews 1:8 a quotation is used as addressed to Christ. Verse 10 — "Thou, Lord, in the beginning has laid the foundation of the earth" — by applying to Christ an Old Testament ascription of Jehovah, implies His absolute Godhead.

2. Old Testament descriptions of God are applied to Him. This application to Christ of titles and names exclusively appropriated to God is inexplicable if Christ was not regarded as being Himself God. The peculiar awe with which the term *Jehovah* was set apart by a nation of strict monotheists as the sacred and incommunicable name of the one self-existent and covenant-keeping God forbids the belief that the Scripture writers could have used it as the designation of a subordinate and created being (see Matt. 3:3 compared with Isa. 40:3; John 12:41 compared with Isa. 6:10; Eph. 4:8 compared with Ps. 68:18).

3. He possesses the attributes of God. Among these attributes are life, self-existence, immutability, truth, love, holiness, eternity, omnipresence, omniscience, and omnipotence. All these attributes are ascribed to Christ in connections which show that the terms are used in no secondary sense, nor in any sense predicable of a creature (see Prov. 8:23; Matt. 9:4; 27:18; 28:20; Luke 1:35;

John 1:1, 4; 2:24, 25; 5:26; 6:69; 8:58; 14:6; 16:30; 17:5; Acts 1:24; Eph. 1:23; Col. 1:17; 2:3; Heb. 1:11; 7:16, 26; 13:8; 1 John 3:16; Rev. 1:8; 3:7).

4. The works of God are ascribed to Him. We do not here speak of miracles, which may be wrought by communicated power, but of such works as the creation of the world, the upholding of all things, the final raising of the dead, and the judging of all men. Power to perform these works cannot be delegated, because they are characteristic of omnipotence (see Matt. 25:31, 32; John 1:3; 5:27-29; 1 Cor. 8:6; Col. 1:16, 17; Heb. 1:3, 10; Rev. 3:14).

5. He receives honor and worship due only to God. In addition to the address of Thomas in John 20:28 — which we have already cited among the proofs that Jesus is expressly called "God," and in which divine honor is paid to Him — we may refer to the prayer and worship offered by the apostolic and post-apostolic church (see John 5:23; 14:14; Acts 7:59; Rom. 10:9, 13 with Gen. 4:26; 1 Cor. 11:24, 25; Phil. 2:10, 11; 2 Tim. 4:18; Heb. 1:6; 13:21; Rev. 5:12-14).

6. His name is associated with that of God upon a footing of equality. We refer to the baptism formula (Matt. 28:19), to the apostolic benediction (2 Cor. 13:14), and to those passages in which eternal life is said to be dependent equally upon Christ and upon God, or in which spiritual gifts are attributed to Christ equally with the Father (Matt. 11:27; John 5:23; 14:1; 17:3; Rom. 10:17; 1 Cor. 12:4-6; Col. 3:1; 2 Thess. 2:16, 17; Rev. 20:6; 22:3).

7. Equality with God is expressly claimed. Not only is equality with God claimed for Himself by Jesus, but it is claimed for Him by His apostles (John 5:18; Phil. 2:6).

8. Further proof of Christ's deity may be found in the application to Him of the phrases "Son of God" and "image of God"; in the declarations of His oneness with God; and in the attribution to Him of the fullness of the Godhead (Matt. 26:63, 64; John 10:30; 14:9; 17:11, 22; Col. 1:15; Heb. 1:3).

9. These proofs of Christ's deity from the New Testament are corroborated by Christian experience. Christian experience recognizes Christ as an absolutely perfect Savior, perfectly revealing the Godhead and worthy of unlimited worship and adoration; that is, it practically recognizes Him as deity. But Christian experience also recognizes that through Christ it has introduction and reconciliation to God as one distinct from Jesus Christ, as one who

was alienated from the soul by its sin, who is now reconciled through Jesus' death. In other words, while recognizing Jesus as God, we are also compelled to recognize a distinction between the Father and the Son through whom we come to the Father.

The Union of the Two Natures in One Person

As the Scriptures distinctly represent Jesus Christ to have been possessed of a divine nature and of a human nature, each unaltered in essence and undivested of its normal attributes and powers, they with equal distinctness represent Jesus Christ as a single, undivided personality in whom these two natures are vitally and inseparably united, so that He is properly not God-and-man, but the God-man. The two natures are bound together, not by the moral tie of friendship, nor by the spiritual tie which links the believer to his Lord, but by a bond unique and inscrutable, which constitutes them one person with a single consciousness and will, this consciousness and will including within their possible range both the human nature and the divine.

Proof of this union:

1. Christ uniformly speaks of Himself, and is spoken of, as a single person. There is no interchange of "I" and "thou" between the human and the divine natures, such as we find between the persons of the Trinity (John 17:23). Christ never uses the plural number in referring to Himself unless it be in John 3:11 — "We speak that we do know" — and even here *we* is more probably used as inclusive of the disciples. 1 John 4:2 — "is come in the flesh" — is supplemented by John 1:14 — "became flesh"; and these texts together assure us that Christ so came in human nature as to make that nature an element in His single personality (John 1:14; 3:11; 17:23; 1 John 4:2).

2. The attributes and powers of both natures are ascribed to the one Christ, and conversely the works and dignities, in a way which cannot be understood except upon the principle that these two natures are organically and indissolubly united in a single person. Examples of the former usage are Romans 1:3 and 1 Peter 3:18; of the latter, 1 Timothy 2:5 and Hebrews 1:2, 3.

   Hence we can say, on the one hand, that the God-man existed before Abraham, yet was born in the reign of Augustus Caesar; and that Jesus Christ wept, was weary, suffered, and died, yet is the same yesterday, today, and forever; on the other hand, that a divine Savior redeemed us upon the cross, and that the human

Christ is present with His people even to the end of the age (Matt. 28:20; Eph. 1:23; 4:10).

3. The constant scriptural representations of the infinite value of Christ's atonement, and of the union of that part of the human race with God which has been secured in Him, are intelligible only when Christ is regarded not as a man of God, but as the God-man in whom the two natures are so united that what each does has the value of both (Eph. 2:16, 18, 21, 22; 2 Pet. 1:4; 1 John 2:2).

4. It corroborates this view to remember that the universal Christian consciousness recognizes in Christ a single and undivided personality and expresses this recognition in its services of song and prayer.

The real nature of this union:

1. Its great importance. While the Scriptures represent the person of Christ as the crowning mystery of the Christian scheme (Matt. 11:27; Col. 1:27; 2:2; 1 Tim. 3:16), they also incite us to its study (Luke 24:39; John 17:3; 20:27; Phil. 3:8, 10). This is the more needful, since Christ is not only the central point of Christianity, but Christianity itself — the embodied reconciliation and union between man and God. The following remarks are offered, not as fully explaining, but only as in some respects relieving the difficulties of the subject.

2. The chief problems.

   a. One personality and two natures. The one person acts in accord with the properties of the two natures.

   b. Human nature without personality. The human nature has its personal subsistence in the person of the Logos.

   c. The relation of the Logos to the humanity during the earthly life of Christ. There is no interpretation of the two natures, as a result of which the divine is humanized and the human is deified.

   d. The relation of the humanity to the Logos during the heavenly life of Christ. The human nature is not magnified by the divine nature, but remains separate and distinct from the divine nature in its union with the one person of the Logos.

3. Reason for mystery. The union of the two natures in Christ's person is necessarily inscrutable because there are no analogies to it in our own experience. Attempts to illustrate it — on the one

hand, from the union and yet the distinctness of soul and body, of iron and heat; and on the other hand, from the union and yet the distinctness of Christ and the believer, of the divine Son and the Father — are one-sided and become utterly misleading if they are regarded as furnishing a rationale of the union and not simply as a means of repelling objection.

The first two illustrations mentioned above lack the essential element of two natures to make them complete: soul and body are not two natures but one, nor are iron and heat two substances. The last two illustrations mentioned above lack the element of single personality: Christ and the believer are two persons, not one, even as the Son and the Father are not one person but two.

4. Ground of possibility. The possibility of deity and humanity in one person is grounded in the original creation of man in the divine image. Man's resemblance to God, his possession of a rational and spiritual nature, is the condition of incarnation. Brute-life is incapable of union with God. But human nature is capable of the divine, in the sense not only that it lives, moves, and has its being in God, but that God may unite Himself indissolubly to it and endow it with divine powers, while yet it remains all the more truly human. Since the moral image of God in human nature has been lost by sin, Christ, the perfect image of God after which man was originally made, restores that lost image by uniting Himself to humanity and filling it with His divine life and love.

5. No double personality. This possession of two natures does not involve a double personality in the God-man for the reason that the Logos takes into union with Himself, not an individual man with already developed personality, but human nature which has had no separate existence before its union with the divine.

6. Effect upon the human. The union of the divine and the human nature makes the latter possessed of the powers belonging to the former. In other words, the attributes of the divine nature are imparted to the human without passing over into its essence — so that the human Christ even on earth had power to be, to know, and to do as God. That this power was latent, or was only rarely manifested, was the result of the self-chosen state of humiliation upon which the God-man had entered.

In this state of humiliation, the communication of the contents of the divine nature to the human was mediated by the Holy

Spirit. The God-man, in His servant-form, knew and taught and performed only what the Spirit permitted and directed (Matthew 3:16; John 3:34; Acts 1:2; 10:38; Hebrews 9:14). But when thus permitted, He knew, taught, and performed, not like the prophets by power communicated from without, but by virtue of His own inner divine energy (Matthew 17:2; Mark 5:41; Luke 5:20, 21; 6:19; John 2:11, 24, 25; 3:13; 20:19).

7. Effect upon the divine. This communion of the natures was such that, although the divine nature in itself is incapable of ignorance, weakness, temptation, suffering, or death, the one person Jesus Christ was capable of these by virtue of the union of the divine nature with the human nature in Him. As the human Savior can exercise divine attributes, not in virtue of His humanity alone, but derivatively by virtue of His possession of a divine nature, so the divine Savior can suffer and be ignorant as man, not in His divine nature, but derivatively by virtue of His possession of a human nature.

We may illustrate this from the connection between body and soul. The soul suffers pain from union with the body, of which apart from the body it would be incapable. So the God-man, although in His divine nature, insensible to pain and suffering, was capable through His union with humanity of absolutely infinite suffering.

8. Necessity of the union. The union of two natures in one person is necessary to constitute Jesus Christ a proper mediator between man and God. His twofold nature gives Him fellowship with both parties, since it involves an equal dignity with God and at the same time a perfect sympathy with man (Hebrews 2:17, 18; 4:15, 16). This twofold nature, moreover, enables Him to present to both God and man proper terms of reconciliation. Being man, He can make atonement for man; being God, His atonement has infinite value, while both His deity and His humanity combine to move the hearts of offenders and constrain them to submission and love (1 Timothy 2:5; Hebrews 7:25).

9. The union eternal. The union of humanity with deity in the person of Christ is indissoluble and eternal. Unlike the Avatars of the East, the Incarnation was a permanent assumption of human nature by the second person of the Trinity. In the ascension of Christ, glorified humanity has attained the throne of the universe. By His Spirit this same divine-human Savior is omnipresent to secure the progress of His cause. The final subjection of

the Son to the Father, alluded to in 1 Corinthians 15:28, cannot be other than the complete return of the Son to His original relation to the Father, since, according to John 17:5, Christ is again to possess the glory which He had with the Father before the world was (cf. Heb. 1:8; 7:24, 25).[5]

The Two States of Christ

The state of humiliation. As to the nature of this humiliation, we may dismiss as unworthy of serious notice the views that it consisted essentially either in the union of the Logos with human nature — for this union with human nature continues in the state of exaltation; or in the outward trials and privations of Christ's human life — for this view casts reproach upon poverty and ignores the power of the soul to rise superior to its outward circumstances. The humiliation, as the Scriptures seem to show, consisted wholly in —

1. That act of the preexistent Logos by which He gave up His divine glory with the Father in order to take a servant-form. In this act He resigned, not the possession, nor yet entirely the use, but rather the independent exercise of the divine attributes (John 17:5; Phil. 2:6, 7).

2. The submission of the Logos to the control of the Holy Spirit and the limitations of His Messianic mission, and His communication of the divine fullness to the human nature which He had taken into union with Himself (Acts 1:2; 10:38; Heb. 9:14).

3. The continuous surrender on the part of the God-man of the exercise of the divine powers with which His human nature was endowed by virtue of its union with the divine, and in the voluntary acceptance which followed upon this of temptation, suffering, and death (Matt. 26:53; John 10:17, 18; Phil. 2:8).[6]

The state of exaltation. The nature of this exaltation consisted essentially in —

1. A resumption on the part of the Logos of His independent exercise of divine attributes;

2. The withdrawal on the part of the Logos of all limitations in His communication of His divine fullness to the human nature of Christ;

3. The corresponding exercise on the part of the human nature of those powers which belong to it by virtue of its union with the divine (Ps. 8:4-8 with Heb. 2:7-10).

THE SAVING WORK OF CHRIST

The Threefold Office

According to the Scriptures, Jesus Christ has a threefold work-office, i.e., a prophetic ministry, a priestly ministry, and a kingly ministry.

Christ as Prophet. The predictive announcement that Christ should be a prophet is recorded in Deuteronomy 18:18, 19 (see also Matt. 13:57; 16:14; 21:11; John 1:21; 4:19; 6:14; 7:40; 9:17; and especially Acts 3:22; 7:37). Officially the prophetic ministry of Christ began at the River Jordan when He was endued with the Holy Spirit and ended at the cross when He offered Himself as a sacrifice for sin (Matt. 4:23-25; Luke 4:14-27; Acts 2:22-23; Heb. 9:26-28).

The primary idea of the prophetic office is that of one who "brings things to light" or "makes manifest." The secondary is prediction of the future. The Old Testament prophet, then, exercised two functions: insight and foresight. The prophet had also, so to speak, "hindsight," for by revelation of the Spirit He frequently knew things of the past. This was true of Moses when he penned the panorama of creation in Genesis.[7]

1. Manifold character of prophetic ministry. An Old Testament prophet fulfilled his ministry in three ways: by teaching, by predicting, and by healing. Our Lord did all these (Matt. 5:17; 24:8-9).

2. More particularly, Christ fulfilled His prophetic office —
   a. By His gracious words (Matt. 5:2; 7:28-29; John 6:63; Rev. 1:10, 11);
   b. By His wondrous deeds (John 5:36; 10:25; 15:24; Acts 2:22);
   c. By His matchless example (John 13:15; 1 Peter 2:21-23);
   d. By His unparalleled silence (Matt. 27:13, 14; 1 Peter 2:23);
   e. By His gift of the Spirit (John 14:26; 15:26; 1 Peter 1:10, 11; 1 John 2:20-27).

Christ as Priest. The predictive announcement that Christ should be a priest is recorded in Psalm 110:4 (see Heb. 5:6; 6:20; 7:21). Our Lord's priesthood is not in the line of Aaron, but "after the order of Melchizedek" — that is, it is not exercised on earth but in heaven; and it is unchanging and eternal.

Officially, or dispensationally, the priestly ministry of Christ began at the cross, when He offered Himself as a sacrifice for sin, and will end at His return, when as king He will sit on the throne of David (Heb. 8-9).

A priest is a God-appointed mediator between God and man through whose intercession, by the offering of blood, atonement is made and justification obtained for the guilty sinner (Lev. 4:16-18).

1. The threefold scope of priesthood in the Old Testament ministry. The scope of the Old Testament priesthood was threefold: namely, first, to offer sacrifices before the people; second, to go within the veil to make intercession for the people; and third, to come forth to bless the people; or, Reconciliation, Intercession, and Benediction.[8]

2. The threefold scope of priesthood in Christ's ministry. As the great high priest, our Lord fulfills these three functions. The first, reconciliation, He accomplished at His first coming, when on the cross He offered Himself as a sacrifice for sin. The second, intercession, He is accomplishing in heaven between His first and second advents. And the third, benediction, He will accomplish upon His return. (See Rom. 8:34; 2 Thess. 1:10; Heb. 7:25; 9:27, 28; 1 Peter 1:4, 5, 18-20; 2:24; Rev. 1:5; 20:4.)

Christ as King. This office is to be distinguished from the sovereignty which Christ originally possessed by virtue of His divine nature. Christ's kingship is the sovereignty of the divine Redeemer, which belonged to Him of right from the moment of his birth, but which will be fully exercised only when He comes the second time to sit upon "the throne of His father David." His kingship belongs more properly to Eschatology, and in particular to the study of the Millennium. Accordingly, it will be treated under that heading.

The Atoning Death

The Scriptures teach that Christ suffered in our stead to satisfy an immanent demand of the divine holiness and thus remove an obstacle in the divine mind to the pardon and restoration of the guilty. This statement may be expanded and explained in a preliminary way as follows:

The fundamental attribute of God is holiness, and holiness is not self-communicating love, but self-affirming righteousness. Holiness limits and conditions love, for love can will happiness only as happiness results from and consists with holiness, that is, with conformity to God.

The universe is a reflection of God, and Christ the Word (Logos) is its life. God has constituted the universe, and humanity as a part of it, so as to express His holiness, positively by connecting happiness with righteousness, negatively by attaching unhappiness or suffering to sin. Christ is the Logos, the immanent God, God revealed in nature, in humanity, and in redemption. The universe must be recognized as created, upheld, and governed by the same Being who, in the course of history, was manifest in human form and who made atonement for human sin by His death on Calvary. As all God's creative activity has been exercised through Christ, so it is Christ in whom all things consist or are held together. Providence, as well as preservation, is His work. He makes the universe to reflect God, especially God's ethical or moral nature. That pain or loss universally and inevitably follows sin is the proof that God is unalterably opposed to moral evil; the demands and reproaches of conscience witness that holiness is the fundamental attribute of God's being.

Christ, the Logos, as the revealer of God in the universe and in humanity, must condemn sin by visiting upon it the suffering which is its penalty; while at the same time, as the Life of humanity (John 1:1-4), He must endure the reaction of God's holiness against sin which constitutes that penalty. Here is a double work of Christ of which Paul distinctly speaks in Romans 8:3, 4. The meaning is that God did through Christ what the law could not do, namely, accomplished deliverance for humanity; and did this by sending His Son in a nature which in us is identified with sin. In connection with sin, and as an offering for sin, God condemned sin by condemning Christ. When the question is asked, "In what sense did God send His Son in connection with sin?" only one answer is possible. He sent Him to expiate sin by His sacrificial death. This is the center and foundation of Paul's gospel (Rom. 3:25). But whatever God did in condemning sin, He did through Christ (2 Cor. 5:19). Christ was the condemner as well as the condemned; conscience in us, which unites the accuser and the accused, shows us how Christ could be both the judge and the sin-bearer.

Our personality is not self-contained. We live, move, and have our being in Christ, the Logos. Our reason, affection, conscience, and will are complete only in Him. He is generic humanity, of which we are the off-shoots (Acts 17:24-28). When His righteousness condemns sin, and His love voluntarily endures the suffering which is sin's penalty, humanity ratifies the judgment of God, makes full propitiation for sin, and satisfies the demand of holiness.

While Christ's love explains His willingness to endure suffering for us, only His holiness furnishes the reason for that constitution of the universe and of human nature which makes this suffering necessary. In regard to us, His sufferings are sacrificial and substitutionary, since His deity and His sinlessness enable Him to do for us what we could never do for ourselves. Yet this substitution is also a sharing — not the work of one external to us but of one who is the life of humanity, the soul of our soul and the life of our life, and so responsible with us for the sins of the race, yet voluntarily, vicariously, and graciously so.

The historical work of the incarnate Christ is not itself all that is involved in the Atonement — it is rather the revelation of that which projects itself both into the past and into the future, namely, the suffering of God on account of human sin. Yet without the historical work which was finished on Calvary, the age-long suffering of God could never have been made effectual for man or comprehensible to man.

Christ, identified with the human race as the Logos, the immanent God, has suffered in all human sin. "In all our affliction He has been afflicted" (Isa. 63:9); so that the prophet can say, "All we like sheep have gone astray. . . . The Lord hath laid on Him the iniquity of us all" (Isa. 53:6). The historical sacrifice was a burning-glass which focused the diffused rays of the Sun of righteousness and made them effective in the melting of human hearts. The sufferings of Christ take deepest hold upon us only when we see in them the two contrasted but complementary truths: that holiness must make penalty to follow sin, and that love must share that penalty with the transgressor. The Cross was the concrete exhibition of the holiness that required, and of the love that provided, man's redemption. Those six hours of pain and suffering on the cross were a revelation of eternal facts in the being of God. The heart of God and the meaning of all previous history were then unveiled. As He who hung upon the cross was God, manifest in the flesh, so the suffering of the cross was God's suffering for sin, manifest in the flesh.

The fact of the atoning death. By predictions, types, descriptive terms, and explicit statements, the Scriptures clearly set forth the fact of the Atonement.

1. Types. The typology of the Old Testament is full of the Atonement. We may cite a few of the more striking types.

   a. Coat of skins (Gen. 3:21);
   b. Abel's lamb (Gen. 4:4);

   c. The offering of Isaac (Gen. 22);

   d. The passover lamb (Exod. 12);

   e. The levitical sacrificial system (Lev. 1-7);

   f. The brazen serpent (Num. 21; see also John 3:14; 12:32);

   g. The slain lamb (Isa. 53:6; see also John 1:29; Rev. 13:8).

2. Predictions. The Old Testament abounds in predictions concerning the Messiah, His character, and His career. Indeed, there are said to be 333 specific, striking Old Testament pictures of the sacrificial death of Christ. A few of these are —

   a. The seed of the woman (Gen. 3:15);

   b. The sin offering (Ps. 22);

   c. The vicarious Savior (Isa. 53);

   d. The cut-off Messiah (Dan. 9:26);

   e. The smitten Shepherd (Zech. 13:6, 7).

3. Descriptive terms. There are five scriptural descriptions for the sacrificial work of Christ.

   a. Atonement. The word *atonement* occurs only once in the Authorized Version of the New Testament, namely, Romans 5:11. The Greek noun here is *katallage*, which is more correctly rendered *reconciliation* in the American Standard Version. The root of the Hebrew word for *atonement* is *kaphar*, which literally signifies "to cover," i.e., "forgive sin" (see Exod. 30:10). Psalm 32:1 gives us both the figurative and spiritual meanings of *atonement*. [9]

   b. Reconciliation. *Reconciliation* is the translation of the Greek noun *katallage*, which literally signifies an exchange, i.e., of equivalent value in money-changing, or an adjustment, i.e., of a difference. The enmity between God and man has been destroyed, and amity has been restored. "The word is used in the New Testament," says Thayer, "of the restoration of the favor of God to sinners that repent and put their trust into the expiatory death of Christ" (Rom. 5:11, ASV; 11:15; 2 Cor. 5:18, 19).

      Reconciliation has two sides, active and passive. In the active sense, we may look upon Christ's death as removing the enmity existing between God and men, which had hitherto been a barrier to fellowship (Eph. 2:16; Col. 1:20). This state of existing enmity is set forth in such Scriptures as Romans 8:7; Ephesians 2:15; James 4:4. In the passive sense of the word, it may indicate the change of attitude on the part of man toward God, this change being wrought in the heart of man by a vision of the cross of Christ; a change from enmity to friendship thus taking place (2 Cor. 5:20). It is probably better to state the case thus: God is propitiated, and the sinner is reconciled (2 Cor. 5:19, 20).

c. Propitiation. *Propitiation* is the translation of the Greek nouns *hilasmos* and *hilasterion*, literally signifying an appeasing, a placating, an expiation. *Propitiation* comes from the Latin and means "that which renders one propitious or favorably disposed toward the sinner." Christ, in other words, is the propitiation for sin (Rom. 3:25; 1 John 2:2; 4:10; see Heb. 2:17, ASV; also Gen. 32:20 as an illustration).

d. Redemption and Ransom. *Redemption* is the translation of the Greek nouns *lutrosis* and *apolutrosis*, signifying a releasing or liberation from captivity, slavery, or death by the payment of a prce, called a ransom. *Redemption* is from the Latin and signifies a buying back (Luke 1:68; 2:38; Rom. 3:24; 1 Cor. 1:30; Eph. 1:7, 14; 4:30; Col. 1:14; Heb. 9:12, 15). Thus Christ is the ransom, who delivers us from sin and death (Matt. 20:28; Gal. 3:13; 1 Tim. 2:6; 1 Peter 1:18).

The meaning of a ransom is clearly set forth in Leviticus 25:47-49. It is the price paid to buy back a person or thing for which it is held in captivity. So sin is like a slave market in which sinners are "sold under sin" (Rom. 7:14); souls are under sentence of death (Ezek. 18:4). Christ by His death buys sinners out of the market, thereby indicating complete deliverance from the service of sin. He looses the bonds, sets the prisoners free, by paying a price — that price being His own precious blood.

e. Substitution. *Substitution* is not a biblical word, but is is a scriptural idea. It means that one person or thing is put in, or takes the place of, another person or thing. Thus Christ took the place of sinners and died, suffering the penalty of sin which they deserved. This is the significance of the scapegoat (Lev. 16); this is also the meaning of Isaiah 53:6. And it is the clear teaching of the New Testament (Matt. 20:28; Mark 10:45; 2 Cor. 5:21; Gal. 2:20; 1 Peter 3:18).[10]

4. Explicit statements. The New Testament abounds in explicit statements concerning the Atonement. If it be carefully read and

all the passages bearing on this subject marked, and these classified, the results inform us that —

a. The center and heart of the atonement of Christ is declared to be —

   (1) His death (Rom. 5:10; Phil. 2:8; Heb. 2:9-14; 9:16; Rev. 5:6, 9, 12);

   (2) His cross (1 Cor. 1:23; Gal. 3:1; 6:12; Eph. 2:16; Col. 1:20);

   (3) His blood (Matt. 26:28; Mark 14:24; Luke 22:20; Eph. 1:7; 2:13; Col. 1:14; Heb. 9:12, 15; 1 John 1:7; Rev. 1:5; 5:9).

b. The atonement bears a relation to God.

   (1) It is grounded in His love (John 3:16).

   (2) It manifests His righteousness (Rom. 3:25; 2 Cor. 5:21).

   (3) It measures the extent of His sacrifice (John 3:16; Rom. 8:32; 2 Cor. 5:21; 1 John 4:10).

   (4) It is the basis of our reconciliation (Rom. 5:11; 2 Cor. 5:18, 19).

c. The atonement bears a relation to the law.

   (1) Christ was born under the law (Gal. 4:4, 5).

   (2) Christ bore its curse (Gal. 3:13; Phil. 2:8).

   (3) Christ fulfilled its righteousness (Rom. 5:18, 19; 8:3, 4; 10:4).

d. The sacrifice of Christ was necessary (Luke 24:26; Gal. 2:21; 3:21; Heb. 2:10).

e. The sacrifice of Christ was voluntary (John 10:17, 18; Gal. 2:20; Eph. 5:2; Heb. 9:14; 10:7-9).

f. The atonement of Christ was the only sacrifice for sin (Acts 4:12; Rom. 3:20-28; Heb. 1:3; 9:22; 10:10, 12, 14, 26; 1 Peter 3:18).

g. The atonement of Christ was vicarious (Matt. 26:28; Rom. 5:6; 2 Cor. 5:14, 15; Gal. 3:13, 14).

h. The atonement of Christ was for sin (John 1:29; Rom. 3:25; 5:8; 6:10; 8:3; 1 Cor. 15:3; 2 Cor. 5:21; Gal. 3:13; Heb. 9:28; 1 Peter 2:24; 3:18; Rev. 1:5).

i. The atonement of Christ was for various classes of people.

   (1) For His own people (Matt. 1:21; John 10:11; 15:13; Eph. 5:25; Heb. 2:13, 14; 1 John 3:16);

   (2) For the many (Matt. 20:28; Mark 10:45; Heb. 9:28);

(3) For the lost (Matt. 9:12; Mark 2:17; Luke 5:32; 19:10);
(4) For the whole world (John 1:29; 3:16; 6:51; 12:47; 2 Cor. 5:14, 15; 1 Tim. 2:6; Heb. 2:9; 1 John 2:2).

j. The atonement of Christ produces many beneficial effects.
(1) Thereby Jesus becomes the Savior of men (Matt. 1:21).
(2) Thereby justification is received (Acts 13:39).
(3) Thereby cleansing is received (1 John 1:7).
(4) Thereby sanctification is received (Heb. 13:12).
(5) Thereby healing is received (1 Peter 2:24).
(6) Thereby universal blessings are received (John 14:13; Eph. 1:3; Heb. 9:15).

The necessity of the atoning death. Insofar as we can penetrate into the mystery of the Atonement, its necessity was fourfold.

1. The holiness of God was outraged by sin and demanded appeasement by punishment.

2. The law of God was violated by sin and demanded that the penalty of death be inflicted. Law has been called "the expression of will." While all law is of God, we may distinguish between natural and divine law.

a. Natural law underlies the physical constitution of the universe. It has been defined as "the observed uniform action or tendency of the forces or powers of the physical universe, as gravitation, cohesion, chemical affinity, etc." Natural law implies four things: (a) a lawgiver or authoritative will; (b) persons and things whereon the law operates; (c) a command or expression of this will; and (d) a power enforcing the command.

b. Divine law, on the other hand, underlies the moral constitution of the universe. It is twofold, namely; the moral law and the ceremonial law.
(1) The moral law is a transcript of the character of God; that is, it is His essential nature expressed in perceptive form, as the Decalogue, the ethical teaching of the Sermon on the Mount, and the new commandment of Jesus (John 15:12). The moral law, therefore, is elemental, universal, and permanent. It implies six things: (a) a divine lawgiver or ordaining will; (b) subjects, or moral beings upon whom the law terminates; (c) commands, or the expression of this will in the moral constitution of the subjects and in the form

of written perceptive enactments; (d) power enforcing these commands; (e) duty, or obligation to obey; and (f) sanctions, or pains and penalties for disobedience. Now, it is the moral law which the sinner has trangressed and for this transgression the penalty of death is threatened (Ezek. 18:4; Rom. 6:23).

(2) The ceremonial law is the expression in written, perceptive form of the will of God for a specific purpose, as the Levitical system of ablutions and the distinction between clean and unclean animals (Lev. 11-15). The ceremonial law, accordingly, was local in application and temporary in character. Indeed, in Christ and His gospel, the moral law is fulfilled, but the ceremonial law is abrogated (Acts 10:9-16; Rom. 10:4; 1 Tim. 4:1-5).

3. The guilty and defiled conscience of the sinner can be acquitted and cleansed only through punishment — the punishment of the sinner himself or of his substitute, the Savior. Peace and rest cannot come to the condemned heart till it is assured that its just penalty has been borne by the spotless Lamb of God (Heb. 10:1-8).

4. The lost sinner. In hamartiology, or doctrine of sin, it is shown that in consequence of sin man is both helpless and hopeless. He is lost, "having no hope, and without God in the world" (Eph. 2:12). For this reason "the Son of man came to seek and to save that which was lost" (Luke 19:10).[11]

The extent of the atoning death. A distinction must be made between the sufficiency and the efficiency of the Atonement. In its sufficiency, the atonement of Christ is universal, that is, potential provision is made for all mankind. But in its efficiency the Atonement is limited, that is, actual provision is made only for those who accept God's gracious offer of salvation through Christ. Both aspects are presented in 1 Timothy 4:10: "We trust in the living God, who is the Savior of all men, specially of those that believe."[12]

1. Passages bearing on the universality of the Atonement: 1 Timothy 2:6; 4:10; Titus 2:11; Hebrews 2:9; 2 Peter 3:9; 1 John 2:2.

2. Passages bearing on the limitation of the Atonement: John 17:9, 20, 24; Ephesians 1:4, 7; 2 Timothy 1:9, 10.

The philosophical explanation of the Atonement. It must be frankly admitted that a complete and satisfactory philosophy of the Atonement on rational grounds is impossible, for at bottom it is a profound and impenetrable mystery. Indeed, the early church viewed the Atonement as a fact more than as a doctrine, that is, as a historic event, not as a speculative problem. It was the central truth of the gospel. Forgiveness was offered freely through the blood of Christ on the simple conditions of repentance from sin and faith toward God.

It would have been well if this had continued to be the case. But with the Scholasticism of the Middle Ages, the speculative element entered into the view of the Atonement. It has been estimated that fully fifteen so-called theories of the Atonement have been formulated. Of these, six merit our attention, five of which we believe to be untrue to the Scriptures and the last of which we believe to be the truly biblical view.[13]

1. The Socinian or Example Theory of the Atonement.[14] This theory held that subjective sinfulness is the sole barrier between man and God. Not God, but only man, needs to be reconciled. This can be effected by man's own will through repentance and reformation. The death of Christ is but the death of a noble martyr. He redeems us *only* as His human example of faithfulness to duty has a powerful influence upon our moral improvement. This fact the apostle, either consciously or unconsciously, clothed in the language of the Greek and Jewish sacrifices.

   As to objections —

   a. Philosophically this theory is based upon false principles: for example, that will is simply the volitional faculty; that utility is the basis of virtue; that law is the expression of arbitrary will; that penalty is a means of reforming the offender; and that righteousness in either God or man is only the manifestation of benevolence.

   b. Historically it is the outgrowth of the Pelagian view of sin and logically necessitates a curtailment or surrender of every other characteristic doctrine of Christianity — inspiration, sin, the deity of Christ, justification, regeneration, and eternal retribution.[15]

   c. Scripturally it contradicts the fact that sin involves objective guilt as well as subjective defilement; that God's holiness requires Him to punish sin; that the atonement was vicarious and substitutional; and that such vicarious and substitutional bearing of sin was necessary in order to furnish a ground whereby God might show favor to the guilty.

d. It furnishes no proper explanation of the sufferings and death of Christ. The unmartyrlike anguish cannot be accounted for, and the forsaking by the Father cannot be justified upon the hypothesis that Christ died as a mere witness to truth (see Ps. 22). If Christ's sufferings were not propitiatory, they neither furnsih us with a perfect example, nor constitute a manifestation of the love of God.

e. It makes the chief result of Christ's death what at most can be only a subordinate result, for neither Scripture nor Christian experience finds in Christ's example the principle motive of His death. Example is but a new preaching of the law, which repels and condemns. The cross has power to lead men to holiness only as it first shows a satisfaction made for sins. Accordingly, most of the passages which represent Christ as an example also contain references to His propitiatory work (1 Peter 2:21-24).

f. Finally, it contradicts the whole tenor of the New Testament in making the life, and not the death, of Christ the most significant and important feature of His work. The constant allusions to the death of Christ as the source of salvation, as well as the symbolism of the ordinances, cannot be explained upon a theory which regards Christ as a mere example and considers His sufferings as incidents, rather than essentials of His work.

2. The Bushnellian or Moral Influence Theory of the Atonement.[16] This theory holds, like the Socinian, that there is no principle of the divine nature which is propitiated by Christ's death; but that this death is a manifestation of the love of God, suffering in and with the sins of His creatures. Christ's atonement, therefore, is the merely natural consequence of His taking human nature upon Him; and is a suffering, not of penalty in man's stead, but of the combined woes and griefs which the living of a human life involves. The atonement has effect, not to satisfy divine justice, but so to reveal divine love as to soften human hearts and to lead them to repentance; in others words, Christ's sufferings were necessary, not in order to remove an obstacle to the pardon of sinners which exists in the mind of God, but in order to convince sinners that there exists no such obstacle,

As to objections —

a. It is open to the same objection as the Example Theory of the

Atonement in that it magnifies a subordinate into the principal effect of Christ's death. Our Lord's sufferings do produce a moral effect upon men; but suffering *with* the sinner is one thing and suffering *in his stead* quite another.

b. Like the Example Theory, it rests upon false philosophical principles that righteousness is identical with benevolence, instead of conditioning it; that God is subject to an eternal law of love, instead of being Himself the source of all law; that the aim of penalty is the reformation of the offender,

c. It also furnishes no proper reason for Christ's sufferings. Though it shows that the Savior necessarily suffers from His contact with human sin and sorrow, it gives no explanation of that constitution of the universe which makes suffering the consequences of sin, not only to the sinner, but also to the innocent being who comes into contact with sin. The holiness of God, which is manifested in this constitution of things and which requires this atonement, is entirely ignored.

d. It contradicts the teaching of the Scriptures, like the Example Theory, in that it asserts that the Atonement was necessary, not to satisfy God's justice, but merely to reveal His love; that Christ's sufferings were not propitiatory and penal; and that the human conscience does not need to be propitiated by Christ's sacrifice before it can feel the moral influence of His sufferings.

e. It can be maintained only by wresting from their obvious meaning those passages of Scripture which speak of Christ as suffering for our sins; which represent His blood as accomplishing something in heaven when presented there by our Intercessor; which declare forgiveness to be a remitting of past offenses upon the ground of Christ's death; and which describe justification as a pronouncing, not a making, just.

f. This theory confounds God's method of saving men with men's experience of being saved. It makes the atonement itself consist of its effect in the believer's union with Christ and the purifying influence of that union upon the character and life.

g. Finally, the theory confines the influence of the atonement to those who have heard it — thus excluding patriarchs and heathen. But the Scriptures represent Christ as being the

Savior of all men in the sense of securing them grace, which, but for His atoning work, could never have been bestowed consistently with the divine holiness.

3. The Grotian or Governmental Theory of the Atonement.[17] "The vicarious sufferings of Christ are an atonement for sin as a conditional substitute for penalty, fulfilling, on the forgiveness of sin, the obligation of justice and the office of penalty in moral government."[18]

This theory holds that the atonement is a satisfaction, not to any internal principle of the divine nature, but to the necessities of government. God's government of the universe cannot be maintained, nor can the divine law preserve its authority over its subjects, unless the pardon of offenders is accompanied by some exhibition of the high estimate which God sets upon His law and the heinous guilt of violating it. Such an exhibition of divine regard for the law is furnished in the sufferings and death of Christ. Christ does not suffer the precise penalty of the law, but God graciously accepts His sufferings as a substitute for the penalty. This bearing of substituted suffering on the part of Christ gives the divine law such hold upon the consciences and hearts of men that God can pardon the guilty upon their repentance without detriment to the interests of His government.

As to objections —

a. Like the Example and Moral Influence theories, it has the fatal defect of substituting for the principal aim of the Atonement a subordinate one, namely, the securing of the interests of God's government.

b. Like the two former theories, it rests upon false philosophical principles in that utility is the ground of moral obligation; that law is an expression of the will, rather than of the nature, of God; that the aim of penalty is to deter from the commission of offenses; and that righteousness is resolvable into benevolence.

c. It also ignores and virtually denies that immanent holiness of God of which law with its threatened penalties, and the human conscience with its demand for punishment, are only finite reflections. There is something back of government, and if the atonement satisfies government, it must be by satisfying that justice of God, of which government is the expression.

d. This theory makes that to be exhibition of justice which is not an exercise of justice; the atonement being, according to this theory, not an execution of law, but an exhibition of regard for law, which will make it safe to pardon the violators of law.

e. It makes the sufferings of Christ in the garden and on the cross inexplicable upon the theory that the atonement was a histrionic (that is, a kind of theatrical) exhibition of God's regard for His government — those "can be explained only upon the view that Christ actually endured the wrath of God against human sin.

f. The actual power of the atonement over the human conscience and heart is due, not to its exhibiting God's regard for law, but to its exhibiting an actual execution of law and an actual satisfaction of violated holiness made by Christ in the sinner's stead.

g. Finally, the theory contradicts all those passages of Scripture which represent the atonement as necessary; as propitiating God Himself; as being a revelation of God's righteousness; as being an execution of the penalty of the law; as making salvation a matter of debt to the believer, on the ground of what Christ has done; as actually purging our sins, instead of making that purging possible; as not simply assuring the sinner that God may now pardon him on account of what Christ has done, but that Christ has actually wrought out a complete salvation, and will bestow it upon all who come to Him.

4. The Irvingian View or Theory of Gradually Extirpated Depravity.[19] This theory holds that, in His incarnation, Christ took human nature as it was in Adam, not before the Fall, but after the Fall — human nature, therefore, with its inborn corruption and predisposition to evil; that, notwithstanding the possession of this tainted and depraved nature, Christ, through the power of the Holy Spirit or of His divine nature, not only kept His human nature from manifesting itself in any actual or personal sin, but completely purified it through struggle and suffering, until in His death he completely extirpated its original depravity and reunited it to God. This subjective purification of human nature in the person of Jesus Christ constitutes His atonement, and men are saved, not by any objective propitiation, but only by becoming through faith partakers of Christ's new humanity.

As to objections —

a. It recognizes an important truth in the fact of the new humanity of Christ. of which all believers are partakers by faith; but it denies the fact of an objective atonement, through which alone we can receive this new spiritual humanity.

b. It rests upon false fundamental principles, namely: that law is identical with the natural order of the universe, and as such, is an exhaustive expression of the will and nature of God; that sin is simply a power of moral evil within the soul, instead of also involving an objective guilt and desert of punishment; that penalty is the mere reaction of law against the transgressor, instead of being also the revelation of a personal wrath against sin; that the evil taint of human nature can be extirpated by suffering its natural consequences.

c. It contradicts the plain teaching of Scripture with regard to Christ's freedom from all taint of human depravity; misrepresents His life as a growing consciousness of the underlying corruption of His human nature, which culminated at Gethsemane and Calvary; and denies the truth of His own statements when it declares that He must have died on account of His own depravity, even though none were to be saved thereby.

d. It makes the active obedience of Christ and the subjective purification of His human nature to be the chief features of His work, while the Scriptures make His death and passive bearing of penalty the center of all.

e. Finally, this theory requires the surrender of the doctrine of Justification as a merely declaratory act of God; and requires such a view of the divine holiness, expressed only through the order of nature, as can be maintained only upon principles of pantheism.

5. The Anselmic or Commercial Theory of the Atonement.[20] This holds that sin is a violation of the divine honor or majesty, and, as committed against an infinite being, deserves an infinite punishment; that the majesty of God requires Him to execute punishment, while the love of God pleads for the sparing of the guilty; that this conflict of divine attributes is eternally reconciled by the voluntary sacrifice of the God-man, who bears in the virtue of the dignity of His person the intensively infinite punishment of sin, which must otherwise have been suffered extensively and eternally by sinners; that this suffering of the God-man presents to the divine majesty an exact equivalent for the deserved sufferings of

the elect; and that, as a result of this satisfaction of the divine claims, the elect sinners are pardoned and regenerated.

As to objections —

a. It recognized an all-important truth in the fact that Christ's death satisfied a principle of the nature of deity, but it errs in representing the majesty or honor as higher than the holiness of God, while it is seriously at fault in admitting a conflict between the divine attributes.

b. It overlooks entirely the value of the active obedience of Christ via His holy life.

c. It gives disproportionate weight to those passages of Scripture which represent the atonement under commercial analogies, as the payment of a ransom or debt, to the exclusion of those which describe it as an ethical fact, whose value is to be estimated not quantitatively, but qualitatively.

d. It limits the extent of the atonement to the elect, thus ignoring the teaching of the Scripture that Christ died for all.

e. While it correctly holds to an external transfer of the merit of Christ's work, it does not clearly state the internal ground of that transfer in the union of the believer with Christ.

6. The Substitutional or Satisfaction Theory of the Atonement. This theory, the first suggestions of which are found in the writings of Augustine (fourth century), was elaborated by John Calvin (sixteenth century). It is commonly known as Calvinism; sometimes it is called the "Orthodox Theory" or "Ethical Theory." It is, we believe, the truly scriptural view.

a. Preliminary points

(1) The theory holds to a twofold element in Christ's substitution, namely: a vicarious obedience (known theologically as "active obedience") for righteousness, and vicarious punishment (known theologically as "passive obedience") for sin. Thus Christ takes the place of sinners in both penalty and precept, and as their substitute endures the punishment which on account of sin they deserve, and in His obedience fulfills the righteousness required of them.

(2) Two kinds of substitution, namely: Unconditional, which grants full and absolute deliverance to those for whom substitution is made; and Conditional, which grants deliverance to those for whom substitution is made only on

the terms agreed upon between the one who makes the substitution and the one who accepts it. Christ's substitution was conditional, dependent upon the repentance and faith of sinners, with reference to the sins of men (personal sins), and unconditional with reference to the "sin of the world" (the guilt of the Adamic sin, collective sin).

(3) Two kinds of Satisfaction. The satisfaction of Christ means that He has satisfied the demands of the holiness and law of God in the place of and in behalf of sinners. There are two kinds of satisfaction, namely: Pecuniary, a money payment, which can be made by anyone; and Penal, blood payment which can be made only by the guilty. Christ's satisfaction was penal; the Atonement was in His blood.

(4) Three kinds of penal satisfaction.

    (a) Identical. Christ's death, however was not identical, because the death of one could not be the same as the death of many (Mark 10:45);

    (b) Equal. Christ's satisfaction was not equal, because the death of the entire race of finite beings would not be equal to the death of the Infinite Being, Jesus Christ;

    (c) Equivalent. Christ's satisfaction was equivalent, because one infinite factor, Jesus Christ, is inconceivably greater than all the finite factors making up the race of Adam.

b. The two questions stated. Two questions conduct us into the heart of the Atonement, and the answers to these questions give us its true philosophy. First: What did the Atonement accomplish? Or, what was the object of Christ's death? Second: What were the means used? Or, how could Christ justly die? The answer to the former question views the Atonement in its relation to God.[21] The answer to the latter question views the atonement in its relation to man. Again, the answer to the first question is an unfolding of the meaning of Romans 3:25, 26. The answer to the second question is an unfolding of the meaning of 2 Corinthians 5:21.

c. The first question considered. What did the Atonement accomplish? Or, what was the object of Christ's death? Briefly the answer is threefold:

(1) It satisfied the outraged holiness of God (Ps. 22; Isa. 53; Rom. 3:25, 26; 4:25; 8:3; Gal. 1:4; 3:13; Heb. 9:15; 1 John 2:2; 4:10).

(2) It avenged the violated law of God (Gen. 2:17; Ezek. 18:4, 20; Rom. 6:23).

(3) It exhibited the love of God, thereby furnishing man a motive for repentance from sin and faith toward Christ (John 3:16; 15:13; Rom. 5:8; 1 Peter 2:21; 1 John 4:9, 10).

d. The second question considered. With respect to the Atonement, what were the means used? Or, how could Christ justly die? Briefly the answer is threefold.

(1) He took our flesh (John 1:14; Rom 8:3; Gal. 4:4; Heb. 2:14-18).

(2) He inherited our guilt (2 Cor. 5:21; Gal. 3:13).

(3) He bore our penalty (Isa. 53:4-5; Matt. 20:28; 2 Cor. 5:21; Gal. 2:20; 3:13; 1 Peter 2:24).

e. The consequences of Adam's sin, both to himself and to his posterity, are met in the substitutionary sacrifice of Jesus Christ —

(1) First, depravity, or corruption of human nature;

(2) Second, guilt, or obligation to make satisfaction for sin through the holiness and law of God;

(3) Third, penalty, or actual endurance of loss or suffering as punishment for sin.[22]

THE RESURRECTION OF JESUS CHRIST

"If Christ be not risen" is one of the most potent negative suppositions that can be made in connection with Christian faith. "Did Jesus Christ arise from the dead?" is the most cogent query that has ever confronted the serious student of Christianity.

Intelligent infidels are quick to see that this is the battlefield in which victory is to be won for the divine or merely human conception and character of the whole New Testament. Strauss, the ablest of them all, well speaks of it as "the burning question," and as he approaches its discussion he truly says, "Here then we stand on that decisive point, where, in the presence of the accounts of the miraculous resurrection of Jesus, we either acknowledge the inadmissibility of the natural and historical view of the life of Jesus and must consequently retract all that precedes, and so give up our whole undertaking, or pledge ourselves to make out the possibility of the results of these accounts, i.e., the origin of the belief in the resurrection of Jesus, without any corresponding miraculous fact."[23]

Without doubt, the resurrection of Jesus Christ is the most crucial event in history. By the defenders of the Christian faith the Resurrection has been called the "Gibraltar of Christian Evidences and the Waterloo of infidelity." We must come inevitably to the conclusion that the Resurrection is the rock from which all the hammers of criticism have never chipped a single fragment. This will be seen as we proceed with our study.

The Importance of the Doctrine

1. Negatively considered. In 1 Corinthians 15 Paul uses the expression "If Christ be not risen" and then proceeds to show what would be the results if this were true. This is a part of Paul's argument against the materialistic infidelity that had crept into the church of Corinth concerning the resurrection of the dead. Says he, "Now if Christ be preached that he rose from the dead, how say some among you that there is no resurrection of the dead? But if there be no resurrection of the dead, then is Christ not risen" (vss. 12, 13). And if Christ be not risen — then what?

a. "Our preaching is vain," or empty. The gospel has had its heart taken out. Our message is robbed of its vitality — its very life. The denial of the resurrection of Jesus Christ (and by that is meant His bodily or physical resurrection) empties the glad tidings of its gladness.

If Christ be not risen, our preaching is emptied of good news; the gospel has lost its note of joy and is changed into a funeral dirge. It has become a gospel of death, a mere biography of a man who lived an extraordinary life, but died an ordinary though ignominious death — "even the death of the Cross." It is then only a weird story which has for its anticlimax a crown of thorns, a rugged cross, a stiffened corpse, and a cold, dark tomb. What mean you, angels of light, by bringing that message of good cheer on that fair night of His birth, if Christ be not risen? Did angel lips speak lies when they sang, "Behold I bring you glad tidings of great joy, which shall be to all people. For unto you is born this day in the city of David a Saviour, which is Christ the Lord"? If Christ be not risen, they did. Better had those angel voices been forever silent than to awaken hopes never to be realized.

If Christ be not risen, our preaching is emptied of its power. It then becomes only the history of a man who failed, and such a tale could never save anyone. No matter how many good words fell from His lips, or how many good deeds were done by His hands, if Christ be not risen, the gospel is not the power of God unto salvation. It is the resurrection of Jesus Christ that gives the gospel its dynamic and vitalizing power. Unless Jesus Christ gained a victory at Calvary, as evidenced by His resurrection over death, hell, and the grave, then we are still their victims, no matter what may be proclaimed to the contrary.

Unless Jesus lives to enforce the provisions and claims of the gospel, it has no value whatever. The Declaration of Independence without the victory of the Revolutionary War and the triumph of George Washington and the patriot soldiers would have been so much waste paper. The Emancipation Proclamation would have been worthless, and the shackles of slavery would still be upon the Negroes had not the South been subdued and the cause of the Union succeeded. And so is the gospel vain and void if Jesus Christ did not rise from the dead to execute His proclamation of deliverance to the captive and the setting at liberty of them who are bound. It took the victory of the open tomb and the power of the risen Lord to give effectuality to the gospel.

b. "Your faith is also vain." If Christ be not risen, your faith is an empty faith. The hand which you stretched out to a living Christ is empty still, for there is no living Christ if Christ be not risen. All that you have grasped at you have missed; your hand has closed upon nothing. All that you have accepted and received by faith as a free gift from God through Jesus Christ — a divine sonship, eternal life, justification, sanctification, glorification, and a home in heaven — you did not receive at all. If Christ be not risen, these are not yours. You have believed in vain; your faith is empty; it has brought you nothing.

Your faith is a delusion. Your religious experience has been a hallucination, a deception. Twice Paul repeats his expression "Your faith is vain." But in verse 17 it has a somewhat different meaning from that expressed in verse 14. The Greek word there translated "vain" means "useless" or "forceless" and brings this other thought that if Christ be not risen, your faith is impotent. Faith is always impotent unless its object gives it power. May not this be the secret of much of the failure in the Christian life? Perhaps we have believed only half of the gospel — the death of Christ for our sins — and our faith has connected with the Christ of the cross for pardon and peace, and not with the Christ of the throne for power and victory.

c. "Ye are yet in your sins." "There is none other name under heaven, given among men, whereby we must be saved." "Thou shalt call His name Jesus, for He shall save His people from their sins." But if Christ be not risen, His name possesses no more saving efficacy than that of Socrates or Plato or Wilberforce or Savonarola. You are still in your sins, for you are without a Savior. You are the victim of a delusion. You supposed that you obtained from Jesus Christ a guarantee of your forgivness. You thought you had a receipt signed by the eternal God showing that your sin-debt had been paid, that the old account was settled long ago. And that guarantee and that receipt consisted of the empty tomb and the risen Lord.

Renan, the infidel writer of the life of Jesus, did not come so far from the truth when he said, "The Christian faith is based upon the fragrance of an empty vase." Our text says about the same thing: "If Christ be not risen ye are yet in your sins." "For He was delivered for our offences and raised again for our justification." It took the resurrection of Jesus Christ to show the justifying value of His death. If Christ be not risen, where is your justification (your righteous standing before God), your evidence of sins forgiven?

d. But not only so; if this negative is true, it makes a serious reflection upon the holy men of God who gave us this record. Paul goes on to say, "Yea, and we are found false witnesses of God, for we have testified of God that He raised up Christ, whom he raised not up if so be that the dead rise not." The apostles of truth are found to be the apostles of falsehood. And the representatives of God are guilty of gross misrepresentation and damnable deceit. And if this is so, then we are set adrift in midnight darkness on a wild ocean waste, without a star or pilot, without chart or compass to guide us. If Christ be not risen, the whole fabric of Scriptural authority breaks down and leaves us without a shred of revealed truth. The resurrection of Christ is the keystone in the arch of Christianity.

e. But notice again, "If Christ be not risen, . . . then they also which are fallen asleep in Christ are perished. If in this life only we have hope in Christ, we are of all men," not "most miserable," as in the Authorized Version, but "most pitiable."

Paul once wrote to some bereaved Christians at Thessalonica who had lost relatives and friends, "Brethren, I would not have you to be ignorant concerning them which are asleep, that you sorrow not as the rest who have no hope. For if we believe that Jesus died and rose again, even so them that sleep in Jesus will God bring with Him." And then at the close of this message of consolation he says, "Wherefore comfort one another with these words."

Nevertheless, we have been miserable comforters ever since, if Christ is not risen. Better had Paul left those Thessalonians in ignorance, for it is better to sorrow as those who have no hope than to sorrow as those who have a false hope. We are indeed of all men the most pitiable, for then they also which have died perished. Then they whom we have "loved long since, and lost awhile" are lost forever. The hope that sustained the martyrs in their sacrifice and that has strengthened and steadied the multimillions who since have died in the faith was a false hope. They have all perished.

But let us turn from this negative supposition to the inspired statement of the positive fact, "But now is Christ risen from the dead."

2. Positively considered. Its importance is shown by —

a. The place it occupies in the New Testament. It is mentioned directly more than one hundred times;

b. The prominence given it in the apostolic preaching and teaching (Acts 1:21, 22; 2:24, 29-32; 4:33; 17:18; 23:6; 1 Cor. 15:15);[24]

c. The position assigned to it in the gospel — co-equal with that of His death (1 Cor. 15:1, 3, 4);

d. The practical and vital relation it sustains to Christian preaching and Christian faith (1 Cor. 15:14, 17).

The importance of the resurrection of Jesus is seen by the divine emphasis given to it in the proclamation of the truth and by the strategic position occupied by it in relation to the Christian faith.

The Necessity of the Resurrection

The resurrection of Jesus Christ was necessary —

1. As a fulfillment of the prophecies made concerning Christ (Ps.

16:10). His resurrection, as well as His death, was "according to the Scriptures," which means primarily the Old Testament writings. The whole testimony of the Scriptures establishes Christ's resurrection. Christ rebuked His disciples for not believing what Moses and the prophets had spoken on this subject (Luke 24:25-28.)

2. As a fulfillment of the predictions made by Christ (John 2:19). There is no real doubt that Christ anticipated and spoke of His own resurrection. At first He used only vague terms, such as "Destroy this temple, and in three days I will raise it up." But later on in His ministry He spoke quite plainly, and wherever He mentioned His death He added, "The Son of Man . . . must be raised the third day." These references to His resurrection are too numerous to be overlooked, and in spite of all difficulties of detail, they are an integral part of the claim made for Himself by Jesus Christ.

3. As an indication of the propitiatory nature of Christ's death (Rom. 4:25). Christ gave His life a propitiation for believers. He was delivered up for our offenses. The resurrection settles it beyond doubt that God has accepted the propitiation. The resurrection declares our justification. When one agrees to settle or meet the responsibilities or obligations for another, the one for whom the settlement has been made naturally desires to know whether the settlement has been accepted. By the resurrection God declares that He has accepted and is satisfied with the settlement Christ has made. Stated another way: God, who made peace by the blood of the Cross, brought forth from the dead our Lord Jesus, the good Shepherd who gave His life for the sheep. God did this in virtue of His everlasting covenant and in doing it verified the value of the Blood. If the believer is ever troubled with doubts as to whether God has accepted the offering Christ made, he needs only to look at the empty tomb and the risen Lord.

4. As a prerequisite to a fruitful life (Rom. 7:1-4). The only living or doing or accomplishing in the Christian life that is acceptable to God is through union with the risen Christ. Through union with the crucified Christ we get our pardon, our cleansing from guilt, our justification, our perfect standing before God. Through union with the risen Christ we get power for life and fruitfulness.

One reason why there is so little of life and fruitage in many professedly Christian lives is because there is so little knowledge of the risen and living Christ (Col. 2:12; Rom. 6:4). This is the truth which baptism symbolizes. The full power of Christ's resurrection we shall not know until we attain unto the resurrection from the dead (Phil. 3:10, 11; Rom. 8:11). But "the power of this resurrection" in our moral and spiritual lives, begetting "newness of life" and "fruit unto God," we may know even now, through being "joined to Him who was raised from the dead."

The Character of the Resurrection
1. Negatively considered
   a. It was not a resuscitation from a seeming death — not a swoon. The Swoon Theory, advanced by Strauss, holds that Jesus did not really die, but simply swooned from the pain and torture of the cross. The cool air of the sepulcher and the stimulus of the spices used in the embalming revived Him. Those who hold this theory say, "Jesus had failed to purify the messianic idea, as entertained by His disciples, of its political aspects. The only way which He could see to accomplish that end was to undergo crucifixion, and to secure a removal from the cross before actual death occurred by pretending to die, trusting to the skill of His fellow-conspirators to restore Him to health. Thus His disciples would look upon Him as the heavenly King and would preach Him as such."

   Reply: We reply that the blood and water and the testimony of the centurion (Mark 15:45) proved actual death. The rolling away of the stone and Jesus' power directly afterward are inconsistent with an immediately preceding swoon and suspended animation.[25]
   b. It was not due to hallucination caused by an overwrought mind — not a vision. This theory was advocated by Renan: "Referring to the reported interview between Christ and Mary Magdalene on the morning of the resurrection, he exclaims: 'Divine power of love! sacred moments in which the passion of an hallucinated woman gives to the world a resurrected God!' Again, speaking of the alleged appearance of Jesus to the disciples on the night following, he says: 'The doors were closed, for they were afraid of the Jews. Oriental towns are hushed after sunset. The silence accordingly within the house was frequently profound; all the little noises which were accidentally made were interpreted in the sense of the

universal expectation. Ordinarily, expectation is the father of
its object. During a moment of silence some slight breath
passed over the face of the assembly. At these decisive periods
of time a current of air, a creaking of a window, or a chance
murmur, are sufficient to fix the belief of people for ages (!). At
the same time that the breath was perceived they fancied that
they heard sounds. Some of them said that they discovered
the word *shalom* (happiness or peace). This was the ordinary
salutation of Jesus and the word by which He signified His
presence. No possibility of doubt; Jesus is present; He is in the
assembly. That is His cherished voice; each one recognizes it.
This idea was all the more easily entertained because Jesus
had said that whenever they were assembled in His name He
would be in the midst of them.

"'It was, then, an acknowledged fact that Jesus had appeared before His assembled disciples on the night of Sunday.
Some pretended to have observed on His hands and His feet
the mark of the nails and on His side the mark of the spear
which pierced Him. According to a widely spread tradition, it
was the same night as that on which He breathed upon His
disciples the Holy Spirit.'

"Such is Renan's treatment of the greatest event that has
ever occurred, or the greatest lie that has ever been told, in
the history of the world. Renan lived long enough to see his
ludicrous account of the resurrection utterly rejected by
infidelity."[26]

Reply: We reply that the disciples did not expect Jesus'
resurrection. The women went to the sepulcher, not to see a
risen Redeemer, but to embalm a dead body. The only way to
account for Mary's hearing the voice of Jesus from one whom
she did not suppose to be Jesus is the supposition that the one
whom she took for the gardener was Jesus. These appearances
soon ceased, however, unlike the law of hallucinations, by
which they may increase in frequency and intensity with the
passage of time.

c. It was not a mere exaltation or manifestation of the spirit of
Jesus — not a temporary materialization. This theory was held
by Theodor Keim, who says Jesus really died but only His
spirit appeared, assuring them of His continued life and imparting such instructions as were needed to direct them in
spreading His doctrines over the face of the earth. He charged

no fraud either to the disciples or to Jesus, showing that Jesus never intended the disciples to think that His body had risen, but simply wishing them to know that His spirit actually continued as a immortal soul, in which form He would always be with them.[27]

Reply: We reply that Jesus Himself denied that He was a bodiless Spirit — "A spirit hath not flesh and bones as ye see me having" (Luke 24:39). This theory would, however, still involve a miracle, that of materialization, and nothing is gained by substituting one miracle for another.

And, too, it would have been a piece of deception on Christ's part, for then He appeared to His disciples only in a spiritual vision and yet conveyed to their minds the impression that He appeared bodily. But the disciples were not impressible, but exceedingly skeptical, and hence were not in a mood to see visions and mistake them for fleshy realities.

Nor does this theory "do justice to the empty tomb. If that had been what occurred, when the disciples began to preach an actual physical resurrection, the first thing their enemies the Jews would have done would have been to produce the body and show that the disciples were mistaken in thnking that Jesus' body had risen. . . . According to the Gospel accounts, the disciples actually thought they saw a vision, and that He was a spirit, until He convinced them that He had a material body by allowing them to handle Him and by eating in their presence. He thus gave the disciples convincing proof that what they saw was not a supernatural vision or a spirit, but that they were actually having intercourse with their risen Lord in His physical body."[28]

d. It was not an imaginary resurrection based upon the desire and expectation of the disciples — not a myth. Strauss utterly discards the idea of willful deception on the part of those who promulgated the story; but he takes it for granted that a considerable time elapsed before the story was published and that exaggerated statements and unintentional misrepresentations of the fact had meanwhile gained currency. He thinks (contrary to the truth in the case) that the disciples of Jesus expected His resurrection and, owing to a certain elevation of their mental and moral life, they imagined it to have taken place. He tries to satisfy himself and his readers with the view that the resurrection has nothing more of a true and historical basis than the mythology of the ancient Greeks and Romans, that gradually assumed shape and beauty; or the legends associated with some of the world's heroes, that are so often mercilessly exposed by the keen knife of modern criticism.[29]

Reply: The time was too short for legends to arise and gain such power over thousands of people as to lead them to sacrifice property, ease, comfort, position, and even life itself to propagate them. Legends do not arise in that way, nor do they have such power over conviction and life. How could a legend have produced Pentecost? How could it have converted the intimidated Peter and his fellow-disciples into fearless preachers and advocates? How could it have won the scholarly Paul?

3. Positively considered. It was a physical and bodily resurrection, as shown by the following:

a. Other resurrections, according to the Gospel accounts, were bodily resurrections. If we are not to believe in the possibility of physical resurrection, then obviously the miracles recorded as wrought by Christ upon Jairus's daughter, the young man of Nain, and Lararus must be rejected at once, for it is evident to the intelligent reader that these resurrections are represented as being physical and bodily. In the case of the son of the widow of Nain (Luke 7:11-18) the body which was quickened was not yet buried, and after the miracle the young man is represented as giving expression to physical speech and action through the medium of his body.

Similarly, Jairus's daughter (Matt. 9:18-26; Mark 5:21-24, 35-43) is accredited with physical action and eating of material food after her resurrection. Lastly, in Lazarus' case (John 11:32-44) the stone was removed that he might come forth in his risen body, and it was his body that was bound in the grave clothes from which Jesus commanded the disciples to loose him. Afterward Lazarus was present bodily at a supper given in honor of Jesus at Bethany.

b. He appeared in the same wound-printed body in which He was crucified. According to Luke 24:37-39, Jesus invited the close inspection of the resurrection body in which He appeared to the disciples in the upper room. "But they were terrified and affrighted, and supposed that they had seen a spirit. And He said unto them, Why are ye troubled? and why do thoughts arise in your hearts? Behold my hands and my feet, that it is I myself: handle me, and see; for a spirit hath not flesh and bones, as ye see me have."

Similarly, according to John 20:27, He invited Thomas by physical touch to identify that body with the one in which He had been crucified and buried. "Then saith he to Thomas, Reach hither thy finger, and behold my hands; and reach hither thy hand, and thrust it into my side: and be not faithless, but believing."

   c. The apostles believed in His bodily resurrection. The empirical and objective proofs of the resurrection were so complete as to so thoroughly convince the apostles that they staked their lives upon it with no motive for believing it if it were false. They believed it because the evidence compelled them to believe it. Both conscience and common sense reject the idea that they would preach the resurrection with such power and vitality if they did not believe it to be historically true (John 20:3-8; Acts 2:22-24; 1 Cor. 15:5-8).

The Mode of the Resurrection

1. Raised by God the Father (Eph. 1:19, 20; Acts 2:24, 32; 10:40; 13:30; Rom. 6:4; 10:9; Col. 2:12). "Upon this fact depends the evidence, that He truly was what He affirmed to be. If God raised Him from the dead, the sentence pronounced upon Him by the Jews was reversed, and He who had expired in ignominy and torment was proved to be the Lord of glory."[30]

2. Arose by His own power (John 10:18; 1 Cor. 15:4). "The New Testament ascribes the resurrection to our Savior Himself. Thus, we find Him saying, 'I have power to lay down my life, and I have power to take it up again'; and when He speaks of His body under the image of a temple, He represents its restoration as His own work: 'Destroy this temple, and in three days I will raise it up.' In both passages, the resurrection is attributed to Him, because His power was exerted in this, as it is in other external acts, in concurrence with that of His Father; for as they are one in nature, they are united in operation; 'My Father worketh hitherto, and I work.' "[31]

3. Quickened or made alive by the Holy Spirit (Rom. 8:11; 1 Peter 3:18). The Holy Spirit, who represents the personal energy of the Godhead, is accredited with the resurrection of Christ. And thus it comes to pass that Jesus Christ arose from the dead by the

138   CHRISTIAN THEOLOGY: SYSTEMATIC AND BIBLICAL

coordinate power of the Triune God, Father, Son, and Holy Spirit.

The Certainty of the Resurrection

1. Proofs of the truthfulness of the biblical statements concerning the resurrection of Christ as found in the narratives themselves.

   a. They give evidence of being four individual representations of Christ's resurrection; the evidence is their apparent disagreement but real harmony. Dr. L. S. Keyser says: "Even the variant details in the several evangelical narratives of the resurrection add to the proof of its reality. There are no contradictions, though not all minutiae can be explained; but the differences of viewpoint prove that there was no collusion among the writers; rather that each of them wrote an independent account of the events as he observed and understood them. The details in each case give the narrative an atmosphere of verisimilitude, so that it is natural to feel that real occurrences are being recited."[32]

   b. They give evidence of being personal testimonies based upon personal observation and experience.

   c. They give evidence of apparent sincerity and avoidance of studied and literary expressions.

      Luke 24:16: Here and elsewhere we are told that Jesus was not recognized at once by His disciples when He appeared to them after His resurrection. There was no point to be gained by their telling the story in this way. They give no satisfactory explanation of the fact. We are left to study it out for ourselves. Why then do they tell it in this way? Because this is the way it happened, and they are not making up a story, but telling what occurred. If they had invented a story, they would never have done it this way.

      1 Corinthians 15:5-8: Here, as everywhere else, Jesus is represented as appearing only to His disciples, with the single exception of His brother. Why is it so represented? Because it so happened. If the story had been made up years after, Jesus would certainly have been represented as appearing to and confounding some, at least, of His enemies.

      John 20:17: There is no explanation of the words *touch me not*. It has puzzled commentators for centuries. Why is it told this way? Because it occurred this way.

      John 19:34: Why is this told? Modern physiologists tell us

that the physical explanation of this is that Jesus suffered from extravasation of the blood, or in modern language "a broken heart." Other recorded facts testify to the same thing. But John knew nothing of modern physiology. Why did he insert a detail that has taken hundreds of years to explain? Because he is recording things as they occurred and as he saw them.

John 20:24, 25: This is most true to life. It is in perfect harmony with what is told of Thomas elsewhere, but to make it up would require a literary act that immeasurably exceeded the possibilities of the author.

John 20:4-6: This is again striking, but in keeping with what we know of the men. John, the younger, outruns Peter, but hesitatingly, reverently stops outside and looks in. Impetuous Peter, the older, lumbers on behind as best he can, but when he once reaches the tomb never waits a moment outside, but plunges in. Who was the literary artist who had the skill to make this up, if it did not happen?

d. They give evidence of unintentional proof as shown by —

(1) The minute details recorded

John 21:7: Here we have the unmistakable marks of truth. John, the man of quick perception, is the first to recognize his Lord. Peter, the impetuous man of unthinking devotion, tumbles into the water and swims ashore as soon as he is told who it is.

John 20:15: Here is surely a note, a touch, which surpasses the art of any man of that day or this. Mary, with a woman's love, forgets a woman's weakness and cries, "Tell me where thou hast laid him and I will take him away." Of course she lacked strength, but a woman's love never stops at impossibilities.

Mark 16:7: "And Peter." Why "and Peter"? No explanation is vouchsafed, but reflection shows it was an utterance of love toward a despondent and despairing disciple who had thrice denied his Lord. He probably would not have felt included in the general invitation.

John 20:27-29: The action of Thomas here too is natural, and the rebuke of Jesus too characteristic to be attributed to some master of fiction.

John 21:15-17: There is no explanation of why Jesus asked three times or why Peter was grieved because he was asked three times. We must read it in the light of the threefold denial to understand it. But the author does not tell us so; if it were made up, he surely would. He simply tells facts.

John 21:21, 22: This too is a characteristic rebuke on Jesus' part.

(2) The manner of His appearances

    (a) To Mary, by speaking her name (John 20:16);

    (b) To the two on the way to Emmaus, in the breaking of bread (Luke 24:30, 31);

    (c) To Thomas, by appealing to his physical senses (John 20:25-28);

    (d) To John and Peter, in the miraculous draught of fishes, as at another time prior to His death (John 21:5-7).

The internal proof of the truth of the Gospel narratives of the resurrection of Christ and accompanying events is so strong as to be undoubtable to the unbiased mind.[33]

2. Things and events which can be accounted for only by the actual resurrection of Christ.

    a. An empty tomb (Matt. 28:6; Mark 16:6; Luke 24:3, 12; John 21:1, 2). If the belief of the early disciples in the resurrection was due to visions, why were they not permanently silenced by the authorities by clearly demonstrating that Jesus' body was still in the tomb? The Jews were not only silent initially, but perpetually by the lack of proof contrary to the proclamation of Christ's resurrection.

    There are only two alternatives to the resurrection claims: either the body was taken by human hands, or it was resurrected by supernatural power. Surely the foes of Jesus did not take His body and start the commotion, and how did His humble friends accomplish such in the face of personal despair and imperial power? Only the power of God entered the tomb for resurrection, and not theft.

    b. The circumstances under which our Lord was buried and slept in the grave till He arose are such as to render all fraud and imposition impossible.

    (1) The tomb was a new one which had never been occupied before (Luke 23:53); no other bodies were there to be confounded with Christ's body.

    (2) It was hewn out of solid rock (Matt. 27:59, 60).

(3) It was near Jerusalem and therefore was accessible for investigation.

(4) The Jews knew that He had predicted His own resurrection (Matt. 27:62-66).

(5) The most effectual means were adopted to prevent the removal of the body (Matt. 27:63-66): a huge stone at the door of the sepulcher, sealed with the Roman seal; and watched by the Roman guard.

c. The change in the disciples which requires the resurrection of Christ for its production. So great was the contrast between their experience then and what it had been during the betrayal, trial, and crucifixion, that they could not hide the change. Their joy made them conspicuous. It was an irrefutable proof of the resurrection. They had seen their risen Lord and were radiant. When Jesus died upon the Cross, the faith of the disciples also apparently expired. Their love and devotion still lived, but it was love for One whom they had lost; their devotion was to His memory, and it expressed itself in loving ministry to His earthly remains. Joseph of Arimathea and Nicodemus buried in the new tomb, not only the body of Jesus of Nazareth, but also the faith of His followers; thus the faith which they afterward manifested is strong evidence of the reality of the resurrection of Jesus. There is no other way to account for it.

In the hall of judgment when Jesus was on trial, Peter shrank and shivered at the pointed finger of a little maid, and showed the white feather like a craven coward. But on the day of Pentecost and later, he shook his own finger in the face of the chiefest of the Jews and accused them of the murder of Jesus Christ, whom he acknowledged to be the Son of God and the Messiah of Israel. What changed this coward into a hero, this craven traitor into a brave and loyal supporter and adherent of the Christ of God? He had been with Jesus, the risen Christ, and that changed his cowardice for a courage that was adamant and strong.

The irresistible power possessed by the post-resurrection disciples proves that Christ is risen. The Shepherd had been smitten and the sheep had been scattered; they all forsook Him and fled. "Weakness" is the word which describes the Christian cause and constituency on that darkest day of human history. But what has happened? Here are those crying out to those who were members of that same weak, insignificant Christian constituency, and crying out by the hundreds and thousands, "Men and brethren, what shall we do?" They are pricked in their hearts. And later there is another great multitude, perhaps 5,000 more, who pass through the same experience. Some of those men once so weak are doing works of power. There is Stephen, so filled with the heavenly dynamic that we read, "They could not resist the wisdom and Spirit by which he spake."

What did happen? Nothing, only that Jesus Christ had risen from the dead and had ascended into heaven as Advocate and High Priest and had sent down the Holy Ghost, of whom He had previously said, "Ye shall receive power, the Holy Ghost coming upon you." And of whom He had also said before His death, "If I go not away, the Comforter will not come, but if I depart, I will send Him unto you." Jesus had gone through death, resurrection, and ascension to the right hand of God, and the Holy Ghost had come. That explains what had happened; that explains the power.

d. The change in the day of rest and worship (Acts 20:7; 1 Cor. 16:2). The day was changed by no express decree, but by the appropriateness of weekly celebration of the day on which He arose.

e. The resurrection was one of the foundation truths preached in the early history of the Christian church. When we consider the beginnings of the church in the Book of Acts, there are two essential facts: (1) the centrality of preaching; (2) the substance of that preaching — the resurrection of Jesus Christ (Acts 2:36; 4:2; 17:31). Jews should naturally and necessarily reject Jesus because He died on a cross (Deut. 21:33); however, many Jews were led to worship Him (Acts 2:41), including a number of priests (Acts 6:7). The only explanation for so many Jews accepting Jesus as the Messiah is the resurrection. The apostolic church was rooted in and on the fact of the resurrection of Jesus Christ. There is no rationale as to why this was made the cornerstone of the Apostles' Creed if it was not, even then, fully attested and firmly believed.

3. Proof from personal testimony.

a. Christ's own testimony (Rev. 1:18; Matt. 17:23; Luke 24:39). James H. Brooks writes, "Jesus of Nazareth presented Himself as that promised Messiah, and distinctly and repeatedly declared that He would be put to death and would rise again. Each of His four biographers — Matthew, Mark, Luke, and John — affirms that He did rise on the third day after His death; and from that time the doctrine of His resurrection became interwoven in all the preaching and writing of His apostles as the foundation of the Church, and linked it with every hope of the human race."[34]

b. The apostles' testimony (1 Peter 1:3; 3:21; Rom. 8:11; 1 John 1:1). These witnesses are all personally qualified. They were of normal intelligence, with nothing to gain but persecution by the absurd claim of Jesus' resurrection. They were not ambitious for power and likely to deceive through various schemes to gain their ends; nor were they ignoramuses likely to be taken by any cunning knave. Rather, as their subsequent history demonstrates, they were brave and generous souls, and men with unblemished character. No other men had higher morals and greater purity of life than those self-denying fishermen. They were the best of witnesses.

c. The large number of witnesses. There was not one witness, or even a story concocted by two men constantly afraid of contradicting each other, but a historical event substantiated by a large number of independent witnesses who were individually close enough to know the facts under a great variety of circumstances. They saw and touched the very same body that was crucified and buried. There was no better way, even for deity, by which Jesus could have given His disciples proof of His resurrection than the manner in which he appeared to them.

The Value of the Resurrection

1. A sure foundation was provided by it for faith in God. R. A. Torrey notes on 1 Peter 1:21: "Men have been looking constantly for proof of the existence and character of God. There is the argument from the marks of creative intelligence and design in the material universe, the argument from the evidence of an intelligent, guiding hand in human history, the ontological argument, etc., but the resurrection of Jesus Christ points with unerring certainty to the existence, power, and holiness of the God who raised Him. My belief in the God of the Bible is not a felicitous fancy. It is a fixed faith resting upon an incontrovertible, firm fact."[35]

2. A substantial proof of the deity of Christ is given. Commenting on Romans 1:4, Moule writes: "Never for an hour had He ceased to be, in fact, Son of God. To the man healed of birth-blindness He had said, 'Dost thou believe on the Son of God?' But there was an hour when He became openly and, so to speak, officially what He always is naturally — somewhat as a born king is 'made' king by coronation. Historical act then affirmed independent fact and, as it were, gathered it into a point for use. This affirmation took place in power, according to the Spirit of Holiness, as a result of resurrection from the dead. 'Sown in weakness,' Jesus was indeed 'raised in' majestic, tranquil 'power.' Without an effort He stepped from out the depth of death, from under the load of sin. It was no flickering life, crucified but not quite killed, creeping back in a convalescence mis-called resurrection; it was the rising of the sun. That it was indeed day-light, and not day-dream, was shown not only in His mastery of matter, but in the transfiguration of His followers."[36]

3. It gives the believer an everliving High Priest (Heb. 7:25; Rom. 8:34; 1 John 2:1). Salvation is begun by the atoning death of Jesus Christ; it is continued by the resurrection and intercession of Christ. We have not only a Savior who died, and so made atonement for sin, but also a Savior who arose and entered by His own blood into the Holy of Holies — God's very presence — where He ever lives and pleads our case in every new failure (cf. Luke 22:31, 32 with John 11:42).

Adolph Saphir contrasts the levitical and Melchizedek roles of Christ thus: "They were many; He is only one. Their priesthood was successional — the son followed the father; Christ has a priesthood which cannot be transferred, seeing that life is indissoluble. They were sinful, but He is holy, pure, and spotless. They offered sacrifices in the earthly tabernacle; He presents Himself with His blood in the true sanctuary, which is high above all heavens, which is eternal. He appeared in the very presence before the face of God. In Jesus Christ, the Eternal Priest after the order of Melchizedek, all is fulfilled which in the preparatory dispensation could only be shadowed forth imperfectly and by a variety of ordinances.

"Christ in virtue of His priesthood can save completely (in a perfect, exhaustive, all-comprehensive manner) all who through Him come to God, because He ever liveth to intercede for them. Let us remember the importance which is attached in all epistles unto the resurrection life of Christ. He who was our Paschal lamb liveth now, and our only hope is in the risen Lord. . . . We cannot dwell too much on the glorious truth that Jesus Christ was crucified for our sins. Yet it is not on the crucifixion, but on Christ the Lord, that our faith rests, and not on Christ, as He was on the cross, do we dwell, but on Christ who was dead and is risen again, and liveth at the right hand of God, making intercession for us. What does the Apostle Paul mean when he says, 'If we have been justified through His death, *much more* shall we be saved by His life?' There is 'much more,' there is progress, there is a climax. When Jesus died upon the cross, He put away our sins, but this was only removing an obstacle.

"The ultimate object of His death upon the cross was His resurrection and His ascension, that through suffering He should enter glory, that He should be the perfect mediator between God and man, presenting us unto God and bestowing upon us all the blessings which He has purchased for us with His precious blood. He has obtained eternal redemption on the cross. He applies the blessings of eternal redemption from the holy of holies. . . . The law brought neither righteousness nor life; Christ brings both righteousness and life; for He died in our stead and He lived again to be our life. Thus the Apostle says, in the epistle to the Romans, 'Who will condemn? It is Christ who died, yea, rather, that is risen again, who is at the right hand of God, making intercession for us.'

"The Father Himself loveth us; it is the Father's good pleasure that Jesus should thus intercede for us. It is of His own free love and sovereign grace that Jesus intercedes for us, that thus the life that through death He hath brought unto us might be in us abundantly, and that all the spiritual blessings in heavenly places, which are in Him, and all the temporal blessings which we require for our safety, comfort, and usefulness may be bestowed upon us by the love of the Father and through the indwelling of the Holy Ghost. The Lord Jesus, who through death entered into glory, brings us to God, as to His and our Father, and brings God to us by the indwelling of the Holy Ghost. Thus is His Priesthood perfect."[37]

Our abiding security and our assurance of the ultimate, perfect completeness of Christ's work for us and in us lie in His eternal priesthood and continual intercession.

4. There is power resident in the truth of it to save men. Moule

comments: "This message is the utterance of faith, the creed of acceptance by faith alone, which we proclaim; that if thou shalt confess with thy mouth Jesus as Lord, as divine King and Master, and shalt believe in thine heart that God hath raised Him from the dead, owning in thy soul the glory of the resurrection, as revealing and sealing the triumph of the atonement, thou shalt be saved."[38]

5. It is according to God's promises to the fathers and therefore their fulfillment (Acts 13:32, 33). Paul was a conscientious Pharisee. He therefore believed and trusted in the hope of the promise made of God unto Abraham, Isaac, and Jacob. All Israel anticipated the fulfillment of the messianic promises and the national honor and glory. All the prophetic judgments were linked with the Holy One, the Redeemer, and His manifestation in the midst of Israel.

   This hope is fulfilled and the promise kept in the resurrection of Jesus, as Paul understands the Old Testament. The resurrection was not to be received incredulously, as the entire history of Israel bears witness to the fact that God can bring life from the dead, e.g., Sarah's womb (Rom. 4:19-21). The nation herself had been promised a national and spiritual resurrection (Ezek. 37:1-14; Hos. 6:1-3). The resurrection of Jesus Christ proved Him to be the Holy One and the hope of Israel (Acts 2:36). Peter refers to this when he writes, "Blessed be the God and Father of our Lord Jesus Christ, who according to his abundant mercy hath begotten us again unto a living hope by the resurrection of Jesus Christ from the dead" (1 Peter 1:3). The grave of the Lord Jesus was for the disciples the grave of their national hope, but His resurrection from the dead the revival of that hope.

6. It is the pledge and guarantee of our own resurrection (1 Thess. 4:14; 2 Cor. 4:14). We know that God will raise us up because He raised Christ up. We are so united to Christ by faith that if He arose we must rise, "If the Spirit of Him that raised up Jesus from the dead dwell in us, He that raised up Christ from the dead shall also quicken our mortal bodies by His Spirit that dwelleth in us" (Rom. 8:11). The resurrection of Jesus Christ has robbed death of its terrors for the believer (1 Cor. 15:55-57). It is the proof of immortal life beyond the grave — that death does not end all, but the soul lives after the body dies. It is said that once a fox came upon a cave into which he saw many foxes had entered, the sand being full of footprints. He was about to pass in when his cunning eye saw that all the footprints pointed one way. All were turned

inward, and there were none leading out of the cave. We have come to a great cave — the grave — and its entrance is marked by many footprints, all leading in and none out. But Christ has set His feet the other way and now if we go into the cave, we shall follow Him out again.

There was once a famous cape reported to be the fatal barrier to the navigation of the ocean. Of all those whom the winds or the current had drawn into its waters, it was said that none had reappeared. A bold navigator named Bartholmew Diaz in 1482 determined to surmount the obstacles, and he did. He opened the route to the East Indies, acquired for his country the riches of the world, and changed the Cape of Storms to the Cape of Good Hope. So Christ has proved Himself death's conqueror and made the grave to become the gateway of life for us. And those who have the anointed ear can hear Him say, "I am He that liveth and was dead, and behold I am alive forever more. Amen. And have the keys of Hades and of death."

Study Questions on Christology

1. What providential preparation was produced in the heathen world by God's preparation for the coming of Christ?
2. What were the three great truths in which Israel was educated through the positive preparation for Christ's coming?
3. Name and discuss the three agencies used in the education of Israel?
4. Describe the two principal effects of the Exile upon the Jews.
5. Give the main facts concerning the following heresies: Ebionism, Cerinthianism, Docetism, Arianism, Apollinarianism, Nestorianism, and Eutychianism.
6. Relate what is known as the orthodox interpretation concerning the nature and personality of Christ.
7. Quote one passage which proves the preexistence of Christ.
8. Describe the nature of the twofold relation of the preexistence of Christ.
9. What twofold classification may be made of the Old Testament appearings of God?
10. Give some instances of manifestations of the divine appearings through the medium of material symbols.

11. Give some of the names under which the divine manifestations in human or angelic form were made.
12. Quote one passage which shows the identity of the material symbols with the visible manifestations in human or angelic form.
13. What are the two names frequently used for the sensible representations of God, to what do they respectively appeal, and to whom are they applied? Quote one passage as illustration.
14. What three pictures of Christ stand out prominently in Old Testament prophecy and in New Testament fulfillment?
15. Give the meaning of *incarnation*. Quote one passage proving the incarnation of Christ.
16. Give the fivefold manner in which the reality of the humanity of Christ is shown and quote one passage with each phase.
17. What do we mean by the integrity of Christ's humanity?
18. Quote one passage proving the birth of Christ to be unique and supernatural.
19. Give the historical evidence of the virgin birth.
20. How may the argument against the virgin birth from the silence on the part of John, Paul, and Mark be met?
21. In what four ways is the human nature of Christ shown to be free both from hereditary depravity and actual sin? Quote one passage as proof.
22. In what sense was Christ's human nature ideal?
23. In what only does the human nature of Christ find its personality?
24. What does Christ's nature as germinal and capable of self-communication constitute Him?
25. Give nine ways in which the deity of Christ is shown in the Scriptures.
26. Give a summary of the presentation of the Logos or Word in John 1:1.
27. What is the testimony of the following passages to the deity of Christ: John 1:18; 20:28; Titus 2:13; Heb. 1:8?
28. Quote passages from Old and New Testaments in which descriptions of God are applied to Christ and show how this proves the deity of Christ.
29. Give the attributes of God possessed by Christ and quote one passage with one of them.
30. Name some of the works of God which are ascribed to Christ.

31. Quote one passage other than John 20:28, which shows that Jesus received honor and worship as deity.
32. In what association is the name of Jesus Christ found which reveals deity? Quote one passage as an illustration.
33. Quote one passage in which equality with God is expressly claimed by Christ or for Christ.
34. What do the Scriptures teach concerning the union of two natures in one person Jesus Christ?
35. What do the Scriptures teach negatively and positively concerning the tie by which the two natures of Jesus Christ are bound together?
36. Name and define the four proofs of the union of the two natures in the single personality of Christ.
37. Quote one passage which shows the person of Christ to be the crowning mystery of the Christian scheme.
38. Give the four chief problems in connection with the union of the two natures in the one person, and a suggested illumination for each.
39. Give two analogies used to illustrate the union of the two natures in one person, and show why they fail.
40. What constitutes the ground of possibility for the union of the two natures — the human and the divine — in the person of Christ?
41. Why is not a double personality involved in the union of the two natures in Christ?
42. What was the effect of the union of the two natures upon the human nature of Christ?
43. Describe and illustrate the effect of the union of the two natures upon the divine nature of Christ.
44. Wherein is the necessity of the union of the two natures in the one person?
45. What is the nature of this union in relation to the future?
46. To what does the final subjection of the Son to the Father in 1 Corinthians 15:28 most likely refer?
47. Give the threefold description of that which comprised the humiliation of Christ.
48. Of what three things does Christ's exaltation consist?
49. Quote a passage of Scripture containing the predictive announcement that Christ should be a prophet.
50. When did the prophetic ministry of Christ officially begin and end?

51. Give the primary and secondary ideas of the prophetic office and also the functions exercised by the Old Testament prophets.
52. In what three ways did the Old Testament prophet fulfill his prophetic ministry?
53. In what five ways did Christ fulfill His prophetic ministry?
54. Quote one passage from the Old Testament and one from the New Testament showing Christ's priesthood to be a fulfillment of prophecy.
55. Give the threefold scope of priesthood, and show how Christ fulfills these priestly functions.
56. From what is Christ's office as king to be distinguished, of what does it consist, and when will it be fully exercised?
57. What do the Scriptures teach concerning the purpose of Christ's sufferings?
58. What relation does holiness sustain to love and happiness?
59. How does the universe as a reflection of God express His holiness?
60. What twofold work was necessary for Christ to do with reference to human sin?
61. Of what is the historical work of the incarnate Christ the revelation, and what relation does it sustain to that which it reveals?
62. How do the Scriptures set forth the fact of the atoning death of Christ?
63. Give some of the Old Testament types of the Atonement and quote one passage with one of them.
64. Give some of the predictive pictures of the Redeemer.
65. What does the Hebrew root for "atonement," *Kaphar*, signify and mean? Quote one passage which contains both significance and meaning.
66. Give the active and passive sides of Reconciliation, and quote one passage with each.
67. Give the significance of the Greek noun and the meaning of the Latin word which are translated "propitiation," and show how the death of Christ expresses these, quoting one passage proving it.
68. Give the meaning of the two words *redemption* and *ransom,* and show their relation or application to Christ and His death, quoting one passage with each.
69. Give the meaning of "substitution," showing how it is true of Christ's work for sinners, quoting one passage on the idea.

70. What three things are declared to be the center and heart of the Atonement? Quote one passage with each.
71. What threefold relationship does the Atonement sustain to God? Quote one passage with each.
72. Quote one passage showing the Atonement to be the basis of our reconciliation.
73. Give the threefold relation of the Atonement to the law.
74. Quote one passage showing the sacrifice of Christ to have been necessary.
75. Quote one passage showing the death of Christ to have been voluntary.
76. Quote one passage showing the death of Christ to be vicarious.
77. Describe the fourfold necessity for the Atonement.
78. Explain the distinctions to be made in considering the extent of the Atonement, and quote one passage for each of the distinctions.
79. Name and define the twofold element in the substitutionary theory of the Atonement.
80. Give the two kinds of substitution, and show how they apply to Christ and His work.
81. Give the three kinds of penal satisfaction, and show why Christ's could be the third only.
82. Discuss the two questions which conduct us into the heart of the Atonement?
83. What are the three consequences of Adam's sin to himself and to his posterity?
84. Show the fivefold result "if Christ be not risen."
85. In what four ways is the importance of the doctrine of the resurrection of Christ positively shown?
86. Discuss the fourfold necessity of the resurrection of Christ.
87. Describe the false theories of the resurrection of Christ, and reply to each.
88. Show the true character of the resurrection of Christ.
89. Give the threefold mode of the resurrection of Christ and explain how it may be attributed to each member of the Trinity.
90. Discuss the proofs of the resurrection of Christ as found within the Gospel narratives themselves.
91. Give discussion of the proof offered for the resurrection of Christ by the empty tomb.
92. Give the circumstances under which Christ was buried and show how they make fraud and deception impossible.

93. Describe the change wrought in the disciples by the resurrection of Christ, and show how this change establishes that fact.
94. Quote one passage showing that the day of worship was changed from the seventh to the first day of the week and give conclusion drawn from this.
95. Show the resurrection of Christ to have been one of the foundation truths taught by the early church, and give the proof which this offers.
96. Give the proof offered for the resurrection of Christ by the personal testimony of each of the following: Christ; apostles; large number of witnesses.
97. Discuss the value of the resurrection of Christ.

Notes

[1]There are those who assert that, if our first parents had not sinned, Jesus Christ would have been born into the world just the same. This may be true, but we know no Scripture that proves it. On the contrary, the above and many similar passages unmistakably teach that the Incarnation was for the purpose of atonement.

[2]Jesus frequently went up to the temple, but He never offered sacrifice. He prayed, "Father, forgive them" (Luke 23:34), but He never prayed, "Father, forgive Me." He said, "Ye must be born anew" (John 3:7), but the words indicated that He had no such need. At no moment in all that life could a single detail have been altered, except for the worse. He not only yielded to God's will when made known to Him, but He sought it (John 5:30.). See also with reference to His sinlessness, 2 Cor. 5:21; Heb. 4:15; 1 Peter 1:19; 1 John 3:5, 7.

[3]By the impersonality of Christ's human nature we mean only that it had no personality before Christ took it, no personality before its union with the divine. It was a human nature whose consciousness and will were developed only in union with the personality of the Logos.

[4]The passages here alluded to abundantly confute the Docetic denials of Christ's veritable human body and the Apollinarian denial of Christ's veritable human soul. More than this, they establish the reality and integrity of Christ's human nature as possessed of all the elements, faculties, and powers essential to humanity.

[5]The best illustration of the possible meaning of Christ's giving up the kingdom is found in the governor of the East India Company giving up his authority to the queen and merging it in that of the home government. He himself, however, at the same time becomes secretary of state for India. So Christ will give up His vice-regency, but not His mediatorship. Christ will finish His work as mediator and then will reign as God, immediately revealing to us the deity. It is not the giving up of His mediatorial authority — that throne is to endure forever — but it is a simple public recognition that God is all in all, that Christ is God's medium of accomplishing all.

[6]Each of these elements of the doctrine has its own scriptural support. We must therefore regard the humiliation of Christ, not as consisting in a single act, but as involving a continuous self-renunciation, which began with the *kenosis* or self-emptying of the Logos in becoming man, and which culminated in the self-subjection of the God-man to the death of the cross (Phil. 2:6-8).

[7]The original name of the prophet was "seer" (1 Sam. 9:9; 2 Kings 17:13). A seer is one who sees, i.e., who sees things not beheld by mortal eye. The word *prophet* comes from the Greek *pro*, "before" or "forth," and *phemi*, "to speak," signifying "to speak forth or beforehand." Thus a prophet was one who spoke to the people as the mouthpiece of God (Exod. 4:15, 16). On the primary idea of the prophetic office see Exodus 4:10-17.

[8]The priests had access to the Holy Place of the ancient tabernacle; but the high priest alone, and then but once a year, on the great Day of Atonement, could enter the Holy of Holies (Heb. 9:6, 7). The formula of benediction which the high priest used on emerging from the Holy of Holies is believed to be recorded in Numbers 6:22-27.

[9]The lid of the ark called the mercy seat is in Hebrew "the kapporetha," signifying the place of the covering, i.e., of sin.

[10]There are two Greek prepositions which express the substitutional or vicarious idea: *huper* (in behalf of) and *anti* (instead of). The English preposition *for* is ambiguous. It means both "in behalf of" and "instead of." The idea of substitution is well illustrated by the use of the preposition used in connection with this phase of Christ's death. In Matthew 20:28 Christ is said to give His life a ransom for many (also 1 Tim. 2:6). That this preposition means "instead of" is clear from its use in Matthew 2:22 — "Archelaus did reign in the room [in the stead] of his father, Herod." Also in Luke 11:11 — "Will he for [instead of] a fish give him a serpent?" (see Heb. 12:2, 16). Substitution, then, as used here means this: Something happened to Christ, and because it happened to Christ, it need not happen to us. Christ died for our sins; we need not die for them if we accept His sacrifice. For further illustration, see Genesis 22:13 where God provides a ram instead of Isaac; also note how Barabbas is freed and Christ bearing His cross takes his place.

154 CHRISTIAN THEOLOGY: SYSTEMATIC AND BIBLICAL

[11]Heathen sacrifices bear witness to the necessity of atonement for sin. They are best explained as a perversion of an original divine revelation. This perversion is seen in the fact that while in heathen sacrifices the victim is offered to appease an offended deity, the truth as set forth in the Scriptures is that "God was in Christ, reconciling the world unto Himself" (2 Cor. 5:19). That heathen sacrifices are a perversion of an original divine revelation is further seen in the fact that the idea of substitution is uppermost; that is, the worshiper, conscious of his sinfulness, brings his offering by whose innocent blood he believes his guilt is expiated.

[12]Christ is the Savior of all men in the sense that (1) His atonement acts as a stay in the execution of the sentence against sin, securing for all men a space for repentance, and the enjoyment of the common blessings of life, forfeited by transgression (2 Peter 3:9; Matt. 5:45; Acts 14:17); (2) His atonement has made objective provision for the salvation of all, by removing from the divine mind every obstacle to the pardon and restoration of sinners, except their willful opposition to God and refusal to turn to Him (Rom. 5:8-10; 2 Cor. 5:18-20); (3) His atonement has procured for all men powerful incentives to repentance presented in the cross, together with the combining agency of the Christian church and the Holy Spirit (Rom. 2:4; John 16:8; 2 Cor. 5:18-20); (4) His atonement provides for the removal of the curse from nature (Isa. 55:13; Rom. 8:21, 22); and (5) His atonement provides for the salvation of infants (Matt. 18:10; 19:13-15). On the other hand, Christ is the Savior only of those who believe, because repentance and faith are the conditions of salvation (Acts 2:38).

[13]The following section is heavily dependent upon A. H. Strong's Systematic Theology, three volumes in one (Westwood, New Jersey: Fleming H. Revell, 1907, 1962), pp. 728-750.

[14]This theory was fully elaborated by Laelius Socinus and his nephew, Faustus Socinus, of Poland in the sixteenth century. Its modern representatives are Unitarians.

[15]Pelagianism was the denial of total depravity in man and the affirmation of "ability" — that is, that man by his own efforts, with divine help, is capable of salvation. The Socinian theory requires the abandonment of the doctrine of inspiration because throughout the Scriptures a vicarious and expiatory sacrifice is presented; the doctrine of sin, because sin as objective guilt and subjective defilement is denied; the doctrine of Christ's deity, because if man can save himself, he has no need of an infinite sacrifice by an infinite Savior; the doctrine of justification, because it denies our being declared guiltless before the law on account of anything Christ has done; the doctrine of regeneration, because it denies the necessity of the birth from above; and the doctrine of eternal retribution, because this is no longer appropriate to finite transgression of arbitrary law and to superficial sinning that does not involve nature.

[16]This theory was held by Horace Bushnell of New England; by Robertson, Maurice, Campbell, and Young of Great Britain; and by Schleiermacher and Ritschl of Germany.

[17]This theory was originated by Hugo Grotius, the Dutch jurist and theologian (1583-1645). It is commonly known as Arminianism.

[18]John Miley, Systematic Theology (New York: Hunt & Eaton, 1893), II, p. 68.

[19]This theory was elaborated by Edward Irving of England (1792-1834) and is held in substance by some German scholars.

[20]This theory was first held by Anselm of Canterbury (1033-1109), who propounded it as a substitute for an earlier patristic view that Christ's death was a ransom paid to Satan to deliver sinners from his power. Many Scots theologians have held this view.

[21]In viewing this aspect of the Atonement, Dr. Strong declares: "Its necessity is grounded in the holiness of God, of which conscience in man is a finite reflection. There is an ethical principle in the divine nature, which demands that sin shall be punished. Aside from its results, sin is essentially ill-deserving. As we who are made in God's image mark our growth in purity by the increasing quickness with which we detect impurity, and the increasing hatred which we feel toward it, so infinite purity is a consuming fire to iniquity. As there is an ethical demand in our natures that not only others' wickedness, but our own wickedness, be visited with punishment, and a keen conscience that cannot rest till it has made satisfaction to justice for its misdeeds, so there is an ethical demand of God's nature that penalty follows sin. . . . The Atonement is, therefore, a satisfaction of the ethical demand of the divine nature, by the substitution of Christ's penal sufferings for the punishment of the guilty. This substitution is unknown to mere law, and above and beyond the powers of law. It is an operation of grace. Grace, however, does not violate or suspend law, but takes it up into itself and fulfills it. The

righteousness of law is maintained in that the source of all law, the Judge and Punisher Himself voluntarily submits to bear the penalty and bears it in the human nature that has sinned. Thus the atonement answers the ethical demand of the divine nature that sin be punished if the offender is to go free. The interests of the divine government are secured as a first subordinate result of this satisfaction to God Himself, of whose nature the government is an expression; while, as a second subordinate result, provision is made for the needs of human nature — on the one hand the need of objective satisfaction to the ethical demand of punishment for sin, and on the other hand the need of a manifestation of divine love and mercy that will affect the heart and move it to repentance" (*Systematic Theology*, pp. 751-753).

[22]If Christ had entered the world in the natural way, He would have had depravity; but through His virgin birth He escaped it (Luke 1:25; 2 Cor. 5:21; Heb. 7:26). However, because of His partaking of our common humanity, Christ inherited guilt and could therefore justly bear penalty. (The word *guilt* is used in two senses: first, blameworthiness, or depravity; and second, liability to punishment, or obligation to make satisfaction for sin. In the latter sense only can it be applied to Christ.) Moreover, the guilt which our Lord inherited by birth was not, of course, the guilt of personal sin. It could not be. It was primarily the guilt of Adam's sin, the guilt of the first or original transgression. But it was also the guilt of our sin, yours and mine. This is true because as the branches are organically and vitally united to the tree, so we are racially and vitally united with Adam. Thus "the Lord hath laid on Him the iniquity of us all" (Isa. 63:6).

[23]James H. Brooks, *Did Jesus Rise?* (New York: Loizeaux Brothers, n.d.), p. 8.

[24]At Pentecost, Peter, the man who had denied his Lord, stood forth with dauntless courage and proclaimed both the death and the resurrection of Christ. Paul's personal testimony to his own conversion, his interviews with those who had seen Jesus Christ on earth before and after His resurrection, and the prominence given to the resurrection in the apostle's own teaching, challenge our attention afresh to this evidence for the resurrection. Thus, too, did all the apostles preach the resurrection.

[25]L. S. Keyser writes: "It is not likely that Christ, who was so weak that He could not carry His cross, could have survived the ordeal of the crucifixion. When the soldiers came to break his legs, as was the cruel custom, they found Him dead, and therefore they refrained from treating Him in that way. When one pierced His side with a spear, blood and water flowed out, proving that the heart had been broken and serum formed. Surely Pilate and the soldiers would have made sure that He was dead. So would Joseph of Arimathea and Nicodemus, who buried Him. (*A System of Christian Evidences*, 10th ed. [Burlington, Iowa: The Lutheran Literary Board, 1950], p. 109).

[26]Brooks, *Did Jesus Rise?* pp. 12-14.

[27]This theory is embodied in the more modern theory of Russellism (Jehovah's Witnesses), which says, "Our Lord's human body was, however, supernaturally removed from the tomb; because had it remained there it would have been an insurmountable obstacle to the faith of the disciples. . . . We know nothing about what became of it, except that it did not decay or corrupt. . . . Whether it was dissolved into gases or whether it is still preserved somewhere as the grand memorial of God's love, of Christ's obedience, and of our redemption, no one knows; nor is such knowledge necessary" (Series II, pp. 129-131).

[28]Floyd E. Hamilton, *The Basis of Christian Faith*, 3rd ed. (New York: Harper Brothers, 1946), p. 292.

[29]Brooks, *Did Jesus Rise?* pp. 11, 12.

[30]John Dick, *Lectures on Theology* (Philadelphia: J. Whetham, 1836), II, 103.

[31]Ibid.

[32]Leander S. Keyser, *A System of Evidences*, p. 114.

[33]This section is heavily dependent upon R. A. Torrey, *What the Bible Teaches* (Westwood, N. J.: Fleming H. Revell, 1898), pp. 166-186.

[34]Brooks, *Did Jesus Rise?* p. 7.

[35]Torrey, *What the Bible Teaches*, p. 180.

[36]H. C. G. Moule, *The Epistle of St. Paul to the Romans* (London: Hodder & Stoughton, 1893), p. 17.

[37]Adolph Saphir, *The Epistle to the Hebrews* (New York: Gospel Publishing House, n.d.), I, pp. 405-9.
[38]Moule, *Romans*, p. 269.

CHAPTER FIVE

PNEUMATOLOGY: THE DOCTRINE OF THE HOLY SPIRIT

THE PERSONALITY OF THE HOLY SPIRIT

The term *person* immediately introduces an insurmountable difficulty — namely, attempting to express the infinite in finite terms. It has been argued that personality and absolute existence are contradictions: that God cannot be, at one and the same time, a person and infinite. That argument is based upon the assumption that the term *person* is capable of concise and final definition.

This is a false assumption. It supposes that perfect personality exists in human beings. This is not so. God alone has perfect personality; that of every other being is limited. In other words, God is not a magnified man; rather, it may be said that man is a limited God. God is not in the image of man; man is in the image of God, and no definite, final deduction can be made concerning God from the study of human life. If man were the one, the final, the absolute unit, then the argument would hold that God cannot be a person and infinite. If He alone be final and absolute, then personality in man is to be looked upon as being imperfect and limited. It is possible to form some conception of divine personality by a study of the human, because man is made in the likeness of God. But wherever the endeavor is made to build up the divine from the suggestion given in man, it must be remembered that the factors of personality in man are finite, while in God they are infinite.

Three things at least are combined in personality — intelligence,

157

emotion, and volition. These essential parts of personality are limited in human beings, but it is not unthinkable that they may have an illimitable existence and yet be included in personality. It is not unthinkable that man, within a circumscribed area, is a picture of the divine; but that yet, by so much as he is circumscribed and limited, he is not himself divine. In this sense man was made in the image of God; but that of which he is the image is like him, yet unlike him. It is unlike him in the fact that all that is found in man of essential majesty and grandeur in a limited degree is to be found in God Himself unlimited and illimitable. The Holy Spirit, then, is a person possessed of will, intelligence, and emotion in an infinite degree.[1]

The personality of the Holy Spirit is shown by the following:

1. Designations proper to personality are given to Him.
    a. The pronoun used for the Holy Spirit is masculine, though the noun translated *spirit* is neuter (John 16:14).
    b. The name *Paracletos* translated *Comforter* cannot be taken as the name of any abstract influence. The Comforter, Instructor, Patron, Guide, Advocate whom this term brings before us must be a person. This is evident from the application of the term to Christ in 1 John 2:1 (cf. John 15:26).
2. His name is mentioned in immediate connection with other persons, and in such a way as clearly to imply personality.
    a. In connection with Christians (Acts 15:28);
    b. In connection with Christ (John 16:14; 17:4);
    c. In connection with the Father and the Son (Matt. 28:19; 2 Cor. 13:14; Jude 20, 21).
3. He performs acts proper to personality. That which searches, knows, speaks, testifies, reveals, convinces, commands, strives, moves, helps, guides, creates, recreates, sanctifies, inspires, makes intercession, orders the affairs of the church, performs miracles, and raises the dead cannot be a mere influence, efflux, power, or attribute of God, but must be a person (Gen. 1:2; 6:3; Luke 12:12; John 3:8; 16:8; Acts 2:4; 8:29; 10:19, 20; 13:2; 16:6, 7; Rom. 8:11, 26, 27; 15:19; 1 Cor. 2:10, 11; 12:8-11; 1 Peter 1:2; 2 Peter 1:21).
4. He is affected as a person by the acts of others. That which can be resisted, grieved, vexed, and blasphemed must be a person, for only a person can perceive an insult and be offended. The blas-

phemy against the Holy Ghost cannot be merely blasphemy against a power or attribute of God, since in that case blasphemy against God would be a lesser crime than blasphemy against His power. That against which the unpardonable sin is committed must be a person (Isa. 63:10; Matt. 12:31, 32; Acts 5:3, 4, 9; 7:51; Eph. 4:30).

5. The ascription to the Holy Spirit of a personal subsistence distinct from that of the Father and of the Son cannot be explained as personification.

   a. This would be to interpret sober prose by the canons of poetry. Such sustained personification is contrary to the genius of even Hebrew poetry, in which Wisdom itself is most naturally interpreted as designating a personal existence (1 Cor. 1:30, ASV).

   b. Such an interpretation would render a multitude of passages either tautological, meaningless, or absurd as can be easily seen by substituting for the name *Holy Spirit* the terms which are wrongly held to be its equivalents — such as *power* or *influence* or *efflux* or *attribute* of God. Acts 10:38 provides an example: "God anointed Him [Jesus] with the Holy Spirit and with power" — anointed Him with power and with power. Romans 15:13: "Abound in hope in the power of the Holy Spirit" — in the power of the power of God. Romans 15:19: "in the power of signs and wonders, in the power of the Holy Spirit" — in the power of the power of God. 1 Corinthians 2:4: "demonstration of the Spirit and of power" — demonstration of power and of power. Such a substitution is thus shown to be meaningless.

   c. It is contradicted, moreover, by all those passages in which the Holy Spirit is distinguished from His own gifts (Luke 1:35; 4:14; Rom. 8:26; 1 Cor. 12:4, 8, 11).[2]

THE DEITY OF THE HOLY SPIRIT

The Holy Spirit is not only a person, but a divine person.[3] Most assuredly the Scriptures teach not only the personality of the Spirit, but His divine personality.

1. He is spoken of as God (Acts 5:3, 4; 1 Cor. 3:16; 6:19; 12:4-6). Of the passage in 1 Corinthians 12, Meyer says: "The Divine Trinity is here indicated *in an ascending climax* in such a way that we pass from the *Spirit* who bestows the gifts to the Lord [Christ] who is

served by means of them, and finally to *God*, who as the absolute first cause and possessor of all Christian powers works the entire sum of all charismatic gifts in all who are gifted."[4]

2. Divine attributes and perfections are ascribed to Him: life (Rom. 8:2); truth (John 16:13); love (Rom. 15:30); holiness (Eph. 4:30); eternity (Heb. 9:14); omnipotence (Luke 1:35); omniscience (John 14:26; 16:12, 13, ASV; 1 Cor. 2:10); omnipresence (Ps. 139:7-10).

3. Divine works are ascribed to Him: creation (Job 33:4; Ps. 104:30); bestowal of life (Gen. 2:7; John 6:63; Rom. 8:2); prophecy (2 Sam. 23:23; 2 Peter 1:21); regeneration (John 3:3-8; Titus 3:5); resurrection (Rom. 8:11).

4. The name of the Holy Spirit is coupled in equality with the names of God and Christ.
   a. In the apostolic commission (Matt. 28:19, 20);
   b. In the apostolic benediction (2 Cor. 13:14);
   c. In the administration of the church (1 Cor. 12:4-6).
   See also Ephesians 4:4-6, where the name of the Holy Spirit appears first, and Romans 15:30, where it occurs second.

5. The Holy Spirit in the New Testament is identified with Jehovah of the Old Testament (cf. Isa. 6:8-10 with Acts 28:25-27; Jer. 31:31-34 with Heb. 10:15-17; Exod. 16:7 with Heb. 3:7-9 and Ps. 95:8-11; Gen. 1:27 with Job 33:4).

6. The Holy Spirit can be blasphemed, and this is possible only of God. As spirit is nothing less than the inmost principle of life, and the spirit of man is man himself, so the Spirit of God must be God Himself (1 Cor. 2:11). Thus the Scriptures teach that the Holy Spirit is a person having all the divine attributes and able to do all divine works. The mystery is acknowledged, and it is profound. To explain it finally is impossible, but this impossibility is to be accounted for by human limitation, and by the fact that the finite can never fully grasp the infinite. The facts must be reverently accepted as forming an integral part of revealed religion; and this has been done by many throughout the history of the church, thus giving an added argument for the divine personality of the Holy Spirit.

Christian experience, expressed as it is in the prayers and hymns of the church, offers proof of the deity of the Holy Spirit similar to that offered for the deity of Jesus Christ. When our eyes are opened to see Christ as Savior, we are compelled to recognize the work in us of a divine Spirit who has taken of the things of Christ and has shown them to us; and this divine Spirit we necessarily distinguish from the Father and the Son.

THE WORK OF THE HOLY SPIRIT

In considering the work of the Holy Spirit, a popular misconception must be removed. This is the result of the teaching of Sabellius; namely, that in creation, God the Father works; in redemption, God the Son works; and in salvation, God the Spirit works. Another way of putting it is, the Old Testament dispensation was the dispensation of the Father; the New Testament dispensation, the dispensation of the Son; and the present dispensation, the dispensation of the Spirit.

Quite to the contrary, the Scriptures teach that in every manifestation of the works of God, the Father, the Son, and the Spirit are alike active. Thus, to use the classifications of Sabellius, in creation, in redemption, and in salvation we trace the working of each member of the Trinity. And in general, the working of each member of the Trinity is this: In every divine activity, the power to bring forth proceeds from the Father; this might be called the authorship power. The power to arrange proceeds from the Son; this might be called the executive power. And the power to bring to completion or to perfect proceeds from the Spirit; this might be called the energizing power (Job 33:4; Ps. 33:6; John 1:1-3; Rom. 11:36; 1 Cor. 8:6). Consequently the office work of the Holy Spirit in every phase and sphere of the divine activity is to bring forward to completion that which has been conceived by the Father and executed by the Son.

In Relation to Creation

The work of the Spirit in creation, and His perpetual presence and manifestation therein, are subjects full of fascination and yet strangely neglected. So much attention has been given to the regenerative work of the Spirit, that His generative activities have been in a large measure overlooked. The origin and preservation of everything in nature are spiritual.

The sacred writings abound in statements with regard to the creative aspect of the Spirit's work. What magnificent figures are contained in the words of the psalmist in Psalm 18:9-12: "He bowed the heavens also, and came down; and thick darkness was under his feet. And He rode upon a cherub, and did fly; yea, He flew swiftly upon the wings of the wind. He made darkness His hiding-place, His pavilion round about Him; darkness of waters, thick clouds of the skies. At the brightness before Him His thick clouds passed, hailstones and coals of fire." It is evident from a careful reading of this psalm that it is a declaration of the perpetual presence of God in all such manifestations. In every gleam of the glory of nature, there is the evidence of an ever-present God.

The final words of that great doxology which Isaiah heard from the inner temple are of great interest in this connection. Isaiah 6:1-3: "In the year that King Uzziah died I saw also the Lord sitting upon a throne, high and lifted up, and His train filled the temple. Around Him stood the seraphim: each one had six wings; with twain he covered his face, and with twain he covered his feet, and with twain he did fly. And one cried unto another and said, Holy, holy, holy is the Lord of hosts: the whole earth is full of His glory." The uplifted Lord is the center of adoration in the courts of heaven; but not there only is His splendor seen — "the whole earth is full of His glory."[5]

For the purpose of this study, it will be sufficient to consider certain definite statements of Scripture in which the work of the Holy Spirit in creation is clearly set forth in its varied aspects. Remembering that the special work of the Holy Spirit in creation is to lead creation to its destiny, which is the glory of God.

1. Bringing order into the universe (Gen. 1:2). The first picture presented to us in the Scriptures is that of the Spirit brooding over chaos. Science agrees that the earth must have been in such a condition as this before the appearance of man. How this condition of things arose, whether through some mighty catastrophe overwhelming a previous order, or through the omnificent word of God, no man can positively tell. Both science and revelation are silent so far as clear, dogmatic statement is concerned.

These opening words of the Book of Genesis tell us that this planet was or became waste and void, and declare that for the accomplishment of the change from this condition to that of order, the Spirit brooded over the face of the waters. He acted as the administrator of the will of God as expressed by the Word of God. The will of God is that order should supercede disorder. The Word of God announces this will, beginning with the first utterance, "Let there be light." By the brooding of the Spirit over chaos, the light came.

This is the unvarying order of the activity of God in creation. This is not an account of the first creation of matter. Concerning that, man has no definite knowledge, except as we read in

Genesis 1:1, "In the beginning God created the Heaven and the Earth"; and then in the second verse, that the earth was or became waste and void. How long the interval between these verses was, no man can tell. Scripture makes no pronouncement thereupon, and the declarations of science are but surmises.

But when the present order was established, it was by the Spirit of God brooding upon confusion and emptiness, as the Power through which the divine will was realized. The earth as it is today, therefore, excepting the results of the curse caused by the Fall, is the direct outcome of the action of the Holy Spirit.

2. Creating and garnishing the heavens (Job 26:12, 13; Ps. 33:6; Isa. 40:12,13). The words of the psalmist — "By the word of the Lord were the heavens made; and all the host of them by the breath of His mouth" — are full of suggestiveness. The word *breath* here might well be written with a capital letter — "The Breath of God's mouth." Here again is revealed the will of Jehovah uttered by the Word of Jehovah and accomplished by the Breath of His mouth; but the sweep of thought is greater here than in Genesis 1:2. It is not a description of the bringing of order to one small planet, but the record in a sentence of the creation of the heavens and all the host of them. The phrase includes all the myriad wonders of the universe around.

By the Word of God and by the Breath of His mouth came the systems of which man is just beginning to learn that in their entirety they are undiscoverable. The point at which astronomical science has now arrived is an acknowledgment that beyond the utmost reach of anything which can be studied through the agency of the telescope lie illimitable space and innumerable worlds. This harmonizes with Jeremiah's statement, "The host of heaven can not be numbered" (Jer. 33:22).[6]

3. Renewal of the face of the earth. Isaiah 40:7: "The grass withereth, the flower fadeth because the breath of the Lord bloweth upon it." Psalm 104:30: "Thou sendest forth thy Spirit, and thou renewest the face of the ground." The Spirit is the breath of renewal. Through death He ever leads to life.

The declaration of the Isaiah passage at first sight is almost staggering. That the Spirit of God comes as the genial summer's zephyr upon nature is easy to understand; but it is difficult to believe that He comes also as the fierce blast of God. Yet it is certainly true. He brings death as a process and a necessity. The pitiless east wind has in it the breath of health. Let there be no more east wind, no more northeast wind, no more biting, keen blast of death, and what would become of nature? Surely Kingsley entered into the spirit of this when he sang —

> Welcome, wild North-easter!
> Shame it is to see
> Odes to every zephyr,
> Ne'er a verse to thee.
> Through the black fir forest
> Thunder harsh and dry,
> Scattering down the snowflakes
> Off the curdled sky.
> Come: and strong within us
> Stir the Vikings' blood,
> Bracing brain and sinew;
> Blow, thou wind of God.

When the east wind blows and the flowers are nipped, and the blade of grass is curled and shriveled, then the Spirit of God is sweeping the ground and preparing for the springing of life in response to the kiss of His gentler breezes (see Ps. 104:30). Hence, we see in the second passage that what follows the death wind of the Spirit is His life wind. The first is winter, the second is spring. Nothing ever finds its way to spring save through winter. The budding of life and the flowers that blossom upon the sod in springtime are the result of the east wind that swept the hills and valleys during the winter days. These are not mere figures of speech. The cold and icy wind blows under the direction of the Spirit of God; and the wind that kisses earth and makes its smiling flowers is the messenger of the self-same Spirit.

4. Sustaining the present physical order and supporting animal and vegetable life (Ps. 104:10-14, 30). It is evident that, as by the power of the Spirit, cosmos was produced out of chaos, so by the everpresent and active power of the Spirit in the processes of nature, cosmos is maintained and life in its varying forms is supported.

5. Giving life to man (Gen. 2:7; Job 33:4). The second account of man's creation, as found in Genesis 2, is an unfolding of the detailed facts in it, and a revealing of man's nature. Man is now shown as uniting in his own person the material with the spiritual, the earth with the heavens, the things that perish and pass with the things that abide forever. God made man of the dust of the earth — a material basis — and breathed into him the breath of

lives, thus creating a spiritual being. Through that inbreathing by God, the conscious side of man's nature was born, and he became a living soul.

Man's material basis, the earthly dust, was devoid of self-consciousness. Man's power to enter into his new environment, his new relationship, his new companionship was the result of the inbreathing of the Breath of lives by God. Man is not man apart from the direct ministry and sustaining power of the Spirit of God. Everything that man is, in the essential facts of His being, which distinguish him from the animal is due to this peculiar form of inbreathing, whereby man became a conscious soul. He was thus made the offshoot of God. In man life was different from life anywhere else; in man life became light. In this sense Christ "lighteth every man that cometh into the world." There was life in the plant, and life in the lower animals; but when God inbreathed to man the Breath of lives, He bestowed a life in which lay the element of light. In man, creation first looked back into the face of God and knew Him. No lower form of life knows God. In all life there are present the power and energy of God; all things live and move and have their being in Him; but apart from man, none are conscious of it. In man, life became light, consciousness, knowingness. Man entered into the perfect environment of the Garden, knew it, appreciated it, and discovered God in it because there had been inbreathed to him the Breath of lives.

He entered not only into environment, occupation, and government, but also into companionship. God made woman to be his companion. He entered into that new relation which created and conditioned the whole social range of human life in the power of the same Breath of lives.

When man is thus viewed from the standpoint of original intention as seen in the picture of Edenic beauty and power, it is evident that the natural is spiritual and the spiritual is natural, and that there is no single aspect of human life which is not under the government of the inspiring Spirit of God.

In Relation to Revelation
1. Author of the Scriptures.
   a. He gave special gifts and qualifications to the human authors of the books of the Bible for the unique work to which they were appointed (1 Cor. 12:4, 8-11, 28, 29).
   b. He revealed truth to the apostles and prophets which had

been hidden from men and which had not been discovered and could not be discovered by mere human philosophy or the ordinary processes of reasoning by the natural mind (Eph. 3:2-5).

c. He gave revelations to the prophets which were independent of their own thinking (1 Peter 1:10-12).

d. He imparted prophetic knowledge to holy men apart from their own volition, and controlled them in giving it utterance (2 Peter 1:21).

e. He was the real speaker in all the prophetic utterances (cf. Heb. 3:7 with Ps. 95:7, 8; Heb. 10:15, 16 with Jer. 31:33; Acts 28:25, 26 with Isa. 6:9, 10; see also 2 Sam. 23:2; Rev. 3:13).

f. He gave not only the thought, but the words in which the thought was to be expressed (1 Cor. 2:13).

g. He has inspired, or breathed out, the Scriptures in their entirety through the medium of men (2 Tim. 3:16; 2 Peter 3:15, 16).

2. Interpreter of the Scriptures (John 16:14; 1 Cor. 2:9-14). Who better can interpret a writing than the author himself? It is the same with Scripture, since the Holy Spirit is the interpreter of Scripture because He is ultimately its author.

Before Pentecost

1. From the Fall to the Messiah. The whole being of man, was conditioned before he sinned in the energy and wisdom of the Spirit. The knowledge of this fact man had lost by reason of his sin; and the Spirit resisted, was separated from the actualities of human life. From the moment of the Fall, a new form of His ministry began, which was partial, occasional, special, and prophetic of the great dispensation to be ushered in when the true light of sacrifice had made plain the way for the clearer apprehension of God.

The distinction of the work of the Spirit in the Old Testament era from that of the New is a difficult subject. After all is said that can be said, much more light is needed for clearness of apprehension and accuracy of statement. To begin with, it is commonly said that the difference is expressed by two Greek prepositions: "upon" (*epi*) and "in" (*en*), i.e., that the Holy Spirit in the Old Testament dispensation came upon men, while in the New Testament dispensation He indwells them. This, however, will not always hold, because in the Old Testament dispensation, the Holy Spirit at times indwelt men; while in the New Testament, He also came upon men (Gen. 41:38; Exod. 31:3; Num. 27:18; Dan. 5:11; Luke 24:49; Acts 1:8).

Perhaps the best point of approach to the subject is the Christian church. In the Old Testament, except in type and symbol, there is no church, the body of Christ and the temple of the Holy Spirit. Until after the death, resurrection, and ascension of Christ, the Spirit is not spoken of as creating a church by His own abiding indwelling. Neither is He spoken of as the one director and only administrator of the affairs of such a body. And yet again He is not spoken of as her sanctifier. All the other aspects of the Spirit's work are found — not continually or perpetually and in an abiding sense, as they are today, but as special occasions demanded.

We may say, then, that in the Old Testament age, chosen individuals were the objects of the Spirit's grace for life and gifts for service; while in the New Testament and the present age, He works in and upon the body of Christ and individual members of that body. These two expressions, *individual persons* and *the body of Christ*, give us the key to the difference between the two dispensations (1 Cor. 12:13). One other distinction should also be noted in this connection, that in the Old Testament age the Spirit came upon and filled men for specific work without reference to character. In the New Testament age, after the accomplishment of the work of the Cross, this is never so: His filling for service always depends upon His application of the work of the Savior for cleansing and holiness.[7]

The work of the Holy Spirit in the Old Testament dispensation may be classified as follows:

a. Coming upon men (Judg. 6:34; 1 Chron. 12:18; 2 Chron. 24:20). The same thought is expressed in each of these passages in the phrase "the Spirit came upon them." The Hebrew word literally means that the Spirit clothed Himself with them — not that the Spirit fell upon them as anointing, but the Spirit took hold of them, passed into them, and made them the instruments through which He accomplished His work.

b. Coming mightily upon men (Judg. 14:6; 1 Sam. 10:10; 16:13). The phrase here means literally forcing them into something. In these cases an entirely different word is used. The thought of it is that of forcing forward or of pushing. The literal meaning of the words is that the Spirit attacked these men, came upon them with compulsion, forced them forward to a certain activity. Under the compulsion of the Spirit, Samson slew the lion, Saul joined the prophets, and uttered words of prophecy, and David went forward to the work of governing the people. How different is the manifestation of power: the slaying of a lion, the uttering of the truth of God, and the governing of the people; but in each case, the action was under the impulse of the Spirit of God.

c. Indwelling men (Gen. 41:38; Num. 27:18). Pharaoh said that in Joseph there dwelt the Spirit of God, and that, therefore, he was discreet and wise. When a successor to Moses was needed for the government and leadership of the people, Joshua was chosen because in him dwelt the Spirit of God. Whether Pharaoh understood his own expression may be very doubtful, but it is certainly worthy of note that in each of the cases cited the Spirit of God created fitness for government; and this fitness consisted not in autocratic, tyrannical power, but in discretion, wisdom, gentleness, and beauty of demeanor. Such were the manifestations of the indwelling of the Spirit in these men under the old covenant.

d. Fitting and filling men for special service (Exod. 31:1-7). Here we are told the Spirit of God filled certain men; and this expression is used only in connection with the work of making the tabernacle. Thus, the whole of that work in its exquisite perfection and glorious beauty was the outshining of the wisdom of the Holy Spirit.

These illustrations go to show that the Holy Spirit was always interested in and working among men; that He did not abide with them, but that for special purposes and at special points in their history, He equipped them for whatever the particular moment demanded.[8]

2. During the messianic period. The silence that had lasted for centuries, since the last prophet had spoken, was at last broken by John the Baptist, who announced One whose distinguishing work should be that of baptizing with the Holy Ghost and with fire (Luke 3:16).

a. He filled and empowered John the Baptist, the forerunner of Jesus, for the service He was called upon to render (Luke

1:15-17). John's father and mother were also filled with the Holy Ghost (Luke 1:41, 67).

b. It was the generative power of the Holy Spirit that gave Jesus His physical nature and human body, thus making possible His virgin birth and sinless humanity (Luke 1:35).

c. The Holy Spirit anointed Jesus for His messianic office (Luke 3:21, 22; 4:18, 19, 21).[9]

d. The Holy Spirit filled and empowered Jesus as the servant of Jehovah for the accomplishment of His work (Luke 4:1, 14; Acts 10:38).

e. The Holy Spirit directed the earthly life and service of Jesus even after His resurrection (Acts 1:1, 2).

f. It was through the Holy Spirit, in some mysterious way, that Jesus offered Himself in sacrifice to God (Heb. 9:14).

g. The Holy Spirit played an important part in the resurrection of Jesus Christ from the dead (Rom. 1:4; 1 Peter 3:18).

h. It was according to the promise of Jesus Christ and as its fulfillment that the Holy Spirit was given at Pentecost; in a very real sense Jesus was the bestower of the Holy Spirit (Luke 24:49; John 20:22; Acts 2:33).

After Jesus had come on the scene, He assured the disciples that the Holy Spirit could be received in answer to prayer (Luke 11:13). They had requested Jesus to teach them how to pray (Luke 11:1), and this request resulted in their hearing the most startling announcement concerning spiritual matters that had ever fallen upon their ears. They were told that if they asked of God with understanding and importunity they should receive good gifts only, and the especially good gift of the Holy Spirit. The statement must have so staggered them as to surprise them almost into inaction; for it is evident that they never asked for the Spirit and, therefore, never received Him in answer to their own asking.

This text is perpetually quoted as having a present-day application. This is due to a failure to draw the line of distinction between the various phases of the Master's mission. These words were spoken to a handful of Jewish disciples gathered around a Jewish Messiah. He was unveiling to them a great secret in all God's dealings with men — that God would give the Holy Spirit to men who asked, if they did so according to the law of prayer laid down. There is no evidence, however, that they ever had the Holy Spirit until that Spirit came along another line of communication. In Luke 11;13 Jesus revealed to the disciples the Word of God, the attitude of the divine heart, the preparedness of the Father to bestow the wondrous gift of the Holy Spirit upon them, but there is no evidence whatever that they ever asked or ever received it in answer to prayer; and yet they never truly saw Christ or understood His mission, or entered into the deep and underlying secrets of His life, until after the Spirit had come upon them in answer to His asking (John 14:16; Acts 2:33; cf. Luke 12:49, 50 with 3:16; Acts 1:2; 2:3; see also John 4:13, 14; 6:35; 7:37-39; 20:21, 22).

From Pentecost to the Lord's Return

The present age is preeminently the dispensation of the Holy Spirit, in which He has a specific work differing from that of preceding ages. This ministry is based upon the work of Christ and was impossible until He had finished that work and ascended on high (John 7:38, 39).

The Holy Spirit could reveal Christ only when there was a complete Christ to reveal. The Holy Spirit could sanctify fully only after the example and motive of holiness were furnished in Christ's life and death. It has been said that "the divine artist could not fitly descend to make the copy before the original had been provided."

1. In relation to the church.
   a. He gave birth to the church on the day of Pentecost as a body of living members. Christ is the church's risen, exalted, and living Head, changing the company of waiting disciples from an aggregation of units into one corporate whole — the church of the living God (Acts 2:1-4; 1 Cor. 12:12-27; Eph. 1:22, 23).
   b. He possessed and indwelt the church as the temple of God. By the creation of the church, a new temple was given to the world, a new institute for praise, for prayer, and for prophecy. The incense of praise, for instance, is offered by the inspiration of the Spirit (John 4:24). The intercession of prayer is maintained by the whole company of those who pray in the Holy Spirit (Jude 20). Similarly, the work of prophecy, in its fullest meaning of forth-telling, is carried forward by such as are witnesses in cooperation with the Holy Spirit to the eternal verities of God (John 15:26, 27; Luke 24:48, 49; 1 Cor. 2:1-5).
   c. He confers gifts and graces upon the church for life, fruitful-

ness, and service. As the Spirit of life, the Holy Spirit is the Giver of life to the church; otherwise its members would be "dead in trespasses and sins" (John 6:63; Rom. 8:2). As the Fruitbearer, He is "God that giveth the increase." "Ye are God's farm," says Paul to the church at Corinth. Every Christian grace is the fruitage of the Spirit, borne in the soil of surrendered hearts (Rom. 8:23; 5:5; Gal. 5:22, 23; Col. 1:8). All qualification for service is the Spirit's equipment of the members of the body (Rom. 12:6-8; 1 Cor. 12:4-11, 28-31).

d. He has anointing, illumination, and guidance for the church (2 Cor. 1:21; 1 John 2:20, 27). In Exodus we have a beautiful typical illustration of the anointing which is ours in Christ. At Aaron's consecration, the precious ointment was not only poured on his head, but ran down in rich profusion upon his body and upon his priestly garments. This fact is taken up by the psalmist: "Like the precious ointment upon the head, that ran down upon the beard, even Aaron's beard: that went down to the skirts of his garments" (Ps. 133:1, 2). This is all fulfilled in Christ, our great High Priest, who has passed through the heavens — Jesus the Son of God.

He also was anointed (Acts 10:38; Luke 4:18, 21; Heb. 1:9). He the *Christos*, the Anointed, stands above and for the *christoi*, His anointed brethren; from Him, the Head, the unction of the Holy Ghost descended on the day of Pentecost. It was poured in rich profusion upon His mystical body. It has been flowing down ever since and will continue to do so till the last member shall have been incorporated with Himself, and so anointed by the one Spirit in the one body, which is the church.

Jesus appropriated to Himself the anointing spoken of by the prophets. According to the passage referred to in Luke and then in two passages in Acts (4:27; 10:38), His personal anointing is mentioned. And as with the Lord, who is the Head, so with His body, the anointing has been provided and potentially bestowed, for "now He which stablisheth us with you in Christ, and hath anointed us, is God" (2 Cor. 1:21). But there needs to be the recognition and realization of this on the part of the church — the appropriation of faith. Hence, the significance of the instruction in 1 John 2:27.

A student of the Scriptures need not be told how closely the ceremony of anointing was related to all important offices and

ministries of the servants of Jehovah under the old covenant.
The priest was anointed that he might be "holy unto the Lord"
(Lev. 8:12). The king was anointed that the Spirit of the Lord
might rest upon him in power (1 Sam. 15:1, 17). The prophet
was anointed that he might be the oracle of God to the people
(1 Kings 19:16). No servant of Jehovah was deemed qualified
for his ministry without this. Even in the cleansing of the leper
this ceremony was not wanting (Lev. 14:17).

If we ask now what this anointing is, the reply is, obviously,
the Holy Spirit Himself. As He is the seal attesting us, so is He
the Oil anointing us — the same Gift described by different
symbols. And as it was with Aaron — the first anointed — who
was thus qualified to anoint others, so with our great High
Priest. It is He within the veil who gives the Spirit unto His
own, that He may qualify them to be "an elect race, a royal
priesthood, a holy nation, a people for God's own possession"
(1 Peter 2:9, ASV).

To sum up the teaching on the anointing, it seems to include
three things: consecration, the obtaining or impartation of
knowledge, and fitness for service.

e. The Holy Spirit presides over and directs the church into the
will and plan of God (Acts 13:1-3; 15:28; 20:28; 1 Cor. 12:8-11).
He from the day of Pentecost has occupied an entirely new
position. The whole administration of the affairs of the church
of Christ has since that day devolved upon Him. That day
marked the installation of the Holy Spirit as the administrator
of the church in all things, which office He is to exercise until
Her rapture at the Lord's return. As coming to fill the place of
the ascended Christ, the Holy Spirit has been rightly called
the Vicar of Jesus Christ. His oversight extends to the slightest
detail in the ordering of God's house, holding all in subjection
to the will of the Head, and directing all in harmony with the
divine plan. How clearly this comes out in the passage in 1
Corinthians 12. As in striking a series of concentric circles
there is always one fixed center holding each circumference in
defined relation to itself, so here we see all the "diversities of
administrations" determined by the one Administrator, the
Holy Ghost.

Whether this authority of the one ruling, sovereign Holy
Spirit is acknowledged or ignored determines whether the
church shall be an anarchy or a unity, a synagogue of lawless

ones or the temple of the living God. Would one desire to find a clue to the great apostasy whose dark eclipse now covers two-thirds of nominal Christendom, here it is — the rule and authority of the Holy Spirit ignored in the church, the servants of the house assuming mastery and then encroaching more and more on the prerogatives of the Head till at last one man sets himself up as the "Vicar of Jesus Christ." There is but one "Holy See" upon earth, i.e., the seat of the Holy One in the church, which only the Spirit of God can occupy without the most daring blasphemy (see 2 Cor. 3:16-18, Weymouth).

Besides the general statement of the administration of the Holy Spirit, let us note the particular acts and offices in which this authority is exercised.

(1) The Holy Spirit has supervision over the government of the church (Acts 20:28; Eph. 4:8-12, ASV).

It is clearly taught that in the early history of the church, bishops or pastors were governed by the Spirit of God and not by the suffrages of the people. The office and its incumbent were alike by divine appointment. The ascent of the Lord and the descent of the Spirit are here exhibited in their necessary relation. In the one event, Christ took His seat in heaven as "Head over all things to the church"; in the other, the Holy Ghost came down to "build up the body of Christ." Of course, it is the Head who directs the construction of the body, as being "fitly framed together, it groweth into an holy temple in the Lord." And it is the Holy Spirit who superintends the construction, since we are builded together for "an habitation of God in the Spirit." Therefore, all the offices through which this work is to be carried on were appointed by Christ, and instituted through the Spirit whom He sent down.

(2) It is the prerogative of the Holy Spirit to direct the worship and service of the church in every phase. Notice the various parts of the service and their relation to the divine Administrator.

(a) Preaching gets its inspiration, effectuality, and authority from the Holy Spirit (Acts 10:44; 1 Cor. 2:1-5; 1 Thess. 1:5, 6; 1 Peter 1:12).

(b) Prayer is dependent for its acceptableness and achievement upon the power and guidance of the Holy Spirit (Rom. 8:26, 27; Eph. 2:18; 6:18; see also Matt.

18:19).

(c) The service of song should be in the Spirit's fullness and power (1 Cor. 14:15; Eph. 5:18, 19; Col. 3:16; Heb. 13:15).

(d) He is the Spirit of Missions, i.e., the Superintendent and Energizer thereof (Acts 1:8; 16:7). In the simple story of primitive missions in Acts, we see how every step in the enterprise was originated and directed by the presiding Spirit: in the selection of missionaries (Acts 13:2); in sending them out into the fields (13:4); in empowering them to speak (13:9); in sustaining them under persecution (13:50-52); in setting the divine seal upon their ministry among the Gentiles (15:8); in counseling them concerning difficult questions of missionary policy (15:28); in restraining them from entering into fields not yet appointed by the Lord (16:6, 7).

f. He completes the church, the body of Christ, by calling out a people for the name of Christ (Acts 15:14-18). The church, "which is His body," began its history and development at Pentecost. An *ekklesia*, an outgathering, was to be made to constitute the mystical body of Christ, incorporated into Him, the Head, and indwelt by Him through the Holy Ghost.

The church is formed from within — Christ, present by the Holy Spirit, regenerating men by the sovereign action of the Spirit and organizing them into Himself, is the divine center. The Head and the body are therefore one and predestined to the same history of humiliation and glory. And as they are one in fact, so are they one in name. He whom God anointed and filled with the Holy Ghost is called "the Christ," and the church which is His body and fullness is also called "the Christ" (1 Cor. 12:12). Christ is thus both in heaven and on earth: as He is called "the Head of the church," He is in heaven; but in respect to His body, which is called "Christ," He is on earth.

As soon as the Holy Ghost was sent down from heaven, this great work of embodying began and is to continue until the number of the elect shall be gathered and the body be completed (Acts 2:41; 5:14; 11:24; 1 Cor. 12:13; Eph. 4:11-16; 5:30; Col. 1:18; 2:19).

2. In relation to the world. The Spirit strives with men as a Spirit of conviction, of reasoning, moving them in patience to the way of

God. This is the first aspect of the ministry of the Spirit among men. He came not merely to reveal "the things of Christ" to the church, but to convict the world of sin, of righteousness, and of judgment.

In the Authorized Version the word *convict* is rendered "reprove." It is a word the inner thought of which is not revealed by the translation "convict." Bishop Westcott, in his exposition of the Gospel of John, says that this word has in it four shades of meaning: first, an authoritative examination of the facts; second, unquestionable proof; third, decisive judgment; and last, punitive power.

The mission of the Holy Spirit with men is to reveal to them the truth on these subjects in such a way that they will be convinced that it is the truth. Concerning sin, men seek to excuse themselves and try to evade the facts; but when the Spirit deals with a man about sin, he cannot escape; and under His illumination man has the same clear vision of righteousness and judgment. It is clear that these three words cover the past, the present, and the future of the outlook of man as a sinner — the history of past sin, the present demand for righteousness, and the fear of future judgment. The Spirit takes these three cardinal facts, and places them in their true light, so that men may make no mistake concerning them. The Master declared the testimony the Spirit would bear on these subjects: "Of sin, because they believe not on Me; of righteousness, because I go to the Father, and ye behold Me no more; of judgment, because the prince of this world hath been judged" (John 16:9-11). That is the threefold revelation which the Spirit is giving to the world today, and it demands a closer examination.

Three persons are spoken of: Man, Christ, and Satan — man in the realm of sin, Christ in the realm of righteousness, Satan in the realm of judgment. Observe next the interrelation of these three: Man in his relationship to himself, to Christ, and to Satan; Christ in His relationship to Himself, to man, and to Satan; Satan in his relationship to himself, to man, and to Christ.

a. Man in his relationship to the three. Man's relationship to himself is that of a sinner having lost his life, whose sin ceases and is put away when he believes in Jesus. Man's relationship to Christ is that of a sinner for whom He has procured salvation, and through whose triumph of righteousness man may himself do righteously. Man's relationship to Satan is that of a slave under the prince of this world, but from whose power he is set free, for this prince has been defeated.

b. Christ in His relationship to the three. Christ's relationship to Himself is that of righteousness, for He declared His personal triumph when He said, "I go to the Father" (John 16:17). His relationship to man is that of a Savior, and therefore man's sin consists in refusal to believe on Him. Christ's relationship to Satan is that of Conqueror, for "the prince of this world hath been judged" (John 16:11).

c. Satan in his relation to the three. Satan, concerning himself, is conquered — "hath been judged" — and is powerless; concerning man, is conquered — "hath been judged" — and therefore can no longer claim man's service; concerning Christ, is conquered — "hath been judged" — and therefore even he must own Him King. There is no other outlook for evil than that of conquest.

Once again; "He, when He is come, will convict the world in respect of sin . . . because they believe not on me" (John 16:8, 9). With the coming of the Spirit upon all flesh, sin had a new center. Henceforth sin consists in the refusal to accept the divine provision of healing and power. No longer is the root-sin that of impurity, or drunkenness, or lust, or pride, or even law-breaking; the root-sin is the refusal to believe on Jesus. If men will believe on Him, in that relationship to Christ which springs from belief, there is to be found healing for wounds, and strength which issues in victory. The Spirit declares that the sin lies not in the fact of passion, but in the refusal to let the Master master the passion.

The Spirit has also come to reveal the truth about righteousness. If the revelation of sin be that of a new center, the revelation of righteousness is consequently that of a new possibility. "Of righteousness, because I go to the Father" (John 16:10). In the height of that glory, which mortal eyes may by no means look upon, is God's perfect Man, the One who said, "I go to the Father." Not simply by virtue of His own righteousness did He go, but bearing into the presence of the Father the marks of the death on the cross, by which He liberated His life, that it might become the force of renewal for man. The Spirit comes to bring to men the gospel of a new possibility of righteousness.

Lastly, the Spirit's revelation of judgment is concerned with a new exercise thereof. A common mistake, in quoting this passage, is that of adding the words "to come" after judgment." The confusion of thought which this reveals is obvious; for the judgment here referred to is not that which is to come, but that already accomplished. The Judgment Day is not to be of twenty-four hours, but of long duration, an age in itself, of which the closing event will be the final assize before the Great White Throne. That stupendous transaction will simply be the unfolding of the facts which are present today, because the prince of this world has been judged. Righteousness has had its conflict with evil and has won the fight. The head of the enemy of the race has been bruised, even though the heel of the Victor was wounded in the process. "The prince of this world hath been judged"; and the things that must pass and perish are evil things and unrighteous things, while the things that cannot be shaken and that will remain are righteous things, pure things, and beautiful things, yea all the things of God. Judgment is fixed, doom is marked, destiny is sealed, by the Cross of Jesus Christ.

If men fling in their lot with the things which are doomed and judged, then they must share the doom and judgment which have been passed upon them by the cross of Calvary; but if they turn their backs upon doomed things and lift their eyes toward the things that abide, the heavenly things where Christ is — the upper things, the conquering things — then for them judgment was borne upon the cross, and they have entered into justification-life. Thus the ministry of the Spirit in the world today is that of revealing the truth concerning sin, righteousness, and judgment.

3. In relation to the believer. As this topic has been virtually covered in considering the work of the Holy Spirit in relation to the church, we give only a brief summary here. The Holy Spirit —

   a. Makes anew, quickens, or regenerates the believer (John 3:3-5; 2 Cor. 3:6; Titus 3:5);

   b. Takes up His abode in the body of every regenerate believer; it becomes His temple (Rom. 8:9; 1 Cor. 3:16; 6:19);

   c. Seals the believer unto the day of redemption (Eph. 1:13, 14; 4:30);

   d. Infills the believer (Acts 2:4; Eph. 5:18);

   e. Provisionally emancipates the believer from a life of bondage in sin to a life of freedom in righteousness (Rom. 8:2, 12, 13; Gal. 5:17, 22, 23);

f. Guides the believer in his walk of life and sphere of service (Acts 8:27-29; 13:2-4; 16:6, 7; Rom. 8:14; Gal. 5:16, 25);

g. Anoints the believer, giving him spiritual discernment in the understanding of the Word of God and imparting spiritual power to do the work of God (John 14:26; 16:13; cf. 1 John 2:20-27 with 1 Cor. 2:9-14; cf. Luke 4:18 with Acts 10:38).

Study Questions on Pneumatology

1. What difficulty does the doctrine of the personality of the Holy Spirit introduce?
2. Discuss the false assumption that God cannot at one and the same time be a person and infinite.
3. In building up a conception of the divine personality from the suggestion given in man, what must be remembered?
4. Discuss the Socinian teaching concerning the Holy Spirit.
5. What was the effect of the Socinian conception of the Holy Spirit upon the church?
6. What designations proper only to personality are given to the Holy Spirit? Give references.
7. Give the personal connections in which the name of the Holy Spirit is mentioned which imply personality, and quote one passage with one of them.
8. Mention some of the acts performed by the Holy Spirit proving personality, and quote one passage with one of them.
9. Give some of the ways in which the Holy Spirit is affected as a person by the acts of others, and quote one passage with one of them.
10. Give proofs showing that the ascription to the Holy Spirit of a personal subsistence, distinct from that of the Father and the Son, cannot be explained as personification.
11. What was the Arian teaching concerning the Holy Spirit, and how did it differ from the Socinian?
12. Quote one passage in which the Holy Spirit is spoken of as God.
13. Provide references in discussing the divine attributes ascribed to the Holy Spirit.
14. Give the divine works ascribed to the Holy Spirit, with refer-

ences.

15. Give three instances in which the name of the Holy Spirit is coupled in equality with that of God and of Christ.
16. What proof does Christian experience offer concerning the Holy Spirit?
17. In taking up the work of the Holy Spirit, what popular misconception needs to be removed?
18. What do the Scriptures teach concerning the distinctive part taken in the works of Gód by each person of the Trinity?
19. What perhaps is the explanation of the neglect of thought concerning the Holy Spirit's relation to creation?
20. What may be said concerning the origin and preservation of everything in nature?
21. In general what is the special work of the Holy Spirit in creation?
22. What aspect of this work is designated in Genesis 1:2?
23. Give the second aspect of the Holy Spirit's relation to creation, and quote one passage proving it.
24. What is the third aspect of the Holy Spirit's work in relation to nature? Quote one passage proving it.
25. Describe the work of the Spirit in relation to animal and vegetable life or the cosmos which He has produced.
26. What part of man was produced by the inbreathing of God, and what threefold relationship was he thus fitted to enter?
27. Give the sevenfold work of the Holy Spirit as the author of the Scriptures.
28. Quote one passage which shows the Holy Spirit to be the interpreter of the Scriptures.
29. What was man's relation to the Spirit prior to the Fall, and what was the effect of the Fall upon this relation?
30. What were the characteristics of the Spirit's ministry after the Fall?
31. How is the difference of the work of the Holy Spirit in the Old Testament and New Testament dispensations commonly expressed, and why will it not always hold true?
32. What perhaps is the best point of approach to the subject of the difference of the work of the Spirit in the two dispensations?
33. What other distinction should be made with reference to the Spirit's work in the two dispensations?
34. Give a fourfold classification of the work of the Holy Spirit in the Old Testament dispensation, with a scriptural illustration of each.

35. Give the various phases of the Holy Spirit's work during the messianic period, and quote one passage with one of them.
36. What was the first aspect of the Holy Spirit's work in relation to the church?
37. By the creation of the church what was given to the world, and how is its threefold function fulfilled?
38. Discuss the purposes of the Holy Spirit's gifts to the church. Quote one passage as an illustration.
39. How is the typical anointing of Aaron fulfilled in Christ for us?
40. How is the importance of the anointing shown in the Old Testament?
41. Since the day of Pentecost, what new position does the Holy Spirit occupy in relation to the church, and by what name has He been rightly called?
42. What does the recognition of the Holy Spirit's authority or the lack of such recognition determine?
43. What is the Holy Spirit's administrative work in relation to the government of the church? Quote one passage showing it.
44. Give the fourfold work of the Holy Spirit in relation to the worship and service of the church. Quote one passage with each.
45. Show how every step of the missionary enterprise in the early church was originated and directed by the presiding Spirit.
46. What has the Holy Spirit to do with the formation of the church?
47. Give the gist of the work of the Holy Spirit in relation to the world.
48. Give a summary of the work of the Holy Spirit in relation to the believer, quoting one passage of Scripture with one phase of this work.

Notes

[1]In the beginning of the third century of ths Christian era, Paul of Samosata advanced a theory denying the deity of Christ and regarding the Holy Spirit as an influence, as an exertion of a divine energy and power. He attempted finally to explain the terms of the New Testament and of Scripture; and in his attempt to say the last definite, formulated word, he found he must cut away certain supernatural mysteries that surrounded the doctrine of God as contained in revelation; and declared that there was no Trinity, that Jesus was not divine, and that the Spirit was simply the influence moving out from God, the energy of God exerted upon men. About the time of the Reformation, two men — Laelius Socinus and his nephew Faustus Socinus — revived the theory, and many accepted it. These facts in the history of the church are mentioned in order that it may be understood whence came the teaching, the influence of which was like leaven, spreading far more widely through the church than the circle of those who actually called themselves Socinians. This circle of people had a well-defined doctrine to teach. The great mass of Christians refused to accept the doctrine, but nevertheless they passed unconsciously under its chilling influence, and unknowingly, almost the whole church came to think of the Spirit of God as an influence, if not to speak of Him as such.

[2]In the passage in Corinthians after mention of the gifts of the Spirit is made, such as wisdom, knowledge, faith, healings, miracles, prophecy, discerning of spirits, tongues, interpretation of tongues, they all are traced to the Spirit who bestows them. Here is not only giving but giving discreetly in the exercise of an independent will such as belongs only to a person. The passage in Romans 10:26 must be interpreted, if the Holy Spirit is not a person distinct from the Father, as meaning that the Holy Spirit intercedes with Himself.

[3]Another heresy arose in the church in the fourth century. Arius, a presbyter of Alexandria, taught that God is one eternal person; that He created a Being infinitely superior to the angels, His only begotten Son; that this only begotten Son of God did in His turn exercise His supernatural power by the creation of a third person, that third person being the Holy Spirit. The difference between Socinianism and Arianism lies in the recognition by the latter of the personality of the Spirit while denying His proper deity. According to Arius, the Holy Spirit is a person, a created person; and if created, then not Creator; and if not Creator then not divine. The Nicene Creed was drawn up and adopted as a corrective to this error of Arianism, which had obtained a firm hold in the early church.

[4]H. A. Meyer, *Critical and Exegetical Handbook to the Epistles to the Corinthians*, tr. Douglas Bennerman (Edinburgh: T. & T. Clark, 1877), I, 360.

[5]A marvelous declaration of the fact of the presence of God in all nature is to be found also in the great theophany of the Book of Job (see Chapters 38-41).

[6]Take the passage in Job 26:13: "By His Spirit the heavens are garnished; His hand hath pierced the swift serpent." The meaning of the passage is obscure, but light is thrown on it by the context, v. 12, "He stirreth up the sea with His power, and by His understanding He smiteth through Rahab." It is a picture of the bringing back of the blue and the light of the heavens after the sweeping of the storm, the beauty of the stars of light replacing the gloom of the black chaotic clouds of darkness, and this is done, we are told, by the Spirit of God.

[7]Scofield insightfully argues: "In the Old Testament, the Spirit of God is revealed as a Divine person. As such He is associated in the work of creation, strives with sinful man (Gen. 6:3); and enlightens the spirit of man (Gen. 1:2; Job 26:13; 27:3; 32:8; 33:4; Ps. 104:30 Prov. 20:27); gives skill to the hand (Exod. 31:2-5); bestows physical strength (Judg. 14:6); and qualifies the servants of God for a varied ministry (Exod. 28:3; 35:21, 31; Num. 11:25-29; 1 Sam. 16-17; 2 Sam. 23:2). To this should be added that operation of the Spirit by which the men of faith in the Old Testament ages were regenerated. While this doctrine is not explicitly taught in the Old Testament (except prophetically), our Lord's words in John 3:5 and Luke 13:28 leave no doubt as to the fact itself. Since the new birth is essential to seeing and entering the kingdom of God, and since the Old Testament saints are in that kingdom, it follows necessarily that they were born of the Spirit. The redemptive ministry of the Holy Spirit in the Old Testament period is not extensively revealed. Certain basic facts may be discerned: (1) there is evidence of a ministry of conviction (Gen. 6:3; Isa. 63:10); (2) the ministry of the Spirit toward the redeemed remnant of Israel seems to be necessitated by Romans 2:29 and

Deuteronomy 10:16; (3) the ministry of the Spirit toward the redeemed remnant is the only valid explanation of moral obedience and spiritual illumination (Ps. 119:97-99, 86-88); (4) the ministry of the Spirit is only temporary and provisional since it is bound by the provisions of the Old Covenant (Jer. 31:31, 32; Ezek. 36:24-27)." From C. I. Scofield, *Plain Papers on the Doctrine of the Holy Spirit* (Westwood, N.J.: Fleming H. Revell, 1899), p. 30.

[8]Another outline of the Holy Spirit's work in the Old Testament is as follows: (1) His action upon the heart of individuals in saving grace. For example, Abel, Enoch, Noah, Abraham, Moses, Samuel, David; (2) His action upon prophets, priests, and kings — a wholly external operation to qualify them for office (Lev. 8:10); (3) His action upon divinely appointed workmen in conferring gifts and talents for the service of the people (Exod. 31:2, 3, 6; Isa. 45:1; Zech. 4:6).

[9]As the Spirit bore a close relationship to Jesus as a perfect and unfallen man, so also did He in His office and position as the Messiah.

CHAPTER SIX

ANTHROPOLOGY: THE DOCTRINE OF MAN

THE ORIGIN OF MAN

Negatively

Not by Abiogenesis, or Spontaneous Generation. The scriptural doctrine of the origin of man is opposed to that held by many of the ancients, that man is a spontaneous production of the earth. The earth was assumed to be pregnant with the germs of all living organisms, which were quickened under favorable circumstances; or it was regarded as instinct with a productive life, to which is to be referred the origin of all the plants and animals living on its surface.[1]

Scripture is also opposed to the more modern view of abiogenesis, i.e., that life is the product of physical causes, that all that is requisite for its production is to bring together the necessary conditions.

Not by Evolution, or Natural Development. Evolution is a philosophical and speculative theory of recent origin which seeks to account for the various elements and compounds of the inorganic world (cosmic evolution), and also for the countless species in the organic world (organic evolution). By the "inorganic world" is meant the elements and compounds as minerals and gases which are without life; and by the "organic world" is meant organisms (plants and animals) which have life.

Although sometimes spoken of as a scientific theory, evolution is not scientific; for science has to do only with facts. Evolution belongs wholly in the realm of speculative philosophy. The basic assumption

183

of this theory is that all things in nature — living and not-living — have a common origin; and that all the diverse elements, compounds, and organisms were developed by the cumulative effect of changes in themselves imperceptibly small, all of which changes were brought about by the energy of "forces resident in nature."

The theory assumes the existence of matter and force, without attempting to account for the origin of either. Matter is supposed to have existed originally in a perfectly simple and undifferentiated condition. Its form is supposed to have been that of an exceedingly tenuous highly heated mist or vapor, filling all space. Force is also assumed to have been exceedingly simple at the first, being nothing more than a tendency on the part of the entire mass of undifferentiated matter to keep in motion. As to where matter and force, and the tremendous uniform heat, necessary to keep matter in a gaseous state came from, the theory is silent.

As we trace in imagination the supposed course of evolution from its assumed beginning in undifferentiated matter, onward and upward, to the infinite diversities of the organic kingdom, we not only encounter difficulties at every step and in connection with every detail, but we also find certain gaps deep and wide for which evolutionists themselves can offer no definite explanation.

1. The first and greatest gap which confronts the evolutionist is that between the living and the not-living. The entire world of living creatures is assumed to have emerged, sometime and somehow, through "resident forces," out of the inorganic realm. Yet no trace of this marvelous process remains, and the inorganic world exhibits no progressiveness at all, no power or disposition to advance one's hair breadth.

2. The next gap is that between the vegetable and animal kingdoms. If the latter, in its entirety, arose out of the former through gradual and infinitesimal changes, no trace of that marvelous development remains; nor can there be found in the vegetable kingdom anything from which the characteristic features of animal life could have evolved.

3. Next we encounter the great gap between the vertebrates and the invertebrates; then that between the mammals and other vertebrates; then the gaps between each of the million or so distinct species of organisms and every other; and finally the immense gap between man and the highest of the brutes.

In considering these great gaps, and the many lesser ones, it should be borne in mind that evolution is set forth expressly as a theory of origins, that is to say, as an explanation of how all the infinite varieties of things, living and not-living, came into existence. But origins, including those of the very broadest kind, are just what the theory conspicuously fails to explain. The evolutionist makes no pretense that his theory can explain the origin of either matter or force. The existence of these he must take for granted, attributing them to an unknowable First Cause.

Positively

The Scriptures clearly and distinctly teach that the origin of man lies in the special, immediate, creative, and formative acts of God (Gen. 1:27; 2:7).[2]

THE UNITY OF THE HUMAN RACE

There is still another question which science has forced on theology, in relation to man, which cannot be overlooked. Has all mankind had a common origin? Have all men a common nature? Are they all descended from one pair, and do they constitute one species? These questions are answered affirmatively in the Bible. The scriptural doctrine concerning man is that the race is not only the same in kind, but the same in origin (Gen. 2:7; 5; 10; Acts 17:26).[3]

Arguments from Scripture

The Scriptures teach that the whole human race is descended from a single pair (Gen. 1:27, 28; 2:7, 22; 3:20; 9:19).

1. This truth is the basis of Paul's doctrine of the organic unity of mankind in the first transgression and of the provision for salvation for the race in Christ (Rom. 5:12, 19; 1 Cor. 15:21, 22; Heb. 2:16).

2. This truth also constitutes the ground of man's obligation of natural brotherhood to every member of the race (Acts 17:26, ASV; Heb. 2:11).

Extrascriptural Arguments

The teaching of Scripture is reenforced by history and science in the following particulars:

Argument from history. So far as the history of nations and tribes in both hemispheres is concerned, it points to a common origin in Central Asia. The European nations are acknowledged to have come in successive waves of emigration from Asia. Modern ethnologists practically agree in saying that the American Indians came from Eastern Asia, perhaps by way of the Aleutian Islands.

Argument from language. Comparative philology points to a

common origin of all the more important languages, and there is no evidence that the less important are not also so derived.

Argument from psychology. The existence among all families of mankind of common mental and moral characteristics is most easily explained in the theory of a common origin. It is probable that certain myths common to many nations were handed down from a time when the families of earth had not yet separated. Among these are the accounts of the making of the world and man, a primeval garden, innocence, a serpent, a tree of knowledge, a temptation and fall, a flood, and sacrifice.

Argument from physiology. All races are fruitful one with another. The normal temperature of the body is the same. The mean frequency of the pulse is the same. There is liability to most of the same diseases. These facts are not true of other animals; and again, human blood can be distinguished by the microscope from that of any other animal.

THE ESSENTIAL ELEMENTS OF MAN

The Scriptures clearly and distinctly teach that man as constituted by creation has a material nature and an immaterial nature. The immaterial nature consists of his soul and spirit.

Proofs of the Immaterial Nature

1. The record of man's creation (Gen. 2:7).

2. Passages in which the human soul or spirit is distinguished, on the one hand from the divine spirit, on the other from the body which it inhabits (Gen. 35:18; Num. 16:22; 1 Kings 17:21; Eccl. 12:7; 1 Cor. 2:11; Heb. 12:9; James 2:26).

3. The mention of the body and soul (or spirit) as together constituting the whole man (Matt. 10:28; 1 Cor. 5:5; 3 John 2).

The detailed account of the creation of man is a subject of the deepest interest, since it forms the only possible basis of true doctrine in regard to the origin and nature of our race. We must, therefore, carefully examine it, but the labor will not be tedious because the whole revelation is contained in the following brief record: "And the Lord God formed man of the dust of the ground, and breathed into his nostrils the breath of life; and man became a living soul" (Gen. 2:7). We have thus three points to consider: the formation of the body, the infusion of the breath of life, and the result that man awoke to consciousness a living soul.

First, then, we are told that the Lord God formed man, that is, molded his bodily shape as the potter does the clay. Indeed, the meaning of the Hebrew verb is so decided that its present participle, used as a substantive, is the ordinary word for a potter. To this first act of God Job refers when he says, "Remember, I beseech Thee, that Thou has made me as the clay; and wilt Thou bring me into dust again?" (Job 10:9); for the material molded was the dust of the ground which had just been moistened by a mist; and hence it is afterward said, "Dust thou are, and unto dust shalt thou return" (Gen. 3:19). The word translated "ground" is *adamah*, which properly means red earth, and from which the name *Adam* seems to be derived. This corresponds to the natural color of Caucasian skin, which is red on white, and in accordance with which Soloman's description of ideal beauty begins with the words, "My beloved is white and ruddy" (S. of Sol. 5:10).

The spirit of man had nothing to do with the formation of its sheath. God first molded the senseless frame, and then breathed into it "the breath of lives." The original of the last word is in the plural. We have not, however, previously noticed this, because it may be nothing more than the well-known Hebrew plural of excellence: the word, which is the common term for life, is rarely found in the singular. But if we wish to give significance to the number, it may refer to the fact that the inbreathing of God produced a twofold life, sensual and spiritual, the distinct existence of each part of which we may often detect within ourselves by their antagonism.

This breath of lives became the spirit of man, the principle of life within him — for as the Lord tells us, "It is the spirit that quickeneth" — and by the manner of its introduction we are taught that it was a direct impartation from the Creator. We must, of course, carefully avoid confusing it with the Spirit of God, from whom the Scriptures plainly distinguish it, and who is represented as bearing witness with our spirit (Rom. 8:16). But as we are told in Proverbs 20:27, it is the candle of the Lord, capable of being lighted by His Spirit, and given by Him as a means whereby man may search into the chambers of his heart and know himself.

Man was thus made up of only two independent elements, the corporeal and the spiritual: but when God placed the spirit within the casing of earth, the combination of these produced a third part, and man became a living soul. Direct communication between spirit and flesh is impossible: their intercourse can be carried on only by means of a medium, and the instant production of one was the result of their contact in Adam. He became a living soul in the sense that spirit and body were completely merged in this third part; so that in his unfallen state he knew nothing of those ceaseless strivings of spirit and flesh which are matters of daily experience to us. There was a perfect blending of his three aspects into one, and the soul as the uniting member became the cause of his individuality, of his existence as a distinct being. It was also to serve the spirit as a covering, and as a means of using the body; nor does Tertullian seem to have erred when he affirmed that the flesh is the body of the soul, the soul that of the spirit.

But it is interesting to note that, while the soul is the meeting-point of the elements of our being in this present life, the spirit will be the ruling power in our resurrection state. For the first Adam was made a living soul, but the Last Adam a quickening Spirit (1 Cor. 15:45); and that which is sown a psychic body is raised a spiritual body (1 Cor. 15:44).

Thus in the very beginning of Scripture we are warned against the popular phraseology of "soul and body," which has long sustained the erroneous belief that man consists of but two parts. There are one or two passages in which a reference to the threefold composition of our being cannot be denied or refuted. Such is the very remarkable verse in the Epistle to the Hebrews — "For the Word of God is quick, and powerful, and sharper than any two-edged sword, piercing even to the dividing asunder of soul and spirit, and of the joints and marrow, and is a discerner of the thoughts and intents of the heart" (Heb. 4:12). Here the writer plainly speaks of the immaterial part of man as consisting of two separable elements, soul and spirit, while he describes the material portions as made up of joints and marrow, organs of motions and sensation. Hence, he claims for the Word of God the power of separating and, as it were, taking to pieces the whole being of man — spiritual, psychic, and corporeal — even as the priest flayed and divided limb from limb the animal for the burnt offering, in order to lay bare every part and discover if there were any hidden spot or blemish.

Another obvious passage is the well-known intercession of Paul for the Thessalonians: "And I pray God your whole spirit and soul and body be preserved blameless unto the coming of our Lord Jesus Christ". (1 Thess. 5:23). The body we may call the sense-consciousness; the soul, the self-consciousness; and the spirit, the

God-consciousness. For the body gives us the use of five senses; the soul compromises the intellect which aids us in the present state of existence, and the emotions which proceed from the senses; while the spirit is our noblest part, which came directly from God, and by which alone we are able to apprehend and worship Him.

This last, as we remarked above, can act upon the body only through the medium of the soul, and we have a good illustration of the fact in the words of Mary: "My soul doth magnify the Lord, and my spirit hath rejoiced in God my Saviour" (Luke 1:46, 47). Here the change in tense shows that the spirit first conceived joy in God, and then, communicating with the soul, roused it to give expression to the feeling by means of the bodily organs.

Origin of the Soul Since the Original Creation

Three theories with regard to this subject have been held, the last of which we deem to be in harmony with the teaching of Scripture.

Theory of Preexistence. This theory was adopted in ancient times to explain the soul's possession of ideas not derived from sense, to account for its imprisonment in the body, and to justify the disparity of conditions in which men enter the world. It has been advocated by later theologians upon the ground that the inborn depravity of the human will can be explained only by supposing a personal act of self-determination in a previous, or timeless, state of being. Objections to the theory of preexistence:

1. If the soul in this preexistent state was conscious and personal, it is inexplicable that we should have no remembrance of such preexistence.[4]

2. While this theory accounts for inborn spiritual sin such as pride and enmity to God, it gives no explanation of inherited sensual sin, which it holds to have come from Adam, and the guilt of which must logically be denied.

Creation Theory. It regards the soul of each human being as immediately created by God and joined to the body either at conception, at birth, or at some time between these two. The advocates of the theory urge in its favor certain texts of Scripture that refer to God as the Creator of the human soul or spirit as well as the fact that there is a marked individuality in the child, which cannot be explained as a mere reproduction of the qualities existing in the parents. Objections to the creation theory:

1. The passages given in its support may with equal propriety be regarded as expressing God's mediate agency in the origination of human souls. It would seem that the general tenor of Scripture, as well as its representations of God as the author of man's body, favor this latter interpretation. Passages commonly relied upon by creationists are the following: Ecclesiates 12:7; Isaiah 57:16; Zechariah 12:1; Hebrews 12:9.

2. Creationism regards the earthly father as begetting only the body of his child — certainly as not the father of the child's highest part. This makes the beast to possess nobler powers of propagation than man, for the beast multiplies himself after his own image.

3. The individuality of the child, even in the most extreme cases — as in the sudden rise in obscure families and surroundings of marked men like Luther — may be better explained by supposing a law of variation impressed upon the species at its beginning, a law whose operation is foreseen and supervised by God.

4. This theory, if it allows that the soul is originally possessed of depraved tendencies, makes God the direct author of moral evil; if it holds the soul to have been created pure, it makes God indirectly the author of moral evil by teaching that He puts this pure soul into a body which will inevitably corrupt it.

Traducian Theory. This view was propounded by Tertullian and was implicitly held by Augustine. It holds that the human race was immediately created in Adam and, as respects both body and soul, was propagated from him by natural generation. All souls since Adam are only mediately created by God, as the upholder of the laws of propagation which were originally established by Him. Arguments in favor of the traducian theory:

1. It seems best to accord with Scripture, which represents God as creating the species in Adam (Gen. 1:27) and as increasing and perpetuating it through secondary agencies (1:28; cf. 22). The breath of life is breathed into man's nostrils only once (2:7, 22; 4:1; 5:3; 46:26; Acts 17:21-26; 1 Cor. 11:8; Heb. 7:10), and after forming man, God ceases from His work of creation (Gen. 2:2).

2. It is favored by the analogy of vegetable and animal life in which increase of numbers is secured, not by multiplicity of immediate creations, but by the natural derivation of new individuals from a parent stock. A derivation of the human soul from its parents no more implies a materialistic view of the soul than the similar derivation of the brute proves the principle of intelligence in the

lower animals to be wholly material.

3. The observed transmission not merely of physical, but also of mental and spiritual characteristics in families and races, and especially the uniformly evil moral tendencies and dispositions which all men possess from their births, are proof that in soul, as well as in body, we derive our being from our human ancestry.

4. The traducian doctrine embraces and acknowledges the element of truth which gives plausibility to the creation view. Traducianism, properly defined, admits a divine concurrence throughout the whole development of the human species and allows, under the guidance of a superintending Providence, special improvements in type at the birth of marked man, similar to those which we may suppose to have occurred in the introduction of new varieties in the animal creation.

THE ORIGINAL STATE OF MAN

God's Image in Man

Man was made in the image of God. We should avoid a twofold danger in the interpretation of Scripture and not put man up so high that he could make no progress, nor on the other hand put him down so low that he could not fall. The image of God in which man was created consisted in a natural and a moral likeness to God.

1. Personality, or natural likeness to God. By personality is meant that twofold power to know self as related to the world and God and to determine self in view of moral ends. This distinguishes man from the brutes. The brute is conscious, but not self-conscious. This natural likeness to God is inalienable. It constitutes the capacity for redemption and gives value even to the life of the unregenerate.

Man cannot lose this element of the divine image without ceasing to be man. Insanity can only obscure it. Bernard said that it could not be burned out even in hell. The lost piece of money (Luke 15:8) still bore the image and superscription of the king, even though it did not know it and did not know that it was lost. Human nature is, therefore, to be reverenced (Ps. 8:5). He who destroyed human life was to be put to death (Gen. 9:6). Even men whom we curse are made after the likeness of God (James 3:9).

The word *image* does not imply perfect representation in man. Christ is the image of God absolutely. Man is the image of God relatively and derivatively. Since God is Spirit, man made in His image cannot be merely a material thing.

2. Holiness, or moral likeness to God. Since holiness is the fundamental attribute of God, it must of necessity be the chief attribute of His image in the moral beings whom He creates. Scripture teaches that original righteousness was essential to this image (Eccl. 7:29: Eph. 4:24; Col. 3:10). This involved the possession of right moral tendencies, such a direction of the will and affections as constitutes God the supreme end of man's being. It is not enough to say that man was created in a state of innocence. Scripture declares that he had a holiness like God's. Holiness has two sides or phases. It is knowledge and perception as well as inclination and feeling.

Man's Original Righteousness

This original righteousness in which man was created is to be viewed in several particulars.

1. It did not constitute the essence of human nature, for in that case human nature would have ceased to exist as soon as man sinned. A man can change his taste or love without changing the substance of his being. When sin is called a nature, it is only in the sense of being inborn. Nature is from *nascor* (to be born). It is as proper to call hereditary taste a nature as it is to identify nature with the substance of one's being.

2. It was not a gift foreign to human nature and added to it after man's creation, for man is said to have possessed the divine image by the fact of creation, not by subsequent bestowal. Adam was created with a holy nature, i.e., tendencies toward God, as all men since Adam are born with a sinful nature, i.e., tendencies away from God.

3. It is rather to be understood as a tendency of man's affections and will, accompanied by the power of evil choice and differing from the perfected holiness of the saints, as instinctive affection and childlike innocence differ from that holiness which has been developed and confirmed by temptation.

4. It was a moral disposition which could be propagated and which if lost would still leave man possessed of a natural likeness to God, making him susceptible to God's redeeming grace. "Only enough likeness to God remained to remind man of what he had lost and to feel the hell of God's forsaking." The moral likeness to God can be restored, but only by God Himself.

THE MORAL NATURE OF MAN

By the "moral nature" of man we mean those powers which fit him for right or wrong action. These powers are intellect, sensibility, and will, together with that peculiar power of discrimination and impulsion which we call conscience. In order to have moral action, man has intellect, or reason, to discern the difference between right and wrong; sensibility, to be moved by each of these; free will, to do the one or the other.

Intellect, sensibility, and will are man's three faculties. But in connection with these faculties there is a sort of activity which involves them all, and without which there can be no moral action, namely, the activity of conscience. Conscience applies the moral law as binding upon us. Only a rational and sentient being can be truly moral; yet it does not come within our province to treat of man's intellect or sensibility in general.

Conscience

As already intimated, conscience is not a separate faculty — like intellect, sensibility, and will — but rather a mode in which these faculties act. Like consciousness, conscience is an accompanying knowledge. Conscience is a knowing of self (including our acts and states) in connection with a moral standard, or law. Adding now the element of feeling, we may say that conscience is man's consciousness of his own moral relations, together with a peculiar feeling in view of them. It thus involves the combined action of the intellect and of the sensibility, and that in view of certain classes, viz., right and wrong.

1. Discriminative and impulsive. We need to define more narrowly both the intellectual and the emotional elements in conscience. As respects the intellectual element, we may say that conscience is a power of judgment. It declares our acts or states to conform, or not to conform, to law; it declares the acts or states which conform to be obligatory; those which do not conform, to be forbidden. In other words, conscience judges, "This is right (or wrong)," "I ought (or, I ought not)." In connection with this latter judgment, there comes into view the emotional element of conscience by which we feel the claim of duty; there is an inner sense that the wrong must not be done.

2. The moral judiciary of the soul. Conscience is the moral judiciary of the soul — the power within of judgment and command.

Conscience must judge according to the law given to it, and therefore, since the moral standard accepted by the reason may be imperfect, its decisions, while relatively just, may be absolutely unjust. Hence the duty of enlightening and cultivating the moral reason so that conscience may have a proper standard of judgment. The office of conscience is to "bear witness" (Rom. 2:15).

3. In its relation to God as lawgiver. Since conscience, in the proper sense, gives uniform and infallible judgment that the right is supremely obligatory, and that the wrong must be forsaken and restricted at every cost, it can be called an echo of God's voice, and an indication in man of that which his own true being requires.

Will

Will is the soul's power to choose between motives and to direct its subsequent activity according to the motive thus chosen — in other words, the soul's power to choose, both an end and the means to attain it. The choice of means we call executive volition.

1. Will and other faculties. We accept the threefold division of human faculties into intellect, sensibility, and will. Intellect is the soul knowing; sensibility is the soul feeling (desires, affections); will is the soul choosing (end or means). In every act of the soul, all the faculties act. Knowing involves feeling and willing; feeling involves knowing and willing; willing involves knowing and feeling. Logically, each latter faculty involves the preceding action of the former; the soul must know before feeling; must know and feel before willing. Yet since knowing and feeling are activities, neither of these is possible without willing.

2. Will and permanent states. Though every act of the soul involves the action of all the faculties, yet in any particular action one faculty may be more prominent than the others. So we speak of acts of intellect, of affection, of will. This predominant action of any single faculty produces effects upon the other faculties associated with it. The action of will gives a direction to the intellect and to the affections, as well as a permanent bent to the will itself. Each faculty, therefore, has its permanent states as well as its transient acts, and the will may originate these states. Hence we speak of voluntary affections and may with equal propriety speak of voluntary opinions. These permanent voluntary states we denominate *character*.

3. Will and motives. The permanent states just mentioned, when they have been once determined, also influence the will. Internal views and dispositions, and not simply external presentations, constitute the strength of motives. These motives often conflict, and though the soul never acts without motive, it does notwithstanding choose between motives and so determines the end toward which it will direct its activities. Motives are not causes which compel the will, but influences which persuade it. The power of these motives, however, is proportioned to the strength of will which has entered into them and has made them what they are.

4. Will and contrary choice. Though no act of pure will is possible, the soul may put forth single volitions in a direction opposed to its previous ruling purpose, and thus far man has the power of a contrary choice (Rom. 7:18 — "to will is present with me"). But insofar as will has entered into and revealed itself in permanent states of intellect and sensibility and in a settled bent of the will itself, man cannot by a single act reverse his moral state, and in this respect has not the power of a contrary choice. In this latter case he can change his character only indirectly by turning his attention to considerations fitted to awaken opposite dispositions, and by thus summoning up motives to an opposite course.

5. Will and responsibility. By repeated acts of will put forth in a given moral direction, the affections may become so confirmed in evil or in good as to make previously certain, though not necessary, the future good or evil action of the man. Thus, while the will is free, the man may be the "bondservant of sin" (John 8:31-36) or the "servant of righteousness" (Rom. 6:15-23; cf. Heb. 12:23 — "spirits of just men made perfect"). Man is responsible for all effects of will, as well as for will itself; for voluntary affections, as well as for voluntary acts; for the intellectual views into which will has entered, as well as for the acts of will by which these views have been formed in the past or are maintained in the present (2 Peter 3:5 — "willfully forget").

THE ENDLESS EXISTENCE OF MAN

Spirit is as truly created a being as matter and is as dependent on omnipotence for continued existence. If the soul of man is to exist forever in its career of activity, it must be because God wills to preserve it thus, for nothing in the universe save God is necessarily self-existent.[5] We cannot prove the endless existence of the soul absolutely any more than we can prove the self-existence of God. It is not one of those truths that men believe because they have proved it, but they believe it in the first place and are therefore all the time trying to prove it.

Argument From a Progressive Creation

Endless being is a necessary inference from the divine progress manifested in creation. This may be called the argument of creative climax. If man ceases to exist at death or a comparatively short time afterward, nature has reached an anticlimax in his creation. The movement toward a purposeful end is thus defeated.

Argument From Universal Belief

Whatever all men everywhere and always have believed is in accordance with the truth. All men have everywhere and always believed in the doctrine of a future, endless existence. Therefore that doctrine is in accordance with truth.

This is sometimes called the historical argument. The testimony of man's nature to endless being may be regarded as the testimony of God who made the future. It assumes the fact of such universal belief and also that the very belief contains in itself the assurance of its truthfulness. The first premise must be justified by an appeal to facts. The second will be admitted by those who recognize the hand of God in the constitution of man. These two assumptions admitted, the conclusion must follow.

Argument From Universal Desire

Every universal and instinctive longing or pre-assurance of man is destined to be satisfied. Man has such longing for endless being and such pre-assurance of it. Therefore, it is destined to be satisfied.

This may be called the argument from analogy. As there is light for the eye, air for the lungs, food for hunger, water for thirst, and society for the social instincts, so it is argued that God cannot have created this longing for endless being merely to mock and disappoint man.

Argument From Universal Moral Expectation

God will complete, in the present or the future, the work of rendering exact justice to those under His moral judgment. There are manifold promises and beginnings of this work left incomplete here. Therefore, there must be a future existence in which to complete the work of justice.

This is called the ethical argument. It is drawn from God's justice to the endless existence of the wicked, as the preceding argument was drawn from God's love to the endless existence of the righteous.

Argument From Human Capabilities

We are conscious of powers greater than our present opportunity affords employment and exercise. Man is capable of continued improvement and perhaps nearly unlimited potential. This potential must be actualized.

This may be called the argument from temporal limitations. Man is capable of indefinite and seemingly almost infinite growth and development. He beats against the bars of present limitations and longs for a wider range of activities. Endless being is a natural inference from this fact.

Argument From the Scriptures

1. Existence after death in Sheol in a conscious state is the view underlying the Old Testament. In some of the Psalms and later prophets, strong expressions of faith and hope in endless being and immortality are found (Num. 16:30; 2 Sam. 22:6; Job 14:13; 17:13, 16; 19:25; Ps. 16:10; 49:14, 15).

2. In the New Testament, the doctrine finds abundant warrant in the teachings of Jesus and in His own resurrection. The gospel rests upon the infinite worth of individual men; human personality is the supreme value for God. To redeem it was the end of Christ's mission. Only as it has endless being was it worthy of such an end.

THE FALL OF MAN

The Probation of Man

The Scriptures teach that after man's creation, God placed him in a garden in Eden and subjected him to a state of probation (Gen. 2:8-17).[6]

Probation, from a Latin word signifying "to prove" or "test," denotes a period of trial under a law of duty, being a test of obedience that is enforced by the sanctions of reward for a right choice and good conduct, and punishment for a wrong choice and evil conduct. Miley says of it, "probation is a temporary economy. The central reality is responsibility for conduct under a law of duty."[7]

The necessity of the probation. While our first parents were created with holy natures, whose fluctuating emotions and spontaneous tendencies were wholly toward the good, yet they were susceptible to temptation from without. Consequently, a period of probation was essential in order to test their loyalty to God by obedience or disobedience to His command. Thus our divine Lord was likewise susceptible to temptation from without (Heb. 2:18; 4:15).

Dr. Miley says: "With a holy nature, there were yet susceptibilities to temptation. In temptation there is an impulse in the susceptibilities adverse to the law of duty. This it true even where it finds no response in the personal consciousness. Yet, in the measure of it, such impulse is a trial to obedience. The proof of it is in a primitive constitution with susceptibilities which might be the means of temptation. . . . These facts are entirely consistent with the primitive holiness which we have maintained. In such a state primitive man began his moral life. The only way to confirmed blessedness was through a temporary obedience. But obedience requires a law of duty; and, with the natural incidence of trial and the possibility of failure, such a law must be a testing law. It thus appears that a probationary economy was the only one at all suited to the state of primitive man."[8]

The purpose of the probation. The purpose of the probation of our first parents was, so to speak, to test their virtue — to transform their *holy natures* into *holy characters*. Moral character is produced only by probation, by the free personal choice of good in the presence of evil and with full power to choose evil. Now Adam and Eve were created with *holy moral natures*. A right choice — that is, obedience to God's command — would have transformed these holy moral natures into *holy moral characters*. As it was, however, their wrong choice — that is, disobedience to the command — transformed their holy moral natures into *sinful moral characters*, and involved both themselves and their posterity in the guilt of sin and the defilement of depravity.

Some suggest that man was created "on the fence" morally with no positive inclinations one way or another. This position is contrary to Scripture, since man was originally created "upright" (Eccl. 7:29). Others suggest that man had some moral deficiency when created, but this cannot be reconciled with the statements of creation (Gen. 1:26, 31). God did not put inclinations in man which led him to sin, nor did God remove from man His sustaining power.

Man was originally created with a moral nature which was positively good, and so man could be treated as a morally responsible being. (Gen. 1:26, 27, 31; 2:17; Eccl. 7:29).

1. Man did have a holy nature by creation. This may be defined as an

inherent tendency to do good, but with power to choose evil. The inherent tendency to do good is supported by the scriptural statement that he was created "upright"; the power to choose evil is necessary, or there would be no force to the probation;

2. Man did not have a holy character by creation. Character may be defined as a tendency to do right which is acquired by moral experience, i.e., by right choices in the face of moral tests. Before the probation, man had not any moral experience and so had no opportunity to develop a holy character. Now since he had a moral nature with a tendency to do right, it would be reasonable to expect that the test would be the door to moral character. As character was developed, the power of contrary choice would become less and less until the individual was confirmed in a habitual response.

Sin originated in man's free act of revolt from God — the act of will which, although inclined toward God, was not yet confirmed in virtue and was still capable of a contrary choice. The power of contrary choice is the necessary condition for free moral development.

The test of the probation. The probationary or testing law is recorded in Genesis 2:16, 17: "Of every tree of the garden thou mayest freely eat; but of the tree of the knowledge of good and evil, thou shalt not eat of it: for in the day that thou eatest thereof thou shalt surely die."

In character this probationary or testing law was positive, not moral. The difference is that while the obligation of a moral law is intrinsic and absolute, the obligation of a positive law arises from a divine commandment. In other words, a moral command carries its own reason for obedience, but a positive command does not. Thus the Ten Commandments are moral in character, because we realize their necessity. For the Ten Commandments are not right because they were given of God; they were given of God because they are right.

On the other hand, God's call to Abraham to offer up Isaac (Gen. 22) was a positive command, because Abraham did not understand its reasonableness or realize its necessity. Another name for positive command is "personal command." It is of the very essence of moral probation that the testing law should be a positive or personal command, the reasonableness and necessity of which are not made known to the one who is subjected to the probation. In the case of our first parents, as we have seen, the probationary law was a positive or personal command. It was God's right to command: It was the duty of Adam and Eve to obey.

Since man was not yet in a state of confirmed holiness, but rather of simple childlike innocence, he could be made perfect only through temptation. Hence the "tree of the knowledge of good and evil" (Gen. 2:9). The one slight command best tested the spirit of obedience. Temptation did not necessitate a fall; if resisted, it would strengthen virtue. The ability not to sin would have become the inability to sin. The tree was mainly a tree of probation. It is right for a father to make his son's title to his estate depend upon the performance of some filial duty, as Thaddeus Stevens made his son's possession of property conditional upon his keeping the temperance-pledge. Whether, besides this, the tree of knowledge was naturally hurtful or poisonous, we do not know.

The reasonableness of the probation. Its reasonableness is seen —

1. In the love and wisdom of God, who could not and would not have subjected our first parents to any state of trial or probationary test which was not for their highest development and eternal welfare and therefore absolutely necessary. Therefore, the prohibition of Genesis 2:17 must have been just, wise, and good.

2. In the manifold source of delight and satisfaction which were provided for Adam and Eve by their Maker (Gen. 2:9). They had everything.

The Temptation of Man

The Scriptures clearly and distinctly teach that our first parents were tempted to sin by disobeying God's positive command. Genesis 3 gives the fullest account of that which became an awful tragedy in the experience of mankind. Other references to it are found in such passages as 2 Corinthians 11:3; 1 Timothy 2:14.

The agent in man's temptation. The natural agent in the temptation of our first parents was the serpent; the higher and supernatural agent, however, was Satan (Gen. 3:1, 4, 5; 2 Cor. 11:3; Rev. 12:9). The serpent is included among the beasts. He is described as being more subtle than any of them. The Hebrew word translated *subtle* signifies craftiness or cunning. It is likely that originally the serpent was a very beautiful creature; and he seems to have possessed the power of upright locomotion (Gen. 3:14). The devil used the serpent as an instrument in tempting Adam and Eve. Thus back of this "beast of the field" was a higher, even supernatural intelligence. God's curse upon the serpent makes this fact unmistakable (Gen. 3:14, 15).

Satan's motives. Satan and the fallen angels were probably stimulated to secure man's downfall, not only by pure malignity and the wish to oppose God whenever they could do so indirectly, but also by a desire to prolong their reign. For, knowing themselves to be rebels, they were probably well aware that the Almighty never intended sinless man to be subject to them, and that in Adam He was raising up a seed, not merely to inhabit the earth, but also to take possession of the realms of the air.

Hence we can easily understand their desire to retard, at least, the counsel of God by reducing the new creation to their own level of sin and ruin. And perchance, they may have known from experience that the result would be a delay of long ages during which the mercy of the Supreme Being would grant His creatures time for repentance and recovery.

1. As to the reasons for Satan's subtle assault upon Eve, we may say that —

    a. He would not make his assault with power and terror, for that would drive the assailed into the arms of their Protector instead of drawing them away from Him.

    b. He would present himself in the form of an inferior and subject animal from which they would never suspect harm.

    c. He would not approach the man and the woman together, for combined they might uphold one another in the obedience and love of God. And he well knew that if he were once detected and baffled, a second attempt would be attended with far more difficulties — nay, might by some appeal of Adam to God be rendered altogether impracticable.

2. As to Satan's reason for not tempting Adam alone, we may say this: Had he commenced by overcoming the man and then through him work the fall of the woman, her ruin would have been incomplete; she would not have been wholly without excuse before God, since she would have acted under the orders or influence of the one whom He had set over her.

    Satan's basic temptation strategy. Since man had been created upright, Satan had no depraved principle or nature upon which to work. Therefore he could operate only through that which is legitimate, i.e., the legitimate out of control is lust, and lust brings forth sin (James 1:13-17). Satan appealed to the three basic appetites, e.g., physical — "good for food"; emotional — "delight to the eye"; intellectual — "to make one wise."

These basic appetites are not evil in themselves, but must always be subject to the spiritual area of life. Christ in His temptations subjected each of these three areas to preeminent spiritual motivation. God had made adequate provision for the satisfaction of each of these basic appetites in regard to man (Gen. 2:9, 2:19). Eve sinned in that she allowed these appetites to take precedence over the spiritual (Gen. 2:16, 17). The satisfaction of these appetites apart from the spiritual control has given rise to most forms of religious error, e.g., the worship of the body (phallic religions, modern sexualism); the worship of the beautiful (all forms of false ritualism); the worship of the mind (rationalism).

The Fall of Man

The doctrine of the fall of man is not peculiar to Christianity; all religions contain an account of it and recognize the great and awful fact. Yet the doctrine of the Fall has a relation to Christianity that it does not have to other religions or religious systems. The moral character of God as seen in the Christian religion far surpasses the delineation of the Supreme Being set forth in any other religion, and thus heightens and intensifies its idea of sin. It is when men consider the very high character of God as set forth in Christianity, and then look at the doctrine of sin that they find it hard to reconcile the fact that God, being the moral Being He is, should ever allow sin to come into the world.

The scriptural fact of man's fall. The Scriptures clearly and distinctly teach that Adam and Eve fell from their first estate in sinning against God by disobeying His positive and personal command (Gen. 3:6; Rom. 5:12; 1 Tim. 2:14).

The purpose of the scriptural narrative. Its purpose is not to give account of the manner in which sin came into the world, but how it found its advent into the human race. Sin was already in the world, as the existence of Satan and the chaotic condition of things in the beginning strikingly testify.

The reasonableness of the narrative of the Fall is seen in comparing the condition of man after he had sinned with his condition when he left the hand of the Creator (cf. Gen. 1:26 with 6:5 and Ps. 14). If the fall of man were not narrated in Genesis, we should have to postulate some such event to account for the present condition in which we find man. In no part of the Scripture, save in the creation account as found in Genesis 1, 2, does man appear perfect and upright. His attitude is that of rebellion against God, of deepening and awful corruption.

Interpretations of the narrative:

1. Allegorical. Some look upon the whole narrative as being an allegory. Adam is the rational part of man; Eve, the sensual; the serpent, external excitements to evil. But the simplicity and artlessness of the narrative militates against this view.

2. Mythological. Others designate the narrative as being a myth. It is regarded as a truth invested with poetic form, something made up from the folklore of the times. But why should these few verses be snatched out of the chapter in which they are found and be called mythical, while the remaining verses are indisputably literal?

3. Literal. Then there is the literal interpretation, which takes the account as it reads, in its perfectly natural sense, just as in the case of the other parts of the same chapter, not regarding it as mythical or allegorical, but historical. We adopt this view for the following reasons:

   a. There is no intimation in the account itself that it is not historical.

   b. As part of a historical book, the presumption is that it is itself historical.

   c. The later Scripture writers refer to it as veritable history even in its details.

   d. The geographical locations in connection with the story are historical.

   e. Particular features of the narrative, such as the placing of our first parents in a garden and the speaking of the tempter through a serpent form, are incidents suitable to man's condition of innocent but untried childhood.

   f. The curse upon the man, upon the woman, and upon the ground are certainly literal, for it is a fact that death is in the world as the wages of sin.

   g. This view that the narrative is historical does not forbid our assuming that the trees of life and of knowledge were at the same time both symbols of spiritual truths and outward realities.

The essence of man's fall.

1. The sin of our first parents was purely volitional; it was an act of their own determination. Their sin was, like all other sin, a voluntary act of the will.
2. The essence of the first sin lay in the denial of the divine will, and elevation of the will of man over the will of God.
3. It was a deliberate transgression of a divinely marked boundary, an overstepping of the divine limits.
4. In its last analysis, the first sin was what every sin committed since has been, a positive disbelief in the word of the living God, a belief in Satan rather than a belief in God.
5. Finally, it is helpful to note that the same lines of temptation which were presented to our first parents were presented to Christ in the wilderness, and to men ever since then (Matt. 4:1-11; 1 John 2:15-17).

The immediate effects of the first sin. These were six in number (Gen. 3:7-13).

1. A sense of shame. This was due to the awakening of conscience.
2. The covering of fig leaves. This was a bloodless covering (see Gen. 3:21; Phil. 3:9).
3. A feeling of fear. This arose from their guilty conscience.
4. An attempt at concealment. Foolishly Adam and Eve supposed that they could hide from the presence of God.
5. An effort at self-vindication. Though guilty, yet Adam and Eve tried to justify themselves.
6. The shifting of blame. Adam laid the blame for his sin upon Eve, and Eve laid the blame of her sin upon the serpent, i.e., Satan.

The judicial consequences of the first sin:

1. Divine judgment. After this painful scene, the Lord God pronounced a fourfold judgment (Gen. 3:14-19).
   a. Upon the serpent. This was the curse of degradation (Mic. 7:17). Even during the Millennium the curse upon the serpent will not be removed, because the serpent is the type of Satan (Isa. 65:25).
   b. Upon the woman. This was the judgment of sorrow and subjection (John 16:21). The blessing of the gospel, however,

mitigates the rigor of the law (1 Tim. 2:15).

c. Upon the man. This was the judgment of sorrow and toil (Job 5:7; Eccl. 2:22, 23). Work, nevertheless, is a blessing and not a curse (Gen. 2:5, 15). It is only the curse resting upon the ground which makes man's labor vexatious and unremunerative.

d. Upon the ground. This was the curse of thorns and thistles. Like the serpent, the thorn is the natural enemy of man (Matt. 7:16). It is used in Scripture symbolically for evil (Num. 33:55; 2 Cor. 12:7). Our Lord's mock crown was composed of thorns (John 19:2, 5). During the Millennium the curse upon the ground will be removed (Isa. 55:13).

2. Separation. The fourfold divine judgment resulted in a threefold separation (Gen. 3:22-24). Thus Adam and Eve were separated —

a. From the Tree of Life. Dr. Pardington says: "The tree of life represents wisdom (Prov. 3:18). Wisdom personified is Christ (1 Cor. 1:24). So the tree of life was an emblem of Christ (Rev. 2:7; 22:14). Adam's body was mortal (Gen. 2:7; 1 Cor. 15:44, 45, 47). Science teaches us that physical life involves decay and loss. There was, however, a divine provision for checking this decay and loss, and preserving the body's youth. This was by means of the tree of life. It accomplished this through its sacramental value; that is, eating of this tree was symbolical of the communion of Adam and Eve with God and of their dependence upon Him. But this only because it had a physical efficacy. Physical immortality without holiness would have been unending misery. Accordingly, our first parents were shut out from the tree of life, until by redemption and resurrection such of their descendants as accept Christ can be prepared to partake thereof. Thus, our glorified bodies will be preserved throughout eternity by eating of the tree of life which is typical of our blessed Lord Himself (Rev. 2:7; 22:14).

"Physical decay and loss, which ended in the death of their bodies, began the instant Adam and Eve were denied access to the tree of life. The nine hundred and thirty years Adam lived, as also the extraordinary longevity of the antediluvians, is evidence of their wonderful natural vitality. 'If Adam had maintained his integrity, the body might have been developed and transfigured without the intervention of death. In other words, the *posse non mori* (that is, able not to die) might have become a *non posse mori* (that is, not able to die)' (Strong). In his *Crises of the Christ*, Campbell Morgan treats the transfiguration of Christ as the flowering of humanity; he regards it as God's demonstration of the fruition of the body — if there had been no sin."[9]

b. From the Garden. The only way to make the exclusion of Adam and Eve from the Tree of Life effective was to drive them from the Garden of Eden. And this the Lord God did, sending man forth "to till the ground from whence he was taken."

c. From the personal and visible presence of God. Sin separates man from God — and it is the *only* thing that can separate man from God. When Adam and Eve hid themselves from the presence of the Lord God, it was because their sin with its resulting guilt and shame had morally unfitted them for personal and face-to-face communion and fellowship with their Maker. Separation from the Garden of Eden, therefore, simply sealed the spiritual separation of man from God which sin had already brought about.

Henceforth, our first parents and their posterity had only a symbolical representation of deity; the cherubim and the flaming sword placed at the east of the Garden of Eden were the visible manifestation of the Lord God. Thither the godly antediluvians came to worship and sacrifice: for there is no evidence that these primitive types of the presence and power, the mercy and redeeming grace of God did not remain until swept away by the Flood. The flaming sword was the first appearance of that self-luminous flame which, as the Shekinah glory, rested over the mercy seat in the Holy of Holies in the tabernacle and the temple.

3. Death. In connection with the prohibition to eat of the Tree of Knowledge of Good and Evil, the Lord God said, "In the day that thou eatest thereof thou shalt surely die" (lit., dying thou shalt die) (Gen. 2:17). This death, which was the result of sin, was threefold.

a. Physical death. This is the separation of the soul from the body. It is all the temporal evils and sufferings which result from disturbance of the original harmony between soul and body. Some regard physical death as a part of the penalty of sin, while others regard it as rather the natural consequence of sin. In either view, it seems to be clear that weakness and disease followed by death resulted primarily from the exclusion of Adam and Eve from the Tree of Life (Num. 16:29; 27:3; Ps. 90:7-9, 11; Isa. 38:17, 18; Rom. 4:24, 25; 6:9, 10; 8:3, 10, 11; 1 Cor. 15:21, 22; Gal. 3:13; 1 Peter 4:6).

b. Spiritual death. This is the separation of the spirit from God. It means all the pain of conscience, loss of peace, and sorrow of spirit, which result from the disturbance of the normal relation between the soul and God (Matt. 8:22; Luke 15:32; John 5:24; 8:51; Rom. 6:23; Eph. 2:1; 5:14; 1 Tim. 5:6; James 5:20; 1 John 3:14). This death was fully visited upon Adam in the day on which he ate the forbidden fruit (Gen. 2:17). It is in this sense only that death is escaped by the Christian (John 11:26).

c. Eternal death. This is the result and culmination of spiritual death. It would seem to be inaugurated by some peculiar repellent energy of the divine holiness (Matt. 25:41; 2 Thess. 1:9) and to involve positive retribution visited by a personal God upon both body and soul of the evil-doer (Matt. 10:28; Heb. 10:31; Rev. 14:11). Eternal death is the same as hell, or *gehenna*, or the second death (Matt. 10:28; see 2 Kings 23:10; Rev. 20:14). Both spiritual and eternal death were arrested by grace through the institution of sacrifice (Gen. 3:21; 4:4; Heb. 9:22). Thus the Coming One who was to "taste death for every man" saved those in the Old Testament age who through obedience and sacrifice believed in Him (Rom. 3:25; Heb. 2:9).

Study Questions in Anthropology

1. What are the ancient and modern views of abiogensis to which the scriptural doctrine of the origin of man is opposed?
2. What are the basic assumptions of evolution?
3. Describe the gaps which are to be found all the way from the lowest form of matter to the highest form of life.
4. What is the scriptural teaching concerning the origin of man? Quote passage.
5. Discuss the unity of the human race.
6. Quote one or more passages of Scripture which teach that the whole human race descended from a single pair.
7. Why is the unity of the race theologically important?

8. Give the extrascriptural arguments for the unity of the race.
9. Discuss the nature of man as constituted by creation.
10. Give a description of the formation and creation of man in his threefold nature: spirit, soul, and body.
11. In what sense did man become a living soul through the in-breathing of the breath of lives?
12. Show from Scripture what will be the ruling power in our resurrection state.
13. Give scriptural argument for the tripartite being of man, and show the function of each part in human consciousness.
14. Give the Preexistent Theory of the soul's origin and the objections to it.
15. Give the Creationist Theory of the origin of the soul and the objections raised.
16. Give the Traducian Theory of the origin of the soul and the arguments in its favor.
17. What twofold danger needs to be avoided in interpreting the Scriptures concerning the image of God in man?
18. Describe man's personality or natural likeness to God, showing its indestructibility.
19. How does the image of God in man contrast with His image in Christ?
20. Describe man's holiness or moral likeness to God prior to the fall.
21. Describe the original righteousness of man in its several particulars.
22. Give the definition of the moral nature of man and its component parts.
23. Give the definition of conscience.
24. Describe and discuss the role of conscience in man.
25. Give the definition of will and discuss its various functions.
26. Quote a passage of Scripture teaching the endless existence of man, and give corroborative arguments proving it.
27. Describe and discuss the probation of man.
28. Describe the temptation of man.
29. Show the relation of the doctrine of the Fall to other religions and its peculiar relation to Christianity.
30. Give the various interpretations of the Scripture narrative of the Fall and the arguments for accepting the literal interpretation.
31. Elucidate at least three aspects of the essence of man's fall.
32. What were the immediate effects of man's first sin?

33. What were the judicial consequences of the first sin? Quote passages where appropriate.
34. Discuss the threefold separation resulting from the divine judgment.
35. Describe the threefold death involved in the penalty of the first sin, and quote one passage with each point.

Notes

[1]This doctrine of spontaneous generation poses a dilemma for those who attempt to explain the origin of life apart from the consideration of a Creator. On the one hand, all scientific experimentation and observation lead to the conclusion that all life comes from life and produces its own kind of living organism. The other horn of the life dilemma is that, according to purely natural law, life could not have been going on eternally (Second Law of Thermodynamics), and without energy interchanges there can be no natural life. Since these natural life forms tend to increase in number, there must have been a beginning of life. This dilemma can only be resolved in the scriptural doctrine of the God who is the fountain of all life (Ps. 36:9), and who is Himself eternal (1 Tim. 1:17).

[2]The Hebrew word *bara* signifies absolute creation.

[3]There are two points involved in this question: community of origin, and unity of species. All plants and animals derived by propagation from the same original stock are of the same species: but those of the same species need not be derived from a common stock. If God saw fit at the beginning, or at any time since, to create plants or animals of the same kind in large numbers and in different parts of the earth, they would be of the same species (or kind), though not of the same origin. The oaks of America and those of Europe are identical in species, though not derived from one and the same parent oak. It may be admitted that the great majority of plants and animals were originally produced not singly or in pairs, but in groups, the earth bringing forth a multitude of individuals of the same kind. It is, therefore, in itself, possible that all men may be of the same species, although not all descended from Adam. And such has been the opinion of some distinguished naturalists, but we do not accept it.

[4]Christ remembered His preexistent state; why should not we? There is every reason to believe that in the future state we shall remember our present existence; why should we not now remember the past state from which we came?

[5]We use the term *man* in this connection to denote whatever is essential to human personality. So long as the person exists, the man exists. As to the righteous, this is commonly admitted; but as to the wicked, some entertain doubts, yet these doubts cannot spring from any obscurity in the language of Scripture, for the same word is used of both classes in Matthew 25:46.

[6]Eden signifies pleasure, delight. Its exact site cannot be determined. In general terms its location must have been in the Mesopotamian Valley, near the headwaters of the Tigris and Euphrates.

[7]John Miley, *Systematic Theology* (New York: Hunt & Eaton, 1893), I, p. 423.

[8]Ibid., pp. 423-424.

[9]George P. Pardington, *Outline Studies in Christian Doctrine (New York: Christian Alliance Publishing Company, 1916), pp. 174-175.*

CHAPTER SEVEN

HAMARTIOLOGY: THE DOCTRINE OF SIN

THE ORIGIN OF SIN

The origin of sin is wrapped in obscurity as one of the unrevealed mysteries of Scripture. We are, however, given a hint of the entrance of sin into the heart of Satan and also the introduction of sin into the human race.

Its Entrance Into the Angelic Realm

In Isaiah 14:12-17, in the picture of the fall of Lucifer, the son of the morning (the King of Babylon, vs. 4), we have an account, it is believed, of the rebellion of Satan against God. Notice the expression "I will" five times repeated — especially the last sentence: "I will be like the Most High" (vs. 14).

In Ezekiel 28, in the prophet's lamentation upon the king of Tyre, we have a hint, it is believed, that Satan fell by reason of pride of heart (vs. 17).

How a pure being, possessed of those intellectual capacities and moral intuitions which were needful to make him justly responsible to divine law, could and did lapse from his primitive innocence and fall into sin is one of those dark problems which philosophers and theologians have vainly endeavored to solve. No more reliable explanation of sin's entrance into the universe in general and into this world in particular has ever been given than that which is furnished by Scripture.

According to Scripture, sin first made its appearance in the

211

angelic race, though nothing more is recorded than the simple fact that the angels sinned (2 Peter 2:4) and kept not their first estate (or principality) but left their own (or proper) habitation (Jude 6). Their motive or reason for doing so receives scant mention. We deduce that the sin of these fallen spirits was a free act on their part, dictated by dissatisfaction with the place that had been assigned to them in the hierarchy of heaven and by ambition to secure for themselves a loftier station than that in which they had been placed.

Yet this does not answer the question how such dissatisfaction and ambition could arise in beings who must be presumed to have been created sinless. And inasmuch as external influence in the shape of temptation from without, by intelligences other than themselves, is by the supposition excluded, it appears that no other answer is possible than that in the creation of a finite personality endowed with freedom of will, there is necessarily involved the possibility of making a wrong (in the sense of sinful) choice.

Its Entrance Into the Human Race

The introduction of sin into the human race, recorded in Genesis 3, came about in a fourfold way: through deception (1 Tim. 2:14); through man's disobedience (Rom. 5:19); through the serpent's enticement (Gen. 3:1-6); through Satan's malignity (2 Cor. 11:3).

In the case of man, sin's entrance into the world receives a somewhat different explanation by the sacred writers from that given to its entrance into the angelic realm. With one accord they ascribe the sinful actions, words, feelings, and thoughts of each individual to his own deliberate choice, so that he is thereby, with perfect justice, held responsible for his deviation from the path of moral rectitude; but some of the inspired penmen make it clear that the entrance of sin into this world was effected through the disobedience of the first man who stood and acted as the representative and surety of his whole natural posterity (Rom. 5:12), and that the first man's fall was brought about by temptation from without, by the seductive influence of Satan, the lord of the fallen spirits already mentioned, the prince of the power of the air, the spirit who now works in the children of disobedience (Gen. 3:1-6; John 8:44; 2 Cor. 11:3; Eph. 2:2).

They teach that the first man's lapse from a state of innocence brought disastrous consequences upon himself and his descendants. Upon himself it wrought immediate disturbance of his whole nature, implanting in it the seeds of bodily, mental, moral, and spiritual degeneration, filling him with fear of his Maker, laying upon his conscience a burden of guilt, and interrupting the hitherto peaceful relations which had subsisted between himself and the Author of his being. Upon his descendants it opened the floodgates of corruption by which their natures even from birth fell beneath the power of evil, as was soon witnessed in the dark tragedy of Cain's fratricide with which the tale of human history began, and in the rapid spread of violence through the prediluvian world.

This is what theologians call the doctrine of "original sin," by which they mean that the results of Adam's sin, both legal and moral, have been transmitted to Adam's posterity, so that now each individual comes into the world as the inheritor of a nature that has been disempowered by sin.

That this doctrine, though frequently opposed, has a basis in science and philosophy, as well as in Scripture, is becoming every day more apparent. The scientific law of heredity, by which not only physical but mental and moral characteristics are transmitted from parent to child, seems to justify the scriptural statement that "by one man's disobedience sin entered into the world and death by sin and so death passed upon all men, because that all have sinned" (Rom. 5:12).

Whether affirmed or contradicted by modern thought, the doctrine of Scripture shines like a sunbeam, that man is "conceived in sin and shapen in iniquity" (Ps. 51:5), that children are "estranged from the womb and go astray" (Ps. 58:3), that all are by nature "children of wrath" (Eph. 2:3), that "the imagination of man's heart is evil from his youth" (Gen. 8:21), and that everyone requires to have "a clean heart" created in him (Ps. 51:10), since "that which is born of the flesh is flesh" (John 3:6), and "no man can bring a clean thing out of an unclean thing" (Job 15:14).

If these passages do not show that the Bible teaches the doctrine of original, or transmitted and inherited, sin, it is difficult to see in what clearer or more emphatic language the doctrine could have been taught. The truth of the doctrine may be challenged by those who repudiate the authority of Scripture; that it is a doctrine of Scripture can hardly be denied.

THE FACT OF SIN

Sin is a reality and not an illusion, although some have so pronounced it on the ground of fatalism. They say that God has fixed all events by His purpose and agency. As all events must take place as He has determined, and as His purpose is good, there can be therefore no such thing as sin. Others deny its existence on the ground of hereditary depravity. They maintain that as men are born with a damaged and depraved nature, they are not, therefore, blameworthy for their evil conduct.

Nature Proclaims It

Ruskin says, "No good nor lovely thing exists in this world, without its correspondent darkness." Roses have their thorns. Physical death and darkness were in the world before man's sin, but moral and spiritual death and darkness are the result of his sin as far as the race is concerned. Man's sin caused spiritual death to pass through his whole nature, and blighted and cursed creation (Gen. 3:17).

The fact of sin is heard in the minor key of nature's voice. The howl of the tempest, the sigh of the wind, the moan of the sea, the mew of the cat, the bark of the dog, the lowing of the cattle, the cry of the vulture, the shriek of the captured animal, the bleat of the sheep, and the croak of the raven — all tell how

> Disproportioned sin
> Jarred against Nature's chime, and with hoarse din
> Brake the fair music that all creatures made
> To their great Lord, whose love their motion swayed.

Men Acknowledge It

Man knows he is wrong, he fails to do the right, he cannot fulfill his own ideals, he longs for a power to lift him out of himself, and he knows if the past is not blotted out, it will meet him again, to condemn him in the future.

Seneca, the philosopher, confesses, "We have all sinned, some more, some less." Ovid, the writer, says, "We always strive after what is forbidden." Goethe, the seer, remarks, "I see no fault which I might not myself have committed." Coleridge, the thinker, declares, "I am a fallen creature . . . an evil ground existed in my will previously to any given act." The Chinese speak of "two good men; one dead, the other unborn." The poet sighs,

> O that there would arise a man in me
> That the man I am may cease to be.

Law Discovers It

"By the law is the knowledge of sin" (Rom. 3:20). The word *knowledge* (*gnosis*) is more than the recognition or the knowing about anything; it is *epignosis*, which signifies an exact knowledge, a personal acquaintance with a person or thing.

The natural man will recognize that certain acts in the life of an individual are sin, but he is not prepared to acknowledge that the seeds of the same sins are to be found in himself. Religious Saul of Tarsus thought he was free from sin till the Spirit opened his eyes to see himself in the looking-glass of the law; then he found that desire in the heart was action in the life in the sight of the Holy One (Rom. 7:7).

Man does wrong because he is wrong, and the law by its deep spirituality touches the root and core of things and thus reveals to man that the sin within, unseen by men, is as much sin in God's sight as what men see without. The law is —

1. A scale to make known to man his deficiencies (James 2:10);
2. A looking-glass to show man his sinfulness (Rom. 7:7);
3. A stethoscope to discover man's disease (Matt. 5:27-37);
4. A rule to evidence his crookedness (Rom. 7:14);
5. An officer to demand man's condemnation (Gal. 3:10);
6. A judge to condemn him to death (Rom. 7:10).

God Declares It

The highest court of appeal is the sacred oracle of God's truth. There are many similes which God uses to bring home the fact, the force, and the folly of sin. Sin, like the beast in the Book of Revelation, is many-headed and as glaring in its pronounced iniquity. Sin is —

1. A grievous malady contaminating the whole of the being, as the Lord said of the iniquity of Sodom, when He pronounced it "great" and "very grievous" (Gen. 18:20);
2. An obscuring cloud which hides the face of God's approval and blessing: as we read in Isaiah 59:2, "Your sins have hid His face from you";
3. A binding cord that keeps the powers of man from fulfilling their designed functions: the wicked one is said "to be holden with the cords of his sins" (Prov. 5:22);
4. A crouching beast which waits to spring upon its victim to its destruction, as Jehovah reminded Cain when He declared "sin croucheth at the door" (Gen. 4:7);
5. A rest-destroyer unhinging the mind and plunging it into the throes of travail and anguish, as David found when he exclaimed, "There is no rest in my bones because of my sin" (Ps. 38:3);

6. A blessing-robber that strips and starves, to the soul's nakedness and destitution, as Jeremiah reminded Judah when he spoke of the cause of their captivity, and said, "Your iniquities have turned away these things, and your sins have withholden good from you" (Jer. 5:25);

7. A terrible desolater which devastates personhood like an earthquake devastating some fair city to its overthrow: "I will make thee sick in smiting thee, in making thee desolate, because of thy sins" (Mic. 6:13);

8. A tripper-up which continually throws the sinner over to his hurt by the obstacles which it places in his way: as the wise man remarked, "Wickedness overthroweth the sinner" (Prov. 13:6);

9. A written record which leaves its indelible mark upon the man who commits it: "Sin . . . is written with a pen of iron, and with the point of a diamond it is graven upon the heart" (Jer. 17:1);

10. A betraying presence which "will be found out" no matter how carefully one seeks to hide it: "Ye have made your iniquity to be remembered, in that your transgressions are discovered, so that all your sins do appear" (Ezek. 21:24);

11. An accusing witness which points its condemning finger at the prisoner arraigned before the bar of justice: as we read in Holy Scripture, "Our sins testify against us" (Isa. 59:12);

12. A sum of addition, which is ever adding to its catalog of ills: as Jehovah once plaintively said, "Woe to the rebellious children . . . that take counsel, but not of Me; and that cover with a covering, but not of my Spirit, that they may add sin to sin" (Isa. 30:1).

Christ Reveals It

The white light of Christ's holy presence makes known the unholy condition of the sinner, as does every other manifestation of the presence of God. Every recorded manifestation of Christ's holiness made those to whom He revealed Himself conscious of their sinfulness. This may be illustrated by the following "I am's" of confession:

1. Seeing Jehovah in His holiness made Isaiah cry, "I am undone" (Isa. 6:5).

2. The remembrance of God's deliverance moved David to exclaim, "I am a worm" (Ps. 22:6).

3. The manifestation of Christ's power urged Peter to confess, "I am a sinful man" (Luke 5:8).

4. The contemplation of the father's home prompted the prodigal to own, "I am no more worthy . . ." (Luke 15:19).
5. The application of the law of God in its spirituality led Paul to declare, "I am carnal" (Rom. 7:14).
6. The unveiling of God's glory led Job to his heart-cry, "I am vile" (Job 40:4).
7. The consciousness of the Lord's remembrance made the psalmist say, "I am poor and needy" (Ps. 40:17).
8. The sense of Jehovah's presence caused Jacob to acknowledge, "I am not worthy of the least of all Thy mercies" (Gen. 32:10).
9. The knowledge of Christ makes everyone who sees himself in the light of His presence to exclaim, "Christ Jesus came into the world to save sinners, of whom I am chief" (1 Tim. 1:15).

Experience Proves It

The field of universal confession would prove this, but of the confessions found in the expression "I have sinned" recorded in the Bible we have sufficient illustrations.

1. Pharaoh, the hardened coward, says "I have sinned" as he sees the consequence of his rebellion against Jehovah (Exod. 9:27; 10:16).
2. Balaam, the scheming prophet, exclaims "I have sinned" when the angel bars his self-willed way (Num. 22:34).
3. Achan, the covetous rebel, confesses "I have sinned" when his iniquity is brought to light (Josh. 7:20).
4. David, the penitent believer, confesses "I have sinned" as he admits his perverseness (2 Sam. 19:20).
5. Nehemiah, the humble servant, includes himself in the sin of the nation in his "I have sinned" (Neh. 1:6).
6. Job, the emptied saint, acknowledges his iniquity in saying "I have sinned" (Job 7:20).
7. Micah, the self-condemned, says "I have sinned" as he ponders the righteousness of Jehovah (Mic. 7:9);
8. Judas, the wicked betrayer, throws down his ill-gotten gain at the feet of the priests as he remorsefully exclaims "I have sinned" (Matt. 27:4).
9. The completely bankrupt prodigal says to his father "I have sinned" as he comes in repentance to him (Luke 15:21).
10. We are assured by the Spirit that the Lord is seeking to bless

those who will honestly and truly confess "I have sinned" (Job 33:27).

The Believer Knows It

Among the many things which Paul says "I know" is this: "I know that in me dwelleth no good thing" (Rom. 7:18). Luther says, "I am more afraid of my own heart than of the pope with all his cardinals." He who knows most of God, knows most about himself. Many like Hume and others are complacent in their self-esteem, while men like Fénelon, Edwards, and Spurgeon always write bitter things against themselves. When Paul says "I know," he represents what had come to him by personal view and acquaintance.

The word *know* is rendered "saw" in Acts 3:9, "beheld" in Luke 19:41, "look" in John 7:52, "consider" in Acts 15:6, "perceiving" in Luke 9:47, and "aware" in Luke 11:44. The believer has seen the evil of sin and loathes it, he beholds the havoc of sin and avoids it, he looks into the heart of sin and distrusts it, he considers the tendency of sin and judges it, he perceives the allurements of sin and conquers it, and he is aware of the existence of sin and dies to it in the fellowship of Christ's death. This is the doctrine of sin as a state which answers to the experience of religious men. Indeed, at a primitive state of advancement, just as in childhood, men repent of what they have done; but at a more mature stage they repent of what they are.

THE NATURE OF SIN

The nature of sin is expressed in the words which the Spirit uses to describe it. Girdlestone says of those words, "Every word is a piece of philosophy; nay it is a revelation."[1]

Missing the Mark of the Divine Standard

God's standard is expressed in the letter of His holy law, and in the living characters of the life of His holy Son. From both of these standards all have sinned, that is, missed the mark.

New Testament usage. The word *hamartano*, translated "sinned" in Romans 3:23, is rendered "trespass" in Matthew 18:15, "offended" in Acts 25:8, and "faults" in 1 Peter 2:20. In the following illustrations it is given as "sin" and "sinned":

1. Judas missed the mark of love to Christ in betraying Him (Matt. 27:4).
2. The prodigal missed the mark of contentment in the father's will by having his own will (Luke 15:18, 21).

3. The impotent man missed the mark of God's law in sinning against himself (John 5:14).
4. The adulterous woman missed the mark of purity by her sin (John 8:11).
5. The angels missed the mark of God's glory by their pride (2 Peter 2:4).
6. Israel missed the mark of God's rest by their unbelief (Heb. 3:17).
7. The sinner misses the mark of God's salvation by refusing Christ in His atonement (Heb. 10:26).
8. The heretic misses the mark of God's truth by his error (Titus 3:11).

Old Testament usage. The equivalent Old Testament word *chata* is equally expressive. The word is variously rendered in the following passages, in which *to sin* is understood as —

1. To miss an aim. The word is rendered "miss" in speaking of the left-handed Benjamites who did not "miss" the mark in slinging stones (Judg. 20:16). The anathema of Jehovah came upon Ahab, who "made Israel to sin," namely, in swerving from the aim of God's service (1 Kings 21:22).
2. To miss one's step and so trip and fall. The one that "hasteth with his feet sinneth" (Prov. 19:2). He does not consider where he is going and comes to grief. Israel, in their haste, missed the mark of God's commandment in eating cattle with blood; hence, it was told to Saul, "Behold the people sin against the Lord" (1 Sam. 14:33).
3. To miss happiness. Job's friend said to him all would be right if he were right. He would "visit his habitation and shalt not sin" (Job 5:24). The psalmist felt that if God's truth was hid in his heart, he would not "sin" against the Lord (Ps. 119:11). To sin against the God of happiness is to miss the happiness of God.
4. To miss one's self. The mighty are scared out of their wits at the approach of leviathan. "By reason of his breakings they are beside themselves" (Job 41:25, ASV). The sinner is the same; he misses the mark of God's sane command and rushes on in his insanity like Pharaoh, who "sinned" yet more (Exod. 9:34).
5. To miss another's good will. Pharaoh's butler and baker "offended" him; hence they were dismissed from their office and imprisoned (Gen. 40:1). The cause of Jehovah's displeasure with Israel in allowing them to be defeated by Ai was the sin of Achan,

hence His sharp reprimand to Joshua, "Israel hath sinned." When Achan confessed "I have sinned" and was judged, then all was adjusted (Josh. 7:11, 20).

6. To miss the right path. Balaam knew he was on the wrong road. When the angel arrested him, Balaam exclaimed, "I have sinned . . . I will get me back again" (Num. 22:34). David felt the same in his sin with Bathsheba, hence his penitential cry, "I have sinned against Thee" (Ps. 51:4).

7. To miss God. The words *to sin* in Genesis 31:39 are rendered "bear the loss." Jacob told Laban he bore the loss of the sheep which were torn by the beasts. What a loss it is to bear when one misses God; as He Himself says, "He that sinneth against Me [or "misseth Me," ASV] wrongeth His own soul" (Prov. 8:36).

To sin, then is to miss the divine aim of life; to miss God's intention for us is to miss God Himself; and to miss Him is to forsake the Fountain of Living Waters and thus miss everything.

A Deviation, Lapse, or Fall From God's Requirement

The word rendered "trespass" in Matthew 6:14, *paraptoma*, is translated "sins" in Ephesians 1:7; 2:1, 5; "offence" in Romans 5:15-18, 20; "fault" in Galatians 6:1 and James 5:16; and "fall" in Romans 11:11. As a man who slips aside from the path falls into the ditch to his hurt, so the sinner by his deviation from the will of God has lapsed from the truth and trespassed against the God of Truth.

1. Every offence against God's Word means a fall from God, and damage to us and to others (see "offence" in Rom. 4:25; 5:15-18, 20).

2. Every departure from God means a fall from the divine purpose. See what the Spirit says about the "fall" of Israel in Romans 11:11, 12.

3. Every sin committed is a medium to convey spiritual death and condemnation. See the description of the condition of the Colossian and Ephesian believers before conversion (Col. 2:13; Eph. 2:1, 5).

4. Every slip from the path of right and duty is damaging to the one who slips. See the word *fault* in Galatians 6:1 and James 5:16.

5. Every trespass is a falling aside from God Himself and is an affront to Him, which He alone can forgive, but which He does when He acts in grace; He "forgives our trespasses" through the blood of Christ's satisfying and vicarious death. See the words *trespass* and

sins in Matthew 6:15; 2 Corinthians 5:19; Ephesians 1:7; Colossians 2:13.

A *Distortion, Perversion, or Bending of What Is Right*

The Hebrew *avah* corresponds to our word *wrong*, meaning that which is "wrung out of its course."

> For gold his sword the hireling ruffian draws,
> For gold the hireling judge distorts the laws.

Dr. Johnson aptly illustrates the wrong use of the sword and the evil course of a judge who uses a good law for a wrong end. Ruskin gives the same thought: "Every right action and true thought sets the seal of its beauty on person and face; every wrong action and foul thought its seal of distortion."

Avah is rendered "done wrong" in Esther 1:16, "did perversely" in 2 Samuel 19:19, "done wickedly" in 2 Samuel 24:17, "done amiss" in 2 Chronicles 6:37, and "committed iniquity" in Psalm 106:6. The setting of these translations gives interesting illustrations. Vashti did "wrong" in the estimation of Memucan in not obeying the command of Ahasuerus; David confessed he had "done wickedly" when he numbered the people; Shimei owned he "did perversely" in the way he cursed David and threw stones at him. Solomon in his dedicatory prayer tells the Lord that those who come back to Him in real repentance and confess they have "done amiss" will be forgiven; the psalmist in the extremity of his suffering exclaimed, "I am troubled" (margin "bent"); Jeremiah in his anguish lamented to the Lord and said, "He hath made my paths crooked"; the prophet Isaiah was so burdened with God's message that he was like a woman "bowed down" with travail; and the psalmist acknowledges as he thinks of the sins of his fathers, "We have committed iniquity."

The words which in the New Testament accord to the Old Testament *avah* are *adikia* and *adikos*. The former is derived from *adikos*. The latter is rendered "unjust," "unrighteous," and the former is translated "iniquity," "unjust," "unrighteous," and "wrong." The character of the ungodly is wrong and they are, therefore, designated again and again as the "unjust" and "unrighteous" (Matt. 5:45; Luke 18:11; Acts 24:15; 1 Cor. 6:9; 1 Peter 3:18; 2 Peter 2:9, 13). The course of life and specific acts of the ungodly are described as "unrighteous," hence the professor is a worker of "iniquity" (Luke 13:27); the steward in the parable is "unjust" in his methods (Luke 16:8); the field purchased by the blood money of Judas is "the reward of iniquity" (Acts 1:18); Simon Magus was held in the "bond of iniquity" (Acts 8:23); the reprobate are filled with all "unrighteous-ness" (Rom. 1:18); the sinner yields his members as "instruments of unrighteousness" (Rom. 6:13); the Satan-dominated have "pleasure in unrighteousness" (2 Thess. 2:12); the tongue is a "world of in-iquity" (James 3:6); the rioters will receive the "reward of unright-eousness" (2 Peter 2:13); and all "unrighteousness" is summarized as "sin" (1 John 5:17).

One of the most terrible phases of sin is when men bend the right to wrong purpose, as Judah did when they took the serpent of brass and worshiped it instead of God (2 Kings 18:4); to take a position of trust to gain sordid dust of gold, as Balaam did (Jude 11); to use the name of the Lord to carry out one's own will, as King Saul did (1 Sam. 15:16-23); to use God's labels for the devil's merchandise, as profes-sors do when they turn the grace of God into lasciviousness (Jude 4); to be associated with God's people for selfish ends, as Achan was when he took God's devoted things and devoted them to himself (Josh. 7:20, 21); to desire the power of God to add to self's exaltation, as Simon Magus wanted to do (Acts 8:18-23); and to betray Christ and His disciples as Judas did (Acts 1:17).

Passing Over the Prescribed Boundary of God's Law

> Nor can the foot
> Of disembodied Spirit, nor angel wing,
> Transgress the deep inexorable gulf
> Betwixt the worlds of darkness and of light.

What the residents of the unseen world cannot do, the sinner does in his sinning, for he passes over (transgresses) the boundary of right and enters the forbidden land of wrong.

The Hebrew word *avar* is used in a variety of connections. It is rendered "pass over" in describing Israel's passage through Jordan's bed (Josh. 3:16); "passed through" in referring to Abram's pilgrim-age (Gen. 12:6); "current" in speaking of the money which Abraham passed to Ephron (Gen. 23:16); "passeth" in alluding to the Eastern custom of shepherds counting their sheep as they passed under the rod (Lev. 27:32); "went over" in stating that a ferry boat carried the king's household over Jordan (2 Sam. 19:18); "passed through" in using the simile of a river going through a district (Isa. 23:10); and "pass" in denoting the fact that the sea does not pass the command of the Lord (Prov. 8:29).

God's word of restriction is, "Thus far thou shalt go and no farther," but man says, "So far shall I go and as much farther as I like." Balaam recognized God's authority when he said, "I cannot go beyond the Word of the Lord" (Num. 22:18; 24:13); but King Saul did not recognize God's authority, for when he was found out in his disobedience, he said, "I have transgressed the commandment of the Lord" (1 Sam. 15:24). Frequently God charged Israel with having transgressed His law (see Num. 14:41; Josh. 7:11, 15; Isa. 24:5; Dan. 9:11; Hos. 6:7; 8:1).

The New Testament word for *transgress* (*parabaino*) is a compound one, meaning to step on one side, to go aside from what is prescribed. The Pharisees by their question charged the disciples with transgressing, when they said to Christ in Matthew 15:2, 3, "Why do Thy disciples transgress the tradition of the elders?" But Christ retorted, "Why do ye also transgress the commandment of God by your tradition?" Judas by his "transgression" fell from the apostleship (Acts 1:25). He who does not abide in the teaching of Christ "transgresseth" (ASV, "goeth onward") and does not possess God (2 John 9).

An Affront to God As Man Dares to Stand Before Him

One of the most pathetic charges of God against Israel is, "I have brought up children and they have rebelled against Me" (Isa. 1:2); and He has to say of men generally, "they have added rebellion unto their sin" (Job. 34:37). The Hebrew word *pasha* is rendered "rebellion" and "rebelled" in the Scriptures cited above, and it is translated as "offend" in Proverbs 18:19; "trespass" in Genesis 31:36; 50:17; "sin" and "sins" in Proverbs 10:12, 19; 28:13; "transgression" in 1 Kings 8:50; "revolted" in 2 Kings 8:20. In contrast with *avar* — in which the command or covenant intervenes between man and God, and man steps over his rightful limit — *pasha* removes even the laws, and man immediately faces God. For a child to disobey his parent is bad, but for a child to clench his fist and defy his parent to his face is worse. That is what the willful sinner does.

Corresponding and equivalent words in the New Testament are *anomos* and *asebes*. *Anomos* is rendered "transgressors," "wicked," "without law," "lawless," and "unlawful." Thus the two thieves were "transgressors" against lawful authority (Mark 15:28). Those who are "without law" in the Jewish sense are nevertheless under responsibility to God (1 Cor. 9:21); when Christ is revealed from heaven He will destroy the "wicked" (lawless) one who has dared to oppose him (2 Thess. 2:8); the law is restrictive and punitive to those who are "lawless," and who are in rebellion against God (1 Tim. 1:9); and Lot is said to have been vexed with the "unlawful" deeds of the Sodomites (2 Peter 2:8).

Asebes signifies those who are irreverent, impious, ungodly. It is translated "ungodly" in the eight verses where it occurs (see Rom. 4:5; 5:6; 1 Tim. 1:9; 1 Peter 4:18; 2 Peter 2:5; 3:7; Jude 4, 15). A man without God is ungodly, and to be without Him means to be in opposition to Him, no matter what the label may be upon the godless one.

The Betrayal of a Trust, Unfaithfulness

The native meaning of the word *ma'al* is to cover, and thence to act covertly, to deal treacherously. "To his sin, man had added transgression; to his transgression, revolt; and to his revolt, he has joined treachery." Adam missed the mark when he listened to Eve instead of to God. He transgressed when he disobeyed the definite command of God and took the forbidden fruit; and then he covered up his sin by his subsequent action. The Spirit emphasizes this in these words: "But they like Adam have transgressed the covenant; there have they dealt treacherously against Me" (Hos. 6:7, ASV). Job also says, "If I covered my transgression as Adam, by hiding mine iniquity in my bosom" (Job 31:33).

The word *ma'al* is rendered "trespass" in Joshua 7:1 in referring to the covered sin of Achan; "transgression" in 1 Chronicles 10:13 in calling attention to the cause of Saul's untimely death; "sore" in 2 Chronicles 28:19 in describing the intensity of Ahaz's sin, for he "transgressed sore" or he "transgressed a transgression"; "falsehood" in Job 21:34, when Job charged his friends with "falsehood" or faithlessness (margin); "grievously" in Ezekiel 14:13 in God's charge against those who had sinned against Him by trespassing grievously"; and "very much" in 2 Chronicles 36:14, when the Lord calls attention to the depths of sin into which the rulers of Judah had gone.

To sin in a general way is bad, and to break a distinct command is worse; but to cover up the sin is worst of all. It was this last act which brought the scathing words of Christ against the Pharisees, for they "for a pretence" or "cloke" made long prayers (Matt. 23:14). To prate well in prayer and to be ill in practice is to be a whited sepulcher of death.

An Offense, an Error, a Negligence

As *chata* denotes sins of commission, so *asham* designates sins of omission. It is found in connection with the trespass-offering which was for sins of ignorance (see the word *trespass-offering* in Leviticus). Its original application is to negligence in going, carelessness of gait — as a faltering, jaded, slow-paced camel, who saunters along without regard to its steps. The word comes from a root which means "to be in fault," hence, to be guilty, and it is rendered "guilty" in Numbers 5:6; "offend" in Habakkuk 1:11; "desolate" in Psalm 34:21; "trespass" in 2 Chronicles 19:10; and "found faulty" in Hosea 10:2. Again and again it is stated that a man's ignorance of an offense did not absolve him from the guilt of it: "Though he wist it not, yet is he guilty" (see Lev. 4:13, 22, 27; 5:2-4, 17, 19, ASV; 6:4).

Some of the most terrible punishments mentioned in the Word are given because of ignorance and negligence. Meroz is cursed because help was not given the Lord (Judg. 5:23). "Let him be anathema maranatha, accursed when the Lord comes" is the predictive announcement to those who "love not the Lord" (1 Cor. 16:22); "everlasting punishment" will be the portion of those who did not minister to Christ's brethren (Matt. 25:45, 46); "everlasting destruction" will be the lot of those who know not God and who have not obeyed the gospel (2 Thess. 1:8, 9); and those who do not believe in Christ are convicted by the Spirit of this sin of sins — "of sin because they believe not in Me" (John 16:9).

A Debt, a Failure in Duty, a Not Meeting Obligations

Christ taught the disciples to pray "Forgive us our debts (Matt. 6:12). The word *debts (opheilema)* comes from a word which means something owing, a due, to be under obligation. It is rendered "owed" in stating what the two debtors owed (Luke 7:41); "indebted" in Luke's version of the Lord's Prayer (Luke 11:4); "duty" in speaking of the fulfillment of commands (Luke 17:10); "ought," when Christ enjoins the principles to wash each other's feet (John 13:14); "behooved" in referring to the necessity of Christ's becoming like us in order to benefit us (Heb. 2:17); and "bound" when Paul felt he was bound to thank God for the saints at Thessalonica (2 Thess. 2:13).

Failure to discharge duty means a liability. When the unforgiving servant had his forgiveness canceled, he was delivered to the tormentors till he had paid all that was due from him (Matt. 18:34). The unforgiven sinner whose obligations are not met has hanging over him all the dread consequences which Christ indicated when He referred to the eighteen people upon whom the tower of Siloam fell, and said: "Think ye that they were debtors above all men that dwelt in Jerusalem? I tell you, nay; but, except ye repent ye shall all likewise perish" (Luke 13:1-5).

Disobedience, Distrust, a Want of Response

All the other words we have considered depict sin before it comes in contact with the divine remedy. But the words translated "disobedience" (Col. 3:6), "unbelief" (Heb. 4:6), "obey not" (Rom. 2:8), and "believed not" (Heb. 11:31), represent man's disobedience to God's salvation. Disobedience is a Satan-annexer (Eph. 2:2), a wrath-bringer (Eph. 5:6), a life-robber (John 3:36, ASV), a prejudice-producer (Acts 14:2, ASV), a heart-hardener (Acts 19:9, ASV), a God-ignorer (Rom. 10:21), a rest-destroyer (Heb. 3:18, ASV), a Christ-stumbler (1 Peter 2:7, 8), a prison-opener (1 Peter 3:20), and a certain-punisher (1 Peter 4:17).

There is no sin so grievous as the sin which is represented by unwillingness to be persuaded by the love of God and which in its willfulness opposes God's gracious purpose in Christ. Were it sin against law, we might imagine the law too severe; or, against rule, we might find an excuse in its sternness; or, against power, we might possibly find an apology in its despotic severity.

There remains, however, no such palliation of this sin of disobedience, for unlike all other forms of sin, it springs into being and confronts God when He stoops in His gentleness to raise the poor and needy. It is the beggar's refusal of heavenly blessing; it is the stubbornness of man that will not yield to God's way of blessing; it is the scorn of eternal love, love's sacrifice, and love's sweet reasonableness; it is the thrice-ribbed ice of sin that will not melt beneath the warm beam of heavenly pity; it is the triple steel that will not be pierced by the golden-headed arrows of mercy; and the adamant that will neither rend nor dissolve at the expiring cry of the Son of God.

THE CULPABILITY OF SIN

By *culpability* is meant the blameworthiness of sin as an act, inexcusable on the part of its perpetrator, who — being such a personality as he is, endowed with such faculties as are his, placed under a law so good and holy, just and spiritual, simple and easy as that prescribed by God, and having such motives and inducements to keep it as were offered to him, from the first through all his posterity — ought never to have committed it. It also includes the heinousness of sin, as an act done against light and love bestowed upon the doer of it, and in flagrant opposition to the holiness and majesty of the Lawgiver so that He, the Lawgiver, cannot but regard it with abhorrence as an act abominable in His sight, and repel from His presence as well as extrude from His favor the individual who has become chargeable with it. But over and above these representations of sin, which are all scriptural, by the culpability of sin is meant its exposure to the penalty affixed by divine justice to transgression.

That a penalty was affixed by God in the first instance when man was created, the Eden narrative in Genesis declares: "The Lord God commanded the man, saying, Of every tree of the garden thou mayest freely eat, but of the tree of the knowledge of good and evil thou shalt not eat of it, for in the day thou eatest thereof thou shalt surely die" (Gen. 2:16, 17). That this penalty still overhangs the impenitent is not only distinctly implied in our Savior's language — that apart from His redeeming work in the world, i.e., every individual therein was in danger of perishing and was indeed already condemned (John 3:16-18) — but also is expressly declared by John (3:36), who says that "the wrath of God abideth" on the unbeliever, and by Paul, who asserts that "the wages of sin is death" (Rom. 6:23).

Without entering into the vexed question as to how far Adam's posterity are legally responsible for Adam's sin — in the sense that apart from their own transgressions they would be adjudged to spiritual and eternal death — it is manifest that Scripture includes in the just punishment of sin more than the death of the body. That this does form part of sin's penalty can hardly be disputed by a careful reader of the Bible; but Scripture unmistakably implies equally that that penalty includes what theologians call spiritual and eternal death. When it affirms that men are naturally "dead in trespasses and in sins," it obviously purposes to convey the idea that until the soul is quickened by divine grace, it is incapable, not of thinking upon the subject of religion or reading the Word of God or of praying or of exercising faith, but of doing anything spiritually good or religiously saving, of securing their legal justification before a holy God, or of bringing about their spiritual regeneration.

When Scripture further asserts that the unbeliever shall not see life (John 3:36), and that the wicked shall go away into everlasting punishment (Matt. 25:46), it assuredly does not suggest that on entering the other world, the unsaved of earth will have another opportunity of accepting salvation (Second Probation), or that extinction of being will be their lot (Annihilation), or that all mankind will eventually attain salvation (Universalism).

Meanwhile it suffices to observe that the words just referred to seem to teach that the penalty of sin continues beyond the grave. Granting that the words of Christ about the worm-that-never-dies and the-fire-that-shall-not-be-quenched are figurative, they un-questionably signify that the figures stand for some terrible calamity — on the one hand, loss of happiness, separation from the source of life, exclusion from blessedness; and, on the other, access of misery, suffering, wretchedness, woe, which will be realized by the wicked as the due reward of their impenitent and disobedient lives, and which no revolving years will relieve. The pendulum of the great clock of eternity, as it swings through the ages, will seem to be ever saying, "He that is unjust, let him be unjust still; and he that is filthy, let him be filthy still; he that is righteous, let him be righteous still; and he that is holy, let him be holy still" (Rev. 22:11).

THE CONSEQUENCE OF SIN

Sin has dulled the ears of man's attention (Acts 28:27), darkened the eyes of man's understanding (Eph. 4:18), depraved the heart of man's affection (Matt. 13:15), diverted the feet of man's walk (Isa. 53:6), carnalized the thought of man's mind (Rom. 8:7), warped the capacity of man's intellect (1 Cor. 2:9-14), wronged the soul of man's nature (Prov. 8:36), poisoned the tongue of man's speech (Rom. 3:13, 14), contracted the hands of man's labor (Prov. 21:25), deadened the spirit of man's being (Rom. 5:12), deprived man of the comfort of God's home (Luke 15:32), and placed man in the devil's grip of power (Eph. 2:2).

Two words sum up the consequences of sin, namely, pollution and penalty.

Pollution

Every part of man's nature has come under sin's dominion. Man in his sin is compared to —

1. An adder for his venom (Ps. 140:3);
2. An ass for his stubbornness (Job 11:12);
3. A bear for his cruelty (Dan. 7:5);
4. A canker-worm for his destructiveness (Joel 2:25);
5. A dog for his uncleanness (Prov. 26:11);
6. A dragon for his desolateness (Job 30:29);
7. A fox for his cunning (Luke 13:32);
8. A leopard for his fierceness (Dan. 7:6);
9. A lion for his ravening (Ps. 22:13);
10. A moth for his frailty (Job 27:18);
11. A sheep for his stupidity (Isa. 53:6);
12. A spider's web for his flimsiness (Isa. 59:5);
13. A swine for his filthiness (2 Peter 2:22);

14. A viper for his poison (Matt. 23:33);
15. A wolf for his ferociousness (John 10:12).

Penalty

The penalty of sin may be summed up in seven words: death, lost, condemnation, guilt, perdition, punishment, eternal.

1. *Death* is the denotative word. Death means separation. Physical death is the separation of the spirit from the body (James 2:26); spiritual death is the separation of man from God (Luke 15:24; John 5:24; Rom. 5:12; 6:23; 1 Tim. 5:6; 1 John 3:14; Rev. 3:1); and the second death is eternal separation from God (James 1:15; 5:20; Rev. 20:14; 21:8).

   Death is said to have "passed upon all men." The word *passed* in Romans 5:12 signifies "to go through, to pierce through, to pass through" and is so rendered in Matthew 19:24 in speaking of the impossibility of a camel "to go through" a needle's eye; in Luke 2:35, where Simeon with prophetic insight tells Mary that a sword would "pierce through" her own soul because of the Christ; and 1 Corinthians 10:1, where reference is made to Israel, who "passed through" the Red Sea. Death, because of sin, has passed through man's nature and deadened every part of it, and unless he receives life, the death-state will culminate in the second death. The hell state is the continuation of the sin state (Rev. 20:14, 15). To be separated from all God is, all Christ was and is, and all the Holy Spirit can give; is hell indeed.

2. *Lost* is the descriptive word. The word *apollumi* means "to lose utterly." It is translated "destroy," "die," "lose," "lost," "marred," "perish."

   a. For God to *destroy* in hell is man's loss of heaven (Matt. 10:28);
   b. To *die* is to lose one's earthly existence (John 18:14);
   c. To live for self is to *lose* one's life in uselessness (Luke 9:24);
   d. To be *lost* is to lose God and one's self (Luke 15:17, 24);
   e. For the wineskins to be *marred* is to lose their service (Mark 2:22);
   f. To *perish* is to lose God's salvation (John 3:16).

   Sin has placed man in the condition described as "lost." Man is lost like a strayed sheep, like the woman's piece of silver, and like the prodigal son in the far country (Luke 15:4, 6, 8, 9, 17, 24, 32). Christ came to seek and to save the lost (Mark 2:17;

Luke 19:10); and God gave Christ that man might not perish (John 3:16; 1 Peter 2:9); but the sinner will find that God is able to "destroy" him if he does not repent (Matt. 10:28).

Two thoughts are wrapped up in the word *lost*, what God loses and what man loses. The sheep lost the shepherd and the fold, and the shepherd lost the sheep; the piece of silver lost the position it occupied, and the woman lost her money; the prodigal lost the father's home, money, food, clothes, and protection, and the father lost his son. Sin robs God from man, and man from God.

3. *Condemnation* is the judicial word. The words translated "condemnation" have varying shades of meaning which it is well to state.

a. *Krisis* signifies a judicial decision and is rendered "judgment" (Matt. 11:22, 24; 2 Peter 2:4, 9; 3:7; 1 John 4:17; Jude 6); "accusation" (Jude 9); "damnation" (Matt. 23:33; Mark 3:29; John 5:29); and "condemnation" (John 3:19; 5:24).

God's judgment against sin has been given, especially against the sin of nonbelief in Christ (John 3:19; 16:8), and His final decision, when men will be judged according to their deeds, will be at the Judgment Day. The day of crisis is passed for the believer, for God's Word is that "he shall not come into condemnation" (John 5:24); but the ungodly, God is reserving "unto the day of judgment to be punished" (2 Peter 2:9).

b. *Katakrino* means to give judgment, to passing sentence upon the sinner, hence to condemn the crime, the punishment following being implied. The word is rendered "damned" in Mark 16:16 and "condemn" in the above sense in Matthew 27:3; Romans 8:3; 1 Corinthians 11:32. Where there is no sin, no judgment is passed; but judgment must be passed upon sin and its sentence carried out where sin exists.

4. *Guilt* is the indicative word. Two words are rendered "guilty."

a. *Enockos* means to be held in, to be detained by the lawful authority because of a charge made, hence in danger of having a penalty inflicted. It is translated "in danger of" in Matthew 5:21, 22; "subject to" in Hebrews 2:15; and "guilty" in Matthew 26:66; 1 Corinthians 11:27; James 2:10.

b. *Hupodikos* means a great deal more. It takes one to the prisoner as he is under sentence. The word occurs only in Romans 3:19, where the sinner, because of his sin, is not on probation, but under condemnation.

5. *Perdition* is the prospective word. This points on to the irretriev-able ruin of those who die in their sins. The word *apoleia* is rendered "destruction" in Matthew 7:13; Romans 9:22; Philip-pians 3:19; 2 Peter 3:16; "waste" in Matthew 26:8; "die" in Acts 25:16; "damnation" in 2 Peter 2:3; "pernicious" in 2 Peter 2:2; and "perdition" in John 17:12; Philippians 1:28; 2 Thessalonians 2:3; Hebrews 10:39; 2 Peter 3:7; Revelation 17:8, 11. Interestingly, Judas complained at the "waste" of the precious ointment that Mary poured on Christ, but he became a "son of waste" by his conduct. The words "waste" and "perdition" are one and the same.

6. *Punishment* is the conscious word. The "goats" in the day of Christ's judgment will go into "everlasting punishment" (Matt. 25:46). The word *kolasis* means penal infliction and comes from a word which means to prune, to dwarf, to curtail, to chastise. It is rendered "torment" in 1 John 4:18.

   There is a whole volume of meaning in two words. *Paidia* is the word used for fatherly chastisement (Heb. 12:5), and *kolasis* is applied to the judicial punishment of the wicked. The former is never applied to the wicked; the latter is never applied to the righteous.

   The nature of scriptural punishment is a result and not a process. Eternal punishment is an expression analogous to "eter-nal judgment" (not judging), eternal redemption (not redeem-ing), eternal salvation (not saving), namely, the eternal effect of an act. "The wrath of God abideth" (John 3:36) on the unbeliever; therefore eternal punishment implies an object to punish. If there are no lawbreakers in prison, there are no law-administrators in action.

7. *Eternal* is the durative word. One cannot escape the doctrine of eternal punishment without lowering the standard of inspiration. One inspired word, the Greek adjective *aionios*, embodies the whole truth. It is used in seven senses in the New Testament —

   a. To the Father as the "eternal God" (Rom. 16:26);
   b. To Christ as the "eternal Life" (Heb. 9:14);
   c. To the Spirit as the "eternal Spirit" (Heb. 9:14);
   d. To the past "times eternal" (Rom. 16:25; 2 Tim. 1:9; Titus 1:2);
   e. To the "eternal Gospel" (Rev. 14:6);

f. To the believer in Christ, who possesses "eternal life" (John 3:15); who is secured in "an eternal covenant" (Heb. 13:20); who is saved in an "eternal salvation" (Heb. 5:9); who is liberated in an "eternal redemption" (Heb. 9:12); who is called to "eternal glory" (1 Peter 5:10); who is kept for an "eternal inheritance" (Heb. 9:15); who is cheered by "eternal comfort" (2 Thess. 2:16); who is assured of "an eternal weight of glory" (2 Cor. 4:17); who should be thinking of "eternal habitations" (Luke 16:9); and be aiming at an abundant entrance into the "eternal kingdom" (2 Peter 1:11);

g. To the unbeliever in his doom, who is said to be cast into "eternal fire" (Matt. 18:8; 25:41; Jude 7); to be under the sentence of "eternal judgment" (Heb. 6:2); because of eternal sin (Mark 3:29, ASV), which means "eternal destruction" (2 Thess. 1:9) and "everlasting punishment" (Matt. 25:46).

We sow a thought and reap a word; we sow a word and reap an act; we sow an act and reap a habit; we sow a habit and reap a character; and we sow a character and reap a destiny.

THE UNIVERSALITY OF SIN

According to the Bible, sin is not a quality or condition of soul that has revealed itself only in exceptional individuals like notorious offenders — prodigals, profligates, criminals, and vicious persons generally; or in exceptional circumstances, as for instance in the early ages of man's existence on the earth, or among half-developed races, or in lands where the arts and sciences are unknown, or in civilized communities where the local environment is prejudicial to morality; but different from this, sin is a quality or condition of soul which exists in every child born of woman, and not merely at isolated times but at all times, and at every stage of his career, though not always manifesting itself in the same forms of thought, feeling, work, and action in every individual or even in the same individual.

Extensively

Sin has affected the whole race of man in every age from the beginning of the world downward, in every land beneath the sun, in every race into which mankind has been divided, in every situation in which the individual has found himself placed.

Scripture utters no uncertain sound on the world-embracing character of moral corruption, saying in the prediluvial age of the world that "all flesh had corrupted his way upon the earth" (Gen. 6:12); in David's generation, that all mankind had "gone aside" and "become filthy," so that "there is none that doeth good, no, not one" (Ps. 14:3); in Isaiah's time, that "all we like sheep have gone astray and have turned every one to his own way" (53:6); in the opening of the Christian era, that "all have sinned and come short of the glory of God" (Rom. 3:23); and generally Solomon's verdict holds good of every day, "There is no man that sinneth not" (1 Kings 8:46) — not even the best of men who have been born again by the Spirit and the incorruptible seed of the Word of God, renewed in their minds and created anew in Christ Jesus. Even of these one writer says: "If we say we have no sin, we deceive ourselves, and the truth is not in us" (1 John 1:8); while another counsels Christians to mortify the deeds of the body, and to put off the old man, which is corrupt according to the deceitful lusts of the flesh (Rom. 7:13; Col. 3:5-10); and a third asserts that "in many things we all offend" (James 3:2).

How true this is may be learned from the fact that Scripture mentions only one person in whom there was no sin, viz., Jesus of Nazareth. But besides Him not a single person figures on the page of Holy Writ of whom it is said, or indeed could have been said, that he was sinless. Neither Enoch nor Noah in the antediluvial age; neither Abraham nor Isaac in patriarchal times; neither Moses nor Aaron in the years of the Israelite wanderings; neither David nor Jonathan in the days of the undivided monarchy; neither Peter nor John, neither Barnabas nor Paul, in the apostolic age — none could have claimed such a distinction; and these were some of the best men that have ever appeared on this planet.

Intensively

Sin has affected every individual, in every department and faculty of his nature, from the circumference to the center, or from the center to the circumference of his being.

It is not a malady which has affected only one part of man's complex constitution: every part thereof has felt its baleful influence. It has darkened his understanding and made him unable, without supernatural illumination, to apprehend and appreciate spiritual things. "The natural man receiveth not the things of the Spirit of God, neither can he know them, because they are spiritually discerned" (1 Cor. 2:14); and again, the "Gentiles walk in the vanity of their minds, having the understanding darkened, being alienated from the life of God through the ignorance that is in them, because of the blindness of their hearts" (Eph. 4:17, 18). It defiles the heart, so that if left to itself, it becomes "deceitful above all things and desperately wicked" (Jer. 17:9), so "full of evil" (Eccl. 9:3) and "only evil continually" (Gen. 6:5), that out of it proceed "evil thoughts, murders, adulteries, fornication," and such like (Matt. 15:19), thus proving it to be a veritable cage of unclean birds.

Sin paralyzes the will, if not wholly, at least partially, in every case, so that even regenerated souls have often to complain like Paul that when they would do good, evil is present with them; that they are carnal, sold under sin; that what they would they do not, and what they hate they do; that in their flesh, i.e., their sin-polluted natures, dwelleth no good thing; and that while to will is present with them, how to perform that which is good they know not (Rom. 7:14-25). It dulls the conscience, that vicegerent of God in the soul, and renders it less quick to detect the approach of evil, less prompt to sound a warning against it, and sometimes so dead as to be past feeling about it (Eph. 4:19). In short there is not a faculty of the soul that is not injured by it. "Sin when it is finished bringeth forth death" (James 1:15).

Study Questions on Hamartiology

1. Describe the origin of sin.
2. Show the difference between the Scripture writers' explanation of the entrance of sin into the angelic realm and that of the entrance of sin into the human race.
3. Give the meaning of *original sin* and quote passages which support it.
4. Discuss the fact of sin.
5. Give some translations and illustrations of the New Testament word *hamartano* and its Old Testament equivalent *chata*.
6. Discuss the Greek word *paraptoma*.
7. Give some translations and illustrations of the Old Testament word *avah* and its New Testament equivalents *adikia* and *adikos*.
8. Give some translations and illustrations of the Old Testament word *avar* and its New Testament equivalent *parabaino*.
9. Give some translations and illustrations of the Old Testament word *pasha* and its New Testament equivalents *anomos* and *asebes*, and also show the distinctive meaning of the Hebrew word *pasha* as contrasted with *avar*.
10. Describe sin as the betrayal of a trust or faithfulness, giving

illustrations from the Old and New Testaments.

11. Give the meaning of the Old Testament word *asham* as compared with *chata*.
12. Give translations and illustrations of the Greek word *opheilema*.
13. Describe sin as disobedience, distrust, unbelief, and a want of response to God, giving illustrations of their use, showing the heinousness of this form of sin.
14. Describe the culpability of sin, showing how it was recognized by God at the time of the Fall, and by the Holy Spirit in various parts of the Scripture.
15. Discuss the various ways in which the consequence of sin is seen in its effect upon men in general.
16. Give some comparisons from Scripture showing man's pollution as a consequence of sin, with references.
17. Give the threefold meaning of death as a penalty of sin, and illustrate the meaning of the phrase "death hath passed upon all men."
18. Give the meaning and translations of the Greek word for *lost*, and give illustrations from Scripture of man's lost condition.
19. Give the meaning of *condemnation* as set forth under the two Greek words *krisis* and *katakrino*.
20. Give the meaning of *guilt* as shown by the two Greek words *enockos* and *hupodikos*.
21. Give the meaning of *perdition* and the translation of the Greek word *apoleia*.
22. Give the meaning of *punishment* and show the distinction between the two Greek words *kolasis* and *paidia*.
23. Give the sevenfold use of the Greek word *aionios*, which is translated "eternal" and "everlasting."
24. What is true of sin as a quality or condition of the soul, negatively and positively, according to the Bible?
25. Describe the universality of sin extensively, and give illustrative proofs from Scripture.
26. Describe the universality of sin intensively, and give illustrative proofs from Scripture.

Notes

[1]Robert Baker Girdlestone, *Synonyms of the Old Testament* (Grand Rapids: Wm. B. Eerdmans Publishing Co., 1897), p. 76.

CHAPTER EIGHT

SOTERIOLOGY: THE DOCTRINE OF SALVATION

Election

Election is that eternal act of God by which, in His sovereign pleasure and on account of no foreseen merit in them, He chooses certain, out of a number of sinful men, to be the recipients of the special grace of His Spirit and so to be made voluntary partakers of Christ's salvation.

Preliminary statements. The Scriptures forbid us to find the reasons for election in the moral action of man before the new birth, and refer us merely to the sovereign will and mercy of God, i.e., they teach the doctrine of personal election. Before taking up the proof of the doctrine, three preliminary statements should be made for which there is scriptural warrant.

1. God has a sovereign right to bestow more grace upon one subject than upon another — grace being unmerited favor to sinners (Matt. 20:12-15; Rom. 9:20, 21).

2. God has been pleased to exercise this right in times past in dealing with men (Ps. 147:20; John 15:16; Acts 9:15; Rom. 3:1, 2).

3. God must have some other reason than that of saving as many as possible in light of the way in which He distributes His grace (Matt. 11:21; Rom. 9:22, 23).

Scriptural proof of the doctrine:

1. Declarations are made of God's purpose to save certain individuals (Mark 13:27; Luke 18:7; Acts 13:48; Rom. 9:11-16; Eph. 1:4, 5, 9, 11; Col. 3:12; 2 Thess. 2:13).
2. Declarations are made of God's foreknowledge of those individuals whom He has purposed to save, whom He has made the object of His special attention and care (Gen. 18:19; Rom. 8:27-30; 11:2; 1 Peter 1:1, 2).
3. Declarations are made that God's choice of those who are to be saved is a matter of grace, or unmerited favor, bestowed in eternity past (Eph. 1:5-8; 2:8; 2 Tim. 1:9).
4. Declarations are made that the Father has given certain persons to the Son to be His peculiar possession (John 6:37; 17:2, 6, 9).
5. Declarations are made that the uniting of believers to Christ is due wholly to God (John 6:44; 10:29).
6. Declarations are made that those who are written in the Lamb's book of life, and they only, shall be saved (Phil. 4:3; Rev. 20:15; 21:27).
7. Declarations are made that believers are the recipients of a special call of God (Rom. 8:28, 30; 9:23, 24; 11:29; 1 Cor. 1:24-29; Gal. 1:15, 16).
8. Declarations are made that regeneration is effected, not by virtue of man's will, but of God's will (John 1:13; James 1:18; see also 1 John 4:10).
9. Declarations are made that repentance, faith, holiness, and good works are the gifts of God (Acts 5:31; 11:18; 2 Tim. 2:25; see also Ps. 51:10; John 6:65; Acts 15:8, 9; 1 Cor. 12:3, 9; Gal. 5:22; Phil. 2:13; Eph. 1:4; 2:9, 10; 6:23; Titus 1:11; 1 Peter 1:2).

"The Spirit breatheth where He wills, and thou (as a consequence) hearest His voice" (John 3:8, Bengel's translation).

These passages furnish an abundant and conclusive refutation, on the one hand, of the view that election is simply God's determination from eternity to provide an objective salvation for univeral humanity; and, on the other hand, of the view that election is God's determination from eternity to save certain individuals upon the ground of their foreseen faith.

Reasonable proof of the doctrine:

1. What God does He has eternally purposed to do. Since He bestows special regenerating grace on some, He must have eternally purposed to bestow it — in other words, He must have

chosen them to eternal life. Thus the doctrine of election is only a special application of the doctrine of decrees.

2. This purpose cannot be conditioned upon any merit or faith of those who are chosen, because faith is neither a work nor merit, but a trusting receptivity (John 1:12). Since faith is the expression of election, it cannot at the same time be the cause of election. There is an analogy between prayer and its answer, on the one hand, and faith and salvation on the other. God has decreed answer in connection with prayer, and salvation in connection with faith. But He does not change His mind when men pray or when they believe. Augustine said, "He chooses us, not because we believe, but that we may believe; lest we should say that we first chose Him. (See John 15:16; Rom. 9:16, 21.)

3. The depravity of the human will is such that, without this decree to bestow special divine influences upon some, all without exception would have rejected Christ's salvation after it was offered to them; and so all without exception must have perished. Election, therefore, may be viewed as a necessary consequence of God's decree to provide an objective redemption, if that redemption is to have any subjective result in human salvation.

4. The doctrine of election becomes more acceptable to reason when we remember, first, that God's decree is eternal and in a certain sense is contemporaneous with man's belief in Christ; and second, that God's decree to create involves the decree of all that in the exercise of man's freedom will necessarily follow.

Objections to the doctrine:

1. It is unjust to those who are not included in this purpose of salvation. Answer:

Election deals, not simply with creatures, but with sinful, guilty, and condemned creatures. That any should be saved is a matter of pure grace, and those who are not included in this purpose of salvation suffer only the due reward of their deeds. There is, therefore, no injustice in God's election. We may better praise God that He saves any, than charge Him with injustice because He saves so few.

God can say to all men, saved or unsaved, "Friend, I do thee no wrong. . . . Is it not lawful for Me to do what I will with Mine own?" (Matt. 20:13, 15). The question is not whether a father will treat his children alike, but whether a sovereign must treat condemned rebels alike. It is not true that, because the governor pardons one convict from the penitentiary, he must, therefore, pardon all. When he pardons one, no injury is done to those who are left. But in God's government, there is still less reason for objection, for God offers pardon to all. Nothing prevents men from being pardoned except their unwillingness to accept His pardon. Election is simply God's determination to make certain persons willing to accept it.

2. It represents God as partial in His dealings and a Respecter of persons. Answer:

Since there is nothing in men that determines God's choice of one rather than another, the objection is invalid. It would equally apply to God's selection of certain nations, as Israel, and certain individuals, as Cyrus, to be recipients of special temporal gifts. If God is not to be regarded as partial in not providing a salvation for fallen angels, He cannot be regarded as partial in not providing a regenerating influence of His Spirit for the whole race of fallen men (Ps. 44:3; Isa. 55:1, 4, 5; Luke 4:25-27; 2 Peter 2:4).

3. It represents God as arbitrary. Answer:

It represents God, not as arbitrary, but as exercising the free choice of a wise and sovereign will, in ways and for reasons which are inscrutable to us. To deny the possibility of such a choice is to deny God's personality. To deny that God has reasons for His choice is to deny His wisdom. The doctrine of election finds these reasons, not in men, but in God.

4. It tends to immorality by representing men's salvation as independent of their own obedience. Answer:

The objection ignores the fact that the salvation of believers is ordained only in connection with their regeneration and sanctification; and that the certainty of final triumph is the strongest incentive to strenuous conflict with sin.

5. It inspires pride in those who think themselves elect. Answer:

This is possible only in the case of those who pervert the doctrine. On the contrary, its proper influence is to humble men. Those who exalt themselves above others, upon the ground that they are special favorites of God, have reason to question their election.

6. It discourages effort for the salvation of the impenitent, whether on their own part or on the part of others. Answer:

Since it is a secret decree, it cannot hinder or discourage such effort. On the other hand, it is a ground of encouragement and thus a stimulus to effort; for, without election, it is certain that all would be lost (cf. Acts 18:10). While it humbles the sinner, so that he is willing to cry for mercy, it encourages him also by showing him that some will be saved, and (since election and faith are inseparably connected) that he will be saved if he will only believe. While it makes the Christian feel entirely dependent on God's power in his efforts for the impenitent, it leads him to say with Paul that he endures "all things for the elect's sakes, that they also may attain the salvation that is in Christ Jesus with eternal glory" (2 Tim. 2:10).[1]

7. The decree of election implies a decree of reprobation. Answer:

The decree of reprobation is not a positive decree, like that of election, but a permissive decree to leave the sinner to his self-chosen rebellion and its natural consequences of punishment. Election and sovereignty are only sources of good. Election is not a decree to destroy — it is a decree only to save. When we elect a president, we do not need to hold a second election to determine that the remaining millions shall be non-presidents.

It is needless to apply contrivance or force. As water naturally runs downhill, so sinners if let alone will go down to ruin. The decree of reprobation is simply a decree to do nothing — a decree to leave the sinner to himself. The natural result of this judicial forsaking on the part of God is the hardening and destruction of the sinner. But it must not be forgotten that this hardening and destruction are not due to any positive efficiency of God — they are a *self*-hardening and a *self*-destruction — and God's judicial forsaking is merely the just penalty of the sinner's guilty rejection of offered mercy (Hos. 4:17; 11:8; Matt. 25:34, 41; 1 Peter 2:8; Jude 4). There is an election to life, but no reprobation to death; a "book of life," but not a book of death.

Calling

Calling is that act of God by which men are invited to accept, by faith, the salvation provided by Christ.

Two kinds of calling:

1. The general, or external, call to all men through God's providence, Word, and Spirit (Isa. 45:22; 55:6; Ezek. 33:11; Matt. 11:28; John 12:32; Rev. 3:20);
2. The special, efficacious call of the Holy Spirit to the elect (Luke 14:23; Rom. 1:7; 8:30; 1 Cor. 1:23, 24; 1 Thess. 2:12; 2 Tim. 1:9; 2 Peter 1:10).

Two key questions:

1. "Is God's general call sincere?" This is denied, upon the ground that such sincerity is incompatible, first with the inability of the sinner to obey, and second, with the design of God to bestow only upon the elect the special grace without which they will not obey.

    a. To the first objection we reply that — since this inability is not physical but moral, consisting simply in the settled perversity of an evil will — there can be no insincerity in offering salvation to all, especially when the offer is in itself a proper motive to obedience.

    b. To the second, we reply that the objection, if true, would equally hold against God's foreknowledge. The sincerity of God's general call is no more inconsistent with His determination that some shall be permitted to reject it, than it is with the foreknowledge that some will reject it.

2. "Is God's special call irresistible?" We prefer to say that this special call is efficacious — that is, that it infallibly accomplishes its purpose of leading the sinner to the acceptance of salvation. This implies two things —

    a. That the operation of God is not an outward constraint upon the human will, but that it accords with the laws of our mental constitution. We reject the term *irresistible* as implying a coercion and compulsion which is foreign to the nature of God's working in the soul (Phil. 2:12, 13).

    b. That the operation of God is the originating cause of that new disposition of the affections and that new activity of the will by which the sinner accepts Christ. This is not any mere cooperation of the will of man with the will of God, but is an almighty act of God in the will of man, by which man's freedom to choose God as his end is restored and rightly exercised (John 1:12, 13).

UNION WITH CHRIST

Spiritual Union

The Scriptures declare that, through the operation of God, there is constituted a union of the soul with Christ — a union of life in which the human spirit, while still most truly possessing its own individuality and distinctness, is interpenetrated and energized by the Spirit of Christ and made inscrutably but indissolubly one with Him, thus becoming a member and partaker of that regenerated, believing, and justified humanity of which He is the Head.

Scriptural proof of the union:

1. The believer is said to be in Christ (John 14:20; Rom. 8:1; 2 Cor. 5:17; Eph. 1:4; 2:13).
2. Christ is said to be in the believer (John 14:20; Rom. 8:9, 10; Gal. 2:20).
3. The Father and the Son are said to dwell in the believer (John 14:23; Eph. 3:17; 1 John 4:16).
4. The believer is said to have life by partaking of Christ, as Christ has life by partaking of the Father (John 6:53, 56, 57; 1 Cor. 10:16, 17).
5. All believers are said to be one in Christ (John 17:21-23).
6. The believer is declared to be a partaker of the divine nature (2 Peter 1:4).
7. The believer is said to be made one spirit with the Lord (1 Cor. 6:17).

The nature of the union. We have here to do not only with the fact of life, but with a unique relation between the finite and the Infinite. Our description, therefore, must be inadequate. Yet in many respects we know what this union is not; in certain respects, we can positively characterize it.

1. Negatively, it is not —
   a. A merely natural union, like that of God with all human spirits — as held by rationalists;
   b. A merely moral union or union of love and sympathy, like that between teacher and pupil, friend and friend — as held by Socinians and others (see 1 Sam. 18:1);
   c. A union of essence, which destroys the distinct personality and subsistence of either Christ or the human spirit — as held by many of the mystics;
   d. A union mediated and conditioned by participation in the sacraments of the church — as held by some ecclesiastical bodies.
2. Positively, it is —
   a. An organic union — in which we become members of Christ and partakers of His humanity (Eph. 5:29, 30);
   b.. A vital union — in which Christ's life becomes the dominating principle within us (Gal. 2:20; Col. 3:3, 4);

   c. A spiritual union — that is, a union whose Source and Author is the Holy Spirit (Rom. 8:9, 10; Eph. 3:16, 17);

   d. An indissoluble union — that is, a union which, consistent with Christ's promise and grace, can never be dissolved (Matt. 28:20; John 10:28; Rom. 8:35, 38, 39; 1 Thess. 4:14, 17);

   e. An inscrutable union — mystical, however, only in the sense of surpassing in its intimacy and value any other union of souls of which we know (Col. 1:27; Eph. 5:32).

The symbolism of the union:

1. From the union of a building and its foundation (Ps. 118:22; Isa. 28:16; Eph. 2:20-22; Col. 2:7; 1 Peter 2:4, 5). Each living stone in the Christian temple is kept in proper relation to every other and is made to do its part in furnishing a habitation for God, only by being built upon and permanently connected with Christ, the chief Cornerstone.

2. From the union between husband and wife (Rom. 7:4; 2 Cor. 11:2; Eph. 5:31, 32; Rev. 19:7). Union with Christ is illustrated by the indissoluble bond that connects husband and wife and makes them legally and organically one.

3. From the union between the vine and its branches (John 15:1-10; see also Rom. 6:5; 11:24; Col. 2:6, 7). The roots of this new Vine, Christ, are planted in heaven, not on earth; and into it the half-withered branches of the old humanity are to be grafted that they may have divine life.

4. From the union between the members and the head of the body (1 Cor. 6:15, 19; 12:12; Eph. 1:22, 23; Eph. 4:15, 16; 5:29, 30). As the members of the human body are united to the head, the source of their activity and the power that controls their movements, so all believers are members of an invisible body, whose head is Christ.

5. From the union of the race with the source of its life in Adam (Rom. 5:12, 21; 1 Cor. 15:22, 45, 49). As the whole race is one with the first Adam, in whom it fell and from whom it has derived a corrupted and guilty nature, so the whole race of believers constitutes a new and restored humanity whose justified and purified nature is derived from Christ, the Last Adam.

Regeneration

Union with Christ involves a change in the dominant affection of the soul. This change we call *regeneration*.

The nature of regeneration:

1. Theological definitions

   a. Regeneration is a spiritual work wrought by the Spirit of God in the spirit of man. This, however, does not define regeneration as it could be applied to any work of the Spirit in the Christian life.

   b. Regeneration is the giving of a bent or direction to the affections and will. This is an inadequate description of regeneration since it covers a part, but not the whole.

   c. Regeneration is that act of God by which the governing disposition of the soul is made holy and by which, through the truth as a means, the first holy exercise of this disposition is secured. This is a good definition, but it fails to make plain what the regenerating act of God is.

   d. The most complete definition would seem to be that regeneration is the communication of the divine nature to man by the operation of the Holy Spirit through the Word. It is an instantaneous change and can, by the nature of the case, occur but once.

2. Biblical descriptions

   a. It is described as a new birth (John 3:3-7; James 1:18; 1 Peter 1:23).

   b. It is described as a spiritual quickening or resurrection (Eph. 2:1, 10).

   c. It is described as the impartation of a new nature, a new creation (2 Cor. 5:17; 2 Peter 1:4).

   d. It is described as a spiritual translation (Col. 1:13).

The necessity of regeneration. That all men without exception need to be changed in moral character is manifest not only in Scripture, but from the following rational considerations:

1. Holiness, or conformity to the fundamental moral attribute of God, is the indispensable condition of securing the divine favor, of attaining peace of conscience, and of preparing the soul for the associations and employments of the blest.

2. The condition of universal humanity as by nature depraved and, when arrived at moral consciousness, as guilty of actual transgression is precisely the opposite of that holiness without which the soul cannot exist in normal relation to God, to self, or to holy beings.

3. A radical internal change is, therefore, requisite in every human soul — a change in that which constitutes its character. Holiness cannot be attained, as the pantheist claims, by a merely natural growth or development, since man's natural tendencies are wholly in the direction of selfishness. There must be a reversal of his inmost dispositions and principles of action, if he is to see the kingdom of God.

The efficient cause of regeneration. Three views only need be considered — all others are modifications of these. The first view puts the efficient cause of regeneration in the human will; the second, in the truth considered as a system of motives; the third, in the immediate agency of the Holy Spirit.

1. The human will as the efficient cause of regeneration. This view takes two forms, according as the will is regarded as acting apart from or in conjunction with special influences of the truth applied by God.

   a. To the view that regeneration is solely the act of man and is identical with self-reformation, we object that the sinner's depravity — since it consists in a fixed state of the affections which determines the settled character of the volitions — amounts to a moral inability. Without a renewal of the affections from which all moral actions spring, man will not choose holiness or accept salvation.

   b. To the view that regeneration is the act of man cooperating with divine influences applied through the truth (synergistic theory), we object that no beginning of holiness is in this way conceivable. For so long as man's selfish and perverse affections are unchanged, he cannot see in God or His service anything productive of happiness; or, if he could see in them anything of advantage, his choice of God and His service from such a motive would not be a holy choice and, therefore, could not be a beginning of holiness.

2. The truth as the efficient cause of regeneration. According to this view, the truth as a system of motives is the direct and immediate cause of the change from unholiness to holiness. This view is objectionable for two reasons.

   a. It erroneously regards motives as wholly external to the mind that is influenced by them. This is to conceive of them as mechanically constraining the will and is indistinguishable from necessitarianism. On the contrary, motives are compounded of external presentations and internal dispositions. It is the soul's affections which render certain suggestions attractive and others repugnant to us. In brief, the heart makes the motive.

b. Only as truth is loved can it be a motive to holiness. But we have seen that the aversion of the sinner to God is such that the truth is hated instead of loved, and a thing that is hated is hated more intensely the more distinctly it is seen. Hence no mere power of the truth can be regarded as the efficient cause of regeneration.

3. The immediate agency of the Holy Spirit as the efficient cause of regeneration. In ascribing to the Holy Spirit the authorship of regeneration, we do not affirm that the divine Spirit accomplishes His work without any accompanying instrumentality. We simply assert that the power which regenerates is the power of God, and although it is conjoined with the use of means, there is a direct operation of this power upon the sinner's heart which changes its moral character.[2]

We add two remarks by way of further explanation.

a. The scriptural assertions of the indwelling of the Holy Spirit and of His mighty power in the soul forbid us to regard the divine Spirit in regeneration as coming in contact, not with the soul, but only with the truth. If any change is wrought, it must be wrought, not in the truth, but in the soul, since even God cannot make the truth more true.

b. No mere increase of light can enable a blind man to see; the disease of the eye must first be cured before external objects are visible. So God's work in regeneration must be performed within the soul itself. Over and above all influence of the truth, there must be a direct influence of the Holy Spirit upon the heart. Although wrought in conjunction with the presentation of truth to the intellect, regeneration differs from moral suasion in being an immediate act of God.

The instrumentality used in regeneration:

1. The Roman, Anglican, and Lutheran churches hold that regeneration is accomplished through the instrumentality of baptism. The Disciples of Christ make regeneration include baptism as well as repentance and faith. To the view that baptism is a means of regeneration we urge the following objections:

The Scriptures represent baptism to be, not the means, but only the sign of regeneration, and therefore to presuppose and follow regeneration. For this reason only believers — that is, persons giving credible evidence of being regenerated — were baptized (Acts 8:12). Not external baptism, but the conscientious turning of the soul to God, which baptism symbolizes, saves us (1 Peter 3:21). Some New Testament verses such as Acts 2:38 and Col. 2:12 are to be explained upon the principle that regeneration, the inward change, and baptism, the outward sign of that change, were regarded as only diffferent sides or aspects of the same fact and either side or aspect might, therefore, be described in terms derived from the other.

Upon this view there is a striking incongruity between the nature of the change to be wrought and the means employed to produce it. It is far more rational to suppose that, in changing the character of intelligent beings, God uses means which have relation to their intelligence. The view we are considering is part and parcel of a general scheme of mechanical rather than moral salvation, and is more consistent with a materialistic than with a spiritual philosophy.

2. The scriptural view is that regeneration, insofar as it secures an activity of man, is accomplished through the instrumentality of the truth. Although the Holy Spirit does not in any way illuminate the truth, He does illuminate the mind so that it can perceive the truth. In conjunction with the change of man's inner disposition, there is an appeal to man's rational nature through the truth. Two inferences may be drawn.

   a. Man is not wholly passive at the time of his regeneration. He is passive only with respect to the change of his ruling disposition. With respect to the exercise of this disposition, he is active. Although the efficient power which secures this exercise of the new disposition is the power of God, yet man is not therefore unconscious, nor is he a mere machine worked by God's fingers. On the other hand, his whole moral nature under God's working is alive and active. We reject the "exercise-system" which regards God as the direct Author of all man's thoughts, feelings, and volitions, not only in its general tenor, but in its special application to regeneration.

   b. The activity of man's mind in regeneration is activity in view of the truth. God secures the initial exercise of the new disposition which He has wrought in man's heart in connection with the use of truth as a means. Here we perceive the link between the efficiency of God and the activity of man. Only as the sinner's mind is brought into contact with the truth does God complete his regenerating work. And as the change of inward disposition and the initial exercises of it are never, as far as we know, separated by any interval of time, we can say in general that Christian work is successful only as it commends the truth to every man's conscience in the sight of God (2 Cor. 4:2).

Conversion

By *conversion* is meant that voluntary change in the mind of the sinner, in which he turns from sin to Christ. The former or negative element in conversion, namely, the turning from sin, we call "repentance." The latter or positive element in conversion, namely, the turning to Christ, we call "faith."

Conversion is the human aspect of the fundamental spiritual change, which, as viewed from the divine side, we call "regeneration." It is simply man's turning. The Scriptures recognize the voluntary activity of the human soul in this change as distinctly as they recognize the causative agency of God. While God turns men to Himself (Ps. 85:4; Jer. 31:18; Lam. 5:21), men are exhorted to turn themselves to God (Prov. 1:23; Isa. 31:6; 59:20; Ezek. 14:6; 18:32; 33:9, 11; Acts 3:19).

This twofold method of representation can be explained only when we remember that man's powers may be interpenetrated and quickened by the divine, not only without destroying man's freedom, but with the result of making man for the first time truly free. Since the relation between the divine and the human activity is not one of chronological succession, man is never to wait for God's working. If he is ever regenerated, it must be in and through a movement of his own will, in which he turns to God as unconstrainedly and with as little consciousness of God's operation upon him as if no such operation of God were involved in the change. And in preaching, we are to impress upon men the claims of God and their duty of immediate submission to Christ, with the certainty that they who do so submit will subsequently recognize this new and holy activity of their own will as due to a working within them of divine power.

From the fact that the word *conversion* means simply a turning, every turning of the Christian from sin subsequent to the first may, in a subordinate sense, be denominated a conversion (Luke 22:32).

Since regeneration is not complete sanctification, and the change of the governing disposition is not identical with complete purification of the nature, such subsequent turnings from sin are necessary consequences and evidences of the first (cf. John 13:10), but they do not, like the first, imply a change in the governing disposition but are rather new manifestations of a disposition already changed. For this reason, conversion proper, like the regeneration of which it is the obverse side, can occur but once. The phrase *second conversion*, even if it does not imply radical misconception of the nature of conversion, is misleading. We prefer, therefore, to describe these subsequent experiences, not by the term "conversion," but by such phrases as "being restored to fellowship," "coming back to Christ," "forsaking sin," "returning from the world," or a kindred expression.

Negative element: Repentance. Repentance is that voluntary change in the mind of the sinner in which he turns from sin. Being essentially a change of mind, it involves a change of view, a change of feeling, and a change of purpose. We may, therefore, analyze repentance into three constituents, each succeeding term of which includes and implies the one preceding.

1. Essential elements involved in repentance

   a. An intellectual element — change of view — recognition of sin as involving personal guilt, defilement, and helplessness (Ps. 51:3, 7, 11). If unaccompanied by other elements, this recognition may manifest itself in fear of punishment, although as yet there is no hatred of sin. For example, the confession "I have sinned" is made by hardened Pharaoh (Exod. 9:27), double-minded Balaam (Num. 22:34), remorseful Achan (Josh. 7:20), insincere King Saul (1 Sam. 15:24), and despairing Judas (Matt. 27:4); but in no one of these cases was there true repentance.

   b. An emotional element — change of feeling — sorrow for sin as committed against goodness and justice, and therefore as hateful to God, and hateful in itself (Ps. 51:1, 2, 10, 14; 2 Cor. 7:10). True repentance takes God's part against ourselves, has sympathy with God, feels how unworthily the Ruler, Father, Friend of men has been treated. It does not ask "What will my sin bring me?" but "What does my sin mean to God?"

   c. A voluntary element — change of purpose — inward turning from sin and disposition to seek pardon and cleansing (Ps. 51:5, 7, 10; Jer. 25:5; Acts 11:18). This includes and implies the two preceding elements and is, therefore, the most important aspect of repentance.[3]

2. Further considerations and qualifications of repentance

   a. Repentance, in each and all of its aspects, is wholly an inward act, not to be confounded with the change of life which proceeds from it. True repentance is, indeed, manifested and evidenced by confession of sin before God (Luke 18:13) and by reparation for wrongs done to men (Luke 19:8). But these do not constitute repentance: they are rather fruits of repentance. Between "repentance" and "fruit worthy of repentance," Scripture plainly distinguishes (Matt. 3:8).

   b. That repentance is only a negative condition, and not a positive means of salvation, is evident from the fact that repentance is no more than a sinner's present duty and can furnish no offset to the claims of the law on account of past transgressions. A truly penitent man feels that his repentance has no merit. Apart from the positive element of conversion, namely, faith in Christ, it would be only sorrow for guilt unremoved.

   c. True repentance never exists except in conjunction with faith. Sorrow for sin, not simply on account of its evil consequences to the transgressor, but on account of its intrinsic hatefulness as opposed to divine holiness and love, is practically impossible without some confidence in God's mercy. It is the Cross which first makes us truly penitent (John 12:32, 33). Hence, all true preaching of repentance is implicitly a preaching of faith (Matt. 3:1-12; cf. Acts 19:4), and repentance toward God involves faith in the Lord Jesus Christ (Luke 15:10; Acts 20:21).

   d. Wherever there is true faith, there is true repentance. Since repentance and faith are but different sides or aspects of the same act of turning, faith is as inseparable from repentance as repentance is from faith. That must be an unreal faith where there is no repentance, just as that must be an unreal repentance where there is no faith. Yet because the one aspect of his change is more prominent in the mind of the convert than the other, we are not hastily to conclude that the other is absent. Only that degree of conviction of sin is essential to salvation which carries with it a forsaking of sin and a trustful surrender to Christ.

Positive element: Faith. Faith is that voluntary change in the mind of the sinner in which he turns to Christ. Being essentially a change of mind, it involves a change of view, a change of feeling, and a change of purpose. We may, therefore, analyze faith also into three constituents, each succeeding term of which includes and implies the preceding.

1. Essential elements involved in faith
   a. An intellectual element — recognition of the truth of God's revelation or of the objective reality of the salvation provided by Christ. This includes not only a historical belief in the facts of the Scriptures, but an intellectual belief in the doctrine taught therein as to man's sinfulness and dependence upon Christ (Rom. 10:17; Heb. 11:1).
   b. An emotional element — assent to the revelation of God's power and grace in Jesus Christ as applicable to the present needs of the soul. Those in whom this awakening of the sensibilities is unaccompanied by the fundamental decision of the will, which constitutes the next element of faith, may seem to themselves — and for a time they appear to others — to have accepted Christ (1 Thess. 2:13).
   c. A voluntary element — trust in Christ as Lord and Savior; or, in other words, to distinguish its two aspects —
      (1) Surrender of the soul, as guilty and defiled, to Christ's control (Matt. 11:28, 29; John 8:12; 14:1; Acts 16:31);
      (2) Reception and appropriation of Christ as the source of pardon and spiritual life (John 1:12; 4:14; 6:53; 20:31; Eph. 3:17).[4]

2. Further considerations and qualifications of faith
   a. Faith is an act of the affections and will, as truly as it is an act of the intellect.
   b. The object of saving faith is, in general, the whole truth of God, insofar as it is objectively revealed or made known to the soul; but in particular, it is the person and work of Jesus Christ, which constitutes the center and substance of God's revelation (Acts 4:12; 10:43; 17:18; 1 Cor. 1:23; Col. 1:27; Rev. 19:10).
   c. The ground of faith is the external word of promise. The ground of assurance, on the other hand, is the inward witness of the Spirit that we fulfill the conditions of the promise (Rom. 4:20, 21; 8:16; Eph. 1:13; 1 John 4:13; 5:10). This new witness

of the Spirit is not a new revelation from God, but a strengthening of faith so that it becomes conscious and unquestionable.

d. Faith necessarily leads to good works, since it embraces the whole truth of God insofar as made known and appropriates Christ, not only as external Savior, but as an internal sanctifying power. The faith which does not lead men to act upon the commands and promises of Christ — or, in other words, does not lead to obedience — is called in Scripture a "dead," that is, an unreal, faith. Such faith is not saving, since it lacks the voluntary element — actual appropriation of Christ (James 2:14-26).[5]

e. Faith, as characteristically the inward act of reception, is not to be confounded with love or obedience, its fruit (Gal. 5:6).

f. Faith is susceptible to increase (Luke 17:5; Mark 9:24; Rom. 10:17). This is evident whether we consider it from the human or divine side. As an act of man, it has an intellectual, emotional, and voluntary element, each of which is capable of growth. As a work of God in the soul of man, it can receive continually, through the presentation of the truth and the quickening agency of the Holy Spirit, new accessions of knowledge, sensibility, and active energy.

Justification

There is no doctrine of the gospel more important than justification. It must ever be a question of intense interest, "How shall man be just with God?" Various answers have been given to this question. Some have insisted that justification is of grace; others have supposed it to be of works; while a third party has virtually attempted to commingle grace and works in a sinner's restoration to the favor of God.

The adoption of correct views on this subject is highly necessary, not only on account of the importance of justification itself, but on account of the relation it bears to the other doctrines of Christianity. It is obvious that our views of other doctrines will be influenced by the conclusions to which we come in regard to the way of acceptance with God.

The meaning of justification:

1. As theoretically and relatively defined. By *justification* we mean that judicial act of God by which, on account of Christ, to whom the sinner is united by faith, He declares that sinner to be no

longer exposed to the penalty of the law, but to be restored to His favor. Or, to give an alternative definition from which all metaphor is excluded: Justification is the reversal of God's attitude toward the sinner because of the sinner's new relation to Christ. God did condemn; He now acquits. He did repel: He now admits to favor. It is a change in a man's legal relation or status before God. It has to do with relations that have been disturbed by sin, and these relations are personal. It is a change from guilt and condemnation to acquittal and acceptance. Regeneration has to do with the change of the believer's nature: justification has to do with the change of his standing before God. The one is subjective: the other is objective.

Justification so defined is, therefore, a declarative act, as distinguished from an efficient act; an act of God external to the sinner, as distinguished from an act within the sinner's nature and changing that nature; a judicial act, as distinguished from a sovereign act; an act based upon and logically presupposing the sinner's union with Christ, as distinguished from an act which causes and is followed by that union with Christ.

2. According to the language and usage of the Scriptures. The Greek word *dikaiosis*, translated "justification," uniformly in both the Old Testament Septuagint and the New Testament — or with only a single exception — signifies, not to make righteous, but to declare just, righteous, or free from guilt and exposure to punishment (Exod. 23:7; Deut. 25:1; Job 27:5; Ps. 143:2; Prov. 17:15; Isa. 5:23; 50:8; 53:11; Rom. 4:25; 5:16, 18). The only Old Testament passage where the meaning is questionable is Daniel 12:3. But even here the proper translation is in all probability not "they that turn many to righteousness," but "they that justify many," i.e., caused many to be justified.

It is worthy of special observation that the terms *justify* and *justification* are contrasted, not with the process of depraving or corrupting, but with the outward act of condemning: and that the expressions used to explain and illustrate them are all derived, not from the inward operation of purifying the soul or infusing into it righteousness, but from the procedure of courts in their judgments, or of offended persons in their forgiveness of offenders. We conclude that these terms, wherever they have reference to the sinner's relation to God, signify a declarative and judicial act of God, external to the sinner, and not an efficient and sovereign act of God changing the sinner's nature and making him subjectively righteous (see also Rom. 4:2-8; Ps. 32:2).

Elements involved in justification:

1. The forgiveness of sin and the removal of its guilt and punishment. God acquits the ungodly who believe in Christ and declares them just. This is not to declare them innocent — that would be a judgment contrary to truth. It declares that the demands of the law have been satisfied with regard to them, and that they are now free from its condemnation (John 3:16: Rom. 4:5; 5:1, 16; Gal. 2:16).

This acquittal, insofar as it is the act of God as Judge or Executive, administering law, may be termed "pardoned." Insofar as it is the act of God as a Father personally injured and grieved by sin, yet showing grace to the sinner, it is termed "forgiveness." Forgiveness may be defined, in personal terms, as a cessation of the anger or moral resentment of God against sin; in ethical terms, as a release from the guilt of sin which oppresses the conscience; in legal terms, as a remission of the punishment of sin, which is eternal death (see Mic. 7:18; Ps. 130:4).

In an earthly tribunal there is no acquittal for those who are proved to be transgressors, but only conviction and punishment. In God's government, however, there is remission of punishment for believers, even though they are confessedly offenders. In justification, God declares this remission (see Rom. 8:1; Heb. 10:17).

The declaration that the sinner is no longer exposed to the penalty of law has its ground, not in any satisfaction of the law's demand on the part of the sinner himself, but solely in the bearing of the penalty by Christ, to whom the sinner is united by faith. Justification, in its first element, is therefore that act by which God, for the sake of Christ, acquits the transgressor and permits him to go free (Acts 13:38, 39; Rom. 3:24, 26; Eph. 1:7). This acquittal is not to be conceived of as the sovereign act of a governor, but rather as a judicial procedure. Christ secures a new trial for those already condemned — a trial in which he appears for the guilty and bears the penalty in the place of the condemned in order to secure a satisfaction to the divine justice.

2. The imputation of divine righteousness and a restoration to a position of favor. This restoration to favor, viewed in its aspect as the renewal of a broken friendship, is denominated "reconciliation"; viewed in its aspect as a renewal of the soul's true relation to God as a Father, it is termed "sonship," sometimes called "adop-

tion" (John 1:12; Rom. 3:22; 5:11; 8:23; 1 Cor.1:30; 2 Cor. 5:20, 21; Gal. 4:4, 5; Eph. 1:5).

In an earthly pardon there are no special helps bestowed upon the pardoned. There are no penalties, but there are also no rewards: law cannot claim anything of the discharged, but then they also can claim nothing of the law. But what, though greatly needed, is left unprovided by human government, God does provide, In justification there is not only acquittal, but approval; not only pardon, but promotion. Remission is never separated from restoration.

The declaration that the sinner is restored to God's favor has its ground, not in the sinner's personal character or conduct, but solely on the basis of satisfied justice (Rom. 3:20-26). God could not justify on the basis of the performance of religious rites (Rom. 4:9-11). God could not justify on the basis of His own love until that love found a way to maintain His justice (Rom. 5:8).

John G. Whittier:

> The hour draws near, howe'er delayed and late,
> When at the Eternal Gate,
> We leave the words and works we call our own,
> And lift void hands alone
> For love to fill. Our nakedness of soul
> Brings to that gate no toll;
> Giftless we come to Him who all things gives,
> And live because He lives.

James Russell Lowell:

> At the devil's booth are all things sold,
> Each ounce of dross costs its ounce of gold;
> For a cap and bells our lives we pay;
> Bubbles we buy with a whole soul's tasking:
> 'Tis heaven alone that is given away,
> 'Tis only God may be had for the asking.

Justification does not simply leave man in the position of Adam before the fall. The Arminians do not all agree on the subject, but in general it may be said that they limit the scope of justification so as to include only the forgiveness of sins. The sinner is accounted righteous only on the basis of his faith or his life of obedience. However, pardon is only one aspect of the declarative act of justification, for a positive standing of righteousness is also reckoned to the account of the believer. One of the best illustrations of that which is secured in the act of justification is the picture Zechariah gives concerning the high priest Joshua in

Zechariah 3:4; "I have caused thine iniquity to pass from thee; I will clothe thee with rich apparel."

The various relationships of justification:

1. Its relation to the requirement of God's law and holiness
   a. Justification has been shown to be a forensic term. A man may, indeed, be conceived of as just, in either of two senses: as just in moral character — that is, absolutely holy in nature, disposition, and conduct; as just in relation to law — or free from all obligation to suffer penalty, and entitled to the rewards of obedience. So, too, man may be conceived of as justified in either of two senses: made just in moral character; or, made just in his relation to law. But the Scriptures declare that there does not exist on earth a just man, in the first of these senses (Eccl. 7:20).

      If, therefore, there be any such thing as a just man, he must be just, not in the sense of possessing an unspotted holiness, but in the sense of being delivered from the penalty of law, and made partaker of its rewards. If there be any such thing as justification, it must be, not an act of God which renders the sinner absolutely holy, but an act of God which declares the sinner to be free from legal penalties and entitled to legal rewards.

   b. The difficult feature of justification is the declaration on the part of God that a sinner, whose remaining sinfulness seems to necessitate the vindictive reaction of God's holiness against him, is yet free from such reaction of holiness as is expressed in the penalties of the law. This fact is to be accepted on the testimony of Scripture. If this testimony be not accepted, there is no deliverance from the condemnation of law. But the difficulty of conceiving of God's declaring the sinner no longer exposed to legal penalty is relieved, if not removed, by the threefold consideration —

      (1) That Christ has endured the penalty of the law in the sinner's stead (Rom. 8:3; Gal. 3:13; cf. Rom. 3:26).
      (2) That the sinner is so united to Christ that Christ's life already constitutes the dominating principle within him (Gal. 2:20).
      (3) That this life of Christ's power in the soul and upon the soul can gradually accomplish a conformity to the divine holiness. This purpose will be completed at the rapture of the church (2 Cor. 3:18; 1 John 3:2).

258 CHRISTIAN THEOLOGY: SYSTEMATIC AND BIBLICAL

2. Its relation to the believer's union with Christ and the work of the Spirit

   a. Since the sinner, at the moment of justification, is not yet completely transformed in character, we have seen that God can declare him just, not on account of what he is in himself, but only on account of the satisfaction rendered to the divine justice by Christ's substitutionary death for sinners. The ground of justification is therefore not, as the Romanists hold, a new righteousness and love infused into us and now constituting our moral character, but that satisfaction rendered fully to the divine moral law by God's own Son when He died for our sins in our place upon the cross. Upon this basis alone God justifies the believing sinner. [6]

   b. The relation of justification to regeneration and sanctification, moreover, delivers it from the charges of externality and immorality. God does not justify ungodly men in their ungodliness. He pronounces them just only as they are united to Christ, who is absolutely just, and who, by His Spirit, can make them just, not only in the eye of the law, but in moral character. The very faith by which the sinner receives Christ is an act in which he ratifies all that Christ has done and accepts God's judgment against sin as his own (John 16:11; Rom. 8:3, 4).

   Justification is possible, therefore, because it is always accompanied by regeneration and union with Christ, and is followed by sanctification. But this is a very different thing from the Romanist confounding of justification and sanctification as different stages of the same process of making the sinner actually holy. It holds fast to the Scripture distinction between justification as a declarative act of God, and regeneration and sanctification as those efficient acts of God, by which justification is accompanied and followed (see Eph. 5:25, 26; 1 Peter 1:1, 2). [7]

   c. Its relation to faith. We are justified by faith, rather than by love or by any other grace: not because faith is itself a work of obedience by which we merit justification — for this would be a doctrine of justification by works; nor because faith is accepted as an equivalent of obedience; nor because faith is the germ from which obedience may spring hereafter — for it is not the faith which accepts, but the Christ who is accepted, that renders such obedience possible; but because faith, and not love or hope, is the medium or instrument by which we receive Christ and are united to Him.

Hence we are never said to be justified on account of faith, but only through faith or by faith. Faith is the mediate or instrumental cause of justification, and the grace of God is the efficient cause of justification. Since the grace of God can be manifested only when a righteous basis for its operation is provided, this was accomplished in the death of Jesus Christ as a satisfaction to the divine justice.

Since the ground of justification is only Christ, to whom we are united by faith, the justified person has peace. If it were anything in ourselves, our peace must needs be proportioned to our holiness. The practical effect of the Romanist's mingling of works with faith as a joint ground of justification is to render all assurance of salvation impossible. But since justification is an instantaneous act of God, complete at the moment of the sinner's first believing, it has no degrees. Weak faith justifies as perfectly as strong faith, although weak faith does not give so strong assurance of salvation.

Justification is instantaneous, complete, and final: instantaneous, since otherwise there would be an interval during which the soul was neither approved nor condemned by God (Matt. 6:24); complete, since the soul, united to Christ by faith, becomes partaker of His complete satisfaction to the demands of law (Col. 2:9, 10); and final, since the union with Christ is indissoluble (John 10:28, 29). As there are many acts of sin in the life of the Christian, so there are many acts of forgiveness following them. But all these acts of forgiveness are virtually implied in that first act by which he was finally and forever justified; so also successive acts of repentance and faith, after such sins, are virtually implied in that first repentance and faith which logically preceded justification.

Adoption

The doctrine of adoption is purely Pauline, and the word *adoption* occurs only five times in the New Testament (Rom. 8:15, 23; 9:4; Gal. 4:5; Eph. 1:5). Some theologians give no special treatment to the subject of adoption. Some regard it merely as an aspect of justification or confuse it with regeneration. However, adoption has an area of meaning not covered by either justification or regeneration.

Meaning of the term. In the analysis of the etymological significance of the terms, it is necessary to relate them to the cultural background from which they came.

1. Adoption. The word means "to place as a son," but it does not have the same force as our English word *adoption*. Its background of Greco-Roman custom is referred to in Galatians 4:1, 2. At a certain time appointed by law, the male child in the family would be formally and legally adopted, i.e., placed in the position of a legal son and given all the privileges of a son. The legal ceremony of adoption did not bring him into the family; it only placed a child of the family as a recognized son in the eyes of the Roman law.

2. Son. The Greek language has two words which are not synonymous, but are actually translated as synonyms in the Authorized Version. This causes confusion in the proper understanding of this doctrine. In Greek and Roman custom *teknon* referred to the child who was born into a family by natural birth; *huios* referred to the same child who at an appointed time was legally declared to be a son. In the theological parallel we become children of God by the new birth (regeneration), and sons of God by adoption. The first term describes our life relation to God: the second our legal relation to God.

Significance of the term:
1. On the human side —
   a. As sons, we have the family name (Eph. 3:14, 15; 1 John 3:1; Rev. 2:17; 3:12).
   b. As sons, we have the family likeness (Col. 3:10; Rom. 8:29; 2 Cor. 3:18).
   c. As sons, we have the parents' nature (2 Peter 1:4; John 1:12, 13; 3:6).
   d. As sons, we have a family affection (1 John 2:9-11; 3:14-18; 4:7, 8; 5:1).
2. On the divine side —
   a. As His children, we are the objects of His peculiar love (John 17:22, 23; 16:27).
   b. As His children, we are the subjects of His fatherly care (Matt. 6:32).
   c. As His children, we are the subjects of His paternal discipline

(Heb. 12:6-11).

d. As His children, we are the subjects of His paternal comfort (2 Cor. 1:4).

e. As His children, we are made heirs to an inheritance (1 Peter 1:3-5; Rom. 8:17).

Sanctification

Erroneous uses of the term:

1. It is not the baptism of the Holy Spirit. The two are constantly confused, but they are not at all one and the same thing, and only confusion and misconception can arise from confounding the two terms. The baptism of the Holy Spirit primarily refers to the event which took place on the day of Pentecost wherein the Holy Spirit made the individual disciples, or believers, to become members of the mystical and corporate body of Christ which is the church. It also includes the successive acts of the Holy Spirit since the day of Pentecost by which He has made individual believers to become members of that same mystical body (1 Cor. 12:12, 13). But, as we shall see later, sanctification describes something entirely separate and distinct from this.

2. It is not perfectionism or the eradication of the Adamic nature, which holds that the Christian may, in this life, become perfectly free from sin. In reply, it will be sufficient to say —

   a. That the theory rests upon false conceptions; first, of law — as a sliding-scale of requirement graduated to the moral condition of creatures, instead of being the unchangeable reflection of God's holiness; secondly, of sin — as consisting only in voluntary acts instead of embracing also those dispositions and states of the soul which are not conformed to the divine holiness; thirdly, of the human will — as able to choose God supremely and persistently at every moment of life, and to fulfill at every moment the obligations resting upon it, instead of being corrupted and enslaved by the Fall. [8]

   b. The theory is not supported, but rather contradicted by the teaching of Scripture. The Scriptures never assert or imply that the Christian may in this life be perfectly sinless. Passages like 1 John 3:6, 9 may seem to, but when properly interpreted they only show the real and contrasting change between the life of the regenerate and of the unregenerate. John paints only in black and white; there are no intermediate tints or colors. Take the words in 1 John 3:6 literally, and there never was and never can be a regenerate person. John recognizes no intermediate state or gradations. He seizes upon the radical point of difference. He contrasts the two states in their essential nature and principle. It is either love or hate, light or darkness, truth or a lie. The Christian life in its essential nature is the opposite of all sin. If there be sin, it must be the after-working of the old nature.

In order to understand John's terms and get his meaning, one must take his own definitions. He defines sin as lawlessness, and hence when he says, "Whosoever abideth in Him sinneth not," he is simply declaring that the abiding one is not lawless and that he that is lawless has not seen Christ, neither known Him. When he says, "Whosoever is born of God doth not commit sin," he simply declares that the begotten one does not practice lawlessness, for God's nature remains in Him and he cannot be lawless in character.

The apostolic admonitions to the early Christians show that no such state of complete sanctification had been attained by them. The party feeling, selfishness, and immorality found among the members of the Corinthian church are evidence that they were far from a state of entire sanctification (1 Cor. 1:1, 2, 10, 11; 3:1-3; 6:4-8; 11:17-19, 29-31; see also 1 John 1:8-10).

We have the record in Scripture of sins committed by some of the most perfect characters of which it bears witness, such as Noah, Abraham, Job, Moses, David, and Peter.

The Greek word *teleios* translated "perfect," as applied to spiritual conditions already attained, can fairly be held to signify only a relative perfection, equivalent to sincere piety or maturity of Christian judgment (1 Cor. 2:6; Phil. 3:15; see also Gen. 6:9; Job 1:1).

The Scriptures distinctly deny that any man on earth lives without sin (1 Kings 8:46; Eccl. 7:20; James 3:2; 1 John 1:8).

c. The theory is disapproved by the testimony of Christian experience.[9] In exact proportion to the soul's advance in holiness does it shrink from claiming that holiness has been already attained, and humbles itself before God in contrition and confession for its remaining apathy, ingratitude, and unbelief (Phil. 3:12-14). But while we show no favor to those who would make sanctification a sudden and paroxysmal act of the human will, we should hold forth the holiness of God as the standard of attainment, and the faith in a Christ of infinite fullness as the medium through which that standard is to be gradually, but certainly realized in us (2 Cor. 3:18).

True meaning of the term. The primary root meaning of the word is "separation." This separation, or setting apart, includes also dedication. Thus sanctification in its general sense is the separation and dedication of a person or object to and for God, to belong wholly to Him and to be used for His glory (Ps. 4:3). This is not only the root meaning, but also the meaning secured by the study of kindred words and their usage in Scripture.

For example, sanctification and holiness are largely the same. The Greek word *hagiasmos* occurs ten times in the New Testament: five times it is translated "holiness" (Rom. 6:19, 22; 1 Thess. 4:7; 1 Tim. 2:15; Heb. 12:14), and five times "sanctification" (1 Cor. 1:30; 1 Thess. 4:3, 4; 2 Thess. 2:13; 1 Peter 1:2). In the American Standard Version of 1901 the same word "sanctification" is used throughout. This is better and more correct. The same word with slight variations in form (*hagiotatos* in Heb. 12:10 and *hagiosunas* in Rom. 1:4; 2 Cor. 7:1; 1 Thess. 3:13) is translated "holiness" four times in both versions; also in the ASV of 2 Corinthians 1:12 (for "simplicity"). The word for "holiness" ("godliness") in Acts 3:12 is different and means piety toward God, godliness, while the one translated "holiness" in Luke 1:75 and Ephesians 4:25 (both versions) is from a word (*hosios*) which means undefiled by sin, free from wickedness, pure, holy. Thus the noun occurs seventeen times in the New Testament (eighteen in the ASV).

The verb (*hagiazo*) is translated "hallow" twice (Matt. 6:9; Luke 11:2) and "sanctify" twenty-seven times. The adjective (*hagios*), from the same root, is translated "holy" eight times and "saints" sixty-two times. The other word for "holy" (*hosios*), adjective and adverb, occurs nine times. There is still another word, meaning sacred, priestly, pertaining to God, which occurs twice (1 Cor. 9:13; 2 Tim. 3:15). The word "holy" in connection with the Spirit occurs nearly one hundred times.

In the Old Testament the word "sanctify" occurs 106 times; "sanctuary," a sanctified place, 135 times (68 times from the same root and 67 from a slightly different one); "consecrate" seven times (Exod. 28:3; 30:30; Josh. 6:19; 2 Chron. 26:18; 29:33; 31:6; Ezra 3:5); "holy" 410 times; "holiness" 30 times; "hallowed" 35 times; "saints" 37 times (18 times from this same word and 19 times from a different one, meaning good, pious). These are all from the same root. They are also from practically the same word except "sanctuary" 67 times, "holy" 8 times, and "saints" 19 times. Even these, with possibly 24 exceptions, have the same meaning as the others. Thus the word in its various forms occurs 300 times in the New Testament and 760 times in the Old, or 1,060 times altogether. Of these, all but 108 are from the same Greek and Hebrew roots and mean the same thing. Of the 108, only 38 have a different meaning from the others, and even their meanings are in harmony with the others.

The term as used in the Bible, then, has a twofold usage: the ceremonial or formal meaning, and the practical or moral meaning.

1. Ceremonial or formal meaning. Here doubtless belong those passages which deal with the thought of the sanctification of God. He is absolutely holy and never needed to be made so. But He is also radically different and separated from the heathen gods and the god of this world (Exod. 15:11-18; 1 Sam. 6:20; Pss. 89:7; 99:2, 3); and when His people or His professed people live like the people of the world, they bring Him and His great name down to the level of the god of this world, at least as far as the world sees. They have profaned Him and His name among the nations. Hence, by cleansing and separating His people and making them different from the world, He separates Himself and His great name and puts them where they belong (cf. Ezek. 20:41; 28:25; 36:20-27; 38:16; 39:27 with Lev. 10:1-3; Num. 20:12, 13; 27:14; Isa. 5:16; 8:13; 29:23). This is also what "hallowed be thy name" means (Matt. 6:9). Therefore, to sanctify God (ASV, "Christ") as Lord in the heart is to separate Him from, and separate from Him, everything which opposes Him and which He opposes (1 Peter 3:15). He Himself does this by separating us to Himself.

That which belonged to Jehovah, set apart for His service, was also considered holy. Nothing is necessarily implied as to moral character, for that which was set apart might be days, seasons, places, objects used for worship, or persons. To sanctify anything in the formal sense was to separate it from common and profane use and to declare that it belonged to God (Num. 3:13; 8:17). Everything thus sanctified was considered holy.

a. Days and seasons were sanctified (Gen. 2:3; Deut. 5:12; Neh. 13:19-22; Joel 1:14; 2:15);

b. Places were sanctified, such as houses (Lev. 27:14) and fields (Lev. 27:16-22). The mount upon which God was to meet Moses with the law was to be sanctified, or set off so that the people could not ascend it or even touch it (Exod. 19:12, 23; Heb. 12:20);

c. The tabernacle and its furniture and the offerings were sanctified also (Exod. 29:27, 33, 36, 37, 44; 30:25-29; 40:10; Lev. 8:10, 11; Num. 7:1). The anointing sanctified. The altar was cleansed before it was sanctified

d. The priests were first cleansed ceremonially by water, a type of regeneration. This had to be done by Moses, not by themselves. After this they were anointed, which sanctified them (Exod. 29:4-9; 40:12, 13; Lev. 8:6, 12);

e. The firstborn of man and of beast was sanctified to God (Exod. 13:2; Num. 8:17);

f. Israel as a nation was sanctified (Exod. 19:5, 6, 10);

g. In the New Testament the formal sense is used sparingly of things (Matt. 23:17, 19; 1 Tim. 4:5; Heb. 9:13);

h. Every child of God is a "saint," or sanctified person, in this formal sense. He is "sanctified in Christ Jesus" — the blood and the work of regeneration does this — and he belongs to God, though he may not be sanctified in the moral sense. This is sometimes called "imputed sanctification."

2. Practical or moral meaning. This aspect is of special interest to the Christian. It is imputed sanctification imparted, or sanctification in the formal sense applied to Christians and made real by the indwelling Holy Spirit.

Since no unclean person or thing can be set apart to God for His use, sanctification includes and presupposes cleansing (cf. John 15:3 with 17:17; Eph. 5:26, ASV, "sanctify, having cleansed"; Lev. 8:6-12). There is but one place where sanctification seems to be synonymous with cleansing, and that is when Hezekiah cleansed the temple after the wicked reign of Ahab (2 Chron. 29:5, 15-18). Even then it is probable that the cleansing preceded the sanctifying, or the setting apart again for the worship of Jehovah.

In the New Testament the work of cleansing is assigned to regeneration and is made a condition for admission into the family of God. Regeneration sanctifies. It is a part of sanctification — the beginning of it, the entrance into it. But the one stops while the other goes on. Both separate —the one separates sin from the sinner and makes him a Christian; the other keeps the Christian separate from sin and makes him a vessel "meet for the Master's use, prepared unto every good work" (2 Tim. 2:21). It is one thing to be cleansed, another thing to be kept clean; one thing to be healed of a disease, another thing to be kept from it so that one may not have it again.

The time of sanctification:

1. The sanctification of the believer begins at his conversion. This might be called "initial sanctification," and it is instantaneous. Sanctification at this stage is both positional and experiential, or objective and subjective. In the former sense, it is closely associated with justification; in the latter sense, it is closely associated with regeneration (1 Cor. 6:11; Heb. 10:10, 14; Titus 3:5; 1 Peter 1:2). With reference to sanctification in this initial sense, Christians are called "saints" (Rom. 1:7; 1 Cor. 1:2; 2 Cor. 1:1). If a man is not a saint, he is not a Christian; if he is a Christian, he is a saint. In some quarters, people are canonized after they are dead; the New Testament canonizes believers while they are alive.

   Note how, in 1 Corinthians 6:11, "sanctified" is put before "justified." The believer grows in sanctification rather than into sanctification out of something else. By a simple act of faith in Christ, the believer is at once put into a state of sanctification. Every Christian is a sanctified man. The same act that ushers him into the state of justification admits him at once into the state of sanctification, in which he is to grow until he reaches the fullness of the measure of the stature of Christ.

2. The sanctification of the believer continues throughout his life upon earth. This is sometimes called "progressive sanctification," and it is the process of that of which the former is the crisis (2 Peter 3:18; 2 Cor. 3:18; 7:1). It includes a subduing of the heart by Jesus, who is now or should be, in a very real sense, Lord; a yielding to Him of the results of the old nature as they come up, the sins, faults, and desires as they are shown in the Word, the mirror and the Spirit's instrument (James 1:22-25; Ps. 119:105; John 17:17; Eph. 5:25, 26); a pruning process (John 15:1-3); often a chastening process (1 Peter 1:7; 4:12, 13); a growing in (not into) grace and the knowledge of Him (2 Peter 3:18); an abounding more and more in love and in a godly walk (1 Thess. 3:12; 4:1, 10); a bringing of every thought into captivity to the obedience of Christ (2 Cor. 10:5).

   The separation from each sin (such as anger, pride) as it comes up and is definitely handed over to the Sanctifier for crucifixion may be instantaneous, but He does not do all His work in an instant, and it seems to be the experience of most people that the things which hinder are dealt with individually. As we look into the mirror and see the blemishes, we do not grieve the Spirit by trying to free ourselves from them, but we deal with Him and trust Him to put them away from us (Eph. 4:30, 31). While it is true that the Spirit does not reveal all defects and unclaimed territory at once, yet it is also true that the moment anything like this is revealed, we can and should claim and secure complete and instantaneous and permanent victory.

3. The sanctification of the believer will be complete at the coming of our Lord Jesus Christ. Then and then only will he have entire sanctification, or be sanctified wholly — spirit, soul, and body. "Wholly" means complete in every part, perfect in evey respect, whether it refers to the church as a whole, or to the individual believer. Some day, the believer is to be complete in all departments of Christian character, with no Christian grace missing; complete in the "spirit" which links him with heaven; in the "body" which links him with earth; in the "soul" as being that on which heaven and earth play; mature in each separate element of Christian character: spirit, soul, and body (1 Thess. 3:12; 13; 5:23, ASV; 1 John 3:2; Phil. 3:20, 21).

The method of sanctification. We come now to the question as to how men are sanctified. What means are used and what agencies employed to make men holy and conform them into the likeness of Christ? The agencies and means are both divine and human: both God and man contributing and operating toward this desired end.

1. From the divine side it is the work of the Triune God.

    a. It is the work of God the Father (John 17:17; 1 Thess. 5:23, 24). It appears from this last verse that sanctification is God's work. The God of peace has called us to it and will accomplish it. He is both the Old and the New Testament Sanctifier (Lev. 20:8; 21:15, 23; Jude 1). Leviticus deals almost entirely with this great subject.

    b. It is the work of the Lord Jesus Christ. He purchased it; His blood was the price paid. God appointed Him to be the sanctification of His people (1 Cor. 1:30).

        (1) He has sanctified all believers by His blood and by His name (Heb. 10:10; 13:12; 1 Cor. 6:9-11);

        (2) He continues the believer's sanctification by His life and

His union with the believer (Heb. 2:11; Eph. 5:25, 26). He Himself is the great wall of separation for the Christian.

   c. It is the work of the Holy Spirit. He is the God-provided Workman to do the work (1 Cor. 6:11; 1 Peter 1:2; Rom. 15:16; 2 Thess. 2:13). Jesus purchased sanctification and the gift of the Spirit by His blood, and He is now at the right hand of God, but He indwells the Christian as subduer and sanctifier through the Holy Spirit.[10]

2. From the human side certain instrumental agencies are used.

   a. An appropriating faith (Acts 15:9; 26:18; 1 Cor. 1:30). Christ is, indeed, made all things needful to the believer, but in reality He becomes such in actual experience only as we appropriate Him for ourselves. Only as the believer daily — yea, even momentarily — takes by faith the holiness of Jesus Christ — His faith, His patience, His love, His grace — to be his own'for the need of that very moment, can Christ, who by His death was made unto him sanctification in the positional sense, become unto him sanctification in the progressive and experiential sense — producung in the believer His own life moment by moment. Herein lies the secret of a holy life — the continuous appropriation of Jesus Christ and all the riches of His grace for every need as it arises. *The degree of our sanctification is the proportion of our appropriation of Christ.*

   b. The study of the Scriptures in subjection to the will of God (John 15:3; 17:17; Eph. 5:26). The Word of God cleanses from the presence of sin, separates us from it, and sets us apart for God. As we bring our lives into daily contact with God's Word, the sins and imperfections of our hearts and lives are disclosed; as we put them away, we become increasingly separated from sin unto God. Our sanctification is limited by our limitation in the knowledge of, and our lack of obedience to, the Word of God. For by the Word sin is made known, conscience is awakened, the character and example of Christ are revealed, and the enabling power of the Holy Spirit is placed at the believer's disposal. There is no power like that of the Word of God for detaching a man from the world, the flesh, and the devil. The Book will separate you from sin, or sin will separate you from the Book.

   c. By judgment of the self-life, personal renunciation of sin and the pursuit of holiness (Rom. 6:19; 1 Cor. 11:18, 31; 2 Cor. 7:1;

Heb. 12:14, asv). Holiness must be the object of one's pursuit. To "follow after" (Heb. 12:14, asv) means to pursue, to persecute, as Saul of Tarsus pursued and followed the early Christians. Sanctification is brought about in the life of the believer by his separating himself deliberately from all that is unclean and unholy, and by presenting continually and constantly the members of his body as instruments unto God for the accomplishment of His holy purposes. Thus, by these single acts of surrender unto holiness, sanctification soon becomes the habit of the life.

d. By subjection to the "Father of spirits" in the exercise of His parental discipline (Heb. 12:5-11).

Prayer

The plausibility of prayer. The belief that specific ends are attained and the granting of special requests is obtained in answer to prayer is considered by many to be inconsistent with the so-called fixity of law and therefore irrational. The reasonableness of prayer may be shown in a way that will be satisfactory to faith, but not to blind unbelief. The fact of prayer and its answer is not contrary to true reason, though it is above and beyond merely natural reason and human philosophy. It is a fact that is understood only in the light of divine revelation.

1. Negatively considered. The difficulty is not to be removed by seeking to eliminate the supernatural from the phenomenal results of prayer.

   a. Prayer is more than the reflex influence upon the one praying. Prayer involves a God who is in personal relations with men, who listens to their petitions and grants their requests. David Hume said truly, "We can make use of no expression or even thought in prayers and entreaties which does not imply that these prayers have an influence." Prayer is not the reflex action of my will upon itself, but rather the communion of two wills, in which the finite comes into connection with the Infinite, appropriating its purpose and power.

   b. The true solution of the problem is not to be found by teaching that God answers prayer only along spiritual lines or in the spiritual realm, such as the action of the Holy Spirit upon the spirit of man.[11] The realm of spirit is no less subject to law than the realm of matter. Moreover, Scripture and experience alike testify that, in answer to prayer, events take place in the outward world which would not have taken place if prayer had not gone before.

c. The question cannot be answered satisfactorily by maintaining that God suspends natural law or breaks in upon the order of nature to gratify every desire expressed or to fulfill every wish made known on the part of man. This view does not take account of natural laws as having objective existence and as revealing the order of God's being. Omnipotence might thus suspend natural law, but wisdom, as far as we can see, would not.[12]

d. The mystery is not explained by considering prayer a physical force, linked in each case to its answer as physical cause is linked to physical effect. We educate our children in two ways: by training them to do for themselves what they can do; and by encouraging them to seek our help in matters beyond their power. So God educates us both by impersonal law and by personal dependence. He teaches us both to work and to ask.

2. Positively considered. Prayer is seen to be plausible from the viewpoint of both Scripture and true reason, by acknowledging that God's answer may involve changes in the sequences or successive actions of nature.

a. God may answer by new combinations or arrangements of natural forces in regions withdrawn from our observation, so that effects are produced which these same forces, left to themselves, would never have accomplished. As man combines the laws of chemical attraction and of combustion to fire the gunpowder and split the rock asunder, so God may combine the laws of nature to bring about the answers to prayers. In all this there may be no suspension or violation of law, but a use of law unknown to us.[13]

Since prayer is nothing more or less than appeal to a personal and present God, whose granting or withholding of the requested blessing is believed to be determined by the prayer itself, we must conclude that prayer moves God, or in other words, induces the putting forth on His part of an imperative volition.

b. God may have so prearranged the laws of the material universe and the events of history that, while the answer to prayer is an expression of His will, it is granted through the working of natural agencies and in perfect accordance with the general principle that results (both temporal and spiritual) are to be attained by intelligent creatures through the use of the appropriate and appointed means. The most formidable objection to this theory is the apparent countenance it lends to the doctrine of necessitarianism. But if it presupposes that free actions have been taken into account, it cannot easily be shown to be false.[14]

The principles of prayer:

1. Negatively considered. At the threshold of this theme, over against all the invitations and promises, we meet certain awful admonitions and prohibitions. In some directions, there is a closed door before prayer. Even its boundless possibilities have a fixed limit, beyond which it is vain to attempt to go. God's restraints are not physical but moral. He can do anything that lies within the range of power, but He cannot deny Himself nor violate moral law. Because prayer pertains to the moral realm, it is subject to moral limitations, and these are its only boundaries. But he who would pray well, both believingly and prevailingly, must learn how far to go, and where to halt. It is of no use to knock at a door that cannot open. We note some of these scriptural limitations.

   a. Man's barter is irrevocable. Esau sold his birthright for a mess of pottage, and the birthright blessing went with the birthright heritage. Though Jacob got the blessing by fraud, behind his trickery lay the permission of the God of the birthright. Jacob's crime of lying succeeded at his father's bedside, but Esau's crime of selling had forfeited what his brother fraudulently obtained. And when the prophetic word had been spoken, it could not be unsaid. Esau sought with tears a change of mind in his father, but in vain. However Isaac himself might regret both Jacob's deceit and his own mistake, he had spoken in the name of God, who had permitted the blessing to go to the brother who had, in Esau's deliberate bargain and barter, bought the right to the birthright succession and all that went with it.

   There are many "profane persons" and "spiritual fornicators" like Esau, not a few of whom are in the church of God, who make a barter of spiritual privileges, opportunities, and blessings — a barter which not even repentance will undo, a forfeiture which not even prayer will restore. Even God cannot give back a lost day or hour. While life is before us, it may be used for God and humanity, or for self and carnality. If wrongly used, and so abused, how can the crime be undone! When life is behind us, it is no longer improvable, but irrevocable. We may repent of what is worse than waste, but the waste remains.

b. God's decrees are irreversible. When Moses again and again pleaded to be permitted to go over Jordan into the Land of Promise, and so complete his work of leadership, God finally said to him, "Speak no more to me of this matter, for thou shalt not go over this Jordan" (Deut. 3:25-27). Moses had publicly dishonored God at Meribah by a second smiting of the once-smitten rock, which was the type of Him who was once for all smitten for us, and yet he had been expressly told to speak to the rock and knew that he was in no respect to depart from "the pattern showed him on the Mount." God, for that offense — which undoubtedly had a deep typical bearing — determined that Moses should not enter with the people into the land of their inheritance; and His decree could not be changed even at Moses' prayer. He who was one of God's mightiest intercessors — ranking with such as Noah and Job, Samuel and Daniel, Elijah and Paul — was told by the very Jehovah whom he knew face to face, as no other had ever known Him, to desist.

c. There are limits of fitness, a time for everything. Prayer cannot take the place of obedience. Only what is seasonable is also reasonable. Jehovah said at the Red Sea, "Wherefore criest thou unto me! Speak unto the children of Israel that they go forward!" It was not a time or place for mere supplication; asking was now to give place to acting. The Lord had already given them assurance of their deliverance, that He would fight for them and destroy their foes. It was not a time to breathe a prayer or cry aloud for help. That cry had been heard and answered, and prompt courageous action and advance were now demanded.

d. Discipline has its necessities. Prayer cannot always avert a providential blow. David had sinned a great sin — and sinned publicly. He had taken another man's wife and, to keep her, had put that other man out of the way; and now the child born of that crime was dying. David went, fasting and praying, before the Lord to plead for the life of the child. But Nathan said, "It shall surely die." No prayer could avert that chastisement. God would not set a premium upon adultery, deception, and murder. The fruit of that abominable and multiplied sin must not abide. It was doomed. The penitent sinner still needed the scourge, and the Father could not spare His rod because of the child's cries.

e. Judicial penalties set limits. Temporal judgments are sometimes necessary as sanctions of God's law. Especially is this true of nations, which as such have no existence beyond this world and whose penalties must come within the bounds of time. There are times when a whole nation has been guilty of some great wrong, and righteousness in God demands retribution.[15]

f. Intercession has its limits. Sometimes the cup of human iniquity becomes full and overflows. When that is the case, no pleas is of any avail. Nothing is left but a deluge of water or a rain of fire. As Noah and Abraham learned, the bounds of God's forbearance were passed. Sin had transcended the limits of even divine patience.

g. Prayer is not to be offered for one who has committed a sin which is unto death (1 John 5:16). What this sin is, we perhaps may not be sure, but because there is such a sin, it behooves us to beware, for no prayer can pierce that death shade.[16]

2. Positively considered

a. It may be offered in the name of Jesus Christ, that is, by virtue of our identity with Him (John 16:23-27). In our Lord's lesson on prayer, which is seven times urged in His last discourse on the eve of His death (John 14:13-24), He teaches the disciples the power of conscious unity and identity with Himself, which makes us even bolder than the sense of our sonship and God's fatherhood. For it is plain that when we ask in Christ's name, He is the real petitioner.

Whenever men use another's name as the authority for approach and appeal to a fellow man, and for a request that they could not urge without such sanction or warrant, it is obvious that he to whom the request is addressed looks past him who presents the petition to the party whom he sees behind the request and for whose sake he grants the favor. Because our name carries no weight, we use another's. So it is no irreverence to say that whenever we ask in the name of Christ, the Father looks past us and sees His Son as the real suppliant. This is emphasized as a new lesson: "Hitherto have ye asked nothing in my name." No Old Testament saint or New Testament disciple had up to that time ever understood this high privilege, because the relation of Christ to His disciples had never been fully revealed.

b. It must be according to the will of God, which is the will of infinite wisdom and infinite love (Matt. 26:39-42; 1 John 5: 14, 15).

c. It is to be by the inward moving and intercession of the Spirit of God (Rom. 8:15, 26, 27; Eph. 2:18; Jude 20). In this aspect of prayer we have God Himself, the Spirit, who is pleading in us. He guides our desires; He shapes our utterance, if indeed the yearnings He awakens do not transcend all language; He displaces carnal by spiritual motives; He teaches us in conscious sonship to cry "Abba, Father" as He Himself virtually does the praying.

d. It is inseparable from our calling and ordination to service (John 15:16).

e. It finds access with boldness in the mediation and priesthood of the Lord Jesus Christ (Heb. 4:15, 16).

f. It should be the expression of true spiritual desire, or yearning, as when David, as God's servant, found in his heart to pray a prayer unto Him (2 Sam. 7:27; Mark 11:24).

g. It should be uttered in simple, trustful faith, the confidence of the child in God as a Father (Mark 11:24; Heb. 11:6; 1 John 5:14, 15).

h. It should be made in dependence upon the sacrificial work of Jesus Christ (Heb. 10:19-22, ASV). It is because of the death of Christ — which removed the barrier that stood between God and us so that he could not consistently hear and answer our prayers — that He can now hear and answer the prayers of His children. As a nineteenth-century preacher remarked, "Prayer is not the conquering of God's reluctance, but the taking hold of God's willingness."

Prohibitions with reference to prayer. Satan knows the importance of prayer, so much so that he would bring and often does bring hindrances into the heart and life. These should be understood and avoided. Some of these are —

1. Wavering (ASV, "doubting"). The doubter is like the waves of the sea, driven by the wind; he must not expect an answer (James

1:6, 7);
2. Asking amiss, to spend it in pleasure (James 4:3);
3. Regarding iniquity in the heart (Ps. 66:18); harboring envy, jealousy, and ill-will;
4. Refusing to forgive or to be forgiven (Matt. 5:23, 24; 6:12, 14, 15; Mark 11:25, 26);
5. Living in sin (Isa. 59:1-3; John 9:31);
6. Refusing to hear the law, the Word of God (Prov. 28:9; Zech. 7:11-13);
7. Refusing to hear the cry of the poor (Prov. 21:13);
8. Discord in the home (1 Peter 3:7);
9. Hypocrisy (Job 27:8, 9; Matt. 6:5);
10. Pride (Job 25:12, 13);
11. Robbing God (Mal. 3:8-10);
12. Idols in the heart (Jer. 11:9-14; Ezek. 8:15-18);
13. Offering unworthy service to God (Mal. 1:6-10);
14. Forsaking God (Jer. 14:10-12).

Study Questions on Soteriology

1. Define election.
2. Discuss the doctrine of election, and refute from Scripture the two extreme views in regard to election.
3. Evaluate the doctrine of election on the basis of reason.
4. Discuss and reflect on the seven objections to the doctrine of election.
5. Define *calling* and distinguish between the general or external, and the special or efficacious, call, quoting one passage with each.
6. Discuss the sincerity of God's general call.
7. Discuss the differences and implications of speaking of God's call as "irresistible" or "efficacious."
8. What do the Scriptures declare concerning the believer's "union with Christ"?

9. Give the scriptural statements concerning the believer's union with Christ, and quote one passage with each.
10. Discuss the negative and positive descriptions of the believer's union with Christ, making reference to Scripture.
11. Give the fivefold symbolism of the believer's union with Christ, and quote one passage with each.
12. Define *regeneration*.
13. Give the biblical descriptions of regeneration, and quote one passage with one of them.
14. Give three reasons for the necessity of regeneration.
15. Discuss the views that teach that either "human will" or "truth" is the efficient cause of regeneration.
16. Give the meaning of the view of "the immediate agency of the Holy Spirit" as the efficient cause of regeneration, and the twofold argument in its favor.
17. Discuss and refute the erroneous view concerning baptism as the instrumentality used in regeneration.
18. Give the scriptural view of the instrumentality used in regeneration, with the two inferences drawn therefrom.
19. Define *conversion*, and give its twofold manifestation.
20. Define the relation that conversion sustains to regeneration, and explain this twofold representation.
21. Discuss the relation that conversion sustains to subsequent acts of turning from sin to Christ.
22. Define *repentance*.
23. Describe the essential elements involved in repentance, and quote one passage with each.
24. Contrast Romanist teaching and Scripture concerning the act of repentance.
25. Discuss repentance under the following headings: as an inward act; as a negative condition; in conjunction with faith.
26. Define *faith*.
27. Describe the essential elements involved in faith, and give an illustration of the part played by each.
28. Discuss faith under the following headings: faith as an act of the affections and will; the object of saving faith; the ground of faith; faith and works; faith as an act of reception; the increase of faith.
29. Discuss the importance of the doctrine of justification.
30. Define *justification*, theoretically and scripturally.
31. Discuss the elements involved in justification, and quote one passage with each.

32. Discuss the relationship sustained by justification to the requirements of God's law and holiness.
33. Discuss the relation of justification to the believer's union with Christ and the work of the Spirit.
34. Discuss justification in its relation to faith.
35. What is it in justification that makes peace and assurance possible?
36. Show how justification can be instantaneous, complete, and final.
37. Discuss the doctrine of adoption. Contrast the Greek words *teknon* and *huios*.
38. Identify what sanctification is not.
39. Discuss the false conceptions of perfectionism. Refute perfectionism from Scripture and Christian experience.
40. Give the positive meaning of *sanctification*.
41. Show from the Scriptures that the meaning of *sanctification* and *holiness* are largely the same.
42. What is the twofold usage of the term *sanctification* in the Scriptures?
43. Discuss the ceremonial or formal meaning of *sanctification*, and show its varied application to things, men, and God.
44. Discuss sanctification with reference to its practical or moral meaning.
45. Discuss the threefold time of the believer's sanctification, and quote one passage with each.
46. Describe the relation of the persons of the Trinity to the work of sanctification, and quote one passage with each.
47. Describe the instrumental agencies from the human side used in the believer's sanctification, and quote one passage with each.
48. What is the attitude taken by many with reference to the plausibility of prayer?
49. Discuss the unsatisfactory attempts to reconcile prayer and natural law.
50. Discuss some of the more feasible reconcililations of prayer and contemporary science.
51. Discuss the scriptural limitations and prohibitions to prayer.
52. Describe the positive principles of prayer, quoting one passage with each.
53. Give the hindrances which constitute prohibitions to prevailing prayer, and quote one passage with each.

Notes

[1]God's decree that the company on Paul's ship should be saved (Acts 27:24) did not obviate the necessity of their abiding in the ship (v. 31). In marriage, man's election does not exclude woman's; so God's election does not exclude man's. There is just as much need of evangelistic effort as if there were no election. Hence the question for the sinner is not, "Am I one of the elect?" but rather, "What shall I do to be saved?"

[2]In any question as to the cause of regeneration it may be asserted immediately that it is not sacramental, i.e., dependent upon the submission of the individual to some ritual; it is not legal, i.e., dependent upon some process of moral development; it is not synergistic, i.e., no cooperation of the human will with the regenerating power of God is involved. Regeneration is an immediate act of God effected by the Holy Spirit within the soul.

[3]In broad distinction from this scriptural doctrine is the Romanist view, which regards the three elements of repentance as the following: (1) contrition; (2) confession; (3) satisfaction. Of these, contrition is the only element properly belonging to repentance; yet from this contrition the Romanist excludes all sorrow for sin of nature. Confession is confession to the priest; and the satisfaction is the sinner's own doing of outward penance, as a temporal and symbolic submission and reparation to violated law. This view is false and pernicious in that it confounds repentance with its outward fruits, conceives of it as exercised toward the church rather than toward God, and regards it as a meritorious ground instead of a mere condition of pardon.

[4]The three constituents of faith may be illustrated from the thought, feeling, and action of a person who stands by a boat, upon a little island which the rising stream threatens to submerge. He first regards the boat from a purely intellectual point of view — it is merely an actually existing boat. As the stream rises, he looks at it, secondly, with some accession of emotion — his prospective danger awakens in him the conviction that it is a good boat for a time of need, though he is not yet ready to make use of it. But thirdly, when he feels that the rushing tide must othewise sweep him away, a volitional element is added — he gets in the boat, trusts himself to it, accepts it as his present and only means of safety. Only this last faith in the boat is faith that saves, although this last includes both the preceding. It is equally clear that the getting into the boat may actually save a man, while at the same time he may be full of fears that the boat will never bring him to shore. These fears may be removed by the boatman's word. So saving faith is not necessarily assurance of faith; but it becomes assurance of faith when the Holy Spirit "beareth witness with our spirit, that we are children of God" (Rom. 8:16).

[5]The sick man's faith in his physician is shown not simply by trusting him, but by obeying him. Doing what the doctor says is the very proof of trust. No physician will long care for a patient who refuses to obey his orders. Faith is self-surrender to the great Physician and the leaving of our case in His hands. But it is also taking His prescriptions and actively following His directions.

[6]As Adam's sin is imputed to us, not because Adam is in us, but because we were in Adam; so divine righteousness is imputed to us, not because Christ is in us, but because we are in Christ — that is, joined by faith to One whose death provided an infinite satisfaction to God which made possible an act of justification. In this sense, we may say that we are justified through a Christ outside of us as we are sanctified through a Christ within us.

[7]The ground of justification cannot be found in any virtue of man, nor in his good works. This position must be maintained over against the Romanist doctrine and the Pelagianizing tendencies of some groups. Rome teaches that the sinner is justified on the basis of the inherent righteousness that has been infused into his heart, and which, in turn, is the fruit of the cooperation of the human will with prevenient grace. This applies to that which is called the first justification; in all the following justification the good works of man come into consideration as the formal cause or ground of justification.

[8]The fundamental error of perfectionism is its low view of God's law; the second is its narrow conception of sin. John Wesley said: "I believe a person filled with love of God is still liable to involuntary transgressions. Such transgressions you may call sins, if you please; I do not."

[9]Some mistake regeneration for sanctification. When led to faith in Christ, finding peace and joy, they think they are sanctified, when they are simply converted or regenerated. Some mistake assurance of faith for sanctification, but joy is not sanctification. It is possible,

however, that one may experience a great crisis in his spiritual life, in which there is such a total surrender of self to God and such an infilling of the Holy Spirit that he is freed from the bondage of sinful appetites and habits and enabled to have constant victory over self instead of suffering constant defeat. If the doctrine of sinless perfection is a heresy, the doctrine of contentment with sinful imperfection is a greater heresy. It is not an edifying spectacle to see a Christian worldling throwing stones at a Christian perfectionist.

[10]Here the question arises, In what sense does the Holy Spirit who sanctifies the believer accomplish His work? In this sense, just as in the Old Testament type the tabernacle, altar, and priest were set apart for God by the anointing oil (Lev. 8:10-12), so in the New Testament anti-type, the believer, who is both tabernacle and priest, is set apart for God by the anointing of the Holy Spirit. Further than that, it is the Holy Spirit's work in the heart that overcomes the flesh and its defilements and thus separates the believer from sin, clothes him with divine graces of character, and makes him fit to be God's own. As Paul puts it in Galatians 5:22, 23, "But the fruit of the Spirit is love, joy, peace, longsuffering, kindness, goodness, faith, meekness, self-control." In opposition to this work of the Holy Spirit we read in the immediately preceding verses what "the works of the flesh" are, an awful catalogue of vileness and sin, and we are told in verse 16, "Walk in the Spirit and ye shall not fulfill the lust of the flesh."

[11]According to this second line of thought, God feeds the starving Elijah, not by a distinct message from heaven, but by giving a compassionate disposition to the widow of Zarephath so that she is moved to help the prophet (1 Kings 17:9: "Behold, I have commanded a widow there to sustain thee"). But God could also feed Elijah by the ravens and the angel (1 Kings 17:4; 19:5); and the pouring rain that followed Elijah's prayer (1 Kings 18:42-45) cannot be explained as a subjective phenomenon.

[12]This third theory might well be held by those who see in nature no force but the all-working will of God. But the properties and powers of nature are revelations of the divine will, and the human will has only a relative independence in the universe. To expect that God would grant our every wish is to desire omnipotence without omniscience. All true prayer is, therefore, an expression of the one petition: "Thy will be done" (Matt. 6:10).

[13]Laws are not our masters, but our servants. They do our bidding all the better because they are uniform. And our servants are not God's masters.

[14]Since God is immanent in nature, an answer to prayer, coming about through the means of natural law, may be as real a revelation of God's personal care as if the laws of nature were suspended and God interposed by an exercise of His creative power. Prayer and its answers, though having God's immediate volition as their connecting bond, may yet be provided for in the original plan of the universe. The universe does not exist for itself, but for moral ends and for moral beings, to reveal God and to furnish facilities of intercourse between God and intelligent creatures.

[15]Though Job, Noah, Moses, Samuel, and Daniel were together to appeal to God, His mind could not be toward His people to save them from judgment (Jer. 15:1; Ezek. 14:14, 20).

[16]Alford makes it an appreciable act, the denying Jesus to be the Christ, the Son of God, which willful, deliberate denial John elsewhere accounts a sufficient ground for not wishing a man "Godspeed" or receiving him into the house. But the state of apostasy which makes such an act possible is undoubtedly included. This sin, whatever it be, is one which may be detected in a "brother" — a professed disciple — which makes the warning more terrible. And no fact is more significant than this — that when a disciple has once radically departed from the faith and practice of godliness, and even goes as far as to deny the Lord that bought him, and to blaspheme His name, history may be safely challenged to produce one unmistakable case of restoration to his lost faith and love! If so, history may perhaps be a sufficient expositor in this case.

CHAPTER NINE

ECCLESIOLOGY: THE DOCTRINE OF THE CHURCH

Ecclesiology is the doctrine or study of the church in its constitution, ordinances, and activities, the last including both work and worship.

There is great danger of losing sight of the church in the endeavor to emphasize the idea of the kingdom of heaven or Christendom. We are prone to think it a small thing to speak of the church; the kingdom and Christendom seem so large in comparison. We are tempted to distinguish and contrast churchism, as it is sometimes called, and Christianity, to the disparagement of the former. It is well to remember: (1) Jesus Christ positively identifies Himself with the church (Acts 9:1-5) and not with Christendom; (2) He gave up His life that He might found the church (Eph. 5:25); (3) the apostle Paul sacrificed himself in his endeavors to build up the church, not Christendom (2 Tim. 2:10; 2 Cor. 11:2, 23-28); (4) he speaks of his greatest sin as consisting in persecuting the church of God (1 Cor. 15:9); (5) the supreme business of God in this age is the gathering of the church ("To take out of them [nations] a people for His name" [Acts 15:13-17]; see also Eph. 4:12).

EXPLANATION OF TERMS

The English Word "Church"

The meaning of this term is determined by its etymology and by its past and present usage.

As determined by its etymology. The English word *church* finds its nearest neighbor and sister in the Scotch *kirk*, and next to that its cousin in the German *kirche*. If it would find its mother, it would look to the old Saxon *circe, cirice,* or *cyrace*. It is evident at a glance that all these are different forms of the same word. Whence did it come? Almost certainly from the Greek *kuriakon*. This word, *kuriakon,* was used by the Greek Christians to designate the house of worship, and it seems clear that the Goths and other Teutonic races got the word, as they got their first knowledge of Christianity, from the Greek Christians.

Now the word *kuriakon* is simply the adjective neuter from *kurios,* "Lord," and means that which is the Lord's, that is, the Lord's place, the Lord's house. This adjective is found in the New Testament, though not with reference to a place. (The passages are in 1 Cor. 11:20, in connection with the Lord's Supper, and in Rev. 1:10, the Lord's Day). In early Greek Christian literature, the neuter adjective with the article, *to,* came to be applied to the house of worship. In usage, the transition was easy from the building to the assembly which worshiped in the building. Thus the word *church* literally means the Lord's place, or the Lord's house, and from that it has been extended to all the various significations which it has acquired in the progress of language.

As determined by its past and present usage. Interesting as its etymology is, the uses of the word in our own day and throughout the history of the church chiefly concern us here. Of these uses we may notice at least five.

1. A particular body of Christians organized for religious purposes and commonly meeting in one place for worship. This is the local church.

2. The general body, or sum total, of Christians, conceived of in the largest inclusive sense, or partially as represented in those under consideration at the time. This is the universal church.

3. The building where the local assembly meets for worship or other purposes. This does not occur in the New Testament, but in early Greek Christian literature the neuter adjective with the article was applied to the house of worship.

4. A body or sect or denomination of Christians having the same general doctrines, organization, and history, including and controlling local bodies of the same faith and order.[1]

5. A group of secondary and derived meanings, more or less vague and growing out of the preceding, may be put together.

a. From the local sense, in such phrases as "a member of the church," "going to church," and the adjectival uses like "church meeting" or "church affairs."
b. From the general sense, as "the church," meaning the whole unorganized mass of Christians — e.g., "church and state," "church history," "church enterprises," or "church people."
c. Somewhat wavering between the two, as "church order" or "church polity."

The Greek Word "Ekklesia"

As determined by its etymology. The word *ekklesia* is derived from *ek*, "out," and *kaleo*, "to call," denoting in good Greek usage the assembly of citizens when *called out* from their homes to gathering places for the discussion of public business.

As determined by its past and present usage. The word *ekklesia* came to mean in a general sense a gathering or assembly of people, even though they might not be summoned specifically for the transaction of public business. From this more general use the word passed to its employment in the Septuagint and the New Testament where its usual meaning is that of assembly or congregation. In the Septuagint it is often used to translate the Hebrew *qahal*, "congregation": either as summoned for a definite purpose (1 Kings 8:65), or for the collective community of Israel regarded as a congregation (Gen. 28:3).

Ekklesia originally referred to a regularly summoned assembly of citizens (e.g., Acts 19:39). It is employed in the New Testament for the congregation of Israel (Acts 7:38), but the more common word so used is "synagogue" (*syn*, together; *ago*, to bring), of which "synagogue" is a transliteration. Matthew 16:18 is the first occurrence of this word in the New Testament. In Christ's words to Peter, *ekklesia* acquires special emphasis from the opposition to the synagogue implied in it. The Christian community in the midst of Israel would be designated as *ekklesia* without being confounded with the *synagogue*, the Jewish community (see Acts 5:11; 8:1; 12:1; 14:23, 27). Nevertheless *synagogue* is applied to a Christian assembly in James 2:2, while *episynagoge* (gathering or assembling together) is found in 2 Thessalonians 2:1; Hebrews 10:25.

Both in Jewish and in New Testament usage *ekklesia* implies more than a collective or national unity, but rather a community based on a special religious idea and established in a special way. In the New Testament the term is used also in the narrower sense of a single church, or a church confined to a particular place. So also of the church in the house of Aquila and Priscilla (Rom. 16:5), the church at Corinth, the churches in Judea, the church at Jerusalem, etc.

There are a few passages in which the word does not connote the Christian church. In Acts 7:38 Stephen mentions the assembly, or congregation, of the people in the wilderness, most probably having in mind the great gathering of the people at Sinai when the law was given. In Acts 19, in reference to the uproar at Ephesus, the word occurs several times, but certainly not in the sense of the church. In verses 41 — and 40 as is evident from the connection — the word simply means the coming together of the people — the crowd; this is not, strictly speaking, a proper use of the word and does not seem to occur elsewhere. In verse 39 there is reference to the lawful assembly as opposed to the confused crowd, and this usage accords with the common classical signification of an assembly of the citizens.

In Hebrews 2:12 is a quotation from the Septuagint version of Psalm 22:22: "In the midst of the congregation will I sing praise to thee." Here there is no description of the New Testament church as such, but simply of a worshiping congregation. Still, it is a suggestive fact that the word occurs in this quotation from the Greek version of the Old Testament. In all the remaining passages of the New Testament, the word *ekklesia* is correctly translated "church."

THE TWOFOLD APPLICATION OF "EKKLESIA"

Its General Aspect, Viewed As an Organism
Definitions, negatively considered:

1. The church is not synonymous or identical with the kingdom of heaven. The phrase *kingdom of heaven* (lit. "of the heavens") is peculiar to Matthew and signifies the messianic earth rule of Jesus Christ, the Son of David. It is called the kingdom of heaven because it is the rule of the heavens over the earth (Matt. 6:10). The phrase is derived from Daniel, where it is defined (Dan. 2:34-36, 44; 7:23-27) as the kingdom which "the God of heaven" will set up after the destruction by the "stone cut out without hands" of the Gentile world-system. It is the kingdom covenanted to David's seed (2 Sam. 7:7-10); described in the prophets (Zech. 12:8); and confirmed to Jesus Christ, the Son of Mary, through the angel Gabriel (Luke 1:32, 33).

The kingdom of heaven has three aspects in Matthew: first, "at hand" from the beginning of the ministry of John the Baptist (Matt. 3:1, 2); second, in seven "mysteries of the kingdom of heaven," to be fulfilled during the present age (Matt. 13:1-52), to which are to be added the parables of the kingdom of heaven which were spoken after those of Matthew 13 and which have to do with the sphere of Christian profession during this age; third, the prophetic aspect — the kingdom to be set up after the return of the King in glory (Matt. 24:29—25:46; Luke 19:12-19; Acts 15:14-17).

The kingdom of heaven is thus seen to be a distinctive Scriptural term having a threefold application, but in none of these is it identical with the church, the body of Christ. The latter, however, is included in the kingdom of heaven in its present mystery form, as is the whole sphere of Christian profession. The church and the kingdom of heaven can be contrasted thus:

a. Contrast in the names. The names are never used interchangeably in Scripture. The church comprises individual believers, "called out ones," a minority, members of His body; the kingdom comprises subjects, and it includes the whole nation of Israel and eventually the whole earth (Zech. 14:9).

b. Contrast of the place of each in the economy of God. The church belongs to the age of grace, the kingdom in its manifestation to the millennial age. The church belongs to the present age, the kingdom to a future age. The church is unknown in the Old Testament; the kingdom is spoken of everywhere in the Old Testament. The church was a secret, or mystery, until Paul's day (Eph. 3:5-9; Col. 1:26; Rom. 16:25, 26); the kingdom was no secret, but was looked for, longed for, prayed for, and expected by every Old Testament seer and saint since David's day. The church is the special theme of Paul's epistles; the kingdom is never mentioned in Paul's epistles.

c. Contrast in terminology. The church is called "His body." Christ is called "the Head of the Church" (Eph. 1:22; 5:23; Col. 1:18); in the kingdom, the Messiah is to be "the King" and is never designated "the King of the Church." The church is spoken of as being "built" upon the foundation of the apostles and prophets (Eph. 2:20-22; 3:5; 4:8-11; 1 Cor. 3:9; Col. 2:7); the kingdom is said to be "set up" (Dan. 2:44; see also Acts 15:16).

The church, when completed, is to be taken away from the earth into heaven (1 Thess. 4:13-18); the kingdom, when set up, is to remain here on the earth (Ps. 145:13). The church is a family — God's heavenly family (Eph. 3:15); the kingdom is a people — God's earthly people. The church comprises believers who have in Christ lost all identity as Jews or Gentiles (Col. 2:11); in the kingdom, national distinctions are to be preserved.

d. Contrast in destiny. The church is heavenly in destiny (Phil. 3:20, 21); the kingdom is earthly in destiny (Dan. 2:44; Zech. 14:9). The church is to be "caught up" into glory (1 Thess. 4:13-18); the kingdom is to remain upon the earth (Zech. 14:9). The glory of the church is celestial (Col. 1:27); the glory of the kingdom is terrestrial (Dan. 7:13, 14, 27).

e. Contrast in proclamation and presentation. The gospel of the grace of God is the message of the church — the good news of God's grace (Acts 20:24; Rom. 1:1); the gospel of the kingdom is the message in connection with the kingdom — the good news of the messianic kingdom (Matt. 4:23; 24:14). The gospel of the glory is another phase of the message of the church (1 Tim. 1:11; 2 Cor. 4:4); the everlasting gospel is another phase of the message of the millennial kingdom (Rev. 14:6, 7).

2. The church is not synonymous or identical with the kingdom of God. The kingdom of God is that sphere or realm in which God is acknowledged and obeyed as sovereign, and comprises all unfallen created intelligence as well as that part of the human race that is included in the redemption which is in Christ Jesus.

a. Contrasts between the church and the kingdom of God. The kingdom of God belongs to all time, i.e., it is contemporaneous with the universe; the church has a specific beginning in time, the day of Pentecost. The kingdom includes both heavenly and earthly beings, while the church includes only earthly beings. The kingdom of God includes unfallen intelligence as well as redeemed men, but the church includes only the redeemed. The kingdom of God includes all the redeemed of all ages; the church includes only those who are redeemed from Pentecost to Parousia, from the resurrection of Christ to His second advent.

b. Comparisons between the kingdom of God and the kingdom of heaven. *The kingdom of God* is a generic term which includes in its force and scope all the other designations of the true kingdom. The kingdom of heaven may be the kingdom of God, but the kingdom of God is not necessarily always the same as the kingdom of heaven, for otherwise both terms would not be employed by Matthew. If Matthew had spoken only of the kingdom of heaven, and Mark and Luke only of the kingdom of God, there might have been good reason for concluding the two expressions were absolutely identical; but the fact that Matthew five times refers to the kingdom of God in a book where the kingdom of heaven is mentioned thirty-two times surely intimates that the two terms are to be distinguished, no matter how closely they may resemble each other in some aspects.

That in certain respects the two expressions are very similar in their scope is clear, and that some of the things predicted of the former are also predicated of the latter cannot be denied. Yet the additional fact that *the kingdom of heaven* which occurs so frequently in Matthew's Gospel — the design of which is to set forth the offer of the messianic kingdom to the Jews, their refusal to comply with the terms of its offer, and the consequences ensuing from their refusal — is never once used by Mark, Luke, or John ought to show that it does bear a different significance from *the kingdom of God*, which is the phrase invariably employed by the other Evangelists. The kingdom of God as administered in Israel of old — whether in the immediate theocracy or by Saul or David and his sons — was not the kingdom of heaven, for its center of dominion and throne were on the earth.

"The kingdom of heaven" in the first twelve chapters of Matthew has an entirely different force and scope from that which it has in the later chapters. In Matthew the kingdom which John announced as "at hand" was the messianic kingdom of Old Testament prophecy, whereas in the parables of Matthew 13, etc., the "kingdom of heaven" has reference to the Christian profession. Yet both of these significations of the "kingdom of heaven" are spoken of as the kingdom of God in the other Gospels. It would therefore be as scriptural to say that the "kingdom of heaven" in Matthew 3 is the kingdom of God, as it would be to say that the "kingdom of heaven" in Matthew 13 is the kingdom of God also; but it would not be accurate to say of other Scriptures that the kingdom of God is synonymous with the "kingdom of heaven" except we qualify our words by adding which aspect of the "Kingdom of heaven" we are referring to.

For instance, when we read in Romans 14:17, "For the kingdom of God is not meat and drink, but righteousness, and peace, and joy in the Holy Spirit," the kingdom of God cannot here be the equivalent of the "kingdom of heaven" which the Baptist announced as recorded in Matthew 3:2, but it would correspond with the "kingdom of heaven" as it is used in the parables of Matthew 13, providing we understand by it the reality of what is there professed.

c. Contrasts between the kingdom of God and the kingdom of heaven. The kingdom of God is universal, including all moral intelligences willingly subject to the will of God, whether angels, the church, or saints of past or future dispensations, (Luke 13:28, 29; Heb. 12:22, 23); the kingdom of heaven is messianic, mediatorial, and Davidic and has for its object the establishment of the kingdom of God in the earth (1 Cor. 15:24, 25).

The kingdom of God is entered only by the new birth (John 3:3, 5-7); the kingdom of heaven, during this age, is the sphere of a profession which may be real or false (Matt. 13; 25:1, 11, 12).

Since the kingdom of heaven is the earthly sphere of the universal kingdom of God, the two have almost all things in common. For this reason many parables and other teachings are spoken of the kingdom of heaven in Matthew and of the kingdom of God in Mark and Luke. The omissions are significant. The parables of the wheat and tares and of the net (Matt. 13:24-30, 36-43, 47-50) are not spoken of the kingdom of God. In that kingdom there are neither tares nor bad fish. But the parable of the leaven (Matt. 13:33) is spoken of the kingdom of God also, for alas, even the true doctrines of the kingdom are leavened with the errors of which the Pharisees, Sadducees, and Herodians were the representatives.

The kingdom of God "comes not with outward show" (Luke 17:20), but is chiefly what is inward and spiritual (Rom. 14:17); the kingdom of heaven is organic and is to be manifested in glory on the earth. The kingdom of heaven merges into the kingdom of God when Christ, having "put all enemies under His feet, . . . shall have delivered up the kingdom to God, even the Father" (1 Cor. 15:24-28).

3. The church is not synonymous or identical with Christendom. The term *Christendom* has a twofold usage. In its limited use it

refers to the professing church or all who make nominal profession of the Christian faith. In its wider significance it has a territorial application and comprises those countries in which Christianity prevails or which is more or less controlled by Christian influences, i.e., nominally Christian lands as opposed to distinctively heathen lands.

Definitions, positively considered. The church is a body of persons called out of the world and separated from sin by the power of God to faith in a crucified and risen Christ, having had wrought in them by the Spirit, through the Word, the nature of the risen Christ, being indwelt by the Spirit, made members one of another, and linked by that Spirit to the risen Man in the heavens—see John 4:23, 24; 15:19; Acts 15:14; 20:28; Rom. 16:16; 1 Cor. 10:32; 11:22; 15:1-4, 9; Eph. 3:10, 21; 4:17; 5:24-26; Phil. 3:3; 1 Tim. 3:5, 15, 16; 2 Tim. 3:16, 17; 1 Peter 1:18, 19; 1 John 2:15-17.

1. Membership of the church as an organism. The word *church* literally means a called-out company, and therefore it comprises only those who are truly called out from the world by Christ unto Himself—in other words, all true believers wherever found. It is not the aggregate of all the churches, constituted as they are at present of both true and false professors, nor is it any particular church on earth, though some churches have formed themselves into what they call a church of the whole, or a catholic church; but it may be seen from the meaning of the word that if the church should ever embrace all the world and become universal, it would cease to be a church or called-out company.

   The church comprises all true Christian believers taken out of all nations, tribes, and tongues and united with their living Head, Jesus Christ, during the age from Pentecost to the Rapture. Induction into the church is the work of Christ through the Holy Spirit.

2. The unity of the church as an organism. This unity is not external, consisting in intellectual belief or form of government; it is wholly spiritual and a result of the unifying power of the Holy Spirit (John 17:21; Rom. 12:5; Gal. 3:28; Eph. 4:13).

The revelation of the church:

1. Foretold by Christ. "On this rock I will build my church" (Matt. 16:18). Here is the church in prophecy and promise, the first mention of the church in the New Testament. The church was not in existence during the earthly life of Jesus; but its establishment

was promised and predicted by Him. It was founded on Peter's confession of Jesus Christ as the Son of the living God.

2. Revealed through Paul. The church doctrinally was alone fully revealed to Paul and by him communicated to man (Eph. 3:1-11).

The symbolism of the church. The relationships existing between Christ and the church are set forth in a variety of symbols. This symbolism consists of numerous descriptive terms applied to the church.

1. The "New Man." "To make in Himself one new man" (Eph. 2:15) — a new, immortal, divine race of men, which is the ultimate answer to God's proposition in Genesis 1:26: "Let us make man in our image." In Genesis we find that Adam and Eve were called by a common name: "He called their name Adam" (Gen. 5:2). Adam and Eve, typically, set forth Christ and His church; therefore we find that Christ and His church have a common name (1 Cor. 12:12). The word *Christ* here is preceded by the article, *the*, the literal meaning thus being "the Christ"; and so the name *Christ* is given to the church as the body of Him who is called, also, the Christ.

2. The "Body of Christ." Two ideas are contained in this symbol: first, the church has a relation which it sustains to Christ, who is its Head (Eph. 1:22, 23; Col. 1:18; 2:19). The church in this aspect is an organism, not an organization. There is a vital relation between Christ and the church, both partaking of the same life, just as there is between the physical head and the body. As the Head of the church, Christ is its Guardian and Director (Eph. 5:23, 24); the Source of its life, filling it with His fullness (Eph. 1:23); the Center of its unity and the Cause of its growth (Eph. 4:15; Col. 2:19). Second, the church has an internal relationship sustained by its members toward each other (1 Cor. 12:12-27; Rom. 12:4, 5; Eph. 4:1-4, 15, 16).

3. The "Temple of God." The church as the temple of God is a building of which Christ is the chief cornerstone, and the apostles and prophets the foundation (Eph. 2:20, 21; 1 Cor. 3:9-17; 1 Tim. 3:15; 1 Peter 2:4-8). The apostles and prophets occupy a foundational position in the church, since they were the first leaders and since the church is established upon the doctrines and practices recorded by them in the New Testament (John 16:13). The church is not built upon weak human beings, but upon the divine truth which they proclaimed.

4. The "Bride of Christ." The church is prospectively the bride of Christ (Eph. 5:31, 32; Rev. 19:7; 21:9). Christ, "the Man," left His Father in heaven and Mary, His mother, on earth, cutting off all ties. He was joined for death and life unto the church as her husband; she is His affianced, and the marriage must necessarily be in the future (2 Cor. 11:2). As there is love and betrothal in the human relationship before the marriage, so there is also in the spiritual relationship. This union, though practically existing with each believer from the very time of his acceptance of Christ, is consummated fully only when the whole church, made ready and perfected, is caught up to heaven and the marriage is celebrated in the heavenly regions (Rev, 19:5-9). Therefore, the first and only Hebrew word in the Apocalypse, *Alleluia*, the supreme shout of praise, is not heard until this event takes place (Rev. 19:1).

The church is to be associated with Christ in His millennial reign, as a queen rules with her husband as royal consort. Her place is above angels, because she rules them (1 Cor. 6:3). This fact seems to indicate that the sphere of government will be heavenly as well as earthly. There is a difference of opinion as to the abode of Christ and the glorified church in their future reign — whether it will be upon or above the earth, since Rev. 5:10 admits of either translation. Since, however, heaven and earth are but divisions of God's great realm, probably the saints will pass as easily from the one to the other as Christ did in the forty days of His resurrection life on earth.

The formation of the church. Historically the church had no existence before the resurrection of Christ (Eph. 3:1-5, 9, 10). The patriarchs — such as Abraham, Isaac, Jacob, and Joseph — were not in the church; they were quickened by the Spirit, but not united to a risen Man in the heavens, since such a person was not yet manifested. The church had no existence when Christ was on earth; it was yet future (Matt. 16:18). The mission of Christ as the Minister of the Circumcision was exclusively to the lost sheep of the house of Israel (Rom. 15:8; Matt. 10:5, 6; 15:24; 27:37).

On the day of Pentecost, the Spirit was made manifest on the earth as the witness of the risen, ascended Christ; then and there the Lord baptized the disciples in the Spirit, into the body in which and through which He was henceforth to manifest Himself on the earth (1 Cor. 12:13).[2] It was then that Christ deposited in this spiritual body, in the person of the Holy Spirit, gifts and powers required for

292   CHRISTIAN THEOLOGY: SYSTEMATIC AND BIBLICAL

service in His name, the ascended Lord.

Its Local Aspect, Viewed As an Organization

The church in the individual or local sense may be defined as that smaller company of regenerate persons who, in any given community, unite themselves voluntarily, in accordance with the principles, precepts, and purposes of Christ as revealed in the New Testament.

By far, the larger number of passages which refer to the church describe it as a local assembly of Christian believers. There is a small number, however, of very important places in which the word has a more general meaning. It is common to distinguish these two classes of meanings by the terms *local church* and *universal church*. It seems, however, in some few passages that, while the local sense of the word is not clearly retained and a more general signification is intended, still the church universal is not meant. Besides, the *church universal* is not itself a New Testament term, and there is no binding reason why it should be employed other than as a convenient designation. The better way is to distinguish between a local and a general meaning of the word *church*, rather than to press an unscriptural distinction between "church local" and "church universal," as if entirely different things were meant. For convenience of discussion, the passages may be divided into those which refer to some particular church or churches; and those which do not point to any specified church and yet retain the local meaning of the term; and these may be further subdivided into passages where the word is used in the singular and in the plural. The passages which describe some particular church, or churches, are as follows:

— Singular: Acts 5:11; 8:1; 11:22, 26; 12:1, 5; 13:1; 14:27; 15:3, 15, 22; 18:22; 20:17; Romans 16:1, 5; 1 Corinthians 1:2; 6:4; 16:19; 2 Corinthians 1:1; Colossians 4:15, 16; 1 Thessalonians 1:1; 2 Thessalonians 1:1; Philemon 2; 3 John 6, 9, 10; Revelation 2:1, 8, 12, 18; 3:1, 7, 14.

— Plural: Acts 15:41; 1 Corinthians 16:1; 2 Corinthians 8:1, 19; 11:8; Galatians1:2, 22; 1 Thessalonians 2:14; Revelation 1:11; 2:7, 11, 17, 29; 3:6; 13:22.

There are passages which do not refer to any specified church, yet clearly exemplify the local meaning. Here again the word is used in the singular and in the plural. The uses are as follows:

— Singular: Matthew 18:17; Acts 14:23; 1 Corinthians 4:17; 11:18, 22; 14:4-35; Philippians 4:15; 1 Timothy 3:5; 5:16; James

5:14.
— Plural: Acts 16:5; Romans 16:4; 1 Corinthians 7:17; 11:16; 14:33, 34; 2 Corinthians 8:18, 23, 24; 11:28; 12:13; 2 Thessalonians 1:4; Revelation 2:23; 22:16.

The organization of the local church:

1. Its formation. There is no account of the act or mode of procedure by which any church mentioned in the New Testament was organized or constituted. The probabilities are that the method was very simple, that the Apostles, or leaders authorized by them, merely recognized the believers in Christ in any one place as a church without any formal or ceremonious act of constitution. We should infer that there would be services of worship and doubtless something in the nature of a covenant or agreement of the members with each other to serve the Lord and maintain the worship and ordinances of His appointment. But this is simply inference; there is no explicit statement.

   Each church was an organized body or society and not simply a loose assembly or meeting. One or two passages may possibly bear the meaning of a "congregation," or "meeting," as the significance of the word *ekklesia*, but the overwhelming implication, where the churches are mentioned or even alluded to as such, is that they were organized bodies and not mere aggregations of followers of Christ. This appears from the names, location, and other characteristics of the New Testament churches. For example, the churches at Jerusalem and Antioch mentioned in Acts could not be regarded as mere gatherings or meetings of the believers who lived at those places. They are mentioned in such a way as to make the invariable impression that they were definite bodies of persons. Even more clearly does this appear from the epistles to individual churches which were addressed as if they were organized bodies, as at Corinth, Philippi, Thessalonica, and Rome; see also the seven churches so often mentioned in the early chapters of the Apocalypse.

2. Its membership. The members of the church are in every case, by either direct statement or necessary implication, represented as actual disciples of Christ. This included, no doubt, in every instance three particulars; namely, conversion (including regeneration, repentance, and faith), confession, and baptism.
   — As to the requirement of conversion: John 3:3, 5, 16, 18, 36; Acts 2:44, 47; Romans 1:6-8; 1 Corinthians 1:2; Colossians 1:2, 4.

— As to the requirement of confession: Matthew 10:32; Romans 10:9, 10; 1 Timothy 6:12; 1 John 4:15.

— As to the requirement of baptism: Mark 16:15, 16; Acts 2:41; 8:12; Romans 6:1-4.

3. Its officers. In studying the officers of the New Testament churches, we have one of the most important and difficult matters connected with our general subject of church polity, and one which has had thorough investigation and discussion from every point of view; because of the necessary limitations under which we are placed, however, we must confine ourselves to a limited discussion.

A rigid classification of the various offices is impossible, for they often seem to touch and include each other. The best that we can do is to group the officers conveniently for discussion rather than to attempt any strict classification. But while exact classification has its difficulties, there yet seems to be a real distinction between those offices which were elective and permanent in the local churches and those which appear to be more general in character and of uncertain permanence. Besides these, there are some official designations which offer special difficulties in interpretation. So in a general way we find three fairly distinct groups of officials mentioned in the New Testament:

a. Offices which are general. Under this first division we consider apostles, prophets, teachers, and evangelists.

(1) Apostles. The Scripture passages which bear upon this office are Matthew 10:2; Luke 6:13; 11:49; 22:14; Acts 1:2, 15-26; 8:1, 14; 11:1; 14:14; 15:2-33; Romans 1:1; 1 Corinthians 1:1; 9:1, 2; 12:28; 2 Corinthians 12:11; Galatians 1:1; Ephesians 2:20; 3:5; 4:11. Without going into a detailed discussion of these passages, we simply set forth some plainly required qualifications for the apostolic office.

(a) The apostle must have a special call and mission. In the case of the original twelve and of Paul, the call came from the Master; the mission in all cases was to proclaim and teach the gospel, and apparently to found and form the churches.

(b) The apostle must be able to render personal testimony to the fact of Christ's resurrection. In the case of Matthias, this was distinctly required. In certain cases the term *apostle* is probably used in the nontechnical sense of messenger (Acts 14:14; Phil. 2:25; Rom. 16:7).

(c) The apostle should have "the signs of an apostle." This seems to mean the power to work miracles as an evidence of apostolic authority. Along with it went, of course, the spiritual work and fruit of a divinely authorized and empowered messenger. Paul claimed these signs in 1 Corinthians 9:2 and 2 Corinthians 12:12.

(d) The apostle should be recognized as such by the rest of the apostolic company. This appears in the prominence given to the Twelve by our Lord, in His special training of them for their work after His departure, in their assumption of their apostolic duties, and their brethren's recognition of their leadership among the disciples after the Ascension, and in many other familiar tokens found in Scripture. See in this connection 1 Corinthians 9:4-6, where Paul claims this authority for himself.

(e) That the apostolic office was not permanent is indicated by the fact that, first, there is no hint anywhere in the New Testament that the office was to be passed on to others; second, personal witness to the resurrection of Christ as an indispensable qualification made it impossible to continue the office; and third, no indication is to be found that the functions of an apostle without the name were to be transferred to any other set of officers and perpetuated in the churches after the apostolic age.

(2) Prophets. The passages alluding to this office are Acts 11:27; 13:1; 15:32; 21:10; 1 Corinthians 12:28; 14:29-40; Ephesians 2:20; 3:5; 4:11. The office of prophet was, in association with the apostolic office, the means for providing a foundation for future ministry (Eph. 2:20). The teachings of the foregoing passages concerning the prophets of the New Testament dispensation and their office may be summarized as follows:

(a) The prophets were not officers elected by the churches. There does not appear in any of the passages noted a trace of election to office. Rather, they were men especially qualified and inspired of God for the benefit of the churches.

(b) They are next in rank to the apostles. It is possible that all the apostles were prophets, but certainly not all the prophets were called apostles.

(c) Their qualification was that of inspiration, sometimes for foretelling the future, as in the case of Agabus, who is mentioned in Acts 11:28 as predicting the famine and in 21:10, 11 as foretelling the trials of Paul at Jerusalem. Generally, however, their function seems to have been to receive and make known new truth by divine inspiration or to give to the brethren better insight into truth already known. In Acts 15, Judas and Silas are mentioned as prophets who exhorted the brethren. Prophecy was, therefore, rather a gift than an office and was probably not confined to any office, but was given to individuals according as God chose and inspired them.

(3) Evangelists. In regard to evangelists there are only a few passages: Acts 21:8; Ephesians 4:11; 2 Timothy 4:5. The statements concerning this office are very limited, and about all that we can say is that the evangelists seem to have been traveling preachers authorized by the apostles and the churches; that they went about preaching but without apostolic rank, and probably in most cases without prophetic inspiration. Their relations to individual churches are unknown, though it is likely that they were supported in their missionary tours by the contributions of their brethren at home, at least in part.

(4) Teachers. In regard to the teachers, we have the following Scripture: Acts 13:1; 1 Corinthians 12:28, 29; Ephesians 4:11; 1 Timothy 2:7; 2 Timothy 1:11; 2:2; Hebrews 5:12; James 3:1. A study of these passages will reveal the probability that the teacher was not, properly speaking, an officer, but his teaching was rather a function which might be joined with other offices and not confined to a special office.

b. Offices which are doubtful as to their functions. In 1 Corinthians 12:28, along with the officers are mentioned "helps, governments." In this much discussed verse we have the offices of apostles, teachers, prophets; and the gifts of healing, of working miracles, of tongues. These last can hardly be considered as offices in any sense — certainly not as distinct and separate offices. The question is whether the remaining two terms, *helps, governments*, constituted separate and distinct offices, and if so, what were they?

It must be admitted that no entirely satisfactory interpretation has been found for this passage, but the best is that which takes the expression "governments," as expressing the duties of the elders in the general oversight of the church, and the phrase "helps," as expressing the duties of the deacons in the care of the poor, the sick and others. So that the offices of elder and deacon, which are not mentioned by name in the text, are at least brought in by notice of their functions.

The "messengers of the churches," mentioned in 2 Corinthians 8:23, where the word in the Greek is *apostle*, may be regarded simply as those who were sent by the church upon a special mission. They were not permanent officers, but were appointed to collect and bear gifts of the churches to the poor saints at Jerusalem. The expression "the angel of the church" in Revelation 2 and 3, doubtless refers to the regenerate portions of the membership of the seven churches in Asia.[3]

c. Offices which are local and permanent. Among the offices of the New Testament churches there were those that were local and designed to be permanent. These were the elders, called also bishops and pastors, and the deacons.

(1) Elders: bishops and pastors. The passages in which the elders appear as church officers are as follows: Acts 11:30; 14:23; 15:2, 4, 6, 22, 23; 16:4; 20:17; 21:18; 1 Timothy 5:17, 19; Titus 1:5; James 5:14; 1 Peter 5:1; 2 John 1; 3 John 1. This term is by far the most frequently used of them all. This probably grew out of the fact that it was already an established word among the Jews, and while it describes the same office as the other two, bishops and pastors, it has rather the idea of maturity and experience, thus describing the character of the officer rather than the function of the office.

Another term for this office is *bishop*. There are only a few places where this term appears: Acts 2:28; Philippians 1:1; 1 Timothy 3:1, 2; Titus 1:7. The word *bishop* from the Greek *(episcopos)* means literally an overseer, and in the margin of the 1901 Version it is so rendered. This title of overseer as applied to an officer in the church looks rather to the functions of the office than to the character of the officer, describing his care and his outlook upon those who are committed to his keeping, as a leader, guide, and teacher. It carries with it more of the idea of authority and rule than does *elder*.

The third title for this same office is *pastor*. There is only one passage where the word is used, Ephesians 4:11, where, in describing the gifts bestowed on the church by the ascended Christ, the apostle says, "and some pastors and teachers." This term seems to have in it the thought of shepherding (see John 10:11; Heb. 13:20; Acts 20:28; 1 Peter 2:25). Thus the term *pastor*, "shepherd," involves the personal care and spiritual concern which the bishop-elder should exercise over his flock.

The duties of the office were oversight, especially spiritual, of the church. This is involved in all three terms employed, and in much else, such as the directions given, the qualifications required, and work enjoined. Another function was teaching, preaching, and edifying the church. This especially appears in the passage in Ephesians where it is said, "some pastors and teachers for the edifying of the church," and in 1 Timothy 3:2, where among the qualifications of the bishop it is said that he must be "apt to teach," and in 1 Timothy 5:17, where the "elders that rule well" are mentioned and described as those who "labor in word and doctrine."

(2) Deacons. The Greek word *diakonos* simply means a servant and in that sense it is often found. There are two passages where the word is used in the official sense: Philippians 1:1; 1 Timothy 3:8-13. While the word in its general signification means a servant, it is clear that it came to be used of a church officer, and this very probably originated in the event mentioned in the sixth chapter of Acts, where the "seven" were set apart to attend to the distribution of the common fund for the benefit of those who needed it.

Perhaps it would be going too far to say that these seven referred to in Acts 6 were actually deacons, in the later sense, of the church at Jerusalem. Two of them, Philip and Stephen, also preached. But thus early in the history of the church it was felt that servants, or officers, to look after the business affairs were needed, so that the spiritual teachers and guides might give more of their time and attention to the ministry of the Word and the devotions of the church.

4. Its function. The local church was possessed of certain rights, duties, and privileges of management and direction.

a. The regulation of its own members.

(1) Their reception. This is argued from the fact that it is the natural right of any society to pass upon the applications of those who would become members and determine the matter by vote. It is also involved in the right to exclude from membership, which is sometimes a duty of the church. See Acts 9:26 and Romans 14:1.

(2) Their discipline. This is taught in such passages as Matthew 18:17; Romans 16:17; 1 Corinthians 5:1-5; 2 Corinthians 2:6-8; Galatians 6:1; 1 Thessalonians 5:14; 2 Thessalonians 3:6, 14, 15. These passages indicate that it was the duty of the church to exercise a watchful supervision over its members, to punish their delinquencies, to rebuke them, and in some cases even to withdraw from them or to exclude them from the fellowship of the church.

(3) Their edification. This is taught in Ephesians 4:11-16; 1 Corinthians 12–14; Colossians 3:12-17. The church is here commanded to edify itself in love, to purge itself from disorders, and to hold fast to the Head, even Christ, making increase of the body. It is the duty of the church to attend to its own orderly growth and to the spiritual nurture and development of its individual members.

b. The election of its officers, servants, and messengers. Some appointments may have been made by the apostles, but doubtless they acted under the direction of the local churches or in cooperation with them by whom these appointments were endorsed or confirmed. See Acts 6:1-6; 14:23; 15:22; 2 Corinthians 8:23; Philippians 2:25; Titus 1:5.

c. The maintenance of worship and the ordinances. In 1 Corinthians 11, the apostle gives extended directions about the observance of the Lord's Supper, rebuking the Corinthian church for their misconceptions and unseemly conduct in regard to that sacred rite. This, together with the following passages, shows the maintenance of worship and the ordinances to be one of the recognized functions of the local church: Acts 1:13, 14; 2:1, 42, 46, 47; 11:26; 13:1, 2; 1 Corinthians 14.

d. The management of its own affairs. Each church judged for itself and acted for itself as a unit, and attended to its own business (1 Cor. 14:40). This is to be inferred from the natural reason that any organized body is properly charged with the management of its own affairs; besides that, the general tenor of the Scripture language is such as to show this; then the descriptions of the churches, the responsibilities enjoined upon them, and the commands given to them indicate that they were charged with the direction and control of their own concerns.

The ordinances of the local church. The word *ordinance* is derived from the Latin *ordo*, a row or order, and so *ordinare* meant to put in the right place in the row, or set in order, and then consequently to establish, to command; so that "ordinance" comes to mean something established, commanded, enforced by proper authority, and the term has been applied to the sacred rites of baptism and the Lord's Supper as institutions or commandments of the Lord.

1. The purpose of the ordinances. The ordinances are certain symbolic acts which Christians are commanded to observe as setting forth great truths of their religion. The purpose of the ordinances may be set forth in three parts, all of which are essential to a complete statement:

   a. They symbolize by vivid action essential Christian truth, expressing in an outwardly observed rite, inwardly accepted and fundamental Christian doctrine.

   b. They are to be kept as observances for the sake of the Lord Jesus, in simple obedience to His positive commands and in grateful recognition of His claims to our love and duty.

   c. They are, therefore, distinctly Christian ceremonies, marking those who rightly observe them as the true followers of Jesus Christ.

2. The custodians of the ordinances. It is the duty and privilege of the organized churches of Christ to keep or observe the ordinances. While there is no definite command which lays the performance of the ordinances upon the churches, yet it appears to be the natural, if not necessary, deduction from the whole trend and tenor of the New Testament teaching. This is a fair inference from the following:

a. The fact of the establishment of churches as the custodians of Christian truth and customs;

b. The absence of continuous apostolic authority in the churches;

c. The principle that definite observances are more properly performed by regularly organized and accredited bodies than by unorganized and unaccredited individuals.

3. The ordinances themselves. Among Protestants generally the term *ordinance* is applied only to baptism and the Lord's Supper.

a. Baptism. The ground of the obligation for the observance of the ordinance of baptism is furnished in the express will of Jesus Christ by His example, practice, and command; and also by the authority of the apostles, their practice, and teaching (see Matt. 3:13-15; 28:19; John 4:1, 2; Acts 2:41; 8:12, 36, 38; 9:18; 10:46-48; 16:15, 33; 19:1-5; Rom. 6:1-4; Col. 2:12; 1 Peter 3:21).

b. Lord's Supper. The ground of the obligation for the observance of the Lord's Supper is based upon the example and command of the Lord Jesus together with the practice of the early church and the inspired instruction given through the apostle Paul (see Matt. 26:26-29; Mark 14:22-25; Luke 22:17-20; 1 Cor. 11:23-26).

The relationships of the local church. The ministries of the local church were not to be confined to itself, but were to reach out toward others. Its life was not to be self-centered, but expansive and helpful. Each church stood in intimate relations with other churches, and in more general relations with the world around. We notice then —

1. The relation of the churches to each other. It is convenient to view these in their negative and positive aspects.

a. Negatively

(1) There was no subordination of one church to another. If anything is plain in the Scriptures certainly this is. Acts 15, which has sometimes been adduced to show that the church at Jerusalem exercised a controlling influence over others, if properly understood has just the opposite bearing. Some men had gone down from Jerusalem to Antioch and taught that the Gentile Christians, in order to be saved, must become Jews and keep the whole law by submitting to the rite of circumcision, and be received as

proselytes into the Jewish nation.

On this question, with marked forbearance to both parties, but without departing one iota from the gospel principle of faith in Christ as essential to salvation, the church at Jerusalem sent a courteous and loving letter by the hand of special messengers to say that in their opinion it was not necessary for Gentiles to become Jews first in order to become Christians, but, in order to refrain from wounding the sensibilities of the Jewish brethren, it was right that Gentile converts should avoid certain offensive practices. Here there is no hint of lordship on the part of the Jerusalem church over the church at Antioch, neither does there appear anywhere else in the New Testament any trace whatever of superiority, or lordship, of one church or set of churches over another.

(2) There was no subjection of the churches to any common human authority. The position of the apostles was peculiar, and even if we grant to them the fullest measure of authority over the churches, there is no evidence that any successors were appointed, or intended to be appointed after them. There is also no hint of any council or college, nor of any general organization or body, either hierarchical or representative, which held authority over individual churches. Of course, all the churches were under the supreme headship of Christ and under the superintendence delegated by Him to the apostles, but this apostolic authority was moral and advisory rather than controlling or mandatory, and was exercised with marked moderation (see 1 Cor. 7:6, 10, 17, 25; 9:1-15; 14:37; 16:1; 1 Thess. 2:3-12; 4:2; 2 Thess. 3:6, 10, 12; 2 Peter 3:2; 3 John 9).

(3) There was no territorial union of the churches. We read of the churches of Judea (Gal. 1:22), of Galatia (Gal. 1:2; 1 Cor. 16:1), of Macedonia (2 Cor. 8:1), and of the seven churches of Asia Minor (Rev. 1:4, et al.). But the mention of these churches is not made in any way to suggest anything like a territorial or national organization including them as constituents.

b. Positively. There were positive relations of the churches to each other involving noteworthy points of contact and cooperation. It appears from the preceding discussion that the mutual relation of the apostolic churches was of independence and equality, and this view is confirmed by the general tenor of Scripture teaching and by the way in which the churches are mentioned. Yet there was a certain union and interdependence of these local bodies. It was not organic or governmental, but rather a community of life and interests.

(1) There was a common faith (see Acts 2:42; Rom. 6:17; 1 Cor. 11:2, 23; Eph. 4:5; 1 Tim. 1:15; Titus 1:4; 2 Peter 1:2; Jude 3).

(2) There was a community of life. By this we mean a similarity of organization, of public worship (including ordinances), of character, of customs (see 1 Cor. 7:17; 11:16).

(3) There was a common relation to the apostles and other teachers. The churches had a common possession, so to speak, in those whom the Lord had placed over them for their guidance and instruction (see Acts 18:24-28; 19:1; Rom. 16:3; 1 Cor. 1:12; 16:12).

(4) There were certain common interests. For example, the churches of Galatia had an epistle addressed to them in common because they were exposed to the same danger. Then the churches of Colosse, Hierapolis, and Laodicea are mentioned together in the Epistle to the Colossians as being exposed to danger, a sort of incipient Gnosticism that was beginning to show itself. In 2 Corinthians 1:1 the churches of Achaia and Corinth are mentioned together, and so with the seven of Asia Minor addressed in Revelation 2, 3.

(5) There was a common work. There was a common work in at least one notable instance in which several separate churches took part, and it is not unlikely that there were other similar cases (Rom. 15:26; 16:1; see also 2 Cor. 8, 9; Gal. 2:10; and 3 John 8).

2. The relation of the churches to society.

a. To civil government. Our Lord taught (Matt. 22:15-22) that a citizen should perform his duties of citizenship without conflict with those which he owed to God. Paul acknowledged his earthly citizenship (Acts 21:39) and with Peter taught submission to the civil authorities as a Christian duty (Rom. 13:1; 1 Peter 2:13). It is needless to say that such submission to the duties of citizenship is to be qualified by one's higher obedience to God.

b. To mankind in general. The church in its life and activity was not to withdraw from the world, but to be an illuminating and preservative agency within the world (Matt. 5:13-16; John 17:14-16; Phil. 2:15). All the relations of life were to feel the influence of the church's holy ministry (see also 1 Cor. 7:29-31; Eph. 5:22–6:9).

c. To the world as sinful and condemned. Active work for the salvation of men was the high and holy mission of the New Testament church. This, we infer, was to be done by both individual effort on the part of the members, and more generally also by the united and cooperative efforts of the members in sending the gospel abroad (Acts 13:1-3; 14:26, 27; Phil. 4:10-18; 3 John 5-10).

Study Questions on Ecclesiology

1. Define *ecclesiology.*
2. How is the importance of the church shown?
3. Discuss the etymology and history of the English word *church.*
4. Discuss the etymology and history of the Greek word *ekklesia* as well as its various New Testament meanings.
5. Discuss the significance, origin, meaning, and aspects of the kingdom of heaven.
6. Give in detail the series of contrasts between the church in its general meaning and the kingdom of heaven.
7. Define the kingdom of God.
8. Give the contrasts between the church and the kingdom of God.
9. Distinguish between the kingdom of heaven and the kingdom of God.
10. What is the twofold use of the word *Christendom?*
11. Give a positive definition of the word *church* in its general aspect.
12. Discuss the membership of the church considered as an organism.
13. Define the unity of the church, and quote one passage in its support.

14. Discuss the revelation of the church.
15. Discuss the symbolism of the church.
16. What is to be said concerning the church as the bride of Christ with reference to the present and the future?
17. Discuss the formation of the church.
18. Give the definition of the "local church."
19. Discuss the use of the terms *local church* and *universal church*, and the meanings suggested by each.
20. Give the supposed method by which the formation of the local church was effected, and show how it is inferred that they were organized bodies.
21. Discuss the membership qualifications of a local church, quoting one passage with each.
22. Name the offices which were general in the early New Testament churches.
23. What were the qualifications for the office of an apostle?
24. How is it shown that the apostolic office was not designed to be permanent?
25. Quote one passage alluding to the New Testament prophet, and discuss the threefold summary of this office.
26. Quote one passage referring to the office of evangelist, and make a brief statement concerning it.
27. What does a study of the passages referring to teachers reveal?
28. Discuss the offices of the New Testament churches whose functions are doubtful.
29. Discuss under each title the officer spoken of as elder, bishop, and pastor, and describe the duties of each office.
30. Discuss the office of deacon and its probable origin.
31. Discuss what is involved in the regulation of its own members by the local church.
32. Describe the functions of the local church.
33. Give the definition of the term *ordinances of the church*.
34. Give the purpose of the ordinances, including the threefold statement concerning them.
35. Show who are the custodians of the ordinances, giving the threefold argument leading to this conclusion.
36. Discuss the ordinances themselves, showing the ground of obligation for their observance.
37. Discuss the relationship of local churches to each other.
38. Discuss the relations of the church to society in regard to civil government, mankind in general, the world as sinful and condemned.

Notes

[1]This use of the word is never found in the New Testament and very seldom in the times preceding the Reformation. It is distinctly a modern usage arising from the divisions of Christians. It is not accepted by all. Congregationalists, Baptists, and others who hold to the independency of the local churches do not designate any one of their cooperative bodies as a "church," nor call their total membership by that term, but reserve it to describe their local bodies.

[2]In Acts 11 is the record of the church passing out of the confines of Judaism. In Acts 13:42-44 is the record of the church broadening out to receive the Gentiles.

[3]The seven stars spoken of in Revelation 1:16-20 are there said to be the seven angels of the seven churches. Angels and stars are symbolical figures. The application of these terms to church officers or bishops and pastors is incorrect. Stars are used in Scripture to typify true believers. Stars are heavenly bodies which shine during the night; so are true believers in a heavenly position with the responsibility to shine in the night. The lamp-stands represent the visible, professing church; stars represent the true believing element in the church. They are held securely in the right hand of Christ. Furthermore, only true believers have an ear to hear what the Spirit says.

CHAPTER TEN

ANGELOLOGY: THE DOCTRINE OF ANGELS, DEMONS, AND SATAN

ANGELS (PROPER)

So much is said in the Scriptures of good and evil angels, and such important functions are ascribed to them — both in the providence of God over the world, and especially in the experience of His people and His church — that the doctrine of the Bible concerning them should not be overlooked. That there are intelligent creatures higher than man has been a general belief. It is so in harmony with the analogy of nature as to be in the highest degree probable, apart from any direct revelation on the subject. In all departments of nature there is a regular gradation from the lower to the higher forms of life: from the almost invisible vegetable fungus to the cedar of Lebanon; from the minutest animalcule to the gigantic mammoth. In man we meet with the first, and to all appearances the lowest, of rational creatures. That he should be the only creature of his order is as improbable as that insects should be the only class of irrational animals.

There is every reason to presume that the scale of beings among rational creatures is as extensive as that in the animal world. The modern philosophy which deifies man leaves no room for any order of beings above him. But if the distance between God and man be infinite, all analogy would suggest that the orders of rational creatures between us and God must be numerous. As this is in itself probable, it is clearly revealed in the Bible to be true. The probabil-

307

ity is turned to certainty by the express declarations of Scripture.

The Fact of the Existence of Angels

This is well established as shown by the teaching of the Old Testament, which is unquestionable and clear (Pss. 68:17; 104:4; Dan. 8:15-17). It is also substantiated by the New Testament teaching (Matt. 13:41; 18:10; 26:53; Mark 8:38; 13:32; John 1:51; Eph. 1:21; Col. 1:16).[1]

The Nature of Angels

Created beings. Angels are not eternal, as God is, nor self-existent, but created and dependent creatures (Ps. 148:2-5; Col. 1:16; 1 Peter 3:22).

Incorporeal, spirit beings. Angels in their ordinary form or mode of being are spirits without flesh and blood (Heb. 1:13, 14; Eph. 6:12, asv). The term *spirit* may be regarded in general contrast with *matter.* The two substances embrace all the objects to be found in the wide realm of knowledge. There is no substance which can be said to be neither matter nor spirit. The world of matter is all around us and is capable of great changes, but nothing can endow it with will and thoughtful reflection. These latter are distinctive peculiarities of spirit. They are found in angels, and angels are spirits. They are in perfect contrast with matter, whether in its grosser or more refined form. They are spirit beings, and we, burdened with the encumbrances of matter, can very imperfectly imagine what they are. While we regard spirit in general contrast with matter, we may consider it in particular contrast with body. The words of Jesus authorize us to do this: "Handle me, and see; for a spirit hath not flesh and bones as ye see me have" (Luke 24:39).

Unmarriageable beings. The unfallen angels in heaven neither marry nor are given in marriage. This teaches, not that angels are sexless beings, but simply that marriage is not God's program for this heavenly order of beings (Matt. 22:30).

Personal (intelligent and voluntary) agents. Personal characteristics are ascribed to angels; they are intelligent, voluntary, active, and therefore personal agents (2 Sam. 14:20; 2 Tim. 2:26; Rev. 12:7; 22:8, 9).

Immortal beings. Angels are possessed of immortality, i.e., they do not die. They have no material bodies, therefore know nothing of growth, decrepitude, or death. The immortality of angels and men is derived from God and dependent on His will. Angels are immortal because God has made them so. They will never die nor cease to be, because it is not the divine will that they return to their original nothingness or cease to live their spirit-life (Luke 20:35, 36). Angels, in short, are beings of superhuman dignity and heavenly glory (Luke 9:26).

Beings of superhuman intelligence. Angels are in order of intelligence distinct from man and apparently superior to man in his present state (2 Sam. 14:17, 20; Matt. 24:36).[2]

Swift and powerful beings. They are possessed of superhuman power, yet it has its fixed limits; they are mighty but not almighty (Ps. 103:20; Matt. 28:2; 2 Thess. 1:7, ASV; 2 Peter 2:11; Rev. 20:1-3). Their power is delegated; they are the angels of His might, the ministers through whom God's power is manifested.[3]

Beings of various ranks and orders. Angels, though finite in number, seem to be virtually beyond computation and are organized in various ranks with correspondingly different authorities.

1. They are a great multitude (Deut. 33:2, ASV; Dan. 7:10; Rev. 5:11).

2. They constitute a company as distinguished from a race (Matt. 22:30; Luke 20:36).[4]

3. They have various gradations and endowments (Col. 1:16; 1 Thess. 4:16; 1 Peter 3:22; Jude 9).[5]

4. They have an organization (1 Kings 22:19; Matt. 25:41; 26:53; Eph. 2:2; Rev. 2:13; 12:7).

Moral Character of Angels

They were all created holy. By the character of God which is absolutely holy, by the character of His creative works with which He as a Holy Being was well pleased, and by the record of the angels' fall, the fact is fully established that they were created holy (cf. Gen. 1:31 with Hab. 1:13; Gen. 18:25; 2 Peter 2:4; Jude 6).

They had a probation. Inasmuch as some are spoken of as "the elect angels" (1 Tim. 5:21) and as election is "unto obedience" (1 Peter 1:1, 2), it seems to be intimated that there was a period of probation or testing, as a result of which the elect were manifested as such. The fact of their probation is clearly established by the record of the obedience of some and the failure and sin of others.

Some preserved their integrity. A large number of the angels have maintained their allegiance to God and obedience to His will, thereby preserving holiness of nature and perfecting holiness of character (Ps. 89:7, ASV; Matt. 25:31; Mark 8:38).

Some fell from their state of innocence. Certain angels sinned, who left their habitation, and became identified with the devil and are now known as his angels (Matt. 25:41; 2 Peter 2:4; Jude 6; Rev. 12:7).

The good are confirmed in goodness. The angels who have maintained their personal integrity and loyalty to God are confirmed in holiness; their obedience has become habitual and their goodness a permanent quality of character (Matt. 6:10; 18:10; see also 2 Cor. 11:14).

The evil are confirmed in wickedness. The angels who sinned and fell, through their continued choice of evil, have become confirmed in wickedness and are identified with all the most flagrant forms of sin and rebellion against God (Matt. 6:13; 13:19; John 8:44; 1 John 5:19; Rev. 12:7, 9; 22:11, ASV).

Clarence Larkin, in *The Spirit World*, asks the question, "Who are the angels referred to by Peter and Jude?" (2 Peter 2:4, 5; Jude 6, 7). He then proceeds to answer the question substantially as follows: "They are not Satan's angels, for his angels are free and, like him, roam about, but these angels are 'in prison,' 'in darkness,' and 'reserved in chains' for judgment. The place of their confinement is not hell, but Tartarus. What was their sin? It was 'fornication,' and fornication of an abominable character — the unlawful cohabitation of angelic beings with 'strange flesh,' that is, with beings of a different nature. When was this sin committed? The text says in the 'days of Noah,' and this was the cause of the flood.

For the details we must go back to the time before the flood. In Genesis 6:1-4 we read, 'And it came to pass, when men began to multiply on the face of the earth, and daughters were born unto them, that the sons of God saw the daughters of men that they were fair [beautiful]; and they took them wives of all which they chose. . . . There were giants in the earth in those days; and also after that, when the sons of God came in unto the daughters of men, and they bare children, the same became mighty men which were of old, men of renown.'

"Who were these 'sons of God'? Some claim that they were the sons of 'Seth,' and that the 'daughters of men' were the daughters of 'Cain,' and that what is meant is that the sons of the supposed godly line of Seth intermarried with the godless daughters of Cain, the result being a godless race. That the 'sons of God' were the descendants of Seth is based on the assumption that the descendants of Seth lived apart from the descendants of Cain up to a time shortly before the flood, and that they were a pure and holy race, while the descendants of Cain were ungodly, and their women irreligious and carnal minded and possessed of physical attractions that were foreign to the women of the tribe of Seth. Such an assumption has no foundation in Scripture.

"To be sure, it says in Genesis 4:26 that after the birth of Enos, a son of Seth, that men began to call upon the Lord; but it does not follow that those men were limited to the descendants of Seth, nor that all the descendants of Seth from that time were righteous. As in the early days of the race it was necessary that brothers and sisters and near relatives should marry, it is very unlikely that the descendants of Seth and Cain did not intermarry until some time before the flood, and stranger still that when they did marry, their offspring would be a race of 'giants' or 'mighty men.'

"As the descendants of both Seth (except eight persons) and of Cain were destroyed in the flood, it is evident that they were not separate tribes at that time and were equally sinners in the sight of God. If the sons of Seth and the daughters of Cain were meant, why did not Moses, who wrote the Pentateuch, say so? It is not sufficient to say that the men of Moses' time knew what he meant; the Scriptures are supposed to mean what they say. When men, we are told, began to multiply on the face of the earth and daughters were born unto them, the 'sons of God' saw the 'daughters of men.' The use of the word 'men' signifies the whole Adamic race and not simply the descendants of Cain, thus distinguishing the 'sons of God' from the descendants of Adam. There is no suggestion of contrast if the 'sons of God' were also men.

"A 'son of God' denotes a being brought into existence by a creative act of God. Such were the angels, and such was Adam, and he is so called in Luke 3:38. Adam's natural descendants are not the special creation of God. Adam was created in the 'likeness' of God' (Gen. 5:1), but his descendants were born in his likeness, for we read in Genesis 5:3 that Adam 'begat a son in his own likeness, after his image.' Therefore, all men born of Adam, and his descendants by natural generation, are the 'sons of men,' and it is only by being 'born again' (John 3:3-7), which is a 'new creation,' that they become the 'sons of God' in the New Testament sense. In the Old Testament it applies exclusively to the angels and is so used five times — twice in Genesis (6:2-4) and three times in Job (where Satan, an angelic being, is classed with the 'sons of God' [Job 1:6; 2:1; 38:7]).

Angelic Ministries

Good angels:

1. They stand in the presence of God and worship Him. Angels are called an assembly or congregation, which like the church on earth worships and praises God (Pss. 29:1, 2; 89:7, ASV; Matt. 18:10; Heb. 12:22).
2. They rejoice in God's works (Job 38:7; Luke 15:10).
3. They execute God's will (Ps. 103:20).
4. They guide the affairs of nations (Dan. 10:10-14, 20, 21).
5. They guide and guard the individual believer (Ps. 91:11; Dan. 6:22; Acts 8:26; 12:7; Heb. 1:14).
6. They minister to God's people and defend and deliver God's servants (Gen. 19:11; 1 Kings 19:5-8; Dan. 6:22; Matt. 4:11; Luke 22:43; Acts 5:19, 20; 12:7-11; 27:23, 24; Heb. 1:14).
7. They guard the elect dead (Matt. 28:2-5; Luke 16:22; 24:22-24; John 20:11, 12; Jude 9).
8. They will accompany Christ as His second advent (Matt. 25:31; 13:49; 2 Thess. 1:7, 8).[6]

Evil angels:

1. They oppose God's purposes and execute Satan's. Evil angels are employed in the execution of Satan's purposes, which are diametrically opposed to those of God and have to do with the hindrance and harm of the spiritual life and well-being of God's people (Dan. 10:10-14; Zech. 3:1; Matt. 12:26, 27; 25:41).
2. They afflict God's people (Luke 13:16; Matt. 17:15, 16, 18; 2 Cor. 12:7).
3. They hinder God's saints and servants (Eph. 6:11, 12; 1 Thess. 2:18).
4. They seek to deceive God's elect (2 Cor. 11:13, 14; see also Matt. 24:24).

Practical Values of the Doctrine of Angels

Good angels:

1. It gives us a new sense of the greatness of the divine resources and of God's grace in our creation to think of the multitude of unfallen intelligences who executed the divine purposes before man appeared.
2. It strengthens our faith in God's providential care to know that spirits of so high rank are deputed to minister to creatures who are environed with temptations and are conscious of sin.

3. It teaches us humility in that beings of so much greater knowledge and power should gladly perform those unnoticed services in behalf of those whose only claim upon them is that they are children of the same common God.

4. It helps us in the struggle against sin to learn that the messengers of God are near to mark our wrongdoing if we fall and to sustain us if we resist temptation.

5. It enlarges our conception of the dignity of our own being and of the boundless possibilites of our future existence to remember these forms of typical innocence and love who praise and serve God unceasingly in heaven.

Evil angels:

1. It illustrates the real nature of sin and the depth of the ruin to which it may bring the human soul as we reflect upon the present immoral condition and eternal wretchedness to which these highly endowed spirits have brought themselves by their rebellion against God.

2. It inspires a salutary fear and hatred of the first subtle approaches of evil from within or from without to remember that these may be the covert advances of a personal and malignant being who seeks to overcome our virtue and to involve us in his own apostasy and destruction.

3. It shuts us up to Christ as the only being who is able to deliver us from these enemies of all good.

4. It teaches us that our salvation is wholly of grace, since for such multitudes of rebellious spirits no atonement and no renewal were apparently provided — simple justice having its way with no mercy to interpose or save.

DEMONS

It is evident that the relation of the Scriptures to the doctrine of demons is vital and positive. Actual communication with unseen spirits, their influence on the acts and destinies of individuals and nations, and demon possession are taught clearly and unmistakably in both the Old and New Testaments. These teachings are not occasional and incidental, but underlie all biblical history and doctrine. The Bible recognizes not only the material world, but a spiritual world intimately connected with it, and spiritual beings both good and bad who have access to, and influence for good and ill, the world's inhabitants. The testimony of the Scriptures and what is to be derived from sources outside the Scriptures are mutually confirmatory on this subject. The importance of a careful and unprejudiced consideration of what the Bible teaches is apparent.

The King James New Testament is less clear in its presentation of the subject of demon-possession than is the original Greek, because of its translating *diabolos* and *daimonion* and *daimon* by the one word *devil*. In later versions the first of these words is translated *devil* and the other two *demon*, the important distinction of the original being thus preserved. The word *diabolos* (devil) meaning "slanderer" or "false accuser" is in the New Testament used only in the singular and appears more than thirty times as a descriptive title of Satan. In its adjectival form it is used three times to represent men as accusers or slanderers (1 Tim. 3:1; 2 Tim. 3:3; Titus 2:3). The words *daimonion* and *daimon* are used frequently in the New Testament both in the singular and plural, but never interchangeably with *diabolos*.

The Fact of the Existence of Demons

Their existence recognized by Jesus. Jesus Christ recognized the existence of demons by speaking of them and to them (Matt. 12:27, 28; 8:28-32; see also Matt. 10:8; Mark 16:17, all ASV). There are several theoretical interpretations of this attitude of Christ toward the subject of demons, from which we select the following:

1. The theory is advanced that Jesus, living in a primitive and unscientific age, simply represented, at least so far as regards this subject, the thought and intellectual advancement of that age; and like His contemporaries, accepted and believed in the doctrine of demons and demon possession though in fact, through ignorance and superstition, they were entirely mistaken. It is evident that this theory is utterly at variance with the claim which our Lord made to a knowledge of the unseen world from which He came, and to the views which have been held by the church in all ages respecting the authenticity and divine origin of the Scriptures.

2. A second theory has been adopted by not a few who are regarded as most intelligent and orthodox Christians. This view is a compromise between theological and scientific orthodoxy and asserts that Jesus was free from the ignorance and superstitions of the age in which He lived, but in accordance with the prevailing ideas of His time, and with the ordinary use of language, spoke of cases of demon possession as His contemporaries did. His mission on

earth was not to teach science, or to start curious discussions or controversies on indifferent and unimportant subjects. He came to teach spiritual truths and did so in the language of the people, speaking of phenomena as they did and in terms with which they were familiar. He recognized in men and women, brought to Him as possessed by demons, only different forms of bodily disease, but as the people spoke of these as demon possessions, He also so spoke of them; as they represented the curing of diseases as casting out demons, He so represented it; and when He gave power to His disciples to heal these diseases miraculously, He, accommodating His language to the popular belief, called it the power to cast out demons.

This theory is very intelligible and plausible, but as we believe, open to serious and fatal objections.

a. It represents Him not as instructing but as deceiving His disciples, as encouraging superstition rather than inculcating truth.

b. The above objection acquires additional force when we consider its intimate relations with other teachings of Jesus recorded in Scripture.

c. This theory, when applied in detail, presents our Lord in a light entirely inconsistent with His character as a divine teacher. It represents Him not only as speaking of diseases as possession by demons, but as personifying diseases and actually addressing them as demons.

d. This theory represents Christ as making use of an unfounded superstition to substantiate His claim of divine authority. When He sent forth His disciples to preach "the kingdom of heaven is at hand," the power to cast out demons was given them as a divine attestation to His mission. The disciples and those to whom they were sent regarded as one of the principal reasons for accepting their testimony the fact that "even the demons were subject unto them through Christ's name," which according to this theory was not a fact but a delusion.

Their existence recognized by the Seventy. The seventy whom Jesus appointed and sent out two by two had to cope with demons and returned with the report that demons were subject unto them through the name of Christ (Luke 10:17, ASV).

Their existence recognized by Paul. The Apostle to the Gentiles recognized the reality of demons in his day and gave warning against them (1 Cor. 10:20, 21; 1 Tim. 4:1; see also Acts 16:16-18; James 2:19, ASV).

Their existence recognized by Old Testament authors. Demons were recognized as existing even in the earliest of the Old Testament books (Deut. 32:17). In the Septuagint the word *demon* was used in order to translate the Hebrew words *sedim* (lords) or *elilim* (idols), since the Hebrews very early associated idolatrous images as mere visible symbols of invisible demons (Pss. 96:5; 106:37, 38).

Their existence recognized in classical writings. According to Homer, a demon was to be regarded as a god or deity (cf. the similarity to Ps. 96:5). In the Greek classics after Homer, the term was used to designate an intermediary between the gods and men.

The Nature and Character of Demons

Personal intelligences. Personal characteristics and actions are ascribed to demons which show that they possess personality and intelligence (Matt. 8:29, 31; Luke 4:35, 41; James 2:19, ASV).

Spirit beings. Demons are the same as evil and unclean spirits, as we may see by the following passages: "When the even was come they brought unto him many that were possessed with demons; and He cast out the spirits with His word" (Matt. 8:16). Again, in Luke 10:17, 20 we read: "And the seventy returned again with joy, saying, Lord, even the demons are subject unto us through thy name"; to which the Lord responds: "Notwithstanding in this rejoice not, that the spirits are subject unto you." So in Matthew's account of the lunatic boy, the demon is said to come forth from him (Matt. 17:18); but in Mark's Gospel this same demon is called a foul spirit and also a deaf and dumb spirit (Mark 9:25). And Luke gives us a list of "certain women which had been healed of evil spirits and infirmities," of whom the first mentioned is Mary, called Magdalene, out of whom went seven demons (Luke 8:2, 3). Demons and evil spirits are, therefore, synonymous terms (see also Mark 5:2, 7-9, 12, 13, 15; Luke 9:38, 39, 42, ASV).

Satan's emissaries. Demons are subjects in the kingdom of Satan and servants in his house; their mission seems to be to carry on his warfare and to do his work (Matt. 12:22-30, ASV).[7]

A multitude in number. Demons are so numerous as to make Satan practically ubiquitous, or everywhere present, through their representation. They belong to the "powers of darkness," a great martialed host, veterans in the service of Satan (Mark 5:9; Luke 8:30; see also Matt. 12:26, 27, all ASV).

Degraded and debased in character and moral principle. Demons are beings of a low moral order, vile and malignant in character, vicious in conduct. They are spoken of as unclean or impure (Weymouth — "foul"; see Matt. 10:1; 12:43; Mark 1:23, 24; Luke 4:33, 36, all ASV); as vicious and malicious (Matt. 8:28; Luke 9:39, both ASV). There seem to be degrees of wickedness represented by these spirits; it is stated in Matthew 12:43-45 that the demon returning to his house "taketh with himself seven other spirits more wicked than himself."

Disembodied spirits. Demons are an order of spirit beings apparently distinct and separate from angels, and which, from the intimations of certain passages of Scripture, seem to be in a disembodied state, having existed in some previous period and place in bodily form (Matt. 12:43, 44; Mark 5:10-14, all ASV).

Demons must always be carefully distinguished from angels, bad and good; for angels are not merely disembodied spirits, but — as we may learn from our Lord's declaration that the children of the resurrection shall be equal to the angels — are clothed with spiritual bodies, such as are promised to us (cf. Phil. 3:21 and Luke 24:39) if we "shall be accounted worthy to obtain that age and the resurrection from the dead" (Luke 20:35). This distinction was clearly understood by the Jews; for in Acts we read that the Pharisees cried out concerning Paul: "We find no evil in this man; but if a spirit or an angel hath spoken to him, let us not fight against God" (Acts 23:9). And in the preceding verse we are told that their opponents, the Sadducees, denied the existence of angels and spirits.

What then is the meaning of the term *demon*? Plato derives it from the Greek adjective formed from a Greek root signifying "knowing, intelligent." It was used by him of a sort of intermediate and inferior divinity. "The deity," says Plato, "has no intercourse with man; but all the intercourse and conversation between gods and men is carried on by the mediation of demons." And he further explains that "the demon is an interpreter and carrier from men to gods and from gods to men, of the prayers and sacrifices of the one, and of the injuctions and rewards of sacrifices from the other." If we inquire of these classical writers whence these demons came, we shall be told that they are the spirits of men of the golden age acting as tutelary deities — canonized heroes, precisely similar both in their origin and functions to the Romish saints.

Now, if we remember that, according to biblical teachings, the heathen gods were really evil angels and demons who inspired oracles and received worship, we shall easily understand that the golden age of which the ancient bards so rapturously sang was no reminiscence of Paradise but of the times of that former world when Satan's power was still intact. A change in the heavenly dynasty, the expulsion of Chronos (Saturn), is always mentioned as having brought to a close this age of unmingled joy.

Such, then, are the demons of the classical writers. Nor does there appear to be any reason for changing the meaning of the term in the New Testament. For may not these demons be the spirits of those who trod this earth in the flesh before the ruin described in Genesis 1:2 and who at the time of that great destruction were disembodied by God and left still under the power, and ultimately to share the fate of, the leader in whose sin they acquiesced? The oft-recorded fact that the demons are continually seeking the bodies of men and endeavoring to use them as their own appears to support this position. May not this propensity indicate a wearisome lack of ease, a wandering unrest arising from a sense of incompleteness, a longing to escape the intolerable condition of being unclothed — for which they were not created — so intense that, if they can satisfy its cravings in no other way, they will even go into the filthy bodies of swine? We find no such disposition on the part of Satan and his angels. They doubtless still retain their celestial bodies — for otherwise how could they carry on their conflict with the angels of God?

The Power and Work of Demons

They have knowledge and discernment. They knew Christ and recognized His supreme authority; they were able to recognize individuals and discriminate between them; they also seem to have knowledge of their future doom (Matt. 8:29, 31; Mark 1:23, 24; Acts 19:13-15; James 2:19; see also Luke 8:31, all ASV).

They enter and control the bodies of human beings and beasts. Demons, when permitted, are capable of exercising influence over individuals and also of entering into physical bodies and bringing them under their evil control (Mark 5:8, 11-13; Matt. 4:24; 8:16, 28, 33; Acts 8:6, 7; 16:16, all ASV).

The question is often raised whether demon control obtains at the present time. Although the authentic record of such control is largely limited to the Bible times, it is incredible that demon possession has not existed since. In this connection it should be remembered that these beings are not only intelligent themselves but also directly governed and ordered by Satan, whose wisdom and cunning are clearly set forth in the Scriptures. It is reasonable to conclude that they, like their monarch, are adapting the manner of their activity to the enlightenment of the age and locality. It is evident that they are not now less inclined than before to enter and dominate a body. Demon possession at present is probably often unsuspected because of the unrecognized fact that demons are capable of inspiring a moral and exemplary life, as well as appearing as the dominating spirit of a spiritist medium, or through the grosser manifestations recorded by missionaries from heathen lands. These demons, too, like their king will appear as "angels of light" as well as "roaring lions," when by the former impersonation they can more effectively further the stupendous undertakings of Satan in his warfare against the work of God.

Of the methods of demons in the latter days of the age, the Scriptures bear special testimony. They will cover their lies with the empty form of religion and by every means make them to appear as the truth, that they may draw both the saved and the unsaved from their hope in Christ: "Now the Spirit speaketh expressly, that in the latter times some shall depart from the faith, giving heed to seducing spirits, and doctrines of devils; speaking lies in hypocrisy; having their conscience seared with a hot iron (1 Tim. 4:1, 2). A departure from the true faith is thus predicted to be the evidence of the influence of demons in the last days. This is none other than the great apostasy that must precede the "day of the Lord" according to 2 Thessalonians 2:2, 3.

Demon influence and control in its relation to individuals is exercised in a twofold method: obsession and possession. The first step on the demon's part to gain control is termed *obsession*. It is defined as the "state or act of being influenced by an evil spirit"; also the continued or continual recurrence of an illusion or delusion. This influence is exercised by an external spirit, antecedent to possession. This is the initial stage of demon influence. *Possession* is the result of obsession or attack after entrance is gained by the demon. Possession is the act of taking or occupying complete control over the individual involved.

They afflict men with infirmities and maladies, both physical and mental. They can cause dumbness (Matt. 9:32, 33), blindness (Matt. 12:22), insanity (Luke 8:26-35) and suicidal mania (Mark 9:22), personal injuries (Mark 9:18), supernatural strength (Luke 8:29), and physical defects and deformities (Luke 13:11-17). Once they have gained control over a human body, they can come and go at will (Luke 11:24-26; see also Luke 9:37-42; Mark 5:4, 5, all ASV).

SATAN

Is there such a being as Satan? Multitudes of scholars and intellectual people deny his existence, save in the imagination of ancient and illiterate people. By many, Satan is now looked upon as a product of priestcraft, a relic of superstition, a myth of a bygone age. With others, Satan is merely an abstraction, a mere negation, the opposite of good. "All the devil there is, is the devil within you" are the last words of "modern thought." The words which Goethe puts into the mouth of Mephistopheles — "I am the spirit of negation" — is accepted as a good workable definition of the devil. He is regarded as a mere abstract principle of evil. As someone has quaintly put it, "They spell *devil* without a *d*, as they spell *God* with two *o*'s. Good and evil is their scheme."

But the more general conception of Satan, the one that prevails among the masses, may be gathered from the visual representations of him appearing on street posters, in illustrated magazines, and upon the stage — where he is pictured as a grotesque monster in human form, having horns, hoofs, and forked tail. Such a conception is an insult to intelligent people, and consequently the devil has come to be regarded either as a bogey with which to frighten naughty children, or as a fit subject for jest and joke. Much of this comes from the fact that men have read their fancies and theories into the Scriptures; they have read Milton's *Paradise Lost*, but have neglected the Book of Job; they have considered the experiences of Luther instead of the Epistles of Peter and Jude. To avoid skepticism on the one hand and ridicule on the other, we must resort to the Scriptures to formulate our views of this doctrine.[8]

The Fact of Satan

According to the Scriptures, there is a being called "the Devil" and "Satan" — a real being who has a real existence. Concerning this they leave no room for doubt (Job 1:6-12; 2:1-7; Zech. 3:1, 2; Matt. 4:1-11; 13:19; Luke 10:18; John 13:2; Acts 5:3; Eph. 6:11, 12; 1 Peter 5:8).[9]

The Personality of Satan

In the Bible the personality of the devil is made emphatic. He is not only the source of evil in others, but the embodiment of evil in a person.

1. Personal pronouns are used which unmistakably reveal personality: Job 1:8 (thou); 2:1, 2 (himself, thou); Zechariah 3:2 (thee).

2. Personal characteristics and elements of personality are clearly ascribed to Satan.

   a. Intelligence. His temptations are spoken of as "devices" (2 Cor. 2:11) and as "the wiles of the devil" (Eph. 6:11); similarly in Revelation 2:24 we read of the "depths of Satan" (Greek, "deep things"). Further, in Revelation 12:9 he is termed "that old serpent, called the devil, and Satan, which deceiveth the whole world." To deceive implies design, and design is the product of intelligence, and intelligence is inseparable from personality.

   b. Memory. In his conflict with our Lord in the wilderness, Satan quoted from the Old Testament Scriptures (Matt. 4:6), which is impossible for an abstraction.

   c. Knowledge. When the devil is cast down to the earth, during the tribulation period, we are told he has "great wrath because he knoweth that he hath but a short time" (Rev. 12:12). The impersonal, however, cannot be said to know.

   d. Will. Satan possesses a will or the power of choice, which is further proof that he is a personal being (2 Tim. 2:26; Isa. 14:13, 14).

   e. Emotions. Such emotions as desire (Luke 22:31), pride (1 Tim. 3:6), and wrath (Rev. 12:12) are attributed to Satan. But desire, pride, and wrath cannot be predicted of the law of gravitation — they are inseparable from personality.

   f. Executive and organizing ability. In Revelation 12:7 and 20:7, 8 we find Satan marshaling his legions to engage in warfare, and in Ephesians 6:12 we have the intimation that he is at the head of graded and organized forces.

3.. Personal actions are attributed to him.

   a. He speaks. He is represented as talking with God (Job 1:9, 10) and arguing with our Lord (Matt. 4:1-11). Speech belongs only to personalities.

   b. He tempts. The first time this mysterious being is introduced to us in the Word of God he appears in this capacity, inciting our first parents to disobedience. In Matthew 4:3 he is expressly termed "the tempter." And again, in 1 Corinthians 7:5 and 1 Thessalonians 3:5, the saints are warned against his machinations. To tempt implies design, and design argues intelligence and moral qualities, and these are inseparable from personality.

c. He accuses. To accuse unquestionably argues a conscious and rational entity (Rev. 12:10; Job 1:9-11).

d. He makes war (Rev. 12:7; 20:8, 9).

e. He performs miracles (Exod. 7:11; 2 Thess. 2:9).

f. He is capable of receiving punishment (Matt. 25:41). A mere abstraction cannot be punished. What is nothing more than a negation cannot be tormented. What is incorporeal and intangible cannot be cast into the lake of fire. That the Scriptures declare that Satan shall be punished is conclusive evidence that he is a person, and a person endowed with moral responsibility.

The Original State of Satan

It is obvious from the teaching of various passages of Scripture that Satan was not always the fallen depraved creature he is represented as being since his first appearance to man in the Garden of Eden. This teaching is not so direct as that on other subjects with which Scriptures deal, but sufficient is given upon the origin and character of Satan to show that his first estate was not one of degradation but one of exaltation and perfection.

The origin of Satan. It is evident from the holy and righteous character of God that He could not have created anything that was essentially and originally evil. Man today is a sinful creature, but he has not always been such (Eccl. 7:29). Originally man was created in the image and likeness of God, but by an act of willful disobedience he corrupted his nature and became sinful. The same is true of that part of the angels that apostatized: they were not created in a fallen condition. Peter tells us that the angels "sinned" (2 Peter 2:4), and Jude declares that these angels "kept not their first estate, but left their own habitation" (vs. 6).

From these two examples furnished by sinful man and the fallen angels we might reasonably conclude, from the law of analogy, that the same principle would hold good concerning Satan. It is unthinkable for us to suppose that God would create the devil, though we must believe He created the one who subsequently became the devil. But we are not left to the uncertain speculations of reason, the Word of God itself gives us definite information which establishes this fact (Ezek. 28:13, 15; John 1:1-3; Eph. 3:9; Col. 1:16; Rev. 4:11).

One of the few passages which seem to throw light upon the origin of Satan and of his position and condition before his apostasy is to be found in Ezekiel 28:11-19. A careful reading of these verses produces the conviction that the prophet is here referring to some other than an earthly king or a mere human being. He must have been borne by the spirit of prophecy into some other time and place, and to some other person. Ezekiel must have been taken back to a far distant period of time. While the king of Tyrus was a historical person, we are compelled to conclude that he must also have been a typical character — a figure of Satan himself. Such terms as here found could never have been employed to describe any mere human king, or any human being whatsoever.

Granting that these verses refer to Satan, let us note the description. In verse 13 he is spoken of as being in the garden of God. Satan was indeed in Adam's garden; he did not, however, appear there as a minister of God, but as an apostate and malignant spirit eager for the ruin of the new creation. Hence, the Eden of this passage must have been of a far earlier date. Nor did it at all resemble the garden in which Adam was placed, for we read nothing of trees pleasant to the sight and good for food; but the prominent feature is the covering — that is, probably, the pavilion or palace of Satan — which is described as being made of gold and of every precious stone. Yet, while this description does not in any way remind us of the Adamic Eden, we cannot but be impressed by its resemblance to that of the New Jerusalem, with its buildings of pure gold as it were transparent glass, its foundations garnished with all manner of precious stones, its jasper wall, and its gates of pearl. And that city, be it remembered, seems to be the destined habitation of the church, composed of those who will then be spiritual beings of a higher order equal to the angels, and, with Christ as their head, will have succeeded to that same power which Satan and his angels are now so fearfully abusing (Luke 20:36; Rev. 5:10).

The latter part of verse 13 should be translated "the service of thy tabrets and of thy pipes was prepared with thee on the day when thou wast created." Music is one of the necessary attendants of royal state. In Daniel 3 we have an enumeration of the various instruments which were to signal the time of the king's pleasure (vs. 5); and in Isaiah 14 the pomp of the king of Babylon and the noise of his viols are said to be brought down to the grave with him. The blast of a trumpet accompanied the manifestation of God upon Mount Sinai (Exod. 19:16) and the trump of the archangel will sound at the return in glory of the King of the whole earth. The meaning, then, of this clause seems to be that Satan was from the moment of his creation surrounded by the insignia of royalty; that he awoke to consciousness to find the air filled with the joyful music of those whom God has appointed to stand before Him. In the next verse, we seem to pass from the royalty of Satan to his priestly dignity (Ezek. 28:14). He is said to have been, by God's appointment, the "anointed cherub that covereth." *Anointed* doubtless means consecrated by the oil of anointing, while the Cherubim appear to be the highest rank of heavenly beings, sitting nearest the throne of God and leading the worship of the universe (Rev. 4:9, 10; 5:11-14). Possibly they are identical with the thrones of which Paul speaks in Colossians 1:16. The words *that covereth* indicate an allusion to the cherubim that overshadowed the ark; but we cannot, of course, define the precise nature of the office of Satan. The general idea seems to be that he directed and led the worship of his subjects.

He is also said to have been upon the holy mountain of God and to have walked up and down in the midst of the stones of fire. The mountain of God is the place of His presence in visible glory, where His High Priest would, of course, stand before Him to minister. The "stones of fire" may, perhaps, be explained as follows: we know that the station of the Cherubim is just beneath the glory at the footstool of the throne (Ezek. 1:26). When Moses took Aaron, Nadab, Abihu, and seventy of the elders of Israel up the mountain of Sinai to see the God of Israel, "there was under His feet as it were a paved work of a sapphire stone, and as it were, the body of heaven in its clearness. . . . And the sight of the glory of the Lord was like devouring fire upon the top of the mount" (Exod. 24:10, 17). This paved work of sapphire, glowing with devouring fire, is perhaps the same as the stones of fire; if so, Satan's presence in the midst of them would indicate his enjoyment of the full cherubic privilege of nearness to the throne of God. Verse 15 shows that God is not the Author of evil. For even the Prince of Darkness was by creation perfect in all his ways, and so continued until iniquity was found in him and he fell.

The original perfections of Satan. He possessed the sum of all creature excellencies. No defect was to be found in him: he was created perfect and remained so until he chose to sin (Ezek. 28: 12-17).

1. Fulness of wisdom (vs. 12).
2. Perfection of beauty (vss. 12, 17).
3. Holiness of nature (vs. 14).
4. Perfection of conduct (vs. 15).

In brief, he maintained a perfection of wisdom, beauty, moral nature, and creature conduct until his fall.

The original position of Satan. Satan seems to have been the highest of all of God's created intelligences, and his position and prerogatives seem to have been in accordance with the place given him in God's creative order and as befitting one possessed with his endowments (Ezek. 28:14).

Satan is here described as "the anointed cherub." Scripture furnishes us with a number of examples where "anointing" is connected with induction to an office, and in the verse now before us the reference is apparently to God's appointment of Satan to fill a certain position. Here we see the exercise of divine sovereignty in the statement, "I have set thee so." Satan came to this position, not by inherent right or by struggle, but by the gift of his divine Creator and Sovereign. It is a point of deep interest to observe that in Old Testament times men were anointed to fill but three offices — the prophetic, the priestly, and the kingly (1 Kings 19:16; Lev. 16:32), and there are some who infer from the hints dropped in Scripture that Satan originally filled each of these offices himself (cf. Ezek. 28:13 with Exod. 28:17-20; Isa. 14:13 with Ezek. 28:17).

The original domain of Satan. The general interpretation of Ezekiel 28:13, 14 is that Satan was created as a guard or protector to the throne of the Most High. This is reasonable. Like the golden cherubim, covering the visible mercy seat in the Holy of Holies of the earthly tabernacle, he was created a guard and covering cherub to the heavenly center of glory. It is expressly stated that he was located by the Most High upon the holy mountain of God — the mountain being a symbol of God's power, government, and eternal throne (Pss. 48:1; 68:15; Isa. 2:2). Over this exalted throne Satan was set as a covering cherub. He is also said to have been in "Eden, the garden of God," which is evidently another Eden than that in which Satan appeared as a serpent. It is probably a reference to the primitive creation, and the whole passage suggests a position of great authority for which he was created and anointed.

The Fall of Satan

God did not create evil. "A good tree cannot bring forth evil fruit, neither can a corrupt tree bring forth good fruit" (Matt. 7:17, 18). If God did not create evil, then how did it originate? It will not do to say, "An enemy hath done this," for then the question will arise, "Who made the enemy?" If Satan did not originate evil in his own

326 CHRISTIAN THEOLOGY: SYSTEMATIC AND BIBLICAL

heart, then it must have been implanted in his heart from some outside source. This would require the coexistence of good and evil in the universe and rob God of sovereignty.

When God created the angels, and all the glorious beings of His original creation, there was no sin or evil in the universe. But as free moral agents they had the power of choice between following the will of God or following their own will. As long as Satan chose the will of God, there was no evil in the universe; but the moment he chose to follow his own will, he fell, and by persuading others to follow him he introduced evil into the universe. That Satan did fall is declared not only in the Old Testament Scriptures, but explicitly by the Lord Jesus Himself: "I beheld Satan as lightning fall from heaven" (Luke 10:18).

The cause of the Fall:

1. Pride. Several Scriptures shed light upon this. In Ezekiel 28:17 we read, "Thine heart was lifted up because of thy beauty, thou has corrupted thy wisdom by reason of thy brightness." Here was the first sin that broke up the calm of eternity and stirred up the storm that has not ceased to rage. An ever-increasing violence that will not be quieted until God quells it forever by His word, "Peace be still."

   The words, "Thine heart was lifted up because of thy beauty," suggest that instead of "the anointed cherub" finding his chief delight in the contemplation of the divine excellencies, he became occupied with his own beauty; as Proverbs 16:18 declares, "Pride goeth before destruction, and a haughty spirit before a fall," so these lofty thoughts which Satan had of himself brought about his ruin. With this agrees 1 Timothy 3:6: "Lest being lifted up with pride he fall into the condemnation of the devil."

2. False ambition. The root of sin is selfishness. When Satan said, "I will ascend into heaven [from the original earth over which he was ruling], I will exalt my throne above the stars of God [other ruling powers] . . . I will ascend above the heights of the clouds; I will be like the Most High" (Isa. 14:12-14), then Satan was guilty of treason and started a rebellion against the government of God that will never cease until he and all his followers are cast into the lake of fireto spend eternity.

The result of the Fall:

1. The anointed cherub became the original sinner (1 John 3:8).

2. He became the author, fountainhead, and disseminator of sin (John 8:44).
3. He ceased to abide in the truth, and sin became his inherent nature, element, environment, and delight (1 John 3:8; John 8:44).
4. His wisdom became corrupted (Ezek. 28:17; Rom. 1:21-25).
5. He came under condemnation (1 Tim. 3:6, ASV).
6. He is to be expelled from the heavenlies (Ezek. 28:16, 17; Rev. 12:7-10).
7. His future destruction is determined (Isa. 14:12-17; Ezek. 28:16; Rev. 20:1-3, 7-10).

The Present Abode of Satan

The common notion is that Satan and his angels are imprisoned in hell. This is not true. The angels described in 2 Peter 2:4 and in Jude 6 as having left their "first estate" and being "reserved in everlasting chains under darkness" are not Satan's angels. They are probably a special class of angels whose sin caused the Flood. According to the Scriptures, Satan does not seem to be restricted to one place.

He has access to heaven. In Job 1:6, 7; 2:1, 2 Satan is seen appearing in the midst of other heavenly beings before the presence of Jehovah; and there seems to be nothing unusual in the presence of Satan in this celestial company. To the question of Jehovah, "Whence comest thou?" he replies, "From going to and fro in the earth and from walking up and down in it." From this revelation, the important information is given that Satan is free to appear in the presence of God. This is also seen in Revelation 12:7-10, where he is presented as "the accuser of the brethren, who accuseth our brethren before God day and night" (see also Zech. 3:1).

He dwells in the heavenly realms. Satan and the principalities, the powers, the world rulers of darkness, the spiritual hosts of wickedness have their abiding place in the heavenlies (Eph. 6:11, 12, ASV).

He is active upon the earth. The earth seems to be the special field of Satan's activity; he goes to and fro in the earth and walks up and down in it (Job 1:7; 1 Peter 5:8).

The Present Position of Satan

It seems to be a principle in God's governmental dealings to "bear with much long suffering the vessels of wrath fitted to destruction" (Rom. 9:22). Apparently He gave the antediluvian world 120 years in which to repent of wickedness and accept the overtures of His mercy made through Noah. With infinite patience He dealt with Pharaoh, and it was not until after the ten plagues had failed to soften his heart that he was cut off out of the land of the living. It was the same with Israel: His judgments fell upon the chosen people only after long and repeated provocation, and then but mildly at the first; it was not until after fifteen centuries of unbelief and rebellion that they were dispersed throughout the world.

Likewise, God did not consign Satan to the lake of fire on the occasion of his first sin. Rather, He has permitted him a long spell of freedom in which to demonstrate the inveteracy of his enmity against God, ere he shall be finally cast into that fire "prepared for the devil and his angels."

The present position of Satan which he occupies through this sufferance on the part of God is revealed by the following:

1. Exaltation and honor. The position of Satan is so exalted that even Michael the archangel would not bring any railing judgment against him (Jude 6, 9, ASV).
2. Rulership and authority.
   a. He is called the "prince of the power of the air." Satan is given this title and is credited with possessing a kingdom, indicating his authority and power in relation to the heavenly realms (Eph. 2:2; Matt. 12:26, 29, ASV; see also Acts 26:18 and Col. 1:13).
   b. He is called the "prince of this world." Satan is the head of the present godless world order and system (John 12:31; 14:30; 16:11). The Greek word translated "world" in John 12:31 is *kosmos*, and the thought is of the present world order. How he came to be the prince of this world may be impossible for us to say positively, but that he is so admits of no question if we are to accept the teaching of Jesus. Anyone who will study the ruling principles of commercial life, of political life, of social life, and above all of international relations will find it perfectly evident that the devil is the one who is the master of the present perverted order of things.
   c. He is called the "god of this age." By this title he is presented as the self-constituted object of world worship (2 Cor. 4:3; see also 2 Thess. 2:3, 4 and Rom. 6:16).

The Character of Satan

Can a being created pure ever fall? While no satisfactory answer may be found, nevertheless the fact is clearly established by the teaching of Scripture that Satan, although pure at the time of his creation, did fall. This is implied by the statement of Jesus in John 8:44: "He . . . abode not in the truth." The word *abode* suggests that previously he was in the truth. What is here implied is definitely taught in other parts of Scripture, and Ezekiel 28:15 furnishes us an example: "Thou was perfect in thy ways from the day that thou was created till iniquity was found in thee." But whatever may have been his character at the first, however exalted his position, there came a time when "his heart was lifted up"; pride which "goeth before destruction" entered, and he came under condemnation, was disgraced, and fell. The character of Satan is revealed in a twofold manner.

1. By the significance of the names given to him in the Scriptures
   a. Satan. Fifty-two times he is called "Satan," which means hater, enemy, or adversary. He is the hater of both God and His people, and is the enemy of God and the adversary of man (Job 1:6; 2:1; Zech. 3:1).

   In this title of "Satan" we see him in the character role which dominates all his actions. As Satan he is the hater. Of all the evil passions of the soul, hate is the most terrible. As manifested in human relationships, the hater is a murderer. Somehow hate seems to be a resultant of wrath, malice, envy, jealousy, and revenge. Hatred in the bosom of the weak or cowardly affects only its possessor; but with hatred burning in the soul of one who is strong and courageous, nothing belonging to the object of hatred is secure: life, personal property, or reputation.

   Note the full significance of hatred; then place beside it the one who hates — yes, as no other being in all the universe can hate. He is the father of haters. Tragedies of all kinds, such as murder, bombings, kidnapings, and various other incendiary actions, are but the scattered rays reflected and deflected from this full orb of hate as the hater revolves in his sphere of darkness.

   Satan hates God, hates the Holy Ghost; but the full force of his hate, of necessity, is directed toward the Son of God, his rival for place and power. The supreme work of the Son was atonement; now the interest and anxiety of heaven has been transferred to this planet. The supreme triumph of the Second Person of the Trinity was accomplished on the cross where He paid the price of human redemption. Satan's energies are now directed to the breaking down of all that was accomplished on the cross. Every movement, every motive, every virtue, coming directly or indirectly from the merits of the Atonement, become at once the object of satanic hatred. Therefore every inch of territory conquered by the gospel was and is a victory over this hateful protest.

b. The Devil. Thirty-five times he is denominated "the devil," which means the accuser or slanderer — accusing the saints before God and traducing the character of God before men (Rev. 12:7-10; Matt. 4:1). "Devil" is the English translation of the Hebrew word *sair* and of the Greek word *diabolos*.

The Hebrew word *sair* means hairy goat, he-goat. The he-goat, in the Bible, stands for all that is low and base. Those who partake of the *sair* nature at the judgment of the living nations are called goats. He divides the sheep from the goats. God teaches us spiritual lessons in all nature, especially by the animal kingdom. As the goat is a synonym for the lowest instincts of the animal, we find a being created in the highest realm of spiritual life sinking to the lowest level of brute life. If no further delineation were given — no other name than "devil" — the fall would be seen to be from one extreme to another.

This cognomen carried further has a second meaning: spoiler, one whose touch soils and besmirches, rearranges. Hearts of purity are defiled and debauched; faces of beauty become marred and ugly. Whenever and wherever it serves his purpose, cosmos becomes chaos. The devil is a spoiler. *Diabolos* designates him more as to his ruling and authority than to the elements of his character. We have noticed already the meaning of "devil," but from the original word we get more explicit meaning as to his rank of authority. As Lucifer we do not know his ruling rank, but in his lost estate he ranks as commander-in-chief. Whatever we may say of him, the prefix *arch*, designating his angel rank, can be logically attached: archspoiler — archdeceiver — archaccuser — archslanderer. However, if accurately defined, *diabolus* means calumniator — archcalumniator; a propagator of calumny. Acting in the capacity of calumniator, he seeks out and defames the innocent. He sends out a million rumors daily which would be, if tangible, cases for libel in any court.

c. The Prince of the Power of the Air. This title points to his present abode and sphere of operations (Eph. 2:2 with 6:12).

It is by no means necessary to restrict "the heavenly places" or "the power of the air" to the eighty or a hundred miles of atmosphere supposed to surround the earth. If Satan's power extends to the sun, and so to the whole of our solar system, the kingdom of the air would include the immense space in which the planets of our center revolve. In light of this, it seems not unlikely that the throne of its prince may be situated in the photosphere of the sun.

We should thus find a deep underlying significance in the fact that idolatry has always commenced with, and in no small degree consisted of, the worship of the Sun-god, whether he be called San, Shamas, Bel, Ra, Baal, Moloch, Milcom, Hada, Adrammelech, Mithras, Apollo, Sheik Shems, or by any other of his innumerable names. May there not be great significance in the fact that the very name of Satan passes, through its Chaldaic form *Sheltan*, into the Greek *Titan*, which last word is used by Greek and Latin poets as a designation of the Sun-god? Indeed, it would almost seem as if this connection were understood in the Dark Ages: for Didron, in his Christian iconography, describes three Byzantine miniatures of the tenth century, in which Satan is depicted with a nimbus, or circular glory, the recognized sign of the sun-god of pagan times.

d. The Prince of This World. Satan manifestly holds the legitimate title of "Prince of This World." This dignity, together with the royal prerogatives which of right pertain to it, was conferred upon him by God Himself. There is no other way of explaining the fact that the Lord Jesus not only spoke of the adversary by this title, but plainly recognized his delegated authority in that He did not dispute his claim to the present disposal of the kingdoms of the world and their glory. And it is only by recognizing the legitimacy of that claim that we can understand a passage of Jude in which the conduct of the archangel Michael toward Satan is adduced as an example of due respect for authority, even though it be in the hands of the wicked (Ezek. 28:11-19; John 14:30; Jude 9).

Christ, by the victory of His cross, has wrested the scepter of authority and rule from the hand of Satan, gained by him in his conquest in Eden; therefore, with respect to the believer,

Satan's power and authority is provisionally nullified. At the close of the present age, he will be deprived of his fiefdom; and the basis of real power being thus removed, his usurped authority will be terminated (John 16:11).

e. The God of This Age. He is called the god of this age because he is the inspirer and director of all spurious religion (cf. 2 Cor. 4:4 with Rom. 6:16; see also 2 Thess. 2:3, 4). There is, indeed, reason to believe that the devil has directly received far more personal worship than those who are not accustomed to investigate such matters would imagine. But it is to something more general that Paul refers (Rom. 6:16): "Know ye not, that to whom ye yield yourselves servants to obey, his servants ye are to whom ye obey?" Two laws are set before us, that of God and that of Satan; and whose law we keep, his servants and worshipers we are. Profession, however vehement, goes for nothing in the other world. We may profess the worship of the Supreme God, we may be very sedulous in the outward part of it; but if at the same time we are obeying the law of Satan, his subjects we are reckoned to be, and to him our prayers and praises ascend.

The law of Satan is this: that we seek all our pleasure in and fix all our heartfelt hopes upon this present age over which he presides; and that we use our best endeavors — by means of various sensuous and intellectual occupations and delights, and countless ways of killing time which he has provided — to keep our thoughts from ever wandering into that age to come, which will see him a fettered captive instead of a prince and a god.

f. Abaddon-Apollyon. This name means destroyer. The Hebrew and Greek names are linked together because both have exactly the same meaning. This name links him with the bottomless pit (Rev. 9:11).

Satan under the name of Abaddon-Apollyon is presented as the destroyer or the destructionist. He has been discussed as a "spoiler," but one who destroys carries the work further than the spoiler. As Abaddon or Apollyon, he is the king of the abyss, or "bottomless pit," and when he appears, it is with purpose and equipment for destruction. Just as God sent the "destroying angel" throughout Egypt, bringing a curse upon Pharaoh for his hardness of heart, this mighty messenger of the abyss visits his destruction wherever and whenever he finds, not the absence of the typical blood upon the door, but any evidence of allegiance to the One whose sacrificial blood he seeks to destroy.

As Abaddon-Apollyon he assumes the part of finisher of his task; when we see him a destroyer, we have a full-sized photograph — leaving out not a single line of countenance or a single character or attribute of his composite nature. He may soil, spoil, deceive, traduce, accuse, slander, or wound, but the ultimate aim is destruction. "When sin is finished it bringeth forth death." We see how the two great rivals stand over against each other in their respective spheres: "for this cause the Son of God was manifested, that He might destroy the works of the devil." With the same degree of purpose the devil seeks to destroy the work of the Son of God. He seeks to destroy truth, righteousness, virtue, hope, faith, love, visions of God, power of the Blood, thoughts of eternity and heaven.

g. Other designations of Satan. He is named "Beelzebub" (Matt. 12:24), which regards him as the head of the demons. He is spoken of as "the wicked one" (Matt. 13:19), which is descriptive of his evil character. He is called "the dragon" (Hebrew — *tannoth*, howler, jackal; making the noise like the howling jackal in the wilderness) to enforce and emphasize the dangerous character of him who seeks our destruction (Rev. 12:9), though it is perhaps under the figure of the "Old Serpent" that he is seen in his most dangerous capacity. In the name "Belial" there is suggested the baseness and vileness of his character (2 Cor. 6:15).

2. By the direct teaching of the Scriptures. We are not left solely to the names applied to Satan for the source of our knowledge of his character. The Scripture language is clear and positive in its portrayal of this personage.

a. He is described as cunning and subtle in character.

(1) His devices. The devil has many and subtle devices of which we should not be ignorant (2 Cor. 2:11).

(2) His wiles. Satan is a great strategist and uses so many wiles, i.e., makes so many subtle assaults that we need the whole armor of God to withstand him (Eph. 4:14; 6:11, 12, all ASV).

(3) His wonder-working power. Satan displays such power and signs and wonders of falsehood as to deceive com-

pletely all those who receive not the love of the truth (2 Thess. 2:9, 10; see also Rev. 13:11-14; Matt. 24:24).

(4) His power of self-transformation. Satan is able to fashion himself into an angel of light (2 Cor. 11:14).

b. He is described as wicked and malignant in nature.

(1) He is the evil one. Satan is the impersonation of evil and the source of evil (1 John 5:19; Matt. 5:37; 6:13, all ASV).

(2) He is the original and chief sinner. Satan sins from the beginning and is the arch-sinner of the universe (1 John 3:8).

(3) He is a murderer and the instigator of murder. The devil is cruel and brutal; he is a murderer at heart and the being responsible for the physical and spiritual death of the race (John 8:44).

(4) He blinds men's minds to saving truth. The devil is heartless and designing; he blinds the minds of men to prevent their being saved, and to secure their condemnation with himself (2 Cor. 4:4, ASV).

(5) He steals the saving truth from the hearts of men. Satan takes away the Word of God out of the hearts of men where it has been sown, so that they might not believe and be saved (Luke 8:12).

The Work of Satan

It is a law of scriptural interpretation that the first mention of anything in God's Word determines its meaning throughout Scripture to a very marked degree. An illustration of this is seen in connection with Satan. The first time he is brought before us in Holy Writ his true character is unveiled, the sphere in which he works is clearly revealed, and the methods he employs are expressly set forth. His subtlety is indicated in his using a serpent as his means of approach to our first parents; his cowardice, in his assaulting the woman rather than the man; his evil nature, in his lying to her and seeking her ruin; his character of tempter, in his capturing his victim by means of an attractive bait ("Ye shall be as God"); his sphere of operations in his inciting Eve to commit not a moral but a spiritual sin — transgression of God's command; his real object of attack — God's Word: "Yea, hath God said?"

In the sentence which God pronounced upon that old serpent, the devil, Satan's purpose and program is definitely revealed (Gen.

3:15). There is much in this remarkable announcement which calls for study and comment; but for our present purpose we limit ourselves to one declaration — "enmity . . . between thy seed and her seed." We are here informed that the woman's "Seed" — the Lord Jesus Christ — is to be the object of Satan's unrelenting hatred. This reveals to us in a word the agelong work in which Satan has been engaged. Ever since the first messianic prediction was uttered in Eden, Satan has been the enemy of the woman's Seed. The person and work of the Lord Jesus have been the objects of his attack.

His methods of opposition have primarily followed two lines.

1. A work of anticipation and opposition. Having learned that the woman's Seed was destined to "bruise" his head, Satan, by way of anticipation and opposition, sought to prevent His entry into this world. It may be that his first attempt along this line is to be seen in the death of Abel. Possibly Satan thought Abel was the promised "Seed" of the woman and for that reason stirred up Cain, "who was of that wicked one" (1 John 3:12) to kill his brother. His next attack was more daring. It appears from Genesis 6 that a considerable number of Nephilim, termed "Sons of God" (fallen celestial beings) left their own habitation (Jude 6), came down to this earth, and cohabited with the daughters of men in an attempt to destroy the human species by producing a race of monstrosities. How nearly Satan succeeded in this attempt the student of the Word is well aware — with the exception of a single family, Noah and his house, all mankind was destroyed by God at the Flood.

At a later date God revealed to Abraham His purpose that all the families of the earth should be blessed through his "Seed," in other words, that the coming Redeemer and Bruiser of Satan should be one of his descendants according to the flesh. Hence we may understand why — some four hundred years later when in Egypt the offspring of Abraham began to wax numerous — that Satan again attempted to frustrate the purpose of God by seeking to destroy the channel through which the promised "Seed" was to come. There can be no reasonable doubt that it was Satan who moved Pharaoh to issue the edict commanding that all the male children of the Hebrews should be put to death.

At a still later date God made known the fact to King David that the promised Messiah should be born of the royal tribe of Judah. Shortly afterwards we find Satan making another attempt to thwart God as may be seen in the dividing of the kingdom, when the ten tribes made a determined and prolonged effort to exterminate the tribe of Judah. Other examples might be cited from the Old Testament (e.g., Haman's plot to slay all the Jews) to illustrate the efforts of Satan attempting to prevent the advent of the woman's Seed; but we turn now to the New Testament. When the fullness of time was come and God sent forth His Son, born of a woman (Gal. 4:4), Satan promptly made an effort to destroy the young child's life. Through Herod he slew all the children in Bethlehem from two years old and under. But his effort was in vain, for being warned of God in a dream, Joseph had taken the young child and His mother and had fled into Egypt.

At the commencement of our Lord's ministry, Satan sought to make Him throw Himself down from the temple. A little later he so stirred up the hearts of our Lord's hearers that we read, they "rose up and thrust Him out of the city and led Him unto the brow of the hill whereon their city was built, that they might cast Him down headlong. But He passing through the midst of them went His way" (Luke 4:29, 30). On another occasion — when, wearied from the day's work, our Lord sought sleep in the bow of a boat — another attempt was made upon His life. The Prince of the Power of the Air lashed the Sea of Galilee into a fury, until the storm was so fierce that the disciples feared their ship was doomed, and it was not until the Creator of the sea commanded it to be still that the plot of the devil was foiled.

From Matthew 16:21-23 we may learn how Satan sought to turn our Lord from the purpose of His incarnation and mission, and this he did through the medium of Peter, whom he caused to say with reference to the crucifixion which Jesus had just foretold, "Be it far from Thee, Lord" (marg. — "pity Thyself") — spare Thyself such humiliation as that. But Christ instantly detected the source of this plausible appeal, and He turned and said to Peter, "Get thee behind me, Satan: thou art an offense unto me."

The trail of the serpent is plainly to be seen around the cross itself. For without doubt it was Satan who instigated the challenge to Christ to demonstrate His deity by descending from the cross (Matt. 27:40). But Christ never faltered; patiently and majestically He bore His sufferings, until He cried in triumph, "It is finished," and surrendered His spirit into the hands of His Father. He sought also to keep Christ in the tomb after His burial by instigating the Roman authorities to seal the tomb securely and guard it with a company of soldiers. But here again he is defeated. The grave cannot retain its victim; death cannot hold the Lord of life.

But Satan has not ceased his opposition to the person and work of Christ. He is still prosecuting his wicked designs, still endeavoring to frustrate the purposes of God, and he is now aiming to nullify the virtues of Christ's atoning death.

2. A work of imitation and perversion. The great ambition and determination of Satan is to be like God. The boast of Lucifer was "I will be like the Most High." In Satan's great scheme, he imitates and counterfeits the things God is doing, and so fine is his imitation that vast multitudes of people who are actually following Satan's error think they are serving God. Satan is not an initiator, but an imitator.

For example, God has an only begotten Son — the Lord Jesus; and so has Satan — "the son of perdition" (2 Thess. 2:3). There is a holy Trinity, and there is a triumvirate of evil (Rev. 20:10). Do we read of the "children of God"? So also we read of "the children of the wicked one" (Matt. 13:38). Does God work in the former both to will and to do of His good pleasure? Then, we are told, Satan is "the spirit that now worketh in the children of disobedience" (Eph. 2:2). Is there a "mystery of godliness" (1 Tim. 3:16)? So also is there a "mystery of iniquity" (2 Thess. 2:7). Are we told that God by His angel "seals" His servants in their foreheads (Rev. 7:3)? So also we learn that Satan by his agent sets a mark in the foreheads of his devotees (Rev. 13:16). Are we told that "the Spirit searcheth all things, yea, the deep things of God" (1 Cor. 2:10)? Then Satan also provides his "deep things" (see Greek for Rev. 2:24). Did Christ perform miracles? So also can Satan (2 Thess. 2:9). Is Christ the Light of the World? Then so is Satan himself "transformed into an angel of light" (2 Cor. 11:14). Did Christ appoint "apostles"? Then Satan has his apostles, too (2 Cor. 11:13).

3. Summary of the work of Satan

   a. He originates and instigates sin (Gen. 3:1-6).

   b. He causes affliction and suffering (Luke 13:16; Acts 10:38).

   c. He causes death (John 8:44; Heb. 2:14).

   d. He allures to evil (1 Chron. 21:1, ASV; Matt. 4:1-10; 1 Cor. 7:5; 1 Thess. 3:5).

   e. He brings men into captivity (1 Tim. 3:7; 2 Tim. 2:26).

    f. He inspires wicked thoughts and purposes (John 13:2; Acts 5:3).

    g. He enters into and controls men (John 13:27; Eph. 4:27).

    h. He blinds the minds of men (2 Cor. 4:4).

    i. He dissipates truth from the hearts of men (Matt. 13:19; Mark 4:15; Luke 8:12, ASV).

    j. He produces a fruitage of evildoers (Matt. 13:39).

    k. He accuses believers (Job 1:6-11; 2:3-5; Rev. 12:9, 10).

    l. He authorizes and energizes his ministers (2 Cor. 11:13-15; Rev. 3:9).

    m. He opposes those who are engaged in God's service (2 Cor. 12:7; 1 Thess. 2:18, ASV; Dan. 10:13; Zech. 3:1).

    n. He sifts and tries believers (Luke 22:31).

    o. He will energize the Antichrist (2 Thess. 2:9, 10, ASV; see also Rev. 12:9, 17; 13:1, 2, 7).

The Future Destiny of Satan

The satanic program as outlined in the Scriptures would seem to indicate that Satan cherishes hopes of ultimate victory for his cause; nevertheless, the same Scriptures foretell in awful tones the certainty of his coming defeat and doom. Though the execution of judgment upon him has been long held in abeyance, he shall not escape the due reward of his iniquities. The Serpent's head has not yet been "bruised," but the time of his complete humiliation is not far distant: "And the God of peace shall bruise Satan under your feet shortly" (Rom. 16:20).

There seem to be four stages in the punishment meted out to the devil.

1. The first stage is conterminous with Satan's apostasy (Ezek. 28:16). On the occasion of his apostasy Satan seems to have been cast out of the highest heavens. To this our Lord evidently refers when He says, "I beheld Satan as lightning fall from heaven" (Luke 10:18). Since that time and to the present, the lower heaven (heavenly places, Eph. 6:12) is apparently the abode of the Evil One — though he still has access to both the heaven of heavens and our earth (Job 1:6, 7).

2. The second stage of his punishment will be marked by his being cast out of heaven as the result of the war in heaven between himself and Michael the archangel (Rev. 12:7-9). His sphere of operations thence will be limited to the earth. He is no longer

granted access to God. Here Satan is pictured as being in great wrath as he is banished from heaven into the earth, "knowing that he has but a short time." This will doubtless occur sometime between the rapture of the church, when Christ returns for His saints (1 Thess. 4:16), and the beginning of the Millennium, when our Lord comes back to the earth with his saints to reign in righteousness for a thousand years.

3. The third stage in the execution of his judgment will consist of his arrest and imprisonment in the abyss (Rev. 20:1-3). An angel officer, the High Sheriff of heaven, will break in on the scene of Satan's earthly activities (the great tribulation) and will lay hold on — arrest — the Old Dragon — Satan — Devil — Serpent, and bind him for a thousand years, casting him into the bottomless pit.

4. The fourth stage will be the last, mark his final doom, and seal his eternal destiny (Rev. 20:10). At the close of the Millennium, Satan is released from the bottomless pit and is given a short season of liberty, during which he once more gives evidence of the inveteracy of his wickedness and of the unchangeability of his evil heart (Rev. 20:7-9).

Satan is thus revealed as having been first created perfect in all his ways, mighty in power, and full of beauty and wisdom; but, having apostatized, he was demoted from the exalted position assigned to him. Though cast down but yet having access to God, he is seen wresting the world scepter from man, to rule as the prince of this world until the judgment of the Cross, after which he still rules as a usurper. At the end of the age he is deprived of his position in the heavenlies and cast down to the earth; and thence into the abyss; and finally is banished to the lake of fire forever. Satan *is now* a conquered enemy (John 12:31; 16:8-11; Col. 2:15; Heb. 2:14; 1 John 3:8).

The Believer's Rightful Attitude and Action Toward Satan

The believer is called upon to face a world-ruling foe who, with all his kingdom and power, is seeking to break and mar that life into which the divine nature has been received. The revelation of Satan's present position and power should disarm the believer of all self-confidence respecting his own ability to contend successfully with this foe.

The Scriptures present certain conditions and requirements which are essential to the believer's present victory over Satan. The believer must —

Claim redemption rights. The believer should claim his redemption rights in Christ Jesus, who died to destroy the works of the devil and to render his power null and void (Eph. 6:16; Col. 2:15; Heb. 2:14; 1 John 3:8; Rev. 12:11, all ASV).

Appropriate full equipment. We should put on the whole armor of God that we may be able to stand against the wiles of the devil (Eph. 6:11-18, ASV).

Maintain strict self-control. We should leave no room and give no place to the devil by evil passion or practice (cf. Eph. 4:27 with Gal. 5:22, 23).

Exercise vigilance. The fact of Satan's existence, activity, and power should make us circumspect and watchful (cf. 2 Cor. 2:11 with 1 Peter 5:8, ASV).

Make resistance. We should resist the devil in God's strength for assured victory (James 4:7; 1 John 2:14).

Study Questions on Angelology

1. Discuss the probability of the existence of angels from the analogy of nature.
2. Quote one passage each from the Old and New Testaments proving the fact of the existence of angels.
3. Discuss the ninefold description of the nature of angels.
4. Discuss the sixfold description of the moral character of angels.
5. Give a detailed description of the ministry of good and evil angels.
6. Give the practical values of the doctrine of angels, good and evil.
7. Discuss the lack of clearness in the presentation of the subject of demon possession in the Authorized Version of the New Testament, and show why the American Standard Version is more accurate.
8. List several reasons for accepting the fact of the existence of demons and discuss the theoretical interpretations of the attitude of the Scriptures toward the subject.
9. Discuss fully the nature and character of demons.
10. Discuss the question of demon control in the present time.
11. Discuss the modern conception of Satan and his usual mode of procedure.

12. Discuss the fact of the existence of Satan as shown by the Scriptures, and quote one passage proving it.
13. Give in detail the threefold proof of the personality of Satan.
14. Discuss the origin of Satan and give the essence of the teaching of Ezekiel 28:11-19.
15. Describe the original perfections, original position, and original domain of Satan.
16. Describe the fall of Satan, including its cause and result.
17. Give the threefold description of the present abode of Satan.
18. Describe fully the present position of Satan.
19. Discuss the character of Satan as revealed by the names given him.
20. Describe the character of Satan as revealed by the direct teaching of the Scriptures.
21. Discuss the work of Satan.
22. Give an outline of scriptural teaching on the work of Satan.
23. Discuss the future destiny of Satan.
24. Give the various aspects of the believer's rightful attitude and action toward Satan, and quote one passage of Scripture with each.

CHRISTIAN THEOLOGY: SYSTEMATIC AND BIBLICAL

Notes

[1]The Scholastic subtleties which encumbered this doctrine in the Middle Ages, and the exaggerated representations made in connection with it which then prevailed, have led, by a natural reaction, to an undue depreciation of it in more recent times. For instance, the Scholastics debated such questions as "How many angels could stand at once on the point of a needle?" (relation of angels to space) and "Can an angel be in two places at the same time?" (relation of angels to time).

[2]In these passages it is assumed that angels of God are wise and endowed with superior knowledge. They were, no doubt, created intelligent spirits, their knowledge beginning with their existence. But we may safely conclude that it has been increasing ever since. Their opportunities of observation and the many experiences they have had in connection with direct revelations from God must have added to the stock of their original intelligence. They are finite beings, and their knowledge is therefore limited (1 Peter 1:12); if limited, progressive. The knowledge of God cannot be augmented, because He is infinite; the knowledge of angelic spirits is susceptible of increase, because they are finite.

[3]To give us some idea of the rapidity of their movements, the sacred writers represent the angels as flying on their errands to execute the commands of the Almighty. This form of expression, judged alone by the passages of Scripture containing it, may or may not be understood literally. Wings, and flight by means of wings, pertain to material beings, and we have seen that angels are pure spirits — celestial beings as contrasted with terrestrial beings — and as such may be possessed of celestial bodies which are capable of materialization. Of all creatures coming within the range of our vision, those which have wings and fly exemplify the highest speed. Angelic activity, is, therefore, very impressively taught by this language. There must, however, be a basis and a reason for the use of this language, and they are to be found in the velocity of angelic movement. See in this connection Daniel 9:21 and Matthew 26:53.

[4]We are called "sons of men," but angels are never called "sons of angels." They are not developed from one original stock, and no such common nature binds them together as binds together the race of man. They have no common character and history. Each was created separately, and each apostate angel fell by himself. Humanity fell all at once in its first father. Cut down a tree and you cut down its branches; but angels were so many separate trees. Some lapsed into sin, but some remained holy. This may be one reason why salvation was provided for fallen man, but not for fallen angels. The angels are "sons of God," as having no earthly parentage and no parentage at all except the divine.

[5]Michael (etymologically, "who is like God) is the only one expressly called an archangel in Scripture, although Gabriel ("God's hero") has been called an archangel by Milton.

[6]God's entrance upon new epochs in the unfolding of His plans seems to have been generally marked by angelic appearances. Hence we read of angels at the completion of creation (Job 38:7); at the giving of the law (Gal. 3:19); at the birth of Christ (Luke 2:13); at the two temptations, in the wilderness and in Gethsemane (Matt. 4:11; Luke 22:43); at the resurrection (Matt. 28:2); at the ascension (Acts 1:10); at the judgment of the living nations (Matt. 26:31).

[7]Christ implied, in the controversy with the Pharisees recorded in this passage, that Satan is a king and as such is in authority over a kingdom. This particular discussion concerned the fact that Christ had healed one "possessed with a demon, blind and dumb." The Pharisees claimed the demon had been cast out by Beelzebub, the prince of demons, or the one whom Jesus later in the narrative called Satan. By this Scripture it may be seen that the kingdom of Satan is a host of evil spirits.

[8]The devil has always worked secretly and sought to hide his true identity. It serves his purpose well to keep his dupes in ignorance concerning his real existence. When he beguiled Eve, he did so through a serpent. When he appeared before God to accuse Job, he waited until a day when the "sons of God came to present themselves before the Lord, and Satan came also among them," (Job 1:6). When he sowed his "tares," he did so secretly in the night "while men

slept" (Matt. 13:25). When he betrayed Christ into the hands of His enemies, he worked through Judas. Satan is adept at disguising himself; he comes to us, not as a dragon of darkness, but "an angel of light" (2 Cor. 11:14).

⁹In the Old Testament, Satan is referred to in seven books under different names, namely, in Genesis, 1 Chronicles, Job, Psalms, Isaiah, Ezekiel, Zechariah. In the New Testament, he is referred to by all the writers and is mentioned in nineteen books, namely, the four Gospels, Acts, the Pauline Epistles (Rom, 1 and 2 Cor., Eph., 1 and 2 Thess, 1 and 2 Tim.), Hebrews, James, John, Peter, Jude, and Revelation. Would all these authors, writing during a period of sixteen hundred years, be astray with regard to his existence? The Lord Jesus Christ Himself refers to Satan at least fifteen times, under five different names, and several of these instances are mentioned by three of the four Evangelists. He was the Truth. Would He have spoken of a being as such if he had no existence? He would never thus have spoken of a mere principle of evil. The Lord was sinless in heart and mind; no evil thought ever could or did rise up in His mind; no evil desire could be in His heart. Yet He was tempted of the devil when He was absolutely alone in the wilderness. If no one approached Him, and He was sinless, how could any suggestion arise within Him of a sinful nature that could be called a temptation? How could any evil principle approach Him from without or rise up from within? The very thought is absurd and impossible. If He was tempted, He was tempted by some being, and the narrative declares that it was the devil.

CHAPTER ELEVEN

ESCHATOLOGY: THE DOCTRINE
OF LAST THINGS

Eschatology, or the doctrine of last things, is the completion and climax of the teaching contained in the revelation which God has made to man. There is nothing pertaining to the individual Christian character, nor the Christian Church as a whole, which finds its destined perfection here upon earth, or in this life (Rom. 8:24; 1 Cor. 13:10).

As preparatory for the complete and final manifestation of the kingdom of God, certain events must take place, such as death, Christ's second coming, the resurrection of the body, and the divine judgments. As stages in the future condition of men, there is to be an intermediate and an ultimate state, both for the righteous and for the wicked. These events and states are taken up in the following discussion in what seems to be their logical order.

PHYSICAL DEATH AND THE INTERMEDIATE STATE

Physical Death

Physical death is the separation of the soul, including the spirit, from the body. We distinguish it from spiritual death, or the separation of the soul from God; and from the second death, or the banishment from God and final misery of the reunited soul and body of the wicked (Heb. 9:27; Isa. 59:2; Rom. 7:24; Eph. 2:1; Rev. 2:11; 20:14; 21:8). Although physical death falls upon the unbeliever as part of the original penalty of sin, to all who are united in Christ it loses its aspect of penalty and becomes a means of discipline and of entrance into larger life (see Ps. 116:15; Rom. 8:10; 14:8; 1 Cor. 3:22; 15:55).

To neither saint nor sinner is death a cessation of being. This is in opposition to the position of the annihilationist. We base our position on the following deductions from Scripture:

1. The account of the curse in Genesis and the subsequent allusions to it in Scripture show that while the death then incurred includes the dissolution of the body, it does not include cessation of being on the part of the soul; it only designates that state of the soul which is the opposite of true life, viz., a state of banishment from God, of unholiness and misery (Gen. 2:17; 3:8, 16-19, 22-24; Matt. 8:22; Luke 15:32; John 5:24; 6:49, 53, 58; 8:51; Rom. 5:21; 8:13; Eph. 2:1; 5:14; James 5:20; 1 John 3:14; Rev. 3:1).

2. The scriptural expressions held by annihilationists to imply cessation of being on the part of the wicked are used not only in connections where they cannot bear this meaning (Esth. 4:16), but in connections where they imply the opposite (Matt. 7:13; Rom. 6:23; 2 Thess. 1:9; Rev. 20:14). The most that these terms imply is the complete deprivation of some element essential to normal existence, i.e., the presence and fellowship of God.

3. The passages held to prove the annihilation of the wicked at death cannot have this meaning, since Scripture foretells a resurrection of the unjust as well as of the just; and a second death, or a misery of the reunited soul and body, in the case of the wicked (Acts 24:15; Rev. 2:11; 20:14, 15; 21:8).

4. The words used in Scripture to denote the place of departed spirits have in them no indication of annihilation, and the allusions to the condition of the departed show that death — to the writers of the Old and New Testaments — though it was the termination of man's earthly existence, was not an extinction of his being or his consciousness (Gen. 25:8, 9; 35:29; Num. 20:24; 1 Sam. 28:19; Isa. 66:24; Job 3:13, 18; Mark 9:43; Luke 16:23; 23:43).

5. The terms and phrases which have been held to declare absolute cessation of existence at death are frequently metaphorical; an examination of them in the context and with other Scripture is sufficient to show the untenableness of the liberal interpretation put upon them by annihilationists and to prove that the language is merely the language of appearance (Ps. 146:4; Eccl. 9:10; John

11:11, 14).

6. The most impressive and conclusive of all proofs of endless being, however, is afforded in the resurrection of Jesus Christ — a work accomplished by His own power and demonstrating that the spirit lived after its separation from the body (John 2:19, 21; 10:17, 18). By coming back from the tomb, He proves that death is not annihilation (2 Tim. 1:10).

The Intermediate State

The Scriptures teach the existence of both the righteous and the wicked after death and prior to the resurrection. In the intermediate state the soul is without its permanent body, yet this state is for the righteous one of conscious joy; for the wicked, one of conscious suffering.

That the righteous do not receive their permanent glorified bodies at death is plain from 1 Thess. 4:16, 17 and 1 Cor. 15:52, where an interval is intimated between Paul's time and the rising of those who slept. The resurrection was to occur in the future, "at the last trump." So the resurrection of the wicked had not yet occurred in any single case (2 Tim. 2:18 — it was an error to say that the resurrection was "past already"); it was yet future (John 5:28-30 — "the hour cometh" not "now is," as in vs. 25; Acts 24:15 — "There shall be a resurrection"). Christ was the first fruits (1 Cor. 15:20, 23). If the saints received their permanent body at death, the patriarchs would have received theirs before Christ, and He would not have been the first fruits.

The intermediate state of the righteous:

1. The soul of the believer, at its separation from the body, enters the presence of Christ (2 Cor. 5:1-8; Luke 23:43).
2. The spirits of departed believers are with God (Heb. 12:23; Eccl. 12:7).
3. The state of the believer immediately after death is greatly to be preferred to life in the body upon the earth (Phil. 1:23).
4. The departed saints are truly alive and conscious (Matt. 22:32; Luke 16:22; 23:43 ["with me" = in the same state]; 1 Thess. 5:10).
5. Departed believers are in a state of rest and blessedness (Rev. 6:9-11; 14:13).

The intermediate state of the wicked:

1. They are in prison, that is, are under constraint and guard (1 Peter

3:19). There is no need of putting unconscious spirits under guard; restraint implies the power of action.

2. They are in torment, or conscious suffering (Luke 16:23).

3. They are under punishment (Heb. 9:27).

Erroneous views of the intermediate state:

1. The passages cited above refute, on the one hand, the view that the souls of both righteous and wicked sleep between death and the resurrection. This view is based upon the assumption that the possession of a physical organism is indispensable to activity and consciousness — an assumption which the existence of a God who is pure spirit (John 4:24), and of angels who are spirit beings (Heb. 1:14), shows to be erroneous.

   Although the departed are described as "spirits" (Eccl. 12:7; Acts 7:59; Heb. 12:23; 1 Peter 3:19), there is nothing in this "absence from the body" (2 Cor. 5:8) inconsistent with the activity and consciousness ascribed to them in the Scriptures. When the dead are spoken of as "sleeping" (Dan. 12:2; Matt. 9:24; John 11:11; 1 Cor. 11:30; 15:51; 1 Thess. 4:14; 5:10), we are to regard this as simply the language of appearance and as literally applicable only to the body.

2. On the other hand, Scripture refutes the view that the suffering of the intermediate state is purgatorial. According to the doctrine of the Roman Catholic Church, "all who die at peace with the church, but are not perfect, pass into purgatory." Here they make satisfaction for the sins committed after baptism by suffering a longer or shorter time, according to the degree of their guilt. The church on earth, however, has power, by prayers and the sacrifice of the Mass, to shorten these sufferings or to remit them altogether.

   But we urge, in reply, that the passages referring to suffering in the intermediate state give no indication that any true believer is subject to this suffering, or that the church has any power to relieve from the consequences of sin, in either this world or the world to come. Only God can forgive; the church is simply empowered to declare that, upon the fulfillment of the appointed conditions of repentance and faith, He does actually forgive.

   This theory, moreover, is inconsistent with any proper view of the completeness of Christ's satisfaction (Gal. 2:21; Heb. 9:28), of justification through faith alone (Rom. 3:28), and of the condition after death being determined in this life (Eccl. 11:3; Matt. 25:10;

Luke 16:26; Heb. 9:27; Rev. 22:11).[1]

THE SECOND COMING OF CHRIST

The question of the return of the Lord Jesus Christ to this earth challenges most keenly the interest of Christians all over the world today.

Four great advents are spoken of in the Scriptures: the first Adam in creation; the Last Adam in incarnation; the Holy Spirit on the day of Pentecost; and the future return of our Lord. Associated with the advent of the first Adam is the Fall; associated with the Last Adam is the atonement of Christ; associated with the Holy Spirit is the birth of the church; and associated with the return of Christ is the establishment of His kingdom. Standing between the advents of the first Adam and the Second Adam is the altar pointing back to the fall of man and pointing forward to Christ's atoning death. Standing between the two advents of Jesus is the Lord's Supper, pointing backward to His death and looking forward to His coming again. The Lord's Supper will be observed only between the two advents (1 Cor. 11:26). The greatest event of past history is the first advent of Jesus; the greatest event of future history is the second advent of Christ.

The Importance of the Second Coming

The prominence given to it. If prominence is the law of emphasis, and emphasis determines importance, then the importance of the Second Coming of Christ is established.

1. In the New Testament teaching. More space is given to the doctrine of the Second Coming of Christ, it is said, than to the atonement; where the atonement is mentioned once, the second advent is referred to twice. Where the first coming of Christ is mentioned once, His second coming is mentioned eight times. Of the twenty-seven books in the New Testament, all but four of them refer to it. One out of every twenty-five verses makes mention of the Second Coming. Fifty times or more in the New Testament we are exhorted to be ready for the realization of this blessed hope.

    Entire chapters such as Matthew 24 – 25, Luke 21, and Mark 13 are devoted to this subject, as are whole books such as 1 and 2 Thessalonians and Revelation. Each chapter of 1 Thessalonians closes with a reference to the Second Advent (1:10; 2:19; 3:13; 4:14-18; 5:23). In the 216 chapters of the New Testament, it is said, there are 318 references to this doctrine.

2. In Old Testament prophecy. By far the greater number of predictions concerning Christ in the Old Testament are connected with His second coming. The same prophets who spoke of Christ's first coming speak with equal clarity of His second advent into the world. It is said that prophecy occupies one-fifth of the Scripture, and the Second Advent occupies one-third of prophecy.

3. In the teachings of Jesus Christ. Jesus Himself taught in clear, unmistakable language His coming again to the earth, not only in those wonderful words of comfort found in John 14:1-3, but also in many other places in the Gospels. In parable and exhortation, before His disciples, before the multitude, and when arraigned before His judges, He talks of His coming again (Luke 17:20-37; 19:11-27; Matt. 24–25; Mark 13; Luke 21).

4. By the witness of angels. The writer of the Epistle to the Hebrews lays special stress on the trustworthiness of the testimony of angels. He speaks of it as being "steadfast," since angels are ministering spirits, messengers, the very mouthpieces of God. Everything the angels — the annunciators of Christ's first coming — said about that coming was true. The angelic testimony regarding the second coming of Christ is found in Acts 1:10, 11. These words are capable of no other interpretation than that the same Jesus the disciples beheld vanishing from their wondering view would again come to the earth as they had seen Him leave it. The entire Book of Revelation may be regarded as angelic testimony to the Second Advent and the accompanying events, for Christ "sent and signified it by His angel unto His servant John."

5. In the preaching of the apostles. Jesus promised the apostles that He would send unto them the Holy Spirit to "guide you into all truth"; "show you things to come"; and "bring all things to your remembrance, whatsoever I have said unto you" (John 14:26; 15:26, 27; 16:13-15). It is, therefore, important to know what these men thus equipped have to say concerning this subject. These all, with no uncertain sound, give a united testimony to the fact of Christ's coming.

   a. Peter's testimony (Acts 2:30-36; 3:19-26; 1 Peter 1:5, 7, 11, 13; 4:7, 13; 2 Peter 3:3, 4, 7-10, 12, 14);

   b. Paul's testimony (1 Thess. 1:10; 2:19; 3:13; 4:14-18; 5:23; 2 Thess. 1:7-10; 2:1-11; Rom. 2:16; 8:18, 19-23; 11:25, 26; 13:11, 12; 1 Cor. 1:7, 8; 5:5; 2 Cor. 5:1-10; Phil. 1:6; 3:21; 2 Tim. 4:1, 8; Titus 2:13);

c. John's testimony (John 14:1-3; 21:22; 1 John 2:28; 3:2; Rev. 1:7; 11:15-17; 22:7, 12, 20);
d. James's testimony (James 5:7-9);
e. Jude's testimony (Jude 14, 21, 24).

The vital relationship it holds to other doctrines. It is easily demonstrated that the statement of the second coming of Christ as recorded in the New Testament is bound up with every fundamental doctrine. It is so woven into these basic doctrines of the Christian faith that the one cannot be denied without denying the others. Like the ephod of the high priest which was so wrought of gold and linen that the linen could not be extracted without pulling apart the gold wire, neither could the gold wire be removed without destroying the linen, so the Second Coming and the great fundamentals and all the flowering beauties of the Christian faith are so inextricably inwrought that the hand which damages the one destroys the other.

The doctrine is bound up with —

1. The doctrine of the Resurrection (1 Cor. 15:23; cf. John 5:28, 29 with 1 Thess. 4:16-18);
2. The doctrine and promise of the transformation of the living (1 Cor. 15:51, 52);
3. The doctrine of sonship with God and likeness to Christ (1 John 3:1, 2);
4. The doctrine and promise of rewards (2 Tim. 4:7, 8; Rev. 22:12; 1 Peter 5:4);
5. The doctrine of the Atonement (cf. Heb. 9:14-28 with Luke 1:8-10);
6. The doctrine of future judgment (2 Tim. 4:1);
7. The doctrine of sanctification (1 Thess. 3:12, 13; 5:23, ASV).

The practical value of the doctrine. The truth of the Second Coming is eminently practical. It is bound up with every practical exhortation to Christian obligation, service, and attainment, including exhortations —

1. To meet together on the Lord's Day (Heb. 10:25);
2. To observe properly the Lord's Supper (1 Cor. 11:26);
3. To love one another (1 Thess. 3:12, 13);
4. To patience (James 5:7, 8);
5. To holy living (1 John 3:3; Titus 2:11-13; 1 Thess. 5:23);

6. To watchfulness (Mark 13:34-37);
7. To Christian activity (Rom. 13:11, 12);
8. To abide in Him (1 John 2:28);
9. Not to judge one another (1 Cor. 4:4, 5);
10. To pastoral fidelity (2 Tim. 4:1, 2; 1 Peter 5:2-4);
11. To comfort and console those who mourn their Christian dead (1 Thess. 4:16-18);
12. To zeal for the salvation of souls (2 Cor. 4:3-5; cf. 1 Thess. 2:19, 20 with 1 Thess. 1:9, 10).

The emphasis placed upon it by the early church. The early Christian church believed in and ardently longed for the coming of Christ to overthrow the powers of evil and paganism as represented by the Roman Empire and to reign victorious in lands over which Caesar's eagles had never flown (1 Thess. 1:9, 10; Titus 2:13; Heb. 9:28).

Schaff, the eminent church historian, writes: "The most striking point in the eschatology of the Ante-Nicene age is the prominent chiliasm, or millenarianism, that is, the belief of a visible reign of Christ in glory on earth with the risen saints for a thousand years before the general resurrection and judgment. It was a widely current opinion of distinguished teachers, such as Barnabas, Papias, Justin Martyr, Irenaeus, Tertullian, Methodius, and Lactantius. The Christian chiliasm is the Jewish chiliasm spiritualized and fixed upon the second, instead of the first, coming of Christ. It distinguishes, moreover, two resurrections, one before and another after the Millennium, and makes the millennial reign of Christ only a prelude to His eternal reign in heaven, from which it is separated by a short interregnum of Satan. The Millennium is expected to come not as the legitimate result of a historical process, but as a sudden supernatural revelation."[2]

The Fact of the Second Coming

From Genesis to Revelation, the Bible is filled with the teaching of the second coming of Christ. It is set forth not only in type, figure, symbol, parable, and illustration, but also by direct statement. These passages establish this fact beyond question: John 14:3; Acts 3:19-21, ASV; Phil. 3:20, 21; 1 Thess. 4:16, 17; Heb. 9:28.

Misinterpretations:

1. It is misinterpreted to mean the coming of Christ in the Holy

Spirit on the day of Pentecost. That this is erroneous is seen by the following:

a. On the day of Pentecost, immediately after the coming of the Holy Spirit, Peter urged the Jews to repent in order that Jesus, whom for a time "the heavens had received," might be sent back again (Acts 3:19-21). This could not be done if His promised coming had already taken place.

b. It was not Christ, but the Holy Spirit, who came on Pentecost, and His coming was conditioned on Christ's absence, for Jesus said, "It is expedient for you that I go away; for if I go not away, the Comforter will not come unto you; but if I depart, I will send Him unto you" (John 16:7). If the Holy Spirit is only another manifestation of Christ, then they are identical. This repudiates the doctrine of the Trinity.

c. The Acts and the Epistles were all written after Pentecost, and these contain many references to the Second Coming as still future.

d. None of the predicted events which are to accompany the return of Christ occurred at Pentecost (see 1 Thess. 4:14-17).

e. The coming of the Holy Spirit at Pentecost marked the inception of the church; the second coming of Christ marks the completion and removal of the church.

f. Christ did not receive believers unto Himself at Pentecost, but rather came to them in the person of the Holy Spirit. Though it may be admitted that the coming of the Holy Spirit — the one who was to take the place of Jesus, Jesus' other Self — was in a sense a coming, and a fulfillment of the promise of Jesus in John 14:17-23 to come and dwell with His disciples, yet it was not *the* coming.

2. It is misinterpreted to refer to His providential coming at the destruction of Jerusalem. This tragedy of history is supposed by many to fulfill the prophecies spoken by Christ in His great discourse on the Mount of Olives, recorded in Matthew 24 and Mark 13, and the one also recorded in Luke 21. From a study of at least two of these passages (Mark 13 and Luke 21), it becomes evident that the capture of the Holy City by Titus may have been a real but only partial fulfillment of the words of Christ.

As in the case of so many Old Testament prophecies, the nearer event furnished the colors in which were depicted scenes and occurrences which belong to a distant future, and in this case to the "end of the age." That this does not fulfill the predictions made concerning the second coming of Christ is made clear by the following:

a. The destruction of the city of Jerusalem did not bring deliverance to the people of Israel or punishment to the enemies of Israel. In the Old Testament these events are always the consequence of the advent of the Messiah in power and glory (Joel 3:12-17).

b. The Lord was not manifestly present at the destruction of Jerusalem; it was destroyed by Roman soldiers.

c. None of the events that are to occur at the Second Coming happened at the destruction of Jerusalem, such as the resurrection of the dead, the translation of living saints, and the physical changes predicted at Jerusalem and in the land of Palestine at Christ's coming (Ezek. 47:1-12; Zech. 14:4-11).

d. Jerusalem must be trodden down of the Gentiles until the "times of the Gentiles" are fulfilled, and "then shall they see the Son of man coming in a cloud with power and great glory" (Luke 21:24-28). The purpose of this coming is thus not to destroy Jerusalem, but to restore it.

e. Jerusalem was destroyed by Titus in A.D. 70, yet John in the Revelation, written about A.D. 96 (twenty-six years later), speaks of the Second Coming as still future (Rev. 22:12, 20).

3. It is misrepresented as meaning the conversion of the sinner. This cannot be for the following reasons:

a. At conversion the sinner comes to Christ by faith for salvation (Matt. 11:28; John 5:40; 6:37), but Christ does not come to the sinner to affect his bodily transformation and translation as He shall at His second coming.

b. The Holy Spirit comes into the newborn soul at regeneration (Rom. 5:5; Gal. 4:4-6), but Christ does not come in His own personality as set forth in predictive prophecy.

c. None of the events to occur at Christ's coming take place at conversion.

4. It is misinterpreted to signify the diffusion of Christianity throughout the world. These are not identical, for —

a. The diffusion of Christianity is gradual, while the Scriptures declare that the return of the Lord shall be sudden and unexpected, as a "thief in the night" (Matt. 24:27, 36, 42, 44; 1

Thess. 5:2; Rev. 3:3).

b. The diffusion of Christianity is a process, while the Scriptures invariably speak of the return of the Lord as an event.

c. The diffusion of Christianity brings salvation to the wicked, where as the return of the Lord is said to bring them, not salvation, but sudden destruction (1 Thess. 5:2, 3; 2 Thess. 1:7-10).

5. It is misinterpreted to mean death — that when we die, Jesus comes to us. This is the most common theory, but that it is erroneous and false is shown by the following:

a. The absurdity of this position is seen if we substitute the word *death* for the coming of the Lord in such passages as deal with that subject (John 14:3; Acts 1:9-11; Phil. 3:20; 1 Thess. 4:16; Titus 2:13; Heb. 9:28).

b. Jesus makes a distinction between His coming and the believer's death. John 21:22 shows how utterly impossible it is to make Christ's coming refer to death. "Jesus saith unto him, If I will that he tarry till I come, what is that to thee? Follow thou me." "If I will that he tarry" evidently means "If I will that he remain alive." Now put Christ's coming at the believer's death into these words and you get this nonsense: "If I will that he remain alive until he die what is that to thee?" (See also Matt. 16:28.)

c. At death the believer goes to be with the Lord; death is a departure, not a coming (2 Tim. 4:6; Phil. 1:23; 2 Cor. 5:6-8).

d. His coming is not to be in connection with death but with resurrection (John 5:28, 29). He is the "resurrection and the life," and when He comes He will raise the dead and change the bodies of the living (Phil. 3:20, 21).

e. A soul passes into eternity every second. It would be absurd to claim that Jesus leaves His place at the Father's right hand and comes in the clouds with a shout, the voice of the archangel, and the trump of God, every time a believer dies.

f. The Scriptures distinctly teach that at the coming of Christ we overcome, not succumb to, death. Death, the last enemy, is then abolished.

The Character of the Second Coming

It will be personal. By the "personal coming" of Christ, we mean His literal, visible, bodily return as contrasted with a coming which is merely figurative, spiritual, or providential. In other words, it means He will come again in like manner as He went away (Acts 1:11).

1. It will be visible. Jesus Christ in His Second Coming shall be seen by all, both the church and the world: the one at the Rapture, the other at the Revelation (Heb. 9:28; Rev. 1:7; Matt. 24:26, 27). In Acts 1:11 we read, "This same Jesus, which is taken up from you into heaven, shall so come in like manner as ye have seen Him go into heaven."

   The word *seen* always has reference to what is tangible and is discovered with the eyes — something that one views with attention. For this reason it is used in Matthew 6:1: "Do not your alms before men to be seen of them." It is a word closely related to the Greek word for "theater" (*theatron*). Matthew 26:64 states: "Ye shall sée the Son of man coming on the clouds." The word *see* signifies what one is permitted to see with the eyes. From both these passages, as well as from the others referred to, it seems clear that a visible return of the Lord is meant. If the ascension of Christ was spiritual and metaphorical, then perhaps His return may be also. The ascension, however, was a literal fact manifest to the physical senses, and so also shall be the second coming of Christ.

2. It will be bodily. He is to come in like manner as He went away. He ascended in a literal body, the body in which He was crucified, which was raised from the dead — transformed and changed, yet real and tangible, capable of being touched and handled, in which He ate "a piece of broiled fish, and of an honey comb." In His incarnation He became indissolubly united with our humanity, linking it up with His deity. He lived as a man, He was crucified as a man, He was resurrected as a man, He ascended and is seated as the Mediator between God and man, the Man Christ Jesus, and as the Son of Man He is coming again (Matt. 16:27; Acts 1:11; 1 Tim. 2:5.)[3]

It will be glorious. The Son of man is coming in the clouds of heaven in splendor, with power and great glory, the glory of His Father and of the holy angels (Matt. 16:27; 24:30; Mark 8:38; 2 Thess. 1:7, 8, ASV; cf. Matt. 24:30 with the following texts: Exod. 19:9; 34:5; Pss. 97:1, 2; 104:3; Isa. 19:1; Matt. 17:5; Acts 1:9-11).

It will be sudden. Jesus Christ will come as a thief, unannounced to the world at large — without warning, unexpectedly, suddenly (Rev. 22:7, 12, 20). The Greek word *tachu*, translated "quickly," does not necessarily mean soon or without delay, but here it has the thought of speed or suddenness (see also 1 Thess. 5:2, 3; Matt. 24:37-39; Luke 21:34, 35).

It will be a twofold. Just as the first coming of the Lord extended over a period of thirty years, so His second coming involves a period of time and includes a series of events. At the first coming He was revealed as a babe in Bethlehem, later as the Lamb of God at His baptism, and as the Redeemer at Calvary. At the second coming He will suddenly appear to His own and catch them away to the Marriage Supper of the Lamb. This appearance is called the Rapture.

Immediately after the Rapture there comes a period of terrible tribulation known as the day of "Jacob's trouble." Following this, there is another sudden but open manifestation of the Lord from heaven with His accompanying saints and holy angels for the purpose of establishing the long-promised messianic kingdom in the earth. This is called the Revelation.

1. The first stage — the Rapture. At this stage Christ comes in the air, and His believing saints are caught up to meet Him (1 Thess. 4:13-17). The term *rapture* is not found in the Scriptures, but the thought which it expresses — snatching or catching away — is contained in the principle passage referring to this stage of our Lord's coming (1 Thess. 4:16, 17). At this stage there are two important events which transpire: the resurrection of the dead saints, and the transformation or bodily change of the living saints. After this they shall all be caught up together (raptured) to meet the Lord in the air.

2. The second stage — the Revelation. At this stage Christ comes to the earth and His saints come with Him (Col. 3:4, ASV; 2 Thess. 1:7-9; 2:7, 8). There may not be scriptural warrant for confining the application of this term (*revelation*) to the second stage of the return of the Lord, since it is used in the Scriptures in connection with both stages; but that it is especially applicable to the latter stage there can be no doubt. This stage embraces the judicial and punitive aspect of the Second Coming and includes the events immediately preparatory to the establishment of the millennial kingdom.

3. Rapture and Revelation differentiated. The coming again of Christ is twofold: not two comings, but two stages in the one coming, one great event with two separate parts. In the first stage He comes as the "Morning Star" (Rev. 22:16); in the second, as the "Sun of Righteousness" (Mal. 4:1, 2). In the first He comes

"into the air" (1 Thess. 4:17); in the second, He descends to the Mount of Olives (Zech. 14:3, 4). In the first, He comes to receive His bride to Himself (John 14:3); in the second, He comes to be received by repentant Israel (Zech. 12:10). The first stage is called "our gathering together unto Him" (2 Thess. 2:1); while the second stage is called "The revelation of Jesus Christ from heaven" (2 Thess. 1:7).

It will be premillennial. By "premillennial" we mean before the Millennium, that is, before the period of a "thousand years" spoken of in Revelation 20:1-6. This period is spoken of in other Scriptures as "the kingdom" and is described in glowing terms by the prophets as a time when the earth shall be blessed with a universal rule of righteousness. The passage in Revelation 20:1-6 tells us that the length of the period shall be one thousand years. The whole tenor of Scripture teaching demands that Christ shall return before the Millennium.

1. The doctrine of the second coming of Christ is used as a basis for practical exhortation and as an incentive to holy living and devoted service; but if this coming cannot take place until one thousand years after the conversion of the world, as held by the postmillenarians, then it loses all value as a stimulant and an incentive.

2. The blessings of the Millennium are to be introduced by judgments, and these judgments are associated with the second coming (see Ps. 2; Isa. 2:1, 3, 10-19; 11:4, 9; 25:7; cf. Isa. 66:23 with 66:15, 24; cf. Mic. 4:3 with 4:12, 13; cf. Zech. 14:2-5 with 14:9).

3. When Christ comes, He will raise the dead, but the righteous dead are to be raised before the Millennium that they may reign with Christ during the one thousand years; hence there can be no Millennium before Christ comes (Rev. 20:4, 5).

4. When Christ comes, He will separate the "tares" from the "wheat," but as the Millennium is a period of universal righteousness, the separation of the "tares" and "wheat" must take place before the Millennium; therefore there can be no Millennium before Christ comes (Matt. 13:40-43).

5. When Christ comes, He will bind Satan; but as Satan is to be bound during the Millennium, there can be no Millennium until Christ comes (Rev. 20:1-3).

6. When Christ comes, Antichrist is to be destroyed; but as Anti-

christ is to be destroyed before the Millennium, there can be no Millennium until Christ comes (2 Thess. 2:8; Rev. 19:20).

7. When Christ comes, the Jews are to be restored to their own land; but as they are to be restored to their own land before the Millennium, there can be no Millennium before Christ comes (Ezek. 36:24-28; Zech. 12:10; Rev. 1:7).

8. When Christ comes, it will be unexpectedly, and thus we are commanded to watch lest He take us unawares. Now, if He is not coming until after the Millennium, and the Millennium is not yet here, why command us to watch for an event that is over one thousand years off?

9. The Scriptures teach that during the present dispensation sorrow, suffering, and conflict with foes within and without will be the portion of the saints. The true church is to be a persecuted, suffering, cross-bearing people by divine appointment, and this she will continue to be until Christ comes, which precludes any Millennium until after His coming (John 15:19-21; 16:33; 1 Thess. 3:3; 2 Thess. 1:7-9; 2 Tim. 3:12).

10. There is an absence in the New Testament of any hint or allusion whatever to the universal triumph of the church in this age upon the earth — thus making the Millennium, which is a triumphal period for the people of God, absolutely impossible until the translation of the church at Christ's coming and her return with Him in glorious manifestation.

11. The scriptural demand of the literal reign of Christ upon the earth requires that His coming should be premillennial.[4] From the time that the first Adam surrendered the kingdom to Satan, the effort to reestablish it with man has been a continual failure, though it was given to Noah, Saul, Nebuchadnezzar, and others; and it will be a failure in this sin-cursed earth until the Second Adam, who has overcome Satan, returns to purify the earth and establish righteousness (Gen. 9:1, 2; Isa. 9:7; Jer. 3:17; Dan. 2:37, 38; Zech. 14:16; Luke 1:32, 33; Acts 3:20, 21). The millennial kingdom will be a literal and personal reign of Christ (Isa. 32:1; Jer. 23:1-6; Matt. 19:28; Rev. 5:10). Speaking of the kingdom, God says, "I will overturn, overturn, overturn, it: and it shall be no more, until He come whose right it is; and I will give it Him" (Ezek. 21:27).

Jesus is in heaven at the right hand of God upon the throne with the Father, in the holy of holies, making intercession for those who come unto God by Him. But heaven has received

Him only until the time of the restitution of all things which God has spoken by the mouth of all His holy prophets, when He shall come again to sit on the throne of His Father David. This again proves His coming to be premillennial.

Events Associated with the Second Coming

The second coming of Christ is not only a point of time, but also a period. It may be classed as an event, but it also includes a series of events. It will include such events as the rapture of the church which embraces the resurrection of the dead saints, the transformation of living believers, and the translation of both (1 Thess. 4:13-17); the judgment seat of Christ (2 Cor. 5:10); the marriage of the church to her Lord (Rev. 19); the events of the seventieth week of Daniel (Dan. 9:24-27); the great tribulation (Matt. 24:29; Dan. 12:1); the coming of Christ with His saints or holy ones (1 Thess. 3:13; Rev. 19); the great battle of Armageddon (Rev. 16:16); the judgment of the living nations (Matt. 25); the national conversion of the Jew (Rom. 11).

The coming of Christ is, therefore, that composite of events which transfers the presence of Christ from heaven to earth and establishes the rightful supremacy of Christ. Included in this series are necessarily those acts which prepare the saints for the kingdom. These events are presented in their various relations as follows:

With reference to the church. We have already seen in our study of ecclesiology that the church is an organism embracing regenerate believers which constitutes the body of Christ, having its inception on the day of Pentecost, and which will find its completion at the first stage of Christ's coming. The Scriptures seem to indicate the following order of events attending this completion:

1. The Rapture. The most startling — and except for the testimony of the "sure word of prophecy," the most incredible — transaction of which we can conceive is that set forth in the words "caught up to meet the Lord in the air" (1 Thess. 4:15-18). The lightning-flash of the advent, dazzling and blinding for a moment; the swift transition of the cloud chariot, and then "forever with the Lord" — this is the brief description of the ecstatic scene which we call the church's translation. The rapture of the church involves a threefold process.

   a. The resurrection of the righteous dead (1 Thess. 4:16; 1 Cor. 15:22, 23). A beautiful miniature of the church is that home in Bethany whose crowning honor is this: "Jesus loved Martha and her sister and Lazarus." Like the body of Christ today, a part living and a part dead — "our friend Lazarus sleepeth" — this household was awaiting the coming of the Lord. But notwithstanding the sickness and dying that were ravaging that home, Jesus "abode two days still in the same place where He was," just as He has already remained away from His church nearly two millenniums — "one day is with the Lord as a thousand years, and a thousand years as one day" — while sickness and mourning and death have been holding sway. Then the advent announcement, for which we also wait, was heard: "Our friend Lazarus sleepeth; but I go that I may awake him out of sleep." Such will be the blessed errand on which our Lord will come when the time of His return arrives.

They hear the Lord's great advent exposition: "I am the resurrection and the life: he that believeth in Me, though he were dead, yet shall he live; and whosoever liveth and believeth in Me shall never die." It is no mere rhetorical amplification which we find here. This double office of Christ and the corresponding twofold work exactly match the declarations which we have in Thessalonians and Corinthians (1 Thess. 4:16; 1 Cor. 15:51). He is the "resurrection" to those who shall be in their graves at the time of His coming; He is the "life" to those who shall then be on the earth. To the first class He alludes when He says, "Though he were dead yet shall he live"; to the second He refers in the saying, "Whosoever liveth and believeth in Me shall never die." But both, in a moment, in the twinkling of an eye, shall be brought into the same condition of "glorified corporeity" at the sound of the last trump.

b. The transformation of living believers (1 Cor. 15:51, 52). In the transfiguration scene, Moses and Elijah were the representatives of the two classes named above. Moses, coming up from his unknown sepulcher in the valley of Moab, as the forerunner of the dead who shall be raised at the advent of Christ; and Elijah returning from the presence of the Lord, as the representative of those who taste not of death, but are translated — both standing together with the Lord in transfiguration glory on the mount present to us a radiant rehearsal, a glowing epitome, of the coming and kingdom of Jesus Christ (cf. Matt. 16:28 with 2 Peter 1:16-18).

In the great resurrection discourse (1 Cor. 15) we find at the culmination of the argument the same double reference: "For the trumpet shall sound, and the dead shall be raised incorruptible, and we shall be changed." Here are the two parties to the final tranfiguration; and they are in an instant brought into the company of One for whom they had been waiting.

c. The translation of all believers (1 Thess. 4:16, 17). The words "Caught up to meet the Lord in the air" are crowded with suggestions, since they always signify "to meet and return with." As the disciples in Rome went out to meet Paul when they heard of his approach and accompanied him to the city; as the wise virgins are pictured as going forth to meet the bridegroom and attending him to the house of the bride — so by the same form of speech it is here implied that the church will be raptured away to join the Lord on His advancing way and will escort Him back to earth.

2. The examination and reward of believers (the judgment seat of Christ). Immediately following the rapture, believers will be brought before the judgment seat of Christ for their examination, manifestation, and rewards. This subject will be dealt with at length in connection with "The Judgments" (pp. 387ff.).

3. The marriage supper. After the saints have been "caught up" and "judged," they, as the "church," will become the "bride of Christ." The marriage of the church is prophetically referred to by Jesus in the parable of the marriage of the king's son (Matt. 22:1-14), and is consummated in Revelation 19:7-9 (see also Eph. 5:25-27; 2 Cor. 11:2).[5]

4. Manifestation with Christ. The manifestation of glorified believers will be coincident with the manifestation or revelation of Jesus Christ at His coming. True believers are sons of God now, but they are not manifest as such. They are traveling through the world incognito, with no recognition given of their divine lineage. But at the second coming of Christ, their divine sonship will be recognized and acknowledged; then they will come into the full realization of all its privileges and prerogatives (Col. 3:4; 1 John 3:1, 2; Jude 14).

With reference to apostate Christendom. After the true church — which is the "body" and the "bride" of Christ (Rev. 19:6-9; 21:2, 9; cf. Eph. 5:25-32) — is translated, the professing church will doubtless go on with its worship, services, and numerous activities just as before the saints were raptured. There will be, however, a marked growth in the apostasy within the professing church — the ecclesiastical organization left on the earth — until finally this false religious system, which in contradistinction to the true church is called "the harlot" (cf. Rev. 17:1-7 with 2 Cor. 11:2, 3), has become so morally and religiously corrupt that it is destroyed by the power of the Antichrist and the ten kings whose favor and protection it has so long enjoyed (Rev. 17:13-18).

The doctrine of the decline and apostasy of this false ecclesiastical system is in strict harmony with the teaching of the Scriptures as shown by the following passages: 2 Thessalonians 2:3, 4; 1 Timothy 4:1, 2; 2 Timothy 3:1-5; 4:1-4; Luke 18:8, ASV. The seeds of this apostasy are already in the church, indeed they have germinated and brought forth a too abundant harvest which will find its culmination in the great apostasy succeeding the removal of the true church.

With reference to Israel. Prophetic truth concerning the coming of the Messiah in relation to Israel is so abundant and comprehensive that it can be dealt with only in outline form.

1. Israel is to be restored to her native land in an unconverted state (Ezek. 36:24-28; 11:16-20; 39:25, 27-29; Jer. 32:37-41; 33:7-9; see also Isa. 11:11-16). These passages indicate that Israel is to be restored to her land in unbelief and that her conversion is to be subsequent to that restoration.

2. The Jewish nation will rebuild the temple and restore its worship. The temple here referred to is not the millennial temple, but a temple to be built and also destroyed during the interval between the rapture and the revelation. It is in this temple that the Antichrist causes the oblation to cease and sets up the abomination spoken of by Daniel (Dan. 9:27), where he "exalteth himself above all that is called God, or that is worshipped; so that he as God sitteth in the temple of God, shewing himself that he is God" (2 Thess. 2:4). This blasphemous act apparently takes place in the middle of the seven-year period of Israel's tribulation (Dan. 9:27).

3. A covenant will be made between Israel and the Antichrist for one week (seven years), but in the midst of the week the Antichrist will replace Israel's religious service by the worship of himself. "And he shall confirm the covenant with many for one week: and in the midst of the week he shall cause the sacrifice and the oblation to cease, and for the overspreading of abominations he shall make it desolate, even until the consummation, and that determined shall be poured upon the desolate" (Dan. 9:27). "Many" refers to Israel, with whom he confirms the covenant.

The Hebrew word *heptade*, translated "week," signifies a period of seven, as "decade" signifies ten, and here stands for seven years. In the midst of the seven years, the Antichrist demands worship from Israelites and sets up his image in Jerusalem — the image spoken of in Revelation 13:14, 15.

4. They will pass through the great tribulation called the time of "Jacob's trouble" (Jer. 30:6, 7; Dan. 7:25; 12:1; Matt. 24:15-22, 29; Rev. 3:10; 7:14). This has its inception in the setting up of the abomination of desolation in the temple area at Jerusalem. This tribulation will be worldwide, but its focal point of most intense trial will be Jerusalem and Judea, where the great oppressor and his armies will be destroyed by the appearing of the Lord "to punish the host of high ones that are on high, and the kings of the earth that are on the earth" (Isa. 24:21). It has to do particularly with the Jew for his rebellion against God, but also in a more limited sense with the world (Rev. 3:10).

"The tribulation" describes a period of suffering unsurpassed, "such as was not since there was a nation, no, nor shall be" (Dan. 12:1). The suffering is to be greater than anything that has yet been seen.

5. Israel will be converted as a nation at Christ's return (Zech. 12:10; Rom. 11:26; Rev. 1:7). Israel will be converted, as was Saul of Tarsus, by a personal revelation of Jesus Christ: "Behold He cometh with clouds; and every eye shall see Him, and they also which pierced Him." Then shall be fulfilled the prediction that a nation shall be born in a day.

6. They will become missionaries to the nations (Ps. 67:1, 2; Isa. 2:1-3; 27:6; Zech. 8:13, 21-23; Rom. 11:12, 15). The Jews as a nation will be converted and become the great missionaries of the world (Acts 15:14-17). The Word of the Lord shall go forth from Jerusalem in worldwide evangelism. Redeemed and regenerate Israel will be the ministers; as it is written: "Ye shall be named the priests of the Lord; men shall call you the ministers of our God" (Isa. 61:6). With their polyglot tongue they shall carry the tidings to the ends of the earth.

7. They will be permanently established in the land (Ezek. 34:28; Amos 9:15). The Lord will remember His covenant with all Israel, with the ten tribes as well as with the two, with Ephraim as well as Judah. For twenty-five hundred years their identity has been lost amid the nations of the East whither they were carried, but they have never been hidden from His eyes.

By the exercise of His omnipotent power the Lord will reveal them to the world and to themselves. He will call them out and separate them as fine gold is separated from the dross (Jer. 31:7-10). He will bring them into the land of Palestine, and they shall no longer be two nations — separate peoples, the one wanderers among the Gentiles, and the other sunken in them as those who be in their graves. They shall be one nation upon the mountains of Israel (Ezek. 27:21, 22).

With reference to the Gentile nations:

1. There shall be an amalgamation of the Gentile nations under the leadership of Antichrist whose armies will be assembled against Jerusalem and Israel at the time when Jesus Christ shall be revealed from heaven, taking vengeance on them who know not God and obey not the gospel. Zechariah describes this judgment upon them as a plague that shall cause "their flesh" to "consume away while they stand upon their feet, and their eyes" to "consume away in their holes, and their tongue" to "consume away in their mouth" (Zech. 14:2-4, 12, 13). This is spoken of in Scripture as "the battle of Armageddon."
2. There is to be judgment of these nations, immediately subsequent to the battle of Armageddon, commonly referred to as the judgment of the living nations. This will be dealt with under "The Judgments" (pp. 387ff.).

With reference to the Antichrist. What is revealed concerning the Antichrist may be summed up under five headings.

1. His names
   a. King of Babylon (Isa. 14:4-17). This implies all that is embodied in the Babylonian spirit: pride, power, idolatry, confusion, and iniquity.
   b. Little Horn (Dan. 7:8). He shall arise in the common order of succession among earth's monarchs.
   c. The Foolish Shepherd (Zech. 11:15-17). This individual shall be exactly contrary to the self-sacrificing ministry of the one who came to be the Good Shepherd (John 10:11-14).
   d. Willful King (Dan. 11:36). He shall despise the restraints of wholesome law.
   e. Man of Sin (2 Thess. 2:3). The full development of unregenerate manhood and the complete manifestation of evil are here suggested.

f. Son of Perdition (2 Thess. 2:3). As the son of perdition he will be Satan's exclusive tool, impelled by a diabolical spirit.

g. Antichrist (1 John 2:18). He shall scorn the world's Redeemer and persuade the Jews that he is the true Messiah for whom they have waited so long.

h. The Beast (Rev. 13:4; 17:8-11). As the Beast or "Eighth Head," wounded unto death and revived, he shall be able to furnish a most important link in his chain of assumptions to messiahship — a counterfeit resurrection. The name "Eight" is essential to him; it signifies life after death. And as Christ "died for our sins and rose again for our justification," so in some mysterious and phenomenal manner this false Christ is predicted to simulate the resurrection of the true Christ.

i. The Wicked [One] (Isa. 14:5; 2 Thess. 2:8). This presents him as the exponent and personification of wickedness.

2. His personality. The opinion has prevailed that the titles mentioned above pertain to a system of error rather than to a person. And the papacy, as furnishing more astounding coincidences than any other institution of church or state, has quite generally been agreed upon as being the power which in itself fulfilled all the prophetic requirements relating to the Antichrist. But no representative of the papal system, however high his assumptions, has ever claimed to be more than God's vicegerent upon earth; while Antichrist, as the Man of Sin, is to "exalt himself, and magnify himself above every God," . . . "so that he, as God, sitteth in the temple of God, showing himself that he is God." Hence the papacy in this most essential feature is not appropriate to this prediction.

A series of contrasts have been recorded in the Scriptures which prove the personality and which establish the identity of the Antichrist.

a. The true Christ comes from above. He is the Lord from heaven (John 3:31). Antichrist is from beneath, a denizen of the pit (Rev. 11:7).

b. Jesus came, endorsed of the Father, with manifest seals of divine approval. Antichrist will come in his own name, bearing no credentials but his own presumptions (John 5:43; Dan. 11:37).

c. The Christ of God humbled Himself to the rank of a servant (Phil. 2:8). The Antichrist is to glorify and exalt himself above the heights of the clouds (2 Thess. 2:4).

d. Jesus was despised and lightly esteemed (Isa. 53:3; Luke 23:18). Antichrist shall be the object of universal admiration (Rev. 13:3, 4).

e. Christ did the Father's will and glorified God on the earth (John 6:38; 17:4). Antichrist comes to do his own wicked will and blaspheme the name of God (Dan. 11:36, 37; Rev. 13:6).

f. God, by His Son Jesus Christ, wrought "miracles and wonders and signs" to manifest the truth concerning Him (Acts 2:22). Satan, through his instrument Antichrist, shall also "with all power and signs and wonders" perform marvelous acts, but this he will do to delude and deceive the unfaithful and unwary (2 Thess. 2:9,10; Rev. 13:13, 14).

g. Christ is likened to a good shepherd, who gives his life for the sheep (John 10:14, 15). Antichrist is the false, evil, or idol shepherd who will scatter and destroy the flock (Zech. 11:16, 17).

h. Jesus was called "Wonderful" and "Prince of Salem," which is "peace" (Isa. 9:6). His great opponent, who will be king of Babylon, which is "confusion," shall also be the wonder of the whole world (Rev. 13:3; 17:8).

i. God is to exalt His Son and cause every knee to bow to Him and every tongue to confess His Lordship (Phil. 2:9-11). Satan will exalt the Antichrist and compel all who dwell upon the earth to worship him (Isa. 14:14; Rev. 13:8).

j. The followers of the Lamb are to have His Father's name written in their foreheads (Rev. 14:1). The worshipers of Antichrist will wear a mark of allegiance — the brand of the beast forced upon them, constituting their only title to civil privileges (Rev. 13:16, 17).

k. The Bible testifies to the love, interest, and energy of a triune God (Father, Son, and Holy Spirit) in an established arrangement of relationship on behalf of lost sinners (John 3:16; 5:17; 14:26). So also is there a trio of evil ones: Satan set against the Most High; Antichrist arrayed against the Son; and the False Prophet in opposition to the divine Spirit (Rev. 13).

3. His origin and development. The rise, progress, and downfall of the Man of Sin are events which belong to the future. The Antichrist is to be the last representative of Gentile power in the earth. In the development of the Little Horn out from among the

others (Dan. 7), we are told the origin of Antichrist. By comparing the activities of the Little Horn with the deeds predicted of the Man of Sin in the New Testament, the identity of the two is established beyond question. He is to be Jehovah's last and most cruel instrument of judicial punishment upon the guilty nation of Israel.

The history of the Antichrist is definitely connected with Babylon and Jerusalem. The former, it would seem, is to be the center of his commercial activities; the latter, the seat of his ecclesiastic operations. It is plain that in imitation of the Lord Jesus, God's King-Priest, the Antichrist will unite under his own hand the civil and sacerdotal authority of the world. In Zechariah 5 we get the description of an ephah, heavy with wickedness and no doubt symbolizing the commerce of nations, transported into the land of Shinar, the site of Babel or Babylon. Revelation 17 depicts the woeful ruin of this same Babylon, grown commercially famous under the reign of the Beast; while 2 Thessalonians 2 unmistakably connects the ecclesiastic prominence of the Lawless One with the sanctuary in Jerusalem.

Out of the seething caldron of lawlessness which is rapidly developing, the Man of Sin will some day arise. He is to arise and flourish after the Jews are returned to their own land and their ancient ritual established. The future origin and development of the Antichrist may be summarized as follows:

a. He is to be the world's last Gentile king, the antitype of Nebuchadnezzar's great image.

b. He is to reign after the old Roman Empire is divided among ten rulers (Dan. 7:24; Rev. 17:12).

c. He will appear in connection with Babylon revived and Jerusalem repeopled.

d. He will come when the sanctuary at Jerusalem and its ritual are in some measure restored.

e. He will be revealed only when God begins to deal nationally with the Jews in the land.

f. He will flourish after the church is caught away and the restraining power now holding him back releases him.

g. He is to resist Jesus, the Prince of princes, and be miraculously overthrown by the personal presence of the Lord Himself.

4. His work. Scripture has grouped the deeds of Antichrist under six

acts of distinct prominence.

a. Antichrist will attract attention as a plausible, conservative, and pacific leader. Appearing as the Little Horn, which indicates the political yet restricted character of his origin, he soon reveals the greatness of his power and ambition (Dan. 7:24, 25). He shall come forth as a rider upon a white horse apparently seeking to gain an advantage from behind a mask of piety (Rev. 6:1, 2). Only when his end has been gained does he reveal his true character (Dan. 9:26).

b. He will next appear as the instigator and prominent party in a notable covenant which he and the Jewish poeple shall confirm together. By His magnanimous bearing, pretensions of amity, and promises of restoring ancient privileges, he will lure them into the unhallowed league (Dan. 9:27).

c. In three and a half years he will astonish his beholders by throwing off the garb of meekness and suddenly appearing in his true character as the "Man of Sin," "Lawless One," and "Son of Perdition." The covenant so deceitfully made will be perverted to his own unholy ends (Dan. 9:26, 27).

d. He will then proceed to manifest himself promptly as a merciless and universal oppressor. The leopard king, whose graceful fascinations had so long riveted the admiring gaze of his charmed prey, springs at last to grip as a bear, to rend as a lion, and to devour as a dragon. The daily sacrifice will be taken away; the Jews will be scattered and spoiled; the holy covenant between Jehovah and the fathers in regard to the land will be abhorred and set aside; and Israel will be brought into a bondage so degrading that to it the bitterness of Egypt would be as honey in the mouth (Dan. 12:1; Rev. 11:13-17).

Others beside the chosen people will fall under his crushing supremacy. Times and laws will be changed. None will be able to buy and sell the necessities of life except through the circulating medium of the mark of the beast. This the Jews will especially resist, since they were forbidden by law to "print any marks upon them" (Lev. 19:28). Satan will at last find a man willing to accept the offer of dominion the Son of God refused (Luke 4:5-7); and through him the archdemon will rule the whole prophetic world. While the Mideast is to be the peculiar center of his activity, there is little doubt that distant dominions outside the limit of the old Roman Empire will feel the influence of the reign of the Man of Sin (Rev. 13:4).

e. His next tremendous move will be to declare himself God. Not satisfied with universal power, he will aspire to universal adoration also. With miracles, signs, and lying wonders this false worship will be secured and enforced. An abominable idol, the image of the Beast, will be set up; the command, on penalty of death, will go forth for all to bow down to it; and the fiery trials of the three Hebrew captives will be reenacted (2 Thess. 2:9, 10; Rev. 13:15).

f. Antichrist's final act will be to stand up against Christ, the Prince of princes. This last move will be fatal to him and bring his career to a close.

5. His end and doom. The downfall of the Antichrist involves events more momentous than any that have transpired on the earth. The passage of the Red Sea, the miracle of the manna, the dividing of the Jordan, and the conquest of Jericho are transactions whose luster must grow dim before the incomparable marvel of the divine visitation upon the Antichrist. The end of the Man of Sin marks an era of sublime interest to all believers. It will be the day of our triumphant manifestation, as sons of God, and the jubilee of all creation. Scripture has solemnly recorded the end of various august evil personages who have from time to time set themselves up in rebellion against God. But to no sinful dweller on the earth save that man called "the Wicked one" has been appointed the terrible distinction of being consumed by the brightness of the personal appearance of the Lord Jesus Himself.

Such will be his exalted doom, an end that will suitably climax his ignoble origin, his surprising popularity, and his unexampled blasphemy. In the following Scriptures the manner of Antichrist's overthrow is indicated: Isaiah 10:17; 11:4; 14:18, 19; 30:33; 2 Thessalonians 2:8; Revelation 19:20; 20:10.

With reference to Satan. The second coming of Jesus Christ in its relation to Satan will mark the beginning of his final overthrow. At this time he will be bound and cast into the abyss, there to be imprisoned for the thousand-year period of Christ's millennial reign. The particular object of this binding and imprisonment of Satan is not so much for his due punishment as for the temporary restraint and prevention of his deception of men. It is stated to be that "he should not lead astray the nations any more until the thousand years be accomplished"(Rev. 20:1-4). At the end of the thousand years he will be liberated for a brief period, at which time he will go out to lead astray the nations, Gog and Magog — which are in the four corners of the earth, whose numbers are as the sands of the sea — to gather them together for war.

This brief period of Satan's last freedom proves that he is still Satan and that man is still prone to err, after a thousand years of bonds and imprisonment for the one, and a thousand years' experience of the next thing to paradise for the other — the devil being just as eager to tempt and deceive, and man just as liable to be tempted and deceived. Swift judgment from God immediately falls upon those who allow themselves to be led astray by the devil and are identified with him in this final insurrection, for we read that "fire came down from God out of heaven, and devoured them" (Rev. 20:9). Satan is then "cast into the lake of fire and brimstone, where the beast and the false prophet are, and shall be tormented day and night forever and ever" (Rev. 20:10).

With reference to the millennial kingdom. The Millennium, or the kingdom age, is that era in the future history of the world when the Lord Jesus will receive from God the rule and government of the earth. This era is to last one thousand years; six times in the first seven verses of Revelation 20 we find the expression "the thousand years." It is this that gives rise to the name "Millennium," which comes from the words *mille*, meaning thousand, and *annus* or *annum*, meaning year or years. They are to be understood as defining the duration of Christ's earthly reign.

While it is true that Revelation 20 is the only Scripture which specifically mentions the thousand years, yet there are many passages, in both the Old and New Testaments, that set forth the character and describe the blessing of that age which is to come.[6]

1. Descriptive titles of the Millennium. The Millennium is referred to in the Scriptures under various titles, each of which contributes its own light to our understanding of its scope and character.

   a. The Regeneration (Matt. 19:28). This title views the earthward character of the coming age. Planet earth, which for six thousand years has groaned beneath its burden of sorrow, will be rejuvenated. For sixty centuries it has been but a giant graveyard, but then it shall be endued with new life, so much so that even the desert place will be made to rejoice and the wilderness blossom as the rose. The force and aptness of this title also appear in that as every birth is preceded by travail, so will it be with the ushering in of the coming age. Indeed, the very term *travail* is used by Christ when speaking of the tribulation period which will immediately precede the Millennium. The literal rendering of the Greek in Matthew 24:8 is, "All these are the beginning of the birth pangs." Hence the appropriateness of styling the "Regeneration" the age which issues forth from the travail pangs of the Tribulation.

b. The Last Day (John 6:40). This title views the Millennium in its dispensational relationship. It will be the closing Day of this earth's Week. It will, as far as this earth is concerned, be the antitypical fulfillment of the Sabbath. It will be the time when creation will at last rest from protracted groaning.

A hint of this was given at the beginning when God, after six days' labor, rested from all the works of His hands. Viewing the seven days of that first week in the light of the inspired Word — "one day is with the Lord as a thousand years, and a thousand years as one day" (2 Peter 3:8) — we gather that earth's history is to be completed in seven thousand years. Six thousand years will have passed from the time when the first Adam made his appearance upon earth until the time when the Last Adam appears upon earth in power and glory to reign in righteousness for a thousand years. This thousand-year reign will be earth's "Last Day."

c. Times of Refreshing (Acts 3:19). This title describes the blessedness of the coming age when God will bring to this dreary earth a time of blessed refreshment. It tells of the blessed reviving which will be wrought in and on God's handiwork. It reveals a contrast with the preceding ages. It suggests the new life and fertility which follows a bountiful shower after a long drought. It intimates the beneficient results which will succeed the removal of Satan from the princedom of this world, and the established rule of the Lord of Glory in his stead. It will be a time of refreshing not only for the earth itself, but for Israel, for the nations, and even for God Himself.

d. Times of the Restitution of All Things (Acts 3:21). This title views the results which will be brought about in the coming age. It is the restitution only of those "things which God hath spoken by the mouth of all his holy prophets." What is to be restored in the Millennium is a condition of fertility and blessedness approximating the Edenic state throughout the earth. Israel is to be restored to the place of God's favor as His peculiar and covenant people. The duration of human life is to be restored to that which equals and surpasses the longevity of the patriarchs before the Flood. The animal world will be restored to the state which it had before the effects of the curse were visited upon it. The sun and moon will be restored probably to their pristine glory, for in the age to come their light is to be increased sevenfold.

e. The Dispensation of the Fullness of Times (Eph. 1:10). This title marks the relation of the coming age to God. It reveals the connection between that age and the ages which have preceded it. It tells how the Millennium is the goal toward which the other ages have moved. It points to the completion of the purpose of God concerning the earth in the present dispensational order. The force of this expression may be gathered from the similar one in Galatians 4:4: "When the fulness of time was come, God sent forth His Son." "The fullness of times" signifies ripeness of opportunity and consummation of need. The first advent of Christ and the proclamation of His gospel introduced a new era, but it also marked the climax of the old. The world was prepared through long processes for this advent and proclamation. From Eden to Bethlehem the centuries were preparing for the advent of Immanuel.

As it was in connection with the first advent, so it is concerning the second. Just as there was a definite and unmistakable movement in all history, making ready for the dispensation of grace, so is there a similar one going on now, making ready the world for the dispensation of glory. Just as the world's urgent need was fully demonstrated before the Savior appeared, so will it be before He comes back as the Prince of Peace to take the government upon His shoulders.

f. The Reign of One Thousand Years (Rev. 20:4, 6). This reference to a reign of a thousand years has become the focal point of theological disagreement between premillennialism and amillennialism. In this passage the writer states that some "lived" prior to the thousand years in order to reign with Christ, whereas the remainder "lived not until the thousand years were finished." Context and consistency demand that both verbs be interpreted as referring to resurrection. The first resurrection must be associated with the Parousia of Christ (1 Cor. 15:20-23). The period during which these are to reign must, therefore, be subsequent to the second coming of Christ.

g. The kingdom of Christ (Rev. 11:15). This title has reference to the personal dominion and majesty of our great God and Savior Jesus Christ. Long before the Incarnation, God made known through His prophets that His Son should be the Head of a kingdom, not a spiritual and heavenly kingdom, but a literal and earthly one (Jer. 23:5; Dan. 7:14; Rev. 11:15, ASV). The kingdom over which Christ shall reign is that which God "prepared from the foundation of the world" (Matt. 25:34).

2. Characteristics of the Millennium. The Millennium, or the kingdom reign of one thousand years, is characterized as the long-expected day of Messiah, the day of righteousness and peace, when Jerusalem, rebuilt and adorned, will be the throne of Jehovah and the center of universal law and rule, worship and blessing. It is the time of God's publicly expressed delight in Christ — God's answer to the thirty-three-year life of suffering and reproach of His first advent. In it we witness the grand display of God's purpose and counsels respecting Christ and the church, Israel and the earth. The characteristics of the millennial age have been outlined as follows:

a. Sevenfold manifestation of Christ

(1) He will be manifested as Man at Jerusalem, where He was crucified. From Jerusalem He ascended, and it is to Jerusalem He will return. The place of His humiliation will be the place of His exaltation (Acts 1:11; Zech. 8:3; 12:10-12; 14:4; Ezek. 43:7; 48:35; Joel 3:21; Zeph. 3:15).

(2) He will be manifested as the Son of Abraham, the inheritor of the land of Palestine. He is "the Seed" concerning whom the promise was made to Abraham: "I will give unto thee and to thy seed after thee . . . all the land of Canaan for an everlasting possession" (Gen. 17:8; cf. Gal. 3:16 with Matt. 1:1).

(3) He will be manifested as the Son of David, heir of the throne (Isa. 9:7; Matt. 1:1; Luke 1:32, 33).

(4) He will be manifested as Son of Man, executing judgment (John 5:27).

(5) He will be manifested as King — King of righteousness (Isa. 32:1); King of Israel (John 12:13); King of kings (Rev. 19:16); King over all the earth (cf. Zech. 14:9 with Phil. 2:10).

(6) He will be manifested as the mighty God and God the Son

(Isa. 9:6; Ps. 134:3; Heb. 1:8, 10). The Lord who will be in Zion at that time is the Lord Jesus Christ; He is here affirmed to be the Maker of heaven and earth and therefore, indeed, the mighty God.

(7) He will be manifested as the supreme Teacher of all the earth (Isa. 2:3; Zech. 8:22).

b. Sevenfold blessing and glory for Israel

(1) Israel and Judah are to be restored to the land and reunited under their King (Ezek. 28:25, 26; 36:24; 37:15-28; Amos 9:14, 15; Jer. 31:10).

(2) Jerusalem will be rebuilt unto the Lord (Jer. 30:17-22; 31:38, 39; Joel 3:17-21; Zeph. 3:14-20).

(3) The temple will be rebuilt in splendor (Ezek. 40–48).

(4) The twelve apostles will rule over the reunited twelve tribes (Luke 22:30; Isa. 32:1).

(5) Restored and converted Israel will be the missionaries to the nations (Isa. 61:6, 9-11).

(6) Israel will be the chamberlains of the King (cf. Zech. 8:23 with John 12:20-23).

(7) Israel will be head over all the nations of the earth (Deut. 28:13; Isa. 14:1, 2; 60:12; Ps. 45:16).

c. Sevenfold description of the millennial reign

(1) Christ will rule the nations with a rod of iron, and by means of His judgments the inhabitants of the world will learn righteousness (Isa. 26:9; Pss. 58:11; 101:5-8).

(2) The church will rule and reign with Christ. Corporately, the church will remain in and rule from the heavens. Individually, Christians may reign on the earth. The twelve apostles will be assigned to rule the twelve tribes of Israel. Rulership in the kingdom is to be a matter of reward (Dan. 7:18, 27; Matt. 19:28; Luke 19:15-19; 22:30; 1 Cor. 6:2; Col. 3:4; 2 Tim. 2:12; Heb. 2:5-10; Rev. 3:21; 5:1-10).

(3) There will be universal peace during the thousand years (Isa. 2:4; cf. 11:5-9 with 65:25).

(4) The earth will enjoy her pristine fruitfulness and freedom from the curse (Ps. 67:4-6; Isa. 35:1; 51:3; Ezek. 34:26; 36:30; 47:9-12; Amos 9:13; Rom. 8:19-23).

(5) Human life will be prolonged (Isa. 33:24; 65:20). It will depend not on grace and an over-watching Providence, but

on righteousness; a man will live as long as he is righteous, and no longer; death will be judgment for disobedience (Pss. 72:8, 9; 149:7; Mic. 5:8-15). Satan being bound and the regenerating Lord enthroned in power, there will be no excuse for sin.

(6) The heavens will be opened to the view of earth, and intercourse between them will be established. Apparently this was the condition at the beginning. They were opened to Enoch, Elijah, Jesus, and Paul. They were wondrously opened to Jacob (Gen. 28:10-12). They will be opened by the coming of the Son of God (Rev. 19:11). It is through those opened heavens that the city of God will be seen shining in all its celestial splendor (Rev. 21:9-27). That this description has to do with the millennial period is shown by certain references which seem to be quite impossible in relation to the eternal state (Rev. 20:9; 21:27; 22:2, 14, 15).

(7) The earth will be free from the polluting presence and power of Satan (Rev. 20:1-3).

3. The manner of the inception of the Millennium. The Millennium is to be brought about by nothing else and nothing less than the personal return of Jesus Christ to this earth. Nothing short of divine intervention can bring to an end the present age wherein abound sin, selfishness, and suffering. It was the personal intervention of God which began the Edenic dispensation. So was it with the Mosaic dispensation and the present gospel age. And it is the personal intervention of God which will bring in the kingdom dispensation.

Nothing less than the personal return and presence of the Lord in manifested power and glory can remove Satan from this scene, can lift the curse from the groaning creation, can set up the kingdom of God on earth, and can establish a reign of righteousness, peace, and blessing. There is no kingdom where there is no king, and there can be no Millennium without Christ, no reign of peace without the presence of the Prince of Peace.

THE RESURRECTION OF THE DEAD

While the Scriptures describe the impartation of new life to the soul in regeneration as a spiritual resurrection (John 5:25; Rom. 6:4, 5; Eph. 2:1, 5, 6; 5:14), they also declare that at the Second Coming there will be a resurrection of the body and a reunion of the body with the soul, from which it has been separated during the intermediate state. Both the just and the unjust will be resurrected. To the just, it will be a resurrection unto life, and the body will be a body like Christ's, fitted for the uses of the sanctified spirit. To the unjust, it will be a resurrection unto condemnation or judgment. Analogy would seem to indicate that the outward form will be corrupt and degraded like the soul which inhabits it.

The Resurrection As a Scriptural Doctrine

Our positive information about the resurrection is derived wholly from the Word of God.

1. It is taught in the Old Testament.
   a. By positive statement (Job 19:25-27; Pss. 16:9-11; 17:15; Dan. 12:2);
   b. By plain figure or symbol (Gen. 22:5; Num. 17:6-10; Rom. 4:19, 20; Heb. 11:19);
   c. By predictive prophecy (Isa. 26:19; Hosea 13:14);
   d. By practical demonstration (1 Kings 17:17-24; 2 Kings 4:32-35; 13:20, 21).

2. It is taught in the New Testament.
   a. By positive statement (John 5:21; Acts 23:6-8; 26:8, 22, 23; 1 Peter 1:3);
   b. By predictive prophecy (John 5:28, 29; 6:39, 40, 44, 54; Luke 14:13, 14; 20:35, 36; 1 Cor. 15; Phil. 3:11; 1 Thess. 4:14-16; Rev. 20:4-6, 13-15);
   c. By practical demonstration: Lazarus (John 11:41-44); Jairus' daughter (Luke 8:41, 42, 49-56); the widow's son (Luke 7:12-15); our Lord (Matt. 28; John 20); departed saints (Matt. 27:52, 53).

The Manner of the Resurrection

Literal and bodily: 1 Corinthians 15:22; Revelation 20:12; 2 Corinthians 5:10; Job 19:25-27; Ps. 16:9; cf. John 5:28, 29 with John 5:25.[7]

Universal. The dead will not all be raised at the same time or to the same destiny, but all the dead will be raised (John 5:28, 29; 1 Cor. 15:22; Rev. 20:12-14).

Twofold:

1. The resurrection of the just. The resurrection of the believing dead will take place in a period of time called "the last day" (John 6:39, 40, 44). The term *day* as here used does not mean a period of

twenty-four hours, but a day period, such as the "day of salvation," "the day of judgment," "the day of the Lord" (see 2 Peter
3:8). The believer's resurrection will be the second event in God's
resurrection program, Christ's resurrection being the first; but it
will be the first event of the series of those included in Christ's
second coming (Luke 14:14; 1 Cor. 15:22, 23; 1 Thess. 4:16; see
also John 5:28, 29; Rev. 20:4-6).

2. The resurrection of the unjust. The resurrection of the unbeliev-
ing dead will take place subsequent to the thousand-year reign of
Christ upon the earth, and just preceding the Great White
Throne judgment (Rev. 20:5, 12-14; Acts 24:14, 15; Dan. 12:2;
John 5:28, 29).

The announcement of two resurrections, separated in time by a
thousand years and distinguished in character as unto immortality and unto mortality, seems to be one of the plainest in all
Scripture: "And I saw the souls of them that had been beheaded
for the testimony of Jesus and for the Word of God: and such as
worshipped not the beast, neither his image, and received not his
mark upon their forehead and upon their hand; and they lived and
reigned with Christ a thousand years. The rest of the dead lived
not until the thousand years should be finished. This is the first
resurrection" (Rev. 20:4, 5, ASV). Here is first a vision of disembodied souls, then of their resurrection.

This resurrection must mean a literal rising from the dead, for
two words employed in the passage put the matter beyond dispute. "They lived" *(ezason)* is language which is never, in the
New Testament, applied to the soul disembodied, but to man in
his complete condition of body, soul, and spirit united. "This is
the first resurrection" *(anastasis)* defines this living to be bodily
resurrection, since the word in the New Testament, with perhaps
a single exception, always signifies corporal resurrection. So the
phraseology employed seems to render it impossible to apply the
vision either to the condition of disembodied existence or to the
quickening of spiritual regeneration.

The question may be asked, How is it that this startling doctrine of two distinct resurrections, with a Millennium between, is
not found till the last book of the Bible is reached? The answer is,
it has been found though not defined. In Daniel there is a con-
densed prophecy of the great tribulation which, by our Lord's
interpretation in Matthew 24, is expanded into an agelong period

of Jewish trial; so in John's Gospel (5:28), there is a miniature prediction of the resurrection: "For the hour is coming in which all that are in their tombs shall hear the voice of the Son of God, and shall come forth, they that have done good unto the resurrection of life; and they that have done ill, unto the resurrection of judgment" — which hour in the Apocalypse of John is interpreted as covering the entire millennial era in its fulfillment. This is according to the common method of prophecy.

Holding that the last presentation of the Resurrection — this in the Apocalypse — is the completest and most comprehensive, the important question is whether the statements of the doctrine in other parts of Scripture harmonize with this. Not only do they harmonize, but in several instances they find their only solution in it.

In the first place, attention is to be called to a class of passages which are marked by the peculiarity that they seem to represent the resurrection of believers as selective and special. It is plain, if the scheme based upon Revelation 20 is correct, that the subjects of the first resurrection are called out from the general mass of the dead; or in other words, that a prior resurrection would involve the idea of an elect resurrection. This conception would seem to explain at once our Lord's allusion (Luke 20:35) to those who will be "accounted worthy to obtain that age, and the resurrection out from the dead" *(ek nekron)*. If there be a first resurrection at the opening of the millennial age in which only the righteous share, the significance of this text is apparent at once.

Even more striking are the words of Paul (Phil. 3:11): "I count all things but loss . . . if by any means I might attain unto the out resurrection from the dead" *(ek nekron)*. The words are very strong in the Greek. They cannot possibly refer to anything else than a selective resurrection, a separation and quickening to life out from among the dead ones. Especially would this seem to be so when, in addition to the very emphatic language describing the resurrection itself, there is the expression of intense desire and vehement striving to attain it. Why should one strive to attain what is inevitable — as Paul's resurrection would have appeared to be, had he held that all men will be raised together? And what could our Lord's words — "They which shall be accounted worthy to obtain that age and the resurrection from the dead" — mean on any other view than that presented — the view, namely, that there is a prior age in which the rising of the saints will take place, and a distinct and special and privileged bodily redemption which belongs to them?

This phase of the argument is set in very strong light by the additional fact that the expression "resurrection from the dead" (*anastasis ek nekron*) is so invariable throughout the New Testament in its application to Christ as well as to His saints. There is only one instance where the other phrase *(anastasis nekron)*, the general expression for "resurrection of the dead" is applied to our Lord, and that seems to be on account of a special requirement of the context (Rom. 1:4). He — coming forth from the dead and opening the doors for all believers to come forth with Him in the resurrection unto life — is described just as they are, as rising *(ek nekron)*. Hence, very significantly, it is said in Acts that the apostles "preached through Jesus the resurrection from the dead," not the resurrection of the dead (4:2). This selective conception is admitted even by some who oppose the doctrine of two resurrections. Olshausen goes as far as to declare that "the phrase would be inexplicable if it were not derived from the idea that out of the mass of the dead some would rise first."

Distinct traces of the idea of a selective and precedent resurrection of the just are found in the Old Testament. The passage in Daniel 12:2 (Authorized Version) — "And many of them that sleep in the dust of the earth shall awake, some to everlasting life, and some to shame and everlasting contempt" — is undoubtedly a messianic prediction concerning the time of the end. Tregelles translates the passage as follows, giving not only the authority of his own accurate scholarship for the rendering, but that of two eminent rabbis, Saadia Haggion and Eben Ezra: "And many from among the sleepers of the dust of the earth shall awake, these — that awake — shall be unto everlasting life; but those — the rest of the sleepers who do not awake at this time — shall be unto shame and everlasting contempt." Here again is presented the idea of the first resurrection with its selective and separate character, and its distinct issue in life.[8]

Objections to the Doctrine of a Literal Resurrection

The theological objection. This objection is that such a doctrine rests upon a literalizing of metaphorical language and therefore has no sufficient support in Scripture. To this we reply that —

1. Though the phrase "resurrection of the body" does not occur in the New Testament, the passages which describe the event indi-

cate a physical, as distinguished from a spiritual, change (John 5:28, 29; Phil. 3:21; 1 Thess. 4:13-17). The phrase "spiritual body" (1 Cor. 15:44) is a contradiction in terms if it be understood as signifying "a body which is simple spirit." It can be interpreted only as meaning a material organism, perfectly adapted to be the outward expression and vehicle of a purified soul. The purely spiritual interpretation is, moreover, expressly excluded by the apostolic denial that "the resurrection is past already" (2 Tim. 2:18) and by the fact that there is a resurrection of the unjust as well as of the just (Acts 24:15).

2. The redemption of Christ is declared to include the body as well as the soul (Rom. 8:23; 1 Cor. 6:13-20). The indwelling of the Holy Spirit has put such honor upon the frail mortal tenement which he has made His temple that, it is evident, God would not permit even this wholly to perish (Rom. 8:11).

3. The nature of Christ's resurrection, as literal and physical, determines the nature of the resurrection in the case of believers (Luke 24:39; John 20:27). As in the case of Christ the same body that was laid in the tomb was raised again, though possessed of new and surprising powers, so the Scriptures intimate, not simply that the saints shall have bodies, but that these bodies shall be in some proper sense an outgrowth or transformation of the very bodies that slept in the dust (Dan. 12:2; 1 Cor. 15:53, 54). The denial of the resurrection of the body, in the case of believers, leads to a denial of the reality of Christ's resurrection (1 Cor. 15:13).

4. Since the accompanying events such as the Second Coming and the judgment are literal, it is reasonable to infer that the resurrection is also literal.

The scientific objection. This is threefold.

1. The resurrection of the particles which constitute the body at death is impossible since they enter into new combinations and not infrequently become parts of other bodies which the doctrine holds to be raised at the same time.[9]

   Reply: The Scripture does not compel us to hold but distinctly denies that all the particles which exist in the body at death are present in the resurrection body (1 Cor. 15:37). The Scripture seems only to indicate a certain physical connection between the new and the old, although the nature of this connection is not revealed (1 Cor. 15:37, 38).

All chasing through the universe to get the identical material atoms and molecules to constitute a proper identity is not only a philosophical absurdity, but also a serious misrepresentation of St. Paul. There are, of course, certain serious difficulties attending the ultraliteralistic view of the resurrection. The bodies of the dead *have fertilized* the wheat fields of Waterloo.

Considerations like these have led some, like Origen, to call the doctrine of the literal resurrection of the flesh "the foolishness of beggerly minds" and to say that the resurrection may be only "the gathering around the spirit of new materials and the vitalizing them into a new body by the spirit's God given power." But this view seems as great an extreme as that from which it was a reaction, i.e., complete material identity between the body of the grave and the resurrection body. It gives up all idea of unity between the new and the old. If the body laid in the tomb were wholly dissipated among the elements, and if God created at the end of the age a wholly new body, it would be impossible for Paul to say, "This corruptible must put on incorruption" (1 Cor. 15:53).

In short, it is clearly intimated in Scripture that there is a physical connection between the old body of the grave and the new body of the resurrection. Paul himself gives us an illustration which shows that his view was midway between the two extremes: "That which thou sowest, thou sowest not the body that shall be, but bare grain, it may chance of wheat, or of some other grain" (1 Cor. 15:37). On the one hand, the wheat that springs up does not contain the precise particles that were in the seed. On the other hand, there has been a continuous physical connection between the seed sown and the ripened grain at the harvest. Similarly, the resurrection body will be the same with the body laid away in the earth as the living stalk of grain is identical with the seed from which it germinated. "This mortal must put on immortality" — not the immortal spirit putting on an immortal body, but the mortal body putting on immortality, the corruptible body putting on incorruption (1 Cor. 15:53).[10]

Two things are requisite to make our future bodies one with the bodies we now inhabit: first, that the same formative principle be at work in them; and second, that there be some sort of physical connection between the body that now is and the body that will be. This physical connection the Scripture most plainly and positively teaches will exist (Job 19:25-27; Phil. 3:21). It is not so much a question of material identity, however, as it is of glorified individuality and personal and characteristic identity in which we are the most deeply interested.

2. A resurrection body, having such a remote physical connection with the present body, cannot be recognized by the inhabiting soul or by other witnessing spirits as the same with that which was laid in the grave.

Reply: Bodily identity does not consist in absolute sameness of particles during the whole history of the body, but in the organizing force which, even in the flux and displacement of physical particles, makes the old the basis of the new and binds both together in the unity of a single consciousness. In our recognition of friends, moreover, we are not wholly dependent, even in this world, upon our perception of bodily form; and we have reason to believe that in the future state there may be methods of communication far more direct and intuitive than those with which we are familiar here. On the occasion of the Transfiguration there is no mention of information given to Peter as to the names of the celestial visitants; it would seem that in his state of exalted sensibility, he at once knew them (Matt. 17:3, 4).

3. A material organism can only be regarded as a hindrance to the free activity of the spirit. The assumption of such an organism by the soul, which during the intermediate state had been separated from the body, would indicate decline in dignity and power rather than indicating progress.

Reply: We cannot estimate the powers and capacities of matter when it is brought by God into complete subjection to the spirit. The bodies of the saints may be more ethereal than the air, and capable of swifter motion than the light, and yet be material in their substance. The soul clothed with its spiritual body will have more exalted powers and enjoy a more complete felicity than would be possible while it maintained a purely spiritual existence, as is evident from the fact that Paul represents the culmination of the soul's blessedness as occurring, not at death, but at the resurrection of the body (Rom. 8:23; 2 Cor. 5:4; Phil. 3:11).

Characteristics of the Resurrection Body

The resurrection body of the believer:

1. Negatively considered. Because of some confusion of thought and teaching, it seems necessary to make some negative statements concerning the body which the believer will receive in the resurrection.

a. The resurrection body will not be produced by an indestructible germ that is in the body of this life; resurrection is not resuscitation of unconscious vitality.

b. The resurrection body will not be produced by natural force which belongs to the body of this life; resurrection is not reanimation through resident forces within the body of the grave.

c. The resurrection body will not be the result of any natural law or habitual divine volition such as brings the buds and blossoms in spring; resurrection is not revivification of dormant life. [11]

d. The resurrection body is not an ethereal body which before or at the time of death was within the physical body, as the shell is within the husk of the nut; resurrection is not the spiritualization of the soul or personality.

e. The resurrection body will not necessarily be a reconstructed body, having material identity with the body that descended in the grave; resurrection is not the reconstruction of the old body by use of the identical material substance of which the body at death is composed. [12]

f. It will not be a flesh and blood body. "Now this I say, brethren, that flesh and blood cannot inherit the kingdom of God" (1 Cor. 15:50). It may be that the reason for this is suggested in the following sentence: "Neither doth corruption inherit incorruption." The blood is, without doubt, the vitalizing principle of these mortal bodies: "For the life of the flesh is in the blood" (Lev. 17:11), and blood is subject to corruption. It will therefore be absent from our resurrection bodies and will be replaced by a substance of vitalization not subject to corruption.

2. Positively considered. The resurrection completes the believer's redemption. It is his physical salvation. It is redemption from all physical limitations and imperfections which are man's inheritance through sin. It brings him into possession of the perfected humanity to which Christ has made him heir through His sacrificial and atoning work. The positive aspects of the believer's resurrection body are summarized as follows:

a. It will be a God-given body — a body which God in His sovereignty will bestow upon us, not bound by the laws of this world, but so made by the direct action of God as to be conditioned by the body of the grave: "But God giveth it a body as it hath pleased Him" (cf. 1 Cor. 15:38 with 2 Cor. 5:1-4).

b. It will be "this body of our humiliation fashioned anew." Hence it will be the same body as to personal identity, though not as to complete material identity (Phil. 3:21 ASV).

c. It will not be pure spirit, but will have flesh and bones like the resurrection body of our Lord, who said to His disciples after His resurrection, "Behold my hands and my feet, that it is I myself; handle me and see; for a spirit hath not flesh and bones as you see me have" (Luke 24:39); the body which He had then and still has is the pattern of the body we are to receive in resurrection (cf. Phil. 3:21 with 1 John 3:2).

d. It will be immortal and incorruptible (1 Cor. 15:52-54; Luke 20:35, 36). Immortality may be predicated of the body alone; of the body of the believer alone; of the resurrection body of the believer alone. Immortality is never predicated of the soul in the Scriptures. It is not synonymous with eternal life or endless existence. Believers possess eternal life in the present, but not immortality. All possess endless existence, but only those who have part in the "resurrection unto life" will be made immortal — not subject to death.

e. It will be a powerful body, not subject to weakness or weariness or the limitations of our present physical bodies, but possessed of powers and capacities of which we have had no experience in our present form of existence. "It is sown in weakness, it is raised in power" (cf. 1 Cor. 15:43 with John 20:19; Rev. 7:15).

f. It will be a heavenly or celestial body, i.e., a body adapted to the environment of the heavenlies and suited to heavenly uses and purposes. "The first man is of the earth, earthy: the second man is the Lord from heaven. As is the earthy, such are they also that are earthy: and as is the heavenly, such are they also that are heavenly. And as we have borne the image of the earthy, we shall also bear the image of the heavenly" (cf. 1 Cor. 15:47-49 with 1 Cor. 15:40).

g. It will be a shining, luminous, or glorious body. This is shown by the direct statement, "It is sown in dishonor, it is raised in glory" (1 Cor. 15:43). It is shown also by those passages which teach that our resurrection body is to be like our Lord's. We have an illustration of the luminous, shining appearance of His resurrection body in the transfiguration record, where it is said, "And after six days Jesus taketh Peter, James and John, his brother, and bringeth them up into a high mountain apart, and was transfigured before them: and His face did shine as the sun, and His raiment was white as the light" (Matt. 17:1, 2; see also Luke 9:29).

This harmonizes with the statements in Philippians 3:21 and 1 John 3:2. It is also intimated in such passages as Matthew 13:43: "Then shall the righteous shine forth as the sun in the kingdom of their Father." And Daniel 12:3: "And they that be wise shall shine as the brightness of the firmament; and they that turn many to righteousness as the stars forever and ever."

Apparently our resurrection bodies will be possessed with a glory light, similar to that in which God is said to envelop Himself: "Who coverest thyself with light as with a garment" (Ps. 104:2). It has been conjectured that the bodies of Adam and Eve were so clothed before they sinned, and that these garments of light served as a covering which departed after the fall, so that "they knew that they were naked" (Gen. 3:7). This glorious style of clothing will come into fashion again in the resurrection.

h. The resurrection bodies will have variety, differing one from another. "There is one glory of the sun, another glory of the moon, and another glory of the stars: for one star differeth from another star in glory. So also is the resurrection of the dead" (1 Cor. 15:41, 42). We will not be characterized by monotony or absolute uniformity in appearance, but there will be that which differentiates us the one from the other.

The resurrection body of the unbeliever. The Scriptures state the fact and purpose of the resurrection of unbelievers, but do not describe their bodies. It is strongly implied, however, that they will be mortal, corruptible bodies (Rev. 20:12, 13).

The Scriptures are strangely silent on the subject of the resurrection of the unbeliever's body. The purpose and result of their resurrection — namely, judgment and punishment — are about all that is given. There is detailed information revealed unto us by the Spirit concerning "things that God hath prepared for them that love Him" (1 Cor. 2:9, 10), but only the cold facts are given concerning the judgment and punishment of the wicked. In the genealogy of Genesis 5 no age is given to those not in the chosen line. In the story of Luke 16 no name is given to the godless rich man.

THE JUDGMENTS

The Scriptures represent all punishment of individual transgressors and all manifestations of God's vindicatory justice in the history of men and nations as acts or processes of judgment. They also, however, intimate that these temporal judgments are only partial and imperfect and that they are, therefore, to culminate in a final and complete vindication of God's righteousness. This will be accomplished by making known to the universe the characters of all men, by assigning to them corresponding destinies and distributing to them suitable rewards.

The Necessity of Judgment

Some object to the doctrine of future and final judgment, assuming that the biblical pictures of the last day are designed merely to impress the imagination and to set forth vividly a principle of judgment that is to be recognized as in continual operation throughout history. As Schiller wrote, "The world's history is the world's judgment."

In reply it may be said that the principle of judgment is constantly in operation. In a real sense moral law works itself out inevitably; but its actions are not after the manner of physical law. Human freedom and sin have greatly complicated the mechanism of the moral order. Matter, force, and motion are changeless and remorseless in their results under given conditions. This is because natural law rules in all forms of matter. But in a realm of free personalities, no such mechanical certitude is possible. Human wills are centers of new initiative. As prone to evil, they render the present social order liable to many complexities and forms of injustice. Only another and divine will can readjust these disturbed and abnormal relations. A future judgment is the Christian expression of this fact. It is the final and equitable requirement demanded by the rule and reign of God in all its aspects.

1. It fulfills the final requirement of conscience. The conscience is the witness in man to the immanent moral law of the universe. Its verdicts in ordinary conduct imply the final verdicts of Him who planted the moral nature in us. "Conscience," it has been said, "is the moral glimpse which the soul obtains of the future." Wrongdoing is accompanied by a forward look upon a fiery judgment (e.g., Heb. 10:27). The moral law, written in our nature, is a copy of the eternal moral law written in God's nature. This law, imma-

nent in us, implies a future reckoning, a judgment day, when that which is true (though not apparent) concerning men may become manifestly true and receive full and final justice.

2. It fulfills the final requirement of history. What works in the individual conscience works also in the corporate conscience of the race. The crimes of nations stand out as clearly in the light of conscience as do the crimes of individuals. The wrongs which the innocent suffer, when might rules in the place of right, fill the pages of a large part of human history. Posthumous influence is a large part of a man's moral power. His work is not done when he dies; his deeds live after him and will live in history until the new order which follows judgment arises. Heredity and solidarity are forces which must be reckoned with in the final awards to individuals. So also freedom and corporate choice of low ideals and immoral standards must be applied as principles of judgment in dealing with men in social groups.

The slow progress of the moral ideal in history points to a culmination which will crystallize the contending forces of good and evil and bring about their final separation. This is clear to ordinary human experience, but more so to Christian experience. The redeemed saints in Revelation are represented as calling for the vengeance of God upon evildoers. Perhaps this moral demand enters character in its perfected form as it does not now. We are commanded to forgive and not to avenge ourselves. There is no contradiction here, but the perfected saints share more completely the divine reaction against sin. All morally vigorous natures partake of this quality in large measure. A contemplation of history as a whole deepens it in everyone. A climax which will bring about a suitable adjustment seems most appropriate.

3. It fulfills the final requirement of the theistic view of the world. If God is a person; if He is in moral relations with men, and men are moral personalities in relations with God; if, in short, we live in a universe of freedom and obligation, then God's vindication of His ways to men calls for a final judgment of affairs. He cannot consistently ignore the demand of the human soul for some sort of understanding of the moral universe. Pantheism reduces us to the level of things. We are passing phenomena, like plants and flowers, the product of an eternal substance or force, without moral dignity. But theism puts us on a higher pedestal. We reflect the eternal intelligence and moral cravings.

If we recognize the purposiveness of the moral sense in us, in

Christian experience, history, and the theistic view of the world, we look forward to a higher solution. Teleology implies judgment. We may illustrate by the principles of progress and unity in literature and art generally. The kingdom of God is like a great drama: it moves forward to a climax; all the apparently loose ends of the development are slowly combined and gathered together; the unity of the whole is seen only in the final outcome; without the climax the drama is meaningless; it is mere motion without progress.

In God's kingdom, judgment operates constantly as an immanent principle in the on-going of history. It expresses itself in a gradual process. But it also expresses itself in signal events and great climaxes. In both aspects, judgment is in close agreement with the nature of man and the course of history in other ways: the slow processes followed by the sudden revolution; the beginning, the ascent toward a goal, the climax, and then a new beginning, a new ascent, a new climax. These are familiar processes in history. The final judgment is the biblical expression of this principle in the moral kingdom.

Future and final judgment is made necessary, therefore, in order that the principle of judgment, which is in constant operation, may have its full and complete expression as demanded by conscience, human history, and the Christian conception of God and man in moral relations with each other.

The Purpose of Judgment

The purpose of future judgment is not the discovery of character and conduct, but their manifestation, discrimination, and reward. As Paul expresses it, "We must all be made manifest before the judgment seat of Christ; that each one may receive the things done in the body, according to what he hath done, whether it be good or bad" (2 Cor. 5:10, ASV).

So also in Romans 2:5, 6 men are said to treasure up for themselves wrath in the day of wrath and revelation of the righteous judgment of God, who will render to every man according to his works. They are to give account of "every idle word" that they speak (Matt. 12:36). Again, "There is nothing covered up, that shall not be revealed; and hid, that shall not be known" (Luke 12:2, ASV).

To judge means, literally, to discriminate, and from this follows the idea of separation. In judgment God discriminates between the righteous and the unrighteous and separates them from each other. But this is simply to uncover or make manifest what previously existed in principle. Deeds done in the body are taken as the criterion of judgment, because deeds declare character. The inward state is, of course, presupposed. No secret thing is hidden from God. The union of man by faith with Christ is a cardinal fact which will be recognized.

The great "deed," the true "work of God," is that men believe on Christ (John 6:29). No other deed means so much as this. It is the mother deed, the root principle, of all good deeds. All the good deeds which God approves are in principle the offspring of this. But this is not a meritorious good work which buys salvation. It is the gift of God's grace. And all the deeds which spring from it arise from the same grace. Christians, then, are not saved by works, but by grace through faith. They are rewarded according to the use they make of the grace as manifest in deeds.

The Fact of Divine Judgment

As revealed in the Scriptures:

1. It is taught in the Old Testament (Pss. 9:7, 8; 96:13). A time of reckoning and judgment for the world, by God, is clearly taught in the Old Testament.

2. It is taught in the New Testament (Acts 17:31; Heb. 9:27). Man is appointed unto judgment, according to the New Testament, just as certainly as he is to death; the resurrection of Jesus Christ is God's assurance of this fact.

As corroborated by human experience. In the nature of man, there are corroborations of this scriptural doctrine which are evidences of, and preparations for, the future judgment.

1. The law of memory, by which the soul preserves the records of its acts, both good and evil (Luke 16:25). Memory is a process of self-registry. The mind is a palimpsest; though the original writing has been erased, the ink has penetrated the whole thickness of the parchment, and God's chemistry is able to revive it. Subjective memory (sometimes called "mental latency") is the retention of all ideas, however superficially they may have been impressed upon the objective mind, and it admits of no variation in different individuals. Recollection which varies greatly is the power of recalling ideas to the mind.

2. The law of conscience, by which men involuntarily anticipate punishment for their own sins (Rom. 2:15, 16; Heb. 10:27).[13]

3. The law of character, by which every thought and deed makes an

indelible impression upon the moral nature (Heb. 3:8, 15; Eph. 4:19; Prov. 23:7). Single acts and words are to be brought into the judgment only as indications of the moral condition of the soul (Matt. 12:36; Luke 12:2, 8, 9). This manifestation of all hearts will vindicate not only God's past dealings, but His determinations of future destinies.

The Executor of Future Justice

1. God will be the Judge (Pss. 9:7, 8; 96:13; Rom. 1:32; 2:2, 3, 5). Future judgment will be executed by God, by whom all are held responsible and to whom also they will be held accountable.

2. God in Christ will be the Judge (John 5:22, 23, 27; Acts 10:42; 17:31; Rom. 2:16; 14:10-12; 2 Cor. 5:10). The texts which speak of God as judging the world are to be understood as referring to God the Son. Christ's own declaration was: "For the Father judgeth no man, but hath committed all judgment unto the Son (John 5:22). No appeal can be made from the Son to the Father: His judgment is final.

   The fitness of Christ to be the final judge of men grows out of His twofold relation to God and man. He is the revelation of God to man; God is now dealing with men in and through Christ. Men come unto God through Him; He is the Way, the Truth, and the Life for men. What God requires of men and what God is willing to bestow upon men come into the clearest expression through Christ. The invisible, eternal God thus adopts a historical mode of manifesting Himself, His grace, His holiness, His power. It is fitting, therefore, that the culmination of His plan should find expression in the person of His Son.

   This fitness of Christ is further seen in the fact that He is "a Son of man" as John describes (John 5:27), indicating that He is thus qualified as a judge of men. The perfect human nature of Christ, united as it is to the divine, ensures all that is needful in true judgment. As man, Christ knows men (John 2:24, 25). He was tested in all points like men, sin apart (Heb. 4:15). He thus possesses knowledge and sympathy which are essential to equitable and just decisions regarding men.

3. The saints will share in the execution of judgment (1 Cor. 6:2, 3; Ps. 149:9). Judgment upon kings, nobles, and peoples is an honor which God will confer upon His saints. Instead of standing in the dock as criminals, they will sit on the bench with Christ as judges.

The Character and Course of Divine Judgment

The multiplicity of judgments may surprise those who have not given this matter careful consideration. There have been many judgments or divine visitations upon sin and sinners in the past, such as the primeval earth (Gen. 1, 2); Adam, Eve, and the serpent (Gen. 3); Cain (Gen. 4); the antediluvians (Gen. 7, 8); the race (Gen. 11); Sodom and Gomorrah (Gen. 19); Egypt, her king, and military power (Exod. 8–15); Israel at Sinai (Exod. 32) and in the wilderness (Num. 14); the seven nations of Canaan (Deut. 7); Israel by the Assyrians (2 Kings 17); Judah by the Chaldeans (2 Kings 25) and subsequently by the Romans (Luke 21); Babylon (Jer. 51); and Nineveh (Nah. 3). The last and greatest of the past judgments is that of the Cross.

There are also judgments transpiring at the present time, such as God's providential and disciplinary judgments upon men and nations.

As the rays of the prophetic lamp fall on the yet unwritten pages of history, judgments numerous as those already past, unsparing and final in character, are revealed to our gaze. The future is crowded with distinctive acts of judgment upon individuals and peoples, of which the following furnish examples: the Jew in the coming tribulation (Mark 13); Israel in the wilderness (Ezek. 20:33-38); the nations to whom the gospel of the kingdom is to be preached (Matt. 25:31-46); Russia, Persia, and other allied northeastern powers politically hostile to Israel (Ezek. 38, 39); Philistia, Moab, Amalek, and other tribes and peoples settled within the borders of, or contiguous to, Palestine (Ps. 83); Edom and the heathen (Obadiah and Isa. 63:1-6); nations and armies of the west gathered in mad opposition to God and to the Lamb (Rev. 19:11-21); Christ-rejecting Christendom (2 Thess. 1, 2); the beast and the false prophet (Rev. 19:20); and the wicked dead (Rev. 20:11-15). From all the judgments of the past, the present, and the future, we select these outstanding ones:

The judgment of the Cross. This stands out from all before and all to come. The past and future, heaven and hell, light and darkness, good and evil, love and enmity center and circle around that wondrous meeting place — the Cross — and by it all is eternally fixed and settled.

1. Here Satan was judged, and his power over the believer was potentially and provisionally broken (John 12:31; 16:11; Col. 2:15; Rev. 12:11).

2. Here sin in the flesh or the nature of sin was judged and put to

death in the death of Christ — the new Federal Head (Rom. 5:13, 16-21; 6:1-4; 8:3, 4; Gal. 2:20).

3. Here the believer's sins were judged and punished in the person of his substitute Savior (Isa. 53:6; Rom. 3:25-28; Gal. 3:13; 1 Peter 2:24; 3:18).[14]

The present judgment of the believer's self-life. There is and should be a present judgment upon the believer's self-life. There should be self-examination by the believer himself, in which sin is discerned, judged, confessed, and put away by the blood of Christ in the power of the Holy Spirit (1 Cor. 11:26-32; 1 John 1:5-7). There must be a continual judgment of self — self-discipline going on in the believer's life; otherwise it will call for divine discipline, corrective judgments, and chastening. God deals with believers, not as subjects of a king or as criminals answerable to a judge, but as sons under the control and discipline of a father (Heb. 12:5-11).

The manifestation of the believer and his works. The principal passage which treats of this judgment is 2 Corinthians 5:10: "We must all appear [be made manifest] before the judgment seat of Christ, that every one may receive the things done in his body according to that he hath done, whether it be good or bad." The pronoun *we* occurs twenty-six times in the chapter, and in every instance it means believers; and since the epistle is addressed to the "church" and "saints" at Corinth, the judgment here spoken of is for believers only.

This judgment takes place when the Lord comes (1 Cor. 4:5), and the place is "in the air" (1 Thess. 4:17) and before the judgment seat of Christ. It will not be a judgment in the sense of a trial, to see whether the judged are innocent (saved) or guilty (lost), for it is a judgment of the saved only. It will be like the judge's stand at a fair or racetrack, where rewards are distributed to the successful contestants. Paul describes such a scene in 1 Corinthians 9:24-27.

1. The basis of the examination and manifestation. The manifestation before the judgment seat of Christ will be of "every man's work." The examination will determine "what sort it is," "whether it be good or bad," i.e., whether it is "gold, silver, precious stones" or "wood, hay, and stubble." This is a judgment not for destiny, but for adjustment, for reward or loss, according to our works, for position in the kingdom, every man according to his works. A vast amount of healthy work will be transacted at the judgment seat of Christ.

The statement that "his wife hath made herself ready" (Rev. 19:7) surely intimates that she has been at the judgment seat before the glorious blaze of the searching, revealing light of the presence of Christ; now, all having come out, she can happily take her place at the side of her heavenly Bridegroom. The mistakes of time will there be rectified, wrong judgments reversed, misunderstandings corrected, ungenerous attempts to impute falsehood or evil where such do not exist exposed; in short, persons, ways, words, motives, and acts will then appear in their true light and character.

It will be a clearing-up moment, so that the church and every member of the redeemed company may enter into the enjoyment of eternal blessing in the perfect knowledge that all has been fully exposed between the soul and Christ. Then in the eternal rest of God, no clouds will ever darken our sky, no unsettled question ever arise to dim the joy, no lurking suspicion ever cross the soul. Every difficulty and question between believers and God, between brother and brother, will then be righteously adjusted.[15]

2. The results of the manifestation.

   a. Some will receive rewards (1 Cor. 3:10-15). The reward of the believer will be proportionate to the faithfulness of his service to God in using the talents with which God has endowed him. The rewards, therefore, will differ according to the faithfulness or unfaithfulness of our life and service. Faith in Jesus Christ saves the believer, but his position in the future life, together with the measure of his rewards, will depend upon his works. Thus it comes to pass that a man may be saved "so as by fire," i.e., saved because of his faith, but his life's work lost.

   b. Some will suffer loss (1 Cor. 3:15; 1 John 2:28; 2 John 8; Rev. 3:11).

   c. All will possess rare privileges and positions of royal honor (Matt. 10:32; Luke 12:8; 1 Cor. 2:9, 10; Rev. 3:4, 5). They will be arrayed in white garments, with their names inscribed in the Book of Life, and be confessed before the Father and the holy angels.

3. The rewards are referred to as crowns.

   a. The crown of righteousness — the triumphant soldier's, the successful runner's, the faithful steward's crown, for those who give evidence of self-mastery in various dimensions of the Christian life (2 Tim. 4:7, 8; 1 Cor. 9:25-27);

b. The crown of rejoicing — the soul-winner's crown (1 Thess. 2:19, 20; Dan. 12:1-3);

c. The crown of life — the martyr's crown for those faithful under trial who live the martyr's life and may die the martyr's death (James 1:12; Rev. 2:10);

d. The crown of glory — the under-shepherd's crown, for feeding and caring for those entrusted to his care (1 Peter 5:4).

The judgment of the living nations. There is to be a judgment of the nations at the revelation of Jesus Christ based upon their treatment of Christ's brethren according to the flesh (a Jewish remnant) who are to be the messengers of the gospel of the kingdom during the interval between the Rapture and Christ's revelation (Matt. 25:31-46). The judgment will occur at the beginning of the Millennium. The place, in general, will be the earth; in particular, "the valley of Jehoshaphat" at the base of the Mount of Olives (Joel 3:3-16; Zech. 14:1-9).[16]

The judgment of Israel. There is a judgment predicted for restored Israel preparatory to the reestablishment of the Davidic kingdom (Ps. 50:1-7; Isa. 1:2, 24-26; Ezek. 20:30-38). These passages are prophecies of the future judgment upon Israel, regathered from all nations into the old wilderness of their former wanderings. The issue of this judgment determines who shall enter the land for kingdom blessing. It takes place probably at the end of the Great Tribulation.

The judgment of the fallen angels. The fallen angels are reserved for judgment which will take place during the period known as "the great day" — the day of the Lord (Jude 6; cf. 2 Peter 2:4 with Isa. 24:21). As the final judgment upon Satan occurs after the thousand years and preceding the final judgment of the wicked (Rev. 20:10), it is reasonable to conclude that the other fallen angels will be judged with him at that time and also share his doom. Saints will be associated with Christ in this judgment (1 Cor. 6:3).

The judgment of the great white throne. There is a future and final judgment of the wicked which will forever settle their destiny of eternal doom (Rev. 20:11-15). This is spoken of as the final judgment. It stands at the end of this present dispensational order (1 Cor. 15:24). The judge will be God the Son, unto whom all judgment has been committed by the Father. The judged are the dead — those who did not have part in the first resurrection. The judgment will be based upon the things written in the books, and the final appeal will be to the Book of Life and to the names written therein. The outcome will be the lake of fire for all those whose names are not written in the Lamb's Book of Life.

THE FINAL DESTINY

The Righteous

The final and eternal state of the righteous is the fullness and perfection of holy life in communion with God and with sanctified spirits. There will be degrees of blessedness and honor, proportioned to the capacity and fidelity of each soul (Luke 19:17-19; 1 Cor. 3:13-15), yet each will receive as great a measure of blessing and privilege as its capacity and capability make possible; these will depend largely upon the improvement and use of God's gifts in the present life. This final state, once entered upon, will be changless in kind and endless in duration (Rev. 22:11).

1. They shall never die (John 8:51; 11:25, 26). This does not mean that the believer will not pass through the experience that we call death, but rather, in reality it is not death (at least, not in the sense in which it is death to the unbeliever). The word *see* in John 8:51 means that the believer will not gaze at death protractedly, steadily, exhaustively. Death is not the objective of his gaze. The believer's outlook is life, not death. The death of the body is not to be reckoned as death any more than the life of the body, in the fuller sense, is to be reckoned as life (1 Tim. 5:6).

    The believer is represented in Scripture as having passed out of the realm of death into the realm of life (John 5:24). His back is turned upon death; he faces and gazes upon life. The temporary separation of the soul and body does not even interrupt, much less impair, the soul's true life received from Jesus Christ.

2. Death for the believer is spoken of as sleep (Dan. 12:2; John 11:11-15; 1 Cor. 15:51; 1 Thess. 4:13, 14). In the passage in 1 Thessalonians, the contrast is sharply drawn between death and the experience through which the believer passes in the dissolution of his soul and body. Jesus "died" — He tasted the awfulness of death — the believer in Him "falls asleep." This does not mean that the soul is unconscious between the time of death and the resurrection.

    When the disciples did not understand the figurative language He used on the occasion when He had been notified of Lazarus' death — "Our friend Lazarus sleepeth" — He then told them plainly, "Lazarus is dead." What Jesus meant is that death is something like what takes place when we go to sleep. The current of life does not cease, but continues to go on, and when we awake we feel better and stronger than before. There is a shutting out of all the scenes of the world and time. Just so is it in the case of the believer's death. Three ideas are contained in the word *sleep:* continued existence — for the mind is active even though the body is still; repose — we lose our hold on and forget the things of the world; wakening — we also think of sleep as followed by awakening. Sleep, in this sense, applies primarily to the body, although in respect to the soul there is a severing of physical consciousness and communication.

3. At death the believer goes to be with Christ (2 Cor. 5:6-8; Phil. 1:23, 24). The Bible seems to give but little explicit and detailed information concerning the character of our existence when "absent from the body" and "at home with the Lord," up to the time of the coming of the Lord and our being "clothed upon with our habitation which is from heaven," (2 Cor. 5:2-4, ASV). It does say, however, that this state is "very far better" than our present state (Phil. 1:23, ASV). This leaves no room for purgatorial tortures or for a state of unconsciousness. It is evidently a state of conscious bliss, although not the highest state to which the believer shall attain. The interval between the death of the believer and his resurrection is characterized by conscious life in the presence of Christ.

4. Believers are to be identified with Christ in His millennial reign (2 Tim. 2:12; Col. 3:4; Rev. 2:25-27). The Millennium will have its two distinct spheres of blessing — the one above, the other on the earth. All who share in the blessedness of the "first resurrection" — the righteous dead from Adam — will reign with Christ over the earth, while the Jews and nations will constitute subjects of the kingdom.

5. In the eternal state, the believer will enter into a new condition and abode of life (John 14:2; 17:24; Rom. 8:18; Heb. 11:10, 16; 13:14). The abode will be a prepared place. This is Christ's own answer to the question, "Is heaven a place as well as a state?" His word should be sufficient to establish this, but the probability is also seen by the further fact that Christ's human body is essential to heaven ("That where I am there ye may be also") and that this body requires place. It means, therefore, a new sphere of life and a new home for the saints. There will be a new heaven and a new earth. Paradise will be regained — new spiritual environment,

new physical conditions. We will not be surrounded by the temptations and defects of this mortal life. In Rev. 21:1–22:5 we have a picture of the Holy City, the New Jerusalem, which will doubtless be the final and eternal abode of the people of God.

The eternal state also involves a new condition of life for the redeemed. God's home is the future dwelling place of the believer (Rev. 21:3); thus the believer has unbroken fellowship with God. The things that belonged to the old order in a sinful universe have passed away: death, mourning, curse, tears, sorrow, night. The things which belong to the new and redeemed order appear: the river of life, the tree of life, new service, new relationships, new light.

The Wicked

The final disposition of the wicked has been the subject of dispute and cavil down through the ages, and it is without doubt the most difficult doctrine with which the Scriptures deal. Various explanations are given for this. To some this doctrine is unwelcome because they feel themselves guilty, and their own conscience assures them that unless they repent and turn to God, an awful doom awaits them. The thought of future punishment striking terror to peoples' hearts prejudices the minds of many against the scriptural presentation of this truth.

To others again, the thought of future anguish seems utterly incompatible with the fatherly love of God. Yet, it is acknowledged to be a remarkable fact that both Jesus and John — who more than anyone else in the New Testament represent the trait of love in their lives and teaching — speak most of the future anguish of the wicked.

1. The Scriptures emphatically teach that eternal punishment is to be the final visitation of God upon the wicked. The final state of the wicked is described under the figures of eternal fire (Matt. 25:41); outer darkness (Matt. 8:12); torment (Rev. 14:10, 11); eternal punishment (Matt. 25:46); wrath of God (Rom. 2:5; John 3:36); second death (Rev. 21:8); eternal destruction from the face of the Lord (2 Thess. 1:9, asv); damnation (Mark 3:29).

Summing up all, we may say that it is the loss of all good, whether physical or spiritual, the misery of an evil conscience, banished from God and from the society of the holy, and dwelling under God's positive curse forever. Here we are to remember, as in the case of the final state of the righteous, that the decisive and controlling element is not the outward, but the inward. Hell is the way it is so that the outward state of the lost may correspond to the inward. The outward torments will be fit accompaniments of the inward state of the soul.

2. The future punishment of the wicked is not annihilation. By virtue of its original creation in the image of God, the soul of man is inherently possessed of endless existence; for neither the righteous nor the wicked is death a cessation of being. On the contrary, the wicked enter at death upon a state of conscious suffering which the resurrection and the judgment only augment and render permanent. It is plain, moreover, that if annihilation took place at death, there could be no degrees in future punishment — a conclusion itself at variance with express statements of Scripture.

There are two forms of the annihilation theory which seem plausible to the natural mind and which in recent times have found a large number of advocates.

a. That the powers of the wicked are gradually weakened, as the natural result of sin, so that they finally cease to be. To this it is to be replied, first, that moral evil does not in this present life seem to be incompatible with a constant growth of the intellectual powers, at least in certain directions, and we have no reason to believe the fact to be different in the world to come; second, that if this theory were true, the greater the sin, the speedier would be the relief from punishment.

b. That there is for the wicked, certainly after death and possibly between death and the judgment, a positive punishment proportioned to their deeds, but that this punishment issues in, or is followed by annihilation. To this second form of the theory it is to be replied, first, that upon this view, as upon any theory of annihilation, future punishment is a matter of grace as well as of justice — a notion for which Scripture affords no warrant; second, that Scripture not only gives no hint of the cessation of this punishment, but declares in the strongest terms its endlessness.

3. Punishment after death excludes new probation and ultimate restoration of the wicked. Some have held to the ultimate restoration of all human beings by appeal to such passages as these: Matthew 19:28; Acts 3:21; 1 Corinthians 15:26; Ephesians 1:9, 10; Philippians 2:10, 11; 2 Peter 3:9, 13.

a. These passages are to be interpreted in the light of the plain positive statements of Scripture already cited. Thus interpreted, they foretell only the absolute triumph of the kingdom of God and the subjection of all evil to Him.

b. A second probation is not needed to vindicate the justice or the love of God, since Christ, in the Holy Spirit, is already in this world present with every soul, quickening the conscience, giving to each man his opportunity, and making every decision between right and wrong a true probation. In choosing evil against their better judgment, even the heathen unconsciously reject Christ. Infants and idiots, as they have not consciously sinned, are, as we may believe, saved at death by having Christ revealed to them and by the regenerating influence of His Spirit (Rom. 1:18-28; 2:6-16).

c. The advocates of universal restoration are commonly the most strenuous defenders of the inalienable freedom of the human will to make choices contrary to its past character and to all the motives which are or can be brought to bear upon it. We find in this world that men choose sin in spite of infinite motives to the contrary. Upon the theory of human freedom just mentioned, no motives which God can use will certainly accomplish the salvation of all moral creatures. The soul which resists Christ here may resist Him forever.

d. Upon the more correct view of the will which we have advocated, the case is more hopeless still. Upon this view, the sinful soul, in its very sinning, gives to itself a sinful bent of intellect, affection, and will — in other words, makes for itself a character which, though it does not render necessary, yet does render certain, apart from divine grace, the continuance of sinful action. In itself it finds a self-formed motive to evil strong enough to prevail over all inducements to holiness which God sees it wise to bring to bear. It is in the next world, indeed, subject to suffering. But suffering has in itself no reforming power. Unless accompanied by special renewing influences of the Holy Spirit, it only hardens and embitters the soul. We have no Scripture evidence that such influences of the Spirit are exerted, after death, upon the still impenitent; but abundant evidence, on the contrary, that the moral condition in which death finds men is their condition forever.

e. The declaration concerning Judas in Matthew 26:24 could not be true if based on the hypothesis of a final restoration. If at any time, even after the lapse of ages, Judas be redeemed, his subsequent infinite duration of blessedness must outweigh all the finite suffering through which he has passed. The Scripture statement that "good were it for that man if he had not been born" must be regarded as a refutation of the theory of universal restoration.

4. Scripture declares this future punishment of the wicked to be eternal. It does this by its use of the terms *aion* and *aionios*. Some, however, maintain that these terms do not necessarily imply eternal duration. To this may be replied —

   a. It must be conceded that these words do not etymologically necessitate the idea of eternity and that, as expressing the idea of "agelong," they are sometimes used in a limited or rhetorical sense (2 Tim. 1:9; Titus 1:2; Heb. 9:26).

   b. They do, however, express the longest possible duration of which the subject to which they are attributis capable; so that, if the soul has endless being, its punishment must be without end (Gen. 17:8, 13; 49:26; Exod. 21:6; 2 Chron. 6:2).

   c. If, when used to describe the future punishment of the wicked, they do not declare the endlessness of that punishment, there are no words in the Greek language which could express that meaning.

   d. In the great majority of Scripture passages where they occur, they have unmistakably the signification "everlasting." They are used to express the eternal duration of God, the Father, Son, and Holy Spirit (Rom. 16:26; 1 Tim. 1:17; Heb. 9:14; Rev. 1:18); the abiding presence of the Holy Spirit with all true believers (John 14:16); and the endlessness of the future happiness of the saints (Matt. 19:29; John 6:54, 58; 2 Cor. 9:9).

   e. The fact that the same word is used in Matthew 25:46 to describe both the suffering of the wicked and the happiness of the righteous shows that the misery of the lost is eternal in the same sense as the life of God or the blessedness of the saints.

   f. Other descriptions of the condemnation and suffering of the lost, excluding as they do all hope of repentance or forgiveness, render it certain that *aion* and *aionios* describe a punishment that is without end (Matt. 12:31, 32; Mark 3:29; 9:43, 48; Luke 3:17; 16:26; John 3:36).

   g. While, therefore, we grant that we do not know the nature of eternity or its relation to time, we maintain that the Scripture representations of future punishment forbid both the hypothesis of annihilation and the hypothesis that suffering will end in restoration. Whatever eternity may be, the Scriptures render it certain that after death there is no forgiveness.

5. Everlasting punishment of the wicked is not inconsistent with God's justice, but is rather a revelation of that justice.

    a. The object of penalty is neither reformatory nor deterrent, but simply vindicatory; in other words, it primarily aims, not at the good of the offender, nor at the welfare of society, but at the vindication of law. Justice is not a form of benevolence, but is the expression and manifestation of God's holiness. Punishment, therefore, as the inevitable and constant reaction of that holiness against its moral opposite, cannot come to an end until guilt and sin come to an end.

    b. Guilt or ill-dessert is endless. However long the sinner may be punished, he never ceases to be ill-deserving. Justice, therefore, which gives to all according to their desserts, cannot cease to punish. Since the reason for punishment is endless, the punishment itself must be endless. Even past sins involve an endless guilt, to which endless punishment is simply the inevitable correlate.

    c. Not only eternal guilt, but eternal sin demands eternal punishment. So long as moral creatures are opposed to God, they deserve punishment. Since we cannot measure the power of the depraved will to resist God, we cannot deny the possibility of endless sinning. Sin tends evermore to reproduce itself. The Scriptures speak of an "eternal sin" (Mark 3:29). But it is just in God to visit endless sinning with endless punishment. Sin, moreover, is not only an act, but also a condition or state of the soul; this state as impure and abnormal involves misery; this misery, as appointed by God to vindicate law and holiness, is punishment; this punishment is the necessary manifestation of God's justice. Not the punishing, but the nonpunishing would impugn His justice; or, if it is just to punish sin at all, it is just to punish it as long as it exists (Mark 3:29; Rev. 22:11).

    d. The actual facts of human life and the tendencies of modern science show that this principle of retributive justice is wrought into the elements and forces of the physical and moral universe. On the one hand, habit begets fixity of character, and in the spiritual world sinful acts, often repeated, produce a permanent state of sin which the soul, unaided, cannot change. On the other hand, organism and environment are correlated to each other; and in the spiritual world, the selfish and impure find surroundings corresponding to their nature, while the surroundings react upon them and confirm their evil character. These principles, if they act in the next life as they do in this, will insure increasing and unending punishment (Gal. 6:7, 8; Rev. 22:11).

e. As there are degrees in human guilt, so future punishment may admit of degrees and yet in all those degrees be infinite in duration. The Scriptures recognize such degrees in future punishment, while at the same time they declare it to be endless (Luke 12:47, 48; Rev. 20:12, 13).

f. We know the enormity of sin only by God's own declaration with regard to it and by the sacrifice which He has made to redeem us from it. As committed against an infinite God, and as having in itself infinite possibilities of evil, it may itself be infinite and may deserve infinite punishment. Hell, as well as the Cross, indicates God's estimate of sin (see Ezek. 14:22-23).

6. The everlasting punishment of the wicked is not inconsistent with God's benevolence. It is maintained, however, by many who object to eternal retribution, that benevolence requires God not to inflict punishment upon His creatures except as a means of attaining some higher good. To this it may be replied —

a. God is not only benevolent but holy, and holiness is His ruling attribute. The vindication of God's holiness is the primary and sufficient object of punishment. This constitutes an end which justifies this means, i.e., the infliction of punishment.

b. In this life, God's justice does involve certain of His creatures in suffering which is of no advantage to the individuals who suffer; as in the case of penalties which do not reform and afflictions which only harden and embitter. If this be a fact here, it may be a fact hereafter.

c. The benevolence of God, as concerned for the general good of the universe, requires the execution of the full penalty of the law upon all who reject Christ's salvation. The Scriptures intimate that God's treatment of human sin is a matter of instruction to all moral beings. The self-chosen ruin of the few may be the salvation of the many.

d. The present existence of sin and punishment is commonly

admitted to be in some way consistent with God's benevolence in that it is made the means of revealing God's justice and mercy. If the temporary existence of sin and punishment leads to good, it is entirely possible that their eternal existence may lead to greater good.

e. As benevolence in God seems in the beginning to have permitted moral evil, not because sin was desirable in itself, but only because it was incident to a system which provided for the highest possible freedom and holiness in the creature; so benevolence in God may to the end permit the existence of sin and may continue to punish the sinner, undesirable as these things are in themselves, because they are incidents of a system which provides for the highest possible freedom and holiness in the creature through eternity.

Study Questions on Eschatology

1. Define physical death, showing what it is to be distinguished from and what aspect of it is related to the believer.
2. State deductions from the Scripture which show that death does not mean cessation of being. Quote one passage with each as illustration or proof.
3. Discuss the intermediate state of the dead.
4. Discuss the intermediate state of the righteous, providing scriptural support.
5. Give the threefold description of the intermediate state of the wicked, and discuss the two erroneous views refuted thereby.
6. Discuss the four great advents of Scripture.
7. Discuss the importance of the second coming of Christ as shown by the prominence given to it in the Bible.
8. Discuss the importance of the Second Coming as shown by the vital relation which it holds to the other doctrines of the Christian faith.
9. Give the twelvefold description of the importance of the Second Coming as shown by its practical value.
10. Discuss the importance of the Second Coming as shown by the estimate placed upon it and the emphasis given to it by the early church.
11. Discuss the fact of the Second Coming, and quote one passage in

proof of the same.

12. Discuss and refute the various misinterpretations of the fact of the second coming of Christ.
13. Describe fully the character of the Second Coming under the following aspects: personal, glorious, sudden, twofold, premillennial.
14. Give the essence of the eleven reasons for believing the second coming of Christ to be premillennial.
15. Why is "premillennialism" a relatively recent term?
16. Give a general description of the events associated with the second coming of Christ.
17. Discuss the events associated with the Second Coming with reference to the church: the Rapture, in its threefold aspect; the marriage supper; manifestation with Christ.
18. Discuss the Second Coming with reference to apostate Christendom.
19. Discuss the Second Coming with reference to Israel, giving in outline her prophetic program.
20. Discuss the Second Coming with reference to the Gentile nations.
21. Describe and discuss fully the Antichrist under the following headings: his names; his personality (with contrasts); his origin and development; his work; his end and doom.
22. Discuss the second coming of Christ with reference to Satan.
23. Discuss the second coming of Christ with reference to the millennial kingdom under the following headings: the Millennium defined; descriptive titles of the Millennium; characteristics of the Millennium; the manner of the inception of the Millennium.
24. Show the resurrection of the dead to be a scriptural doctrine.
25. Discuss the manner of the resurrection under the following headings: literal and bodily, universal, and twofold.
26. Discuss the questions concerning the two resurrections and show the correspondence between the passage in Revelation 20 and other key passages.
27. Discuss the theological objection to the doctrine of a literal resurrection as well as the fourfold reply.
28. Discuss the scientific objections and replies to the doctrine of a literal resurrection.
29. Discuss the ultraliteralistic view of the resurrection body, the opposing, extreme view of Origen, and also the view of Paul.

30. Describe the characteristics of the resurrection body, negatively considered.
31. Discuss the characteristics of the resurrection body, positively considered, and quote one passage with each.
32. Discuss the characteristics of the resurrection body of the unbeliever.
33. What do the Scriptures represent and intimate concerning the punishments of individual transgressors and all manifestations of God's vindicatory justice toward men and nations?
34. Discuss the necessity of judgment in light of conscience, history, and theism.
35. Discuss the purpose of future judgment.
36. Show the fact of divine judgment as revealed in the Old and New Testament Scriptures, and quote one passage from each.
37. Discuss the fact of future divine judgment in view of the laws of memory, conscience, and character.
38. Give the threefold description of the Executor of justice, and quote one passage with each.
39. Mention a few of the multiplicity of judgments recorded in Scriptures.
40. Give the threefold description of the judgment of the Cross, and quote one passage with each.
41. Discuss the present judgment of the believer's self-life.
42. Discuss the basis and the results of the believer's manifestation before the judgment seat of Christ.
43. Describe the crowns of reward to be distributed at the judgment seat of Christ, and quote one passage with each.
44. Discuss the judgment of the living nations, and distinguish between this and the final judgment.
45. Discuss the judgment of Israel.
46. Discuss the judgment of the fallen angels.
47. Discuss the judgment of the Great White Throne.
48. Discuss the final destiny of the righteous in some detail.
49. Discuss the final destiny of the wicked. Defend the eternality of God's punishment for sin.

Notes

[1] It should be added that while the Scriptures represent the intermediate state to be one of conscious joy to the righteous and of conscious pain to the wicked, they also represent this state as one of incompleteness. The perfect joy of the saints and the utter misery of the wicked begin only with the resurrection and final judgment.

[2] Philip Schaff, *History of the Christian Church* (Grand Rapids: Wm. B. Eerdmans Publishing Co., 1956), II, 614. Gibbon, in his great work, writes: "The ancient and popular doctrine of the Millennium . . . was carefully inculcated by a succession of Fathers from Justin Martyr and Irenaeus, who conversed with the immediate disciples of the Apostles, down to Lactantius, who was the preceptor of the son of Constantine. . . . It appears to have been the reigning sentiment of all orthodox believers." (Edward Gibbon, *The History of the Decline and Fall of the Roman Empire* (Boston: Estes and Lauriat, 1888), I, 533-534.

[3] The "Parousia" is always a personal presence, never anything else (John 14:3). It is the King Himself—not even His kingdom—that we are to look for. We are told that in papyri from the Ptolemaic period down to the second century A.D., *parousia* (coming presence) is traced in the East to the technical expression for the arrival or the visit of the king or emperor. It is not, therefore, a word peculiar to the New Testament. It was in use in the time of the apostles, and they appropriated it for sacred use (cf. 2 Cor. 10:1, 2, 10, 11 with Matt. 24:3, 27). The "coming," therefore, is the "personal arrival." This is clearly true of both Christ and Antichrist as seen in 2 Thessalonians 2:7-9. The "man of sin" is personal; so is the "Son of man" who destroys him.

[4] *Premillennialism* is a term of comparative newness. It was not needed in theological discussion for centuries. Postmillennialism having become popularized, however, the term must be employed in order to define the view held by the primitive church, that Christ will literally return from the heavens in order to effect the restitution foretold by the holy prophets (Acts 3:19-21). The regenesis of nature and restoration of nations included in the promised restitution will occupy one thousand years, the duration of earth's antitypical Sabbath, including the resurrection of all believers, the imprisonment of Satan, with the destruction of the Antichrist. This hope, as ever imminent, was the strong consolation of early believers, while martyrs in their sufferings were sustained through its constant expectation.

[5] The terms *body* and *bride* are both true of the church: "body" is referred to when the vital and organic relation of the church to Christ is intended; "bride," when its affection and love relation are to be emphasized. The Marriage Supper of the Lamb is a figure under which is depicted the complete union between Christ and His Church.

[6] Premillennialism does not base its claim on any single prooftext, or series of texts, but rather on the whole trend of Scripture revelation. The much controverted passage of Revelation 20:1-6 is explained in the glowing light of multiplied predictions. The learned Alford declared that the whole church for three hundred years understood these verses in a plain literal sense. John Bengel, prince of exegetes, as well as his student John Wesley, gave unequivocal testimony to the view that Christ would come before the Millennium. Premillennialism protests against the application of those parables and discourses of our Lord which clearly point to a new kingdom, introduced and established on His return, to natural phenomena such as death, war, national calamities, and natural convulsions. These frequently recurring events are too superficial as adequate fulfillment of divine prophecy. Premillennialists believe that the Old Testament predictions of the sufferings and glory of Messiah bound the present age. They are as mountain peaks, between which lies the church and beyond which lies the millennial kingdom. Premillennialists believe that the Bible given in the language of men must be interpreted by such rules as govern that language; that the literal meaning of the word be retained until it be determined that the language is figurative. Prophecy frequently appears in symbolic form, but most Scripture symbols are explained in the Scripture.

[7] In 1 Corinthians 15:22 the apostle is speaking of physical death in Adam and of physical resurrection in Christ. These passages show the necessity of the raising of the body in order that judgment and reward may be administered according to things done in the body.

[8] Two texts have been cited as distinctly and unquestionably contradicting the theory of two

resurrections. The first is in 2 Timothy 4:1, reading, according to the Authorized Version: "I charge thee, therefore, before God and the Lord Jesus Christ, who shall judge the quick and the dead at his appearing and his kingdom." It is said that we have here the living and the dead, without distinction or separation, brought together at the coming of Christ. All that need be said in regard to this passage is that, according to the ASV phrasing, the words read: "and by His appearing and kingdom." This change not only relieves the passage of any seeming contradiction of this doctrine, but makes it give emphatic support to it. The other text is John 5:28, ASV: "Marvel not at this; for the hour cometh in which all that are in the tombs shall hear His voice and shall come forth, they that have done good, unto the resurrection of life; and they that have done ill, unto the resurrection of judgment." This, it is said, teaches a simultaneous resurrection, since it declares that, in the hour that is coming, both classes will come forth to their respective rewards. To this it is to be replied, in the first place, that the word *hour* (*hora*), as here employed, refers to an era or lengthened period of time. This is not an unusual meaning of the word, as appears by referring to such examples as 1 John 2:18 and Romans 13:11 and, what is more directly to the point, our Lord's use of the term in this sense in John 5:25: "Verily, verily, I say unto you, the hour is coming, and now is, when the dead shall hear the voice of the Son of God, and they that hear shall live." This refers, doubtless, to that spiritual quickening, under the preaching of the gospel, which began with the time of Christ and is going on today. Therefore the hour referred to must have continued for at least nearly two thousand years. This is the time for the quickening of the living who are dead in sins. It is evidently synchronous with 1 John 2:18 — "It is the last time" (*hora*) — and covers the whole gospel dispensation. Next follows, in our Lord's discourse, a statement in regard to the time involved relative to the two classes referred to as "the dead." The two periods are set in contrast. The first — the hour of spiritual quickening — has already begun; hence it is described thus: "The hour is coming and now is." The second had not yet begun; hence only the words "the hour is coming" are used with reference to it. Is it not fair to presume that the second era, like the first, is a prolonged one? That this is the case cannot be reasonably denied. This seems to be the order: at the appearing of the Lord from heaven, the age will open in which all that are in their graves will come forth, but some at the beginning and some at the end of the age. If it be said that it is a strained and unnatural construction to bring events which are so far apart into such immediate juxtaposition, with no intimation of any time lying between them, it may be replied that it is not at all uncommon in prophecy. Who, for instance, in reading Isaiah's words concerning the Messiah — "To proclaim the acceptable year of the Lord and the day of vengeance of our God" — would have imagined that in this single sentence two grand and distinct eras were brought together and spoken of in a breath, — the era of grace and the era of judgment? But the Lord, by His penetrating exegesis, cleft the passage asunder as He expounded it in the synagogue; breaking off in the middle of the sentence — "to preach the acceptable year of the Lord" — He closed the book and sat down, saying, "This day is this Scripture fulfilled in your ears" (Luke 4:21). In this prophetic passage (John 5:28, 29) there is a similar conjoining of distinct and widely separated acts of the same resurrection drama.

[9]For example, a newspaper article once asked, "Who Ate Roger Williams?" When his remains were exhumed, it was found that one large root of an apple tree followed the spine, divided at the thighs, and turned up at his toes. More than one person had eaten its apples. Or more obviously, the cannibal and his victim cannot both possess the same body at the resurrection.

[10]To use another illustration: My body is the same body that it was ten years ago, although physiologists declare that every particle of the body is changed not simply once in seven years, but once in a single year. Life is preserved only by the constant throwing off of dead matter and the introduction of the new. There is indeed a unity of consciousness and personality, without which I should not be able to say at intervals of years: "This body is the same one I have always had; this body is mine." But a physical connection between the old and the new is also necessary.

[11]Nature has no perfect analogies by which the doctrine of the resurrection of the body may be proved. The illustration from the seed in the earth is no proof. True, it appears to die, and

out of the apparent death comes forth the beautiful life, but every farmer knows it does not die: its very heart and life survive and appropriate the decay of the outer shell. "The disgusting grub," spinning its own shroud and falling into apparent death to bring forth in spring a beautiful butterfly, is no proof of the resurrection, for there is never an hour — from the time when that grub goes into quarters to the day when he comes forth a winged thing of wonderful beauty — that the scientist cannot easily discover life, either latent or active, in the cocoon. The forest standing silent through the cold season, having cast its leaves and lost its sap, is still not dead, but sleeping until the May sun shall rouse it up to activity again, leafing, flowering, fruiting; but in the death of the body, there is not — so far as we know, so far as any thoughtful man has claimed — one principle of life put in the grave. The perfect dissolution that follows is evidence enough of that truth; and so all analogies from nature fall and she joins reason in saying with reference to our buried loved ones, "There is no hope." Revelation is our one and only spokesman on this subject. It dares to set itself up to speak where reason is silent or to oppose reason if she enters into the argument. Nature's agnosticism does not silence revelation's assertions that "all that are in their graves shall come forth."

¹²This may seem to be a departure from the pattern furnished us in Christ's resurrection, which was not only the pledge but the pattern of ours, for His resurrection body was substantially the same material body which was laid in the grave. And yet we do not know what changes may have been wrought in it through the process of resurrection. But, however that may be, we must remember that the condition of Christ's body during the period that it was in the grave was different from the condition of all other bodies of similar experience. For of His body alone has it been said, "Neither wilt thou suffer thy Holy One to see corruption" (Ps. 16:10).

¹²Goethe said that his writings taken together constitute a great confession. Wordsworth wrote:

"For, like a plague will memory break out,
And, in the blank and solitude of things,
Upon his spirit, with a fever's strength,
Will conscience prey."

¹⁴All the divine judgment for the believer was focused upon Christ (Isa. 53:6), and He fully and forever satisfied divine justice on his behalf. There will be no future judgment of the believer for his sins as crimes, for they have already been judged at the Cross. No judgment and no condemnation are the emphatic declarations of Scripture (John 5:24; Rom. 8:1). The weakest and feeblest believers are as free and immune from divine judgment for sin as Christ Himself. It can no more overtake them than it can reach Him. For us and Him it is forever passed. "As He is [beyond judgment], so are we in this world" (1 John 4:17). We will be manifested before the judgment seat, or *bema*, of Christ for rewards, but not judged to reveal guilt or innocence or to determine destiny. No judgment! No condemnation! No separation! is the plain teaching of the New Testament concerning the regenerate believer in Christ.

¹⁵It is suggested that the gold, silver, and precious stones — nondestructible materials — which stand the fire test symbolize the true motive, objective, and energy that should characterize the believer's life and service. Gold, the symbol of the glory of God, suggests the motive (1 Cor. 10:31). Silver, symbolizing the redemption of Christ, suggests the objective, i.e., the carrying out of His redemptive purposes (Exod. 30:11-16; Acts 20:28; 1 Cor. 2:2; Gal. 6:14: 1 Peter 1:18, 19). Precious stones are thought to symbolize the power of the Holy Spirit productive of the Christian graces (Zech. 4:6; Gal. 5:22, 23; Titus 2:10; 1 Peter 3:3-5; 4:11). These materials which stand the fire test are contrasted with wood, hay, and stubble, destructible materials which suggest what is of the earth, earthy; of earthly production, for earthly uses and ends, with earthly motives — worldly, fleshly, and selfish, if not devilish.

¹⁶The popular and prevalent idea of the judgment described in Matthew 25:31-46 is that of an assize in which all those who are alive at that time, together with the resurrected dead of all ages, will be judged to determine their destiny. The following unanswerable objections may be raised against this interpretation: (1) There is no reference whatever to any resurrection; (2) those who are judged are called "the nations." This word is never employed in Scripture

concerning those who have died; (3) there are three classes of persons here instead of two, which a general judgment necessitates. There are the sheep, goats, and brethren, the latter term referring to the Jews, the Lord's kindred after the flesh. The church does not appear here because it has already been raised and translated; the saints have been judged for their works and rewarded accordingly; (4) the Messiah calls unto Him the living Gentiles who are upon the earth following His return, and He determines their eligibility for the Millennium upon the basis of their attitude toward the Jewish brethren. The good works which form the basis of judgment are not in themselves the ground of salvation or admission to the kingdom, but are merely the evidences of regenerated natures. The regenerate ones will enter into the kingdom prepared for them from the foundation of the world; the unregenerate will be cast out into everlasting fire (vss. 34, 41).

Subject Index

personality of 320ff, 328ff
Schaff, Philip 352, 407n
Schiller, Johann C. F. von 1, 387
Scholasticism 119, 342n
Science 162, 183f; and miracle 28; and
  Scripture 18, 51ff
Scofield, C. I. 181nf
Second Coming 31, 111, 286, 312,
  339, 349ff, 407nf; character 355ff;
  erroneous views regarding 352ff;
  related events 360ff
Seneca 214
Socinianism (Socinus) 79, 119f, 154n,
  181n, 243
Soul 54, 101, 107f, 186ff, 242, 345f,
  376f, 396; theories of origin 189ff —
  preexistence 189, creation 189f,
  traducian 190f
Spencer, Herbert 52
Spiritism 26
Spurgeon, Charles Haddon 20, 68,
  218
Strauss, D. F. 127, 133, 135
Strong, Augustus Hopkins 60, 93n,
  121, 154n, 206
Symbols and types 203, 205f, 215f,
  244, 352, 407n; for Scripture 24f; in
  ordinances 120; of Christ in Old

Testament 98f, 113f; of church 167,
  290f

TELEOLOGICAL argument 63ff
Tertullian 188, 190
Theology, as science 13f; necessity of
  14; possibility of 14ff; sources of 18
Torrey, R. A. 143, 155n
Traducianism 190f
Tregelles, Samuel P. 380
Trinity 67, 85ff, 267f, 367; equality of
  persons 87ff, 160; heresies regard-
  ing 86f, 353; Holy Spirit in 159ff
Truth 76, 80, 82f, 103, 120, 246f; and
  miracles 31; (first truths) 60ff; of
  Scripture 46; possibility of 21

UNIVERSALISM 227

VIRGIN birth 101f, 155n, 169

WESLEY, John 278n, 407n
Westcott, B. F. 175
Westminster Catechism 60
Will 242, 269, 279n, 312, 400; of God
  28, 78, 80, 82, 124, 237, 270; of man
  28, 65, 119, 192, 194f, 239f, 242,
  246, 249, 252